THOMAS PERCY

THOMAS PERCY

A Scholar-Cleric in the Age of Johnson

BERTRAM H. DAVIS

UNIVERSITY OF PENNSYLVANIA PRESS

PHILADELPHIA

FRONTISPIECE: Thomas Percy, mezzotint by William Dickinson (from Sir Joshua Reynolds's portrait), 1775

Library of Congress Cataloging-in-Publication Data

Davis, Bertram Hylton.
  Thomas Percy: a scholar-cleric in the age of Johnson / Bertram H. Davis.
    p.   cm.
  Includes index.
  Bibliography: p.
  ISBN 0-8122-8161-6
  1. Percy, Thomas, 1729–1811.   2. Literary historians—Great Britain—
Biography.   3. Bishops—Northern Ireland—Biography.   4. Church of Ireland—
Bishops—Biography.   5. Great Britain—Intellectual life—18th century.   I. Title.
PR29.P4D39   1989
820'.9—dc19
[B]   88-38842
                                                                              CIP

FOR RUTH

CONTENTS

PREFACE

Of the several roads that led from obscurity to recognition in the eighteenth century, Thomas Percy was not content to travel only one. Born a grocer's son, he died a bishop of the Church of Ireland. The friend as he progressed of such men as Samuel Johnson, James Boswell, Oliver Goldsmith, and Sir Joshua Reynolds, he was the senior member of Johnson's famous "Literary Club" some years before his death, a man of letters celebrated throughout the United Kingdom and on the Continent.

He was something of a united kingdom himself. His interest in early British literature took him into Wales and Scotland while he served his two churches in rural Northamptonshire. He was chaplain, successively, to the Earls of Sussex, the Duke of Northumberland, and King George III. As he rose in the church, he moved north to the deanery of Carlisle and then across the Irish Sea to the bishopric of Dromore.

Most of the ten books that he wrote or edited in the 1760s were pioneer works, and ironically the only one about which he had any misgivings was the best of the ten. He described the *Reliques of Ancient English Poetry* apologetically as a mere parcel of old ballads gathered together to amuse his idle hours. But it was the *Reliques* that fired the imaginations of Blake, Scott, Wordsworth, and Coleridge and helped through them to effect a revolution in English poetry. The rise of the obscure ballad paralleled Percy's own.

At best dimly aware of the book's impact, Percy pursued his literary interests and tended his Dromore diocese through the volatile period that erupted in the Irish rebellion of 1798 and then settled into the uneasy union of England and Ireland. He died in 1811 after a long and eventful life. Percy's *Reliques*, one of the great works of its century, lived on to inspire other poets and to introduce generation after generation to the magic of English poetry.

Percy's life and works have been commemorated in only one full-length volume, Alice C. C. Gaussen's *Percy: Prelate and Poet* (1908), of which I have made frequent use. Since 1908, however, a vast amount of new Percy material has been acquired by the major research libraries of Britain and America, by English county libraries, and by libraries as distant as South Africa and New Zealand. A good deal remains in private collections. Since 1944 eight volumes of *The Percy Letters* have been published, a collection indispensable for both the letters themselves and the commentaries of their editors.

In my search for Percy materials I have found librarians and private collectors almost uniformly ready to assist, but I should like to extend special thanks to Charles Miller and the reference and special collections staffs of the Strozier Library, Florida State University; Lady Mary Hyde Eccles; Stephen Parks, Curator of the James Marshall and Marie-Louise Osborn Collection, Yale University; Hugh Amory of the Houghton Library, Harvard University; David Fleeman of Pembroke College and J. F. A. Mason and June Wells of Christ Church, Oxford; W. Gordon Wheeler and Mary Kelly of the Queen's University of Belfast; G. W. Nicholls of the Johnson Birthplace Museum, Lichfield; and His Grace the Duke of Northumberland. To Kenneth Balfour, Percy's direct descendant, I owe a particular debt of gratitude for his hospitality to my wife and me over the past twelve years, and for the access he has given me to his extensive Percy memorabilia.

Other friends in England, Scotland, and Northern Ireland have also provided hospitality that facilitated my research and have at times supplemented it with information from their own experience or inquiries: Audrey and the late Eric Brook, Vera M. Davis, George and Jane Highmore, Ian and Noreen Lightbody, Doris and Edith Mercer, Nora and the late Harry Taggart, and Patsy and George Wright. The late James L. Clifford encouraged the writing of the biography and provided assistance with his unfailing generosity. My wife, to whom the biography is dedicated, has accompanied me patiently down all the Percy byways and has undertaken much of the tedious work of transcription.

For assistance of various kinds I wish also to thank the Reverend Winthrop Brainerd, Margaret Chidell, Andrew Doloughan, Daniel Eisenberg, John J. Fenstermaker, Arthur Freeman, Donald Greene, Clive Gwilt, Arthur Houghton, John H. Middendorf, George F. Miles, the Reverend N. E. Palmer, Betty Rizzo, Brian Sheedy, Arthur Sherbo, Colin Shrimpton, Margaret M. Smith, Fred L. Standley, J. C. Stoneham, John A. Vance, and the late Mrs. A. R. Wallace.

For permission to quote from manuscript material I am indebted to the following: Kenneth Balfour; Arthur Houghton; James Lawson; His Grace the Duke of Northumberland; The Henry W. and Albert A. Berg Collection, New York Public Library, Aston, Lenox, and Tilden Foundations; The Bodleian Library; The British Library; The University of Cape Town Libraries; Strozier Library, Florida State University; The Folger Shakespeare Library; The Houghton Library, Harvard University; The Hyde Collection, Somerville, New Jersey; The National Library of Scotland; The National Library of Wales; The Northamptonshire Record Office; The Yale University Library; The Beinecke Rare Book and Manuscript Library, Yale University; The James Marshall and Marie-Louise Osborn Collection, Yale University. I am indebted to the McGraw-Hill Book Company and the Editorial Committee of the Private Papers of James Boswell for permission to quote from the Yale Editions of the Private Papers of James Boswell, and to the Oxford University Press for permission to quote from *Boswell's Life of Johnson*, edited by George Birkbeck Hill and revised and enlarged by L. F. Powell, 1934–50.

Finally, I express appreciation to the John Simon Guggenheim Foundation, the American Council of Learned Societies, and Florida State University for making possible the year, and later another half year, of continuous research on which this biography is based.

CHAPTER I

Bridgnorth:

1729–1751

Bridgnorth was a leading Shropshire community in the eighteenth century, as lively and attractive as it is in our time. Within hailing distance of the house where Thomas Percy spent his childhood, bargemen eased their cargoes along the Severn River, which swirled between the high town and the low town as it hurried on to Worcester, Gloucester, and the Bristol Channel. Along the river's banks, local merchants like Percy's father loaded or unloaded their wares, and no doubt at select points men and boys cast their fishing lines on summer days, just as they do today. Carts and wagons rumbled into the high town across the Severn bridge and along Underhill Street to the imposing half-timbered Percy house, where teams and drivers could catch their breath before the arduous climb up the Cartway to the High Street. From any of the house's three gabled windows the young Percy could look south to the steep and wooded cliff of the high town, an irresistible challenge for young adventurers, and to the church of St. Mary Magdalene that crowned the hill. Behind the church, though visible from below the cliff only to the mind's eye, the shattered keep of the castle leaned toward St. Mary's as though in thanks for being spared the obliteration suffered by much of the rest of the town during the Parliamentary siege of 1646.

The town had been rebuilt, but its near destruction has given the 1580 Percy house the distinction of being the oldest house in Bridgnorth. Standing at the foot of the Cartway just up from the river's edge, it remains a showpiece, its gables and decorative oak timbers inviting attention from both the far end of the Severn bridge and the Castle Walk along the eastern rim of the cliff. In the eighteenth century, with its ready access to town, bridge, and an active river traffic, it would seem to have been ideally placed for Percy's father to carry on his business as wholesale grocer, tobacconist, chandler, and maltster.

Arthur Lowe Percy was the son of Arthur Percy, who had been born in Worcester in 1668 and apprenticed at an early age to a grocer and distiller in Bridgnorth, where he settled into his own business shortly after the Revolution of 1688. The senior Percy married Margaret Cleiveland in 1699 and thus formed with the family of the poet John Cleiveland a connection in which his grandson was to take almost as much pride as in his Percy ancestry. In an unpublished memoir Thomas recalled his grandfather, who lived until 1741, as "always in very decent circumstances," though not rich because of his assistance in supporting his mother, sister, and sister's children. I "remember the honesty & simplicity of his character with great reverence," he added.[1] He remembered his grandmother, who lived until 1745, for the meekness and gentleness of her temper, her piety and goodness, and above all her beauty: "she was one of the most comely old Personages I ever saw." The two Percy grandparents retired to Worcester when they turned over their house in Oldbury, near Bridgnorth, to their son Edward upon his marriage, but both were buried in the church of St. Leonard's, Bridgnorth.

Thomas Percy's father, Arthur Lowe Percy, was born at Bridgnorth in 1704, the fourth of six children, of whom only three survived childhood. In 1727 he married Jane Nott, daughter of Thomas and Margery Nott of Bridgnorth and nearby Sutton Maddock, who seem to have been not altogether pleased with their son-in-law. Percy's mother had frequently to apologize to her mother and sisters for his father's "miscarriages" and to defend his conduct. Perhaps the first of Arthur Lowe Percy's supposed miscarriages was to leave his father's business at the time of his marriage and strike out on his own as wholesale grocer and tobacconist; but his trade and reputation prospered, so that between 1733 and 1742 he was elected, successively, to the offices of bridgemaster, chamberlain, and bailiff, in the last of which he shared with one other person the responsibilities of justice of the peace and lord of the manor.[2]

His family grew also. Thomas was born on April 24, 1729, and was baptized on May 10 at St. Leonard's, where he was recorded in the parish register as "Thomas son of Arthur Pearcy & Jane his wife."[3] Anthony Percy was born on June 20, 1731, and baptized at St. Leonard's on July 10; and Arthur, the last of the Percy children, was born on April 9, 1734, and baptized at St. Leonard's on April 11. The parish register notwithstanding, Thomas consistently spelled his name Piercy until 1756, when he changed the spelling to Percy.

Officiating at Thomas Percy's baptism was the Reverend Thomas Littleton, an usher at the Bridgnorth Free School near the north end of the high town in the circular walk about St. Leonard's. In Percy's time the headmaster of the school, an ancient one founded at least as early as 1503, was the Reverend Hugh Stackhouse of St. Mary's, a man of apparent learning who left some fourteen hundred books and pamphlets for use by the clergy of the Bridgnorth district when he died. Because Littleton was attached to St. Leonard's, young Thomas, who had probably already learned to read at home, was placed under his tutelage, and at the age of eight he began his formal exposure to the rudiments of English grammar.

Percy provided no details of his course of study at the Free School aside from noting that Littleton, though a man of literature, was unable to accommodate "his knowledge sufficiently to the Capacity of children." Perhaps as a result the most enjoyable parts of Percy's school hours were the walks between the gabled house in Underhill Street and the school building about a quarter of a mile away. The quickest route would have taken him a short distance up the Cartway to St. Leonard's Steps, which cut across the side of the cliff to the church close. A more exciting route, along the west bank of the Severn, held out the lure of boats and busy rivermen, but exacted at last the toll of a sharp climb up the Granary Steps to the close. Still another route, doubtless most attractive on Saturday market days, led up the Cartway to the High Street and then to Church Street by way of the half-timbered town hall that straddled the High Street. In his four years at the Free School, the young Percy must have come to know the high town very well.

At home Percy was fortunate to enjoy an atmosphere in which reading was encouraged. His father, though lacking an "academical education," took great delight in books and had a mind that his son called "extremely well cultivated." Books of chivalry, and of fairies, pirates, and highwaymen, along with Nathaniel Crouch's popular *Extraordinary Adventures, Unparallel'd Varieties,* and *Wonderful Prodigies,* seem to have been the staples of the young Percy's earliest reading. But a pious father and mother probably led him at as tender an age to *The Practice of Piety* and *The Whole Duty of Man,* which he also listed among his boyhood books.[4] Perhaps piety relieved some of the drudgery of formal penmanship, as it did years later for his own son

Henry, who at the age of eight filled an exercise book with commonplaces such as "Praise good men," "Remember past favours,"
and "Time waits for no man," each repeated five or six times in a
column and followed at the bottom of the page by Henry's signature
and the date.[5] The Percy house had its own pious memorial carved
conspicuously above a hearth by the builder, Richard Forester:

> EXCEPT • THE • LORD • BUILD • THE
> OWSE • THE • LABOURERS • THERE • OF
> EVAIL • NOT • ERECTED BY • R • FOR ※   1580

In 1774 Thomas Percy included the word "owse" under the letter
"O" in his sketchy "Bridgnorth Words and Phrases," which survives
in manuscript on the reverse sides of the pages in Henry's exercise
book.

When he was ten or eleven, Thomas's head was shaved and he
was fitted with his first wig, an occasion probably comparable to the
change from knee pants to long trousers in later generations.[6] But if
Percy was acquiring the superficial dignity of approaching adoles-
cence, he was being held back intellectually by Mr. Littleton's want
of a proper instructional method, and after Easter in 1741 he was
enrolled at Newport School, some twenty miles north of Bridgnorth.
At Newport an unsuccessful attempt had been made in 1726 to secure
Samuel Johnson a position as student assistant to the headmaster. After
his enrollment Percy's visits to his family would have been confined
to the regular school recesses, of which he left only a single memorial.
During one of the Christmas holidays, he and his two younger brothers went shooting with one or two other boys, and as they stood in
a small circle the uncocked fowling piece held by one of them went
off in their midst. Fortunately—an "instance of divine mercy,"
Thomas called it—the charge went into the ground between them and
no one was injured.[7]

Newport School had been established in 1656 by William Adams,
and the Reverend Samuel Lea had been appointed headmaster in 1725.
Lea's strength was not intellectual achievement—Percy recalled that
he had "no great depth of learning"—but an excellent method of
instruction that included keeping his boys at their work, and as a
consequence the school flourished. Percy flourished also, perhaps more
than any of the nearly forty boys who boarded at the Lea house. He
began at age twelve in the school's lowest class, where he was initiated

into the simple Latin of *Sententiae Pueriles*, and at the end of five years, with two years still to be completed, he was judged by his headmaster to be ready for the university.

As events later demonstrated, Lea's judgment about his pupil was sound, and even the relevant evidence of Percy's schooldays confirms it. No writing survives.[8] But by the age of seventeen, he had assembled and catalogued a library of about two hundred sixty-five books, most of which remained at Bridgnorth in the care of his younger brother Anthony, who, on April 16, 1746, recorded his office as "Bookeeper."[9] As one might expect of a conscientious mid-century schoolboy, the Latin poets were represented in some profusion, along with such English greats as Shakespeare and Milton. But side by side with this traditional gathering stood a later English pantheon: Samuel Butler's *Hudibras*, the works of Abraham Cowley, and Gerard Langbaine's *Account of the English Dramatick Poets*; the plays of Dryden, Otway, Southerne, and Congreve; and Aphra Behn's novels, *Gulliver's Travels, Robinson Crusoe, Moll Flanders,* and Samuel Richardson's recently published *Pamela*. There were four untitled collections, two each of poems and plays. Germs of later Percy interests can be seen in two volumes of "Antiquities," seven sets of Ovid's poems, and *The Seven Wise Maisters of Rome,* from which he was to take a story for *The Matrons* of 1762.

For all Percy's tender age, this was a young man's rather than a boy's library. Infrequent items like *Extraordinary Adventures* and *Wonderful Prodigies* remained the sole clues to the boy who had entered Newport School in the lowest form. Clearly at seventeen Percy's literary tastes and interests had advanced far beyond those of most contemporaries. Nor was the library less remarkable for the intensity of its religious coloration. Such household texts as *The Whole Duty of Man* and *The Practice of Piety* were supplemented with *The New Whole Duty of Man, The Devout Soul's Exercise, The Practice of the Faithful,* and *A Guide to Heaven*. Perhaps these were simply additions to a young person's standard fare contributed by an overzealous father and mother. But they were only the beginning. Half a dozen Bibles in Greek, Latin, and English, the last in both black letter and modern print, suggest an aspiring cleric's rather than a schoolboy's interest, and other books would seem to reflect a curiosity transcending the need to strengthen one's moral and religious fiber through such everyday works as *The Whole Duty of Man* and *The Practice of Piety*. *The Companion to the Altar, A Persuasive to the Communion, Admonition against Swearing, Torments after Death, The Principles of Religion,* Burgess's sermons, and *A Reply to the Bishop of Exeter* point as surely to the later vicar, dean, and bishop as Percy's literary collection does to the poet and scholar.

In 1746 Samuel Lea nominated Percy as a candidate in the election of exhibitioners to Christ Church, Oxford, on a foundation established by Edward Careswell, who had died in 1691 leaving the income from several estates for the support of eighteen students at Christ Church. These were to be selected from "the most ingenious deserving scholars" in the Shropshire parishes where the Careswell estates lay, including Newport and Bridgnorth. The income had been reserved first, however, for a number of life annuities, and the election of exhibitioners was further delayed by disputes over the will that had to be settled in the Court of Chancery. As a consequence, the 1746 election was the first. On July 8 of that year Percy had the honor of being chosen one of the first exhibitioners from Newport, along with Jonathan Stubbs, son of the Receiver of the Rents of the Careswell estates, and John Lea, son of Headmaster Samuel Lea. Both Stubbs and Lea were from school classes above Percy's own.

The news of the election must have come as a surprise to Percy's father, who had not been consulted by Lea and had not intended to send his son to the university so soon. But the financial assistance was generous, and he must have welcomed it: £18 for each of the four undergraduate years, £21 for each of three years as a Bachelor of Arts, and £27 for each of three as a Master of Arts. For by 1746 Percy's father had experienced a series of misfortunes through his refusal to take legal steps to compel payment from a number of debtors, lest he "pull them to pieces." Other creditors, less tenderhearted, seized everything that they had, and Percy's father, having lost over £3000, was forced to sell estates at Worcester and Bridgnorth and never fully recovered from his setback. By the end of the year he had been ordered to appear before a commission of bankruptcy.[10] "May his integrity, strict honour, humanity & tenderness be revered & imitated by his Descendants!" Thomas Percy wrote of him. "May they pay somewhat more regard to Oeconomy! and may they meet with better Fortune!"

On July 18, in a quick transition from schoolboy to college student, Percy was entered a commoner at Christ Church, and he matriculated on the same day. Shortly thereafter he seems to have returned to Bridgnorth, possibly to assist his father through a difficult period as well as to prepare for his own first college term. Notations on his library list suggest that he gave Anthony his copies of *The London Cuckolds* and *London Jests*, rewards perhaps for Anthony's service as "Bookeeper," selected with an experienced eye to a fifteen-year-old's emerging interests. They suggest also that Thomas himself left Bridgnorth with a small bundle of books befitting the seriousness of the enterprise he was embarking upon, including Bibles, a book of devotions, Greek and Latin grammars, *The Iliad*, and his volumes of antiquities. Books like *Moll Flanders* and Dryden's *Plays*, two of his Newport companions, did not make the trip. The record of his board charges shows him in residence at Christ Church once again on September 2.

The English universities had been slow to respond to the social and scientific changes of the seventeenth and early eighteenth centuries, and their curricula and practices remained largely rooted in the classical and clerical traditions of medieval times. Often ill-paid, and committed by statute to celibate lives, many of the fellows abandoned their positions for more attractive livings in the church or elsewhere, and of those who remained a fair number gave little attention to either their own study or their students'. But there were exceptions among the colleges, and Christ Church was one of them. In 1729, though himself a student at Pembroke, Samuel Johnson had urged his friend John Taylor to enroll at Christ Church, where his inquiry suggested that the tutors and the lectures excelled those of other colleges.[11] The dean in Percy's time was the eminent Dr. John Conybeare, later Bishop of Bristol, who had visited Shropshire to supervise the election of the first Careswell exhibitioners; and Percy had the good fortune to be assigned to the Reverend Richard Hind, whom he later described as an excellent tutor and a very accomplished scholar. All of the Careswell exhibitioners were given rooms in Peckwater Quadrangle, Percy in Room 2 of Staircase 2, where he was close to Thomas Hartshorne from the Bridgnorth Free School and George Bowdler from Shrewsbury. On Lady Day in 1748, Percy moved to Room 1 of Staircase 8 in Peckwater Quadrangle, where he remained until midsummer of 1750.[12]

With the rest of his classmates, Percy was given a first-year course of reading that included eight books of *The Iliad* and six of *The Aeneid*, Cicero, Bishop Pearson's *Exposition of the Creed*, parts of the Old Testament in Hebrew and the New Testament in Greek, and the *Artis Logicae Compendium* of Henry Aldrich, an earlier Dean of Christ Church. In these he did so well that on November 14, 1747, he was

elected one of Bishop Fell's exhibitioners, through a competition held
in the College hall on November 12 and open to "ingenious and
indigent" commoners of Christ Church with a year's residence, who
were examined in classical authors and philosophy. The prize for each
successful candidate was £10 a year during his undergraduate tenure,
with the condition that he reside at the college for at least forty weeks
of each year. When one considers that the preacher of Goldsmith's
Deserted Village was "passing rich with forty pounds a year," Percy's
combined scholarship incomes would seem to have raised him sub-
stantially above a level of indigence.

In their second year Percy and his classmates read another eight
books of *The Iliad*, the final six of *The Aeneid*, and the *Ethicae Compendium*, and they continued with Cicero, Pearson, and their Old and
New Testament studies. In 1748 he compiled a notebook on Euclid,
apparently a special study during either the spring of his second year
or the fall of his third.[13] The third year curriculum was similar to the
second, except that Lucretius replaced Virgil and the *Physicae Compendium* replaced the *Ethicae Compendium*. The final undergraduate year
was given over to a study of John Locke's *Essay Concerning Human
Understanding* and the Thirty-nine Articles.

This was hardly a burdensome schedule for one of Percy's background and quickness of mind, and doubtless he had much time for
pursuits of his own choosing. Additional reading was certainly one
of them, and the nature of other pursuits is suggested in a letter that
he wrote to his second cousin William Cleiveland on March 24, 1756,
when Cleiveland was a student at Oxford's Magdalen Hall: Where
but at a college "shall I meet with that small select Collection of friends,
of my own Age, of my own Turn, of my own Employment &
Persuits, and of my own Leisure? With whom to walk, to converse,
to compare Studies, & to dispel the Gloom contracted by Books &
Solitude."[14]

Walking, as Percy noted, was one of the pleasures that he could
share with his friends, and Oxford and its countryside provided endless
opportunities for exploration. Riding was probably beyond the means
of a scholar dependent upon his exhibitioner's stipends, but perhaps
he joined an occasional group at the nearby Port-Meadow horse rac-
ing, a sport popular in Bridgnorth and attractive to Percy in later
years. He continued to enjoy shooting, although he recorded only
another near accident during a foray alone into the fields around Oxford during the winter of 1747–48. In climbing over a hedge, he pushed

aside the brambles with the butt of his loaded gun, and a briar caught the trigger and discharged the shot so close to his head that the powder and smoke momentarily blinded him and some of the shot went through his hat. Fortunately, his only injury was to his hand, which was holding the end of the barrel and was grazed by the shot—a second instance, he commented, of "Divine Mercy, by which my Life has been wonderfully preserved."[5]

It can be assumed that he did not join his college mates in drinking, not from any objection on principle but simply because he found wine distasteful. Some twenty years later he had still not overcome his distaste sufficiently to share a convivial dinner group's enjoyment of its toasts.[6] As for young women, no record of any acquaintances among them survives for his Oxford period, a consequence, no doubt, of limited opportunities: his close confinement in boys' schools, the exclusive male companionship offered by the university, and the absence of sisters or other young female relations who might have introduced him to their friends. He was also preoccupied with study. Having entered Christ Church with two years less schooling than most of his classmates, he was "deeply conscious," as he wrote his brother Anthony some years later, of his own "defects and inferiority" and of the need for "constant & unremitted application." His "very humble & modest opinion" of himself also led him "to conciliate the favour of all that I conversed with, & to neglect no means to improve myself, & to profit by all opportunities that offered."[7]

His activities, nonetheless, were probably similar to those of many of his classmates from comparable social and economic backgrounds, although the impetus of his boyhood training and his ambition had given him a relish for intellectual pursuits that doubtless some of them did not share. But whatever its impact upon others, Christ Church clearly filled his needs, and he was to remember his college years with fondness, as one is likely to do who has made the best of them. He assured Will Cleiveland in his March 24 letter that he had "never since experienced such pure & undisturbed Happiness" as he had "enjoy'd within the Walls of a College"; and though something must be allowed for his desire to encourage a relation still poring over his college texts, Percy's assessment of his own experience was probably close to the mark.

Percy's undergraduate course was completed on May 7, 1750, when he was awarded the Bachelor of Arts degree, but, with his eye fixed on a master's degree and a clerical career, he had already undertaken work that would keep him in residence at Oxford through much of the next year and a half. On April 19, 1750, he began the study of Hebrew under Mark Moses Vowel, a Polish Jew converted to Christianity and baptized at Oxford, who listed his position as "Teacher of the Hebrew Language at Oxford" in a letter to the *Gentleman's Magazine* published in July 1751.[18] Percy copied Vowel's lectures on Hebrew grammar into the same notebook he had used for his Euclid studies in 1748, although he turned the notebook upside down and over to give himself a clear succession of pages throughout. In the little more than two months that he attended Vowel's lectures, he managed to fill all but a few of the pages.

Percy's Hebrew studies as an undergraduate had probably been fairly elementary. Under Vowel they became intense. In 1751 and 1752 he corresponded with Vowel and fellow Salopian Richard Yate about interpretations of Hebrew language, and he wrote a series of "dissertations" that he was later to offer to an unenthusiastic Ralph Griffiths for possible use in a new Griffiths periodical, *The Library*: "On the original Meaning and Derivation of the Word Shiloh," for example, and "On Naaman's request to Elisha, on his being cur'd of his Leprosy."[19] A curious by-product of Percy's Hebrew studies was his occasional employment of Hebrew script letters as substitutes for English, perhaps at first merely for practice but later apparently to screen a comment from prying eyes. His earliest letter extant was written in Hebrew and then translated rather stiffly into his code, and it was addressed to his Newport and Christ Church colleague John Lea, who had pursued the same studies under Vowel. In the letter, written on September 29, 1750, Percy described himself as "a little angry" because Lea had not acknowledged receipt of papers that would shortly have to be returned to their owner; he sent greetings to Lea's father and other members of his family, and closed by asking when Lea would be ready for the priesthood.[20]

Always adept at languages, Percy also included French and Italian among his graduate studies, the first of which he may have begun at Newport, where a French grammar was listed among his books.[21] Although he was not to receive the master's degree for another two months, he had completed the necessary exercises by the spring of 1751 and was prepared to take the first steps in his chosen career. He secured an appointment as curate, and at Hereford Cathedral on October 31, 1751, he was ordained a deacon by James Beauclerc, Bishop

of Hereford. He promptly assumed his duties at two churches just a
short distance from Bridgnorth.

NOTES

Beginning with chapter 2, information for which no source is given has been
taken from Percy's diary, B.L. Add. MS. 32,336.

1. Following Percy's practice I have consistently spelled the family names
   as Percy and Cleiveland rather than Piercy and Cleveland. Percy's memoir
   is contained in B.L. Add. MS. 32,326, from which this and Percy's other
   autobiographical comments quoted in this chapter are taken. The account
   of his grandparents is at ff. 13–16. Information in this chapter for which
   no other reference is cited is also taken from Percy's memoir or from an
   article by J. F. A. Mason that quotes parts of it and supplements it with
   helpful material related to Percy's school and college years ("Bishop Percy's Account of His Own Education," *Notes & Queries*, New ser. 6 [1959]:
   404–8).
2. B.L. Add. MS. 32,326, ff. 19–23; Salop Record Office 4001/F/120–140
   and 4001/Admin/3/3; *The History of the Ancient Borough of Bridgnorth*
   (Bridgnorth, 1821; reprint, Bridgnorth: Foxall, 1978), 5–6.
3. The baptismal date is given in the parish register as 29 April, in accordance
   with the Julian calendar, which at that time was eleven days behind the
   Gregorian calendar in use on the Continent. England changed to the
   Gregorian calendar on 2 September 1752, and unless otherwise noted, I
   have amended all earlier dates to accord with it.
4. The list of Percy's boyhood library is in Bodl. MS. Percy c. 9, ff. 33–
   42. Notations indicate which books Percy had at Newport and Oxford.
   For his early interest in chivalry see also *Ancient Songs Chiefly on Moorish
   Subjects Translated from the Spanish by Thomas Percy with a Preface by David
   Nichol Smith* (Oxford: Oxford Univ. Press, 1932), xi.
5. Salop Record Office, Shrewsbury, MS. 1175/2.
6. B.L. Add. MS. 32,335, f. 143 (Letter to Anne Percy, 9 March 1799).
7. B.L. Add. MS. 32,326, f. 30.
8. A hymn "written by T. P. at school" (collection of Kenneth Balfour)
   may be by Percy, but his nephew, a precocious poet, had the same initials,
   and it is impossible to make a firm attribution.
9. Bodl. MS. Percy c. 9, f. 33.
10. Public Record Office, B. 4/11, No. 2445, 19 Dec. 1746 (O.S. for 30 Dec.);
    London Gazette, 3–6 Jan. 1746 (O.S. for 14–17 Jan. 1747). The bankruptcy
    records give no indication, as they do for other bankrupts, that Percy's
    father conformed with the requirements of the bankruptcy laws. That

omission, plus the fact that in 1756 Thomas was selling properties in Worcester to pay off his father's indebtedness, suggests that Arthur Lowe Percy was able to make an arrangement whereby he avoided the worst rigors of the bankruptcy laws. In the Public Record Office his creditor is listed as Elizabeth Nott, his sister-in-law, who perhaps advanced the money to his actual creditors and permitted him to repay her over a period of ten years.

11. James L. Clifford, *Young Sam Johnson* (New York: McGraw- Hill, 1955), 116.

12. The information about the exhibitioners' rooms has been kindly supplied by Dr. J. F. A. Mason, Librarian of Christ Church.

13. Bodl. MS. Percy e. 9; Mason, 407.

14. B.L. Add. MS. 32,333, f. 2.

15. B.L. Add. MS. 32,326, ff. 30–31.

16. B.L. Add. MS. 39,547, f. 9 (Letter to Anne Percy, 30 Aug. 1771); Alice C. C. Gaussen, *Percy: Prelate and Poet* (London: Smith, Elder, 1908), 91.

17. Letter to Anthony Percy, 7 Jan. 1781 (collection of Kenneth Balfour).

18. *Gentleman's Magazine* (July 1751), 317–18.

19. Alnwick Castle MSS. 93A/31 and 37.

20. Alnwick Castle MS. 93A/37.

21. Mason, 408.

CHAPTER II

Curate and Vicar:

1751–1756

PERCY'S TWO CHURCHES were St. Calixtus in Astley Abbots, about two miles north of Bridgnorth, and St. Peter and St. Paul in Tasley, about a mile west. Where he lived at this time is not certain, but it would have been natural for him to rejoin his family during this period of apprenticeship for the ministry. By 1751 Percy's father, though not yet recovered from his financial reverses of five or six years earlier, still had sufficient vigor and reputation to be elected to his second term as bailiff, and during the first year of Percy's return he was thus serving again as one of Bridgnorth's two chief magistrates. No doubt he was sustained in good part by Percy's mother, who, though never in good health, had subordinated her own interests to her husband's, "alleviating his Concern...," as Percy wrote, "[and] never dropping the least upbraiding or discontented word under any of their difficulties." About his brothers Percy is silent. Anthony, who did not attend the university, had turned twenty in June and perhaps was working with his father in the grocer's trade. The seventeen-year-old Arthur was probably employed in Birmingham, for in August 1755, while living in that city, he was admitted as a burgess in the Bridgnorth Corporation.[1]

As deacon, Percy was an assistant to the Reverend Daniel Adamson, who was rector of both churches and vicar of Worfield in Shropshire as well. In reality, once he had proved himself to Mr. Adamson, Percy was probably given the authority of an ordained priest except in the administration of the sacraments. He seems very quickly to have stimulated a demand for his services as a preacher. On November 7, 1751, only a week after his ordination as a deacon, he preached the sermon at Sutton Maddock, a homecoming appearance, perhaps, for the grandson of Sutton Maddock's Margery Nott.

On the next Sunday he preached at Newport and at both St. Leonard's and St. Mary Magdelene in Bridgnorth, not an easy task even for a young man of Percy's energies; but perhaps all three churches afforded him the special attraction of homecoming welcomes. There is no record of his preaching at Astley Abbots and Tasley until December 12, 1751, but thereafter Mr. Adamson called upon him regularly at both churches and occasionally at Worfield also. In 1752, in addition to Worfield and his own two churches, he preached again at Sutton Maddock, Newport, and the two Bridgnorth churches, and for the first time in the Shropshire towns of Morville and Oldbury.[2]

All this activity suggests that Percy must have had little time for anything but composing sermons, and no doubt establishing himself in the ministry was not an easy task. Probably his first few sermons were original; the manuscripts, in any event, contain no references to other sermons from which they might have been derived. But Percy learned at the beginning to practice economies that freed him from a constant attendance at his desk. Like other clergymen, he used the same sermon at different churches: the Sutton Maddock sermon of November 7 was preached the next week at St. Leonard's, and the Newport sermon of November 14 was preached at Sutton Maddock on November 21. By 1752 he was adapting the printed books and sermons of other divines to his own uses: a sermon that he preached at Astley Abbots and Tasley on July 9, 1752, was compiled, as he noted in his manuscript, from Thomas Stackhouse's *Complete Body of Divinity* and from sermons by Archbishop Secker and Bishops Zachary Pearce and Isaac Maddox.[3] He developed variants of sermons based on similar but not identical biblical texts, another process more expeditious than original composition. The sermon preached at Astley Abbots on the morning of December 12, 1751, and at Tasley the same evening—"On the Characters of Godliness"—was a variant of "On the Advantages of Piety," which he had preached at St. Mary's on November 14, and by January 9 he had preached two additional variants of the same sermon.

Percy's sermons do not make especially interesting reading today, but his sermon "On the Characters of Godliness" was long remembered by one of his Astley Abbots parishioners who had come of age shortly before Percy was ordained a deacon in 1751. Writing to Percy on January 21, 1801, John Colinge recalled that the text of the sermon, which he described as "Give me neither Riches nor Poverty," was explained by Percy "in such a manner as eminently marked you out for that Superiority which you now possess." Perhaps Colinge's memory was the more vivid because, soon after hearing the sermon, he contracted smallpox and, delirious from a high fever, ran from his bed into the garden and threw himself into the well. Although he was pulled out immediately, he was not expected to live, and Percy was sent for. But from that time, as Percy noted, Colinge grew steadily better and at last recovered, though with the loss of one eye. It was, wrote Percy, "One of the first Instances observed in that Country of the Success of cool Treatment in the Small Pox." It was also another "remarkable Instance of Divine Mercy."[4]

Once Percy had prepared a body of sermons that could be fitted to most regular church services, he had generally only to decide which of them to preach on any given Sunday, a decision aided by his careful notation on each sermon or variant of the dates and places of its use. Some sermons were to have brief careers: "Not fit to be used again," he later noted on a sermon concerning the duty of parents to children.[5] Others fared much better; two or three sermons from his first year at Astley Abbots and Tasley were still in service forty years later. This is not to suggest that his collection did not grow over the years or that he never again composed original sermons. He was constantly discovering sermons that he might adapt, including two by his later Shropshire friend Edward Blakeway.[6] As his reputation increased, he was also invited to preach charity or other special sermons that had to be directed to particular causes, and though he might review other works prepared for similar occasions, he was careful to avoid any slavish imitation. When he himself wanted relief, he could call upon "old John Higgs," curate of Quatford, who would gladly substitute at both churches for five shillings.[7]

Preaching the sermons was probably Percy's most pressing obligation at his two churches, and after he had settled into his position he must have had considerable time to himself. Eighteenth-century clergymen did not commonly make the rounds of hospitals or visit parishioners in their homes with the frequency of many of today's clergy, although Percy doubtless had to respond to other calls like John Colinge's. Nor was the church the center of social activity that it has become in this century. His congregations, moreover, were small. Astley Abbots had a population of four or five hundred, and in 1752 only thirteen baptisms, twelve burials, and three marriages were recorded in the parish register. In 1753 there were eleven baptisms, seven burials, and three marriages. Tasley, with a population of less than a hundred, had only four baptisms, two burials, and two marriages in 1752, and five baptisms with no burials or marriages in 1753.[8] Even if Percy had assisted Mr. Adamson on all these occasions, the demands on his time could not have been great.

On the face of it, such limited activity hardly afforded Percy much of a challenge; yet he seems to have enjoyed these initial years in the church and to have had no desire for a quick change of scene. But he did aspire to the clerical and academic honors appropriate to his work. On June 17, 1753—Trinity Sunday—he was ordained a priest in Hereford Cathedral, once again by Bishop Beauclerc, and from Hereford he proceeded to Oxford, where he was awarded the degree of Master of Arts on July 5. At Oxford he learned that a church living within the gift of Christ Church—the vicarage of Easton Maudit in Northamptonshire—was soon to be vacated by the Reverend Enoch Markham, himself a recent graduate of Christ Church, and Percy obtained an assurance from the dean and chapter that it would be reserved for him.[9]

Probably during the July trip to Oxford, as well as a second trip three months later, Percy stopped off at Halesowen in Shropshire to visit the poet William Shenstone, an Oxford classmate of a good Newport friend, the Reverend Robert Binnel; and he was sufficiently impressed by Shenstone's estate, the Leasowes, to draw up a brief description of it in this year.[10] He was back at Oxford in early October, attending the convocation on October 8 for the installation of a new vice-chancellor, greeting old friends, and perhaps making some new ones: "Tea at Dr. Derham's, saw Gow'r, & walk'd w.th Brooke," he wrote in his diary for October 15.[11] On that day the living was presented to him in a ceremony at Christ Church, and before breakfast the next morning he was on his way to Easton Maudit, where he arrived in the evening to a warm welcome. He had supper and stayed overnight with the churchwarden, Joseph Steer, and the following morning had breakfast at the vicarage with Markham, whom he found packing. He was shown the church—consecrated, like his church at Tasley, to St. Peter and St. Paul; was introduced to the lord of the manor, Augustus, Earl of Sussex, whom he found "very civil"; and made preliminary arrangements for the Reverend Thomas Gery Bennet, rector of Earls Barton and curate of Bozeat, to serve as curate of Easton Maudit during his absence. That evening he joined Lord Sussex for supper at the manor house, and he spent the night again with Joseph Steer.

However much Percy may have wished it, the Earl of Sussex's civility and hospitality did not conclude the formalities of his appointment as vicar of Easton Maudit. Nearly a month after his return to Bridgnorth, he had to travel to London for the Bishop of Hereford to sign appropriate testimonials and for the Bishop of Peterborough, of whose diocese Easton Maudit was a part, to institute him in office. He secured the Bishop of Hereford's signature on November 26 and, in gown and cassock, was formally instituted on November 27. He wrote to Bennet and Dr. Conybeare on the same day, presumably to let them know that everything had gone as planned.

That was the business of Percy's London trip, which lasted from Saturday, November 24, to Thursday, December 13, 1753. The rest seems to have been all pleasure. It was probably his first London visit, and his diary, which unfortunately breaks off after December 1, shows him with money in his pocket and intent upon enjoying it. On his way to London he bought a barrel of oysters to send to his father, and on his arrival he bought a walking stick, apparently for his own use. He stayed with a distant cousin, Tom Woodington, and frequently breakfasted, dined, or supped with a nearer and equally hospitable relation, his father's first cousin Mary Perrins, who had married the distiller John Perrins of Worcester and London.[12] He attended morning and afternoon services at St. Clement Danes the day after his arrival and thought it worth recording that the afternoon preacher made no use of notes. He visited Westminster Abbey, Westminster Hall, the House of Commons, and the recently built Westminster Bridge. He frequented the coffee houses and proved to be an insatiable playgoer. On Tuesday, November 27, he took Mrs. Perrins to Drury Lane to see David Garrick and Hannah Pritchard in Farquhar's *Beaux' Stratagem*, and he returned the next night to see them in *King Richard III*. On Thursday he found time only for the afterpiece at Covent Garden, Lewis Theobald's *Harlequin Sorcerer*. But he was again at Drury Lane on Friday with a young Worcestershire and Oxford friend, George Durant, to see Samuel Foote and Mrs. Pritchard in Congreve's *The Old Bachelor* and Foote in his own afterpiece, *The Englishman in Paris*. On Saturday he and Tom Woodington attended the opening performance at Drury Lane of Richard Glover's *Boadicia*, in which he noted that the players "acted in fear" of the audience throughout the first act and even Mrs. Pritchard was "a little hiss'd." She recovered quickly, however, and the play was applauded.

He also sought out some of the more unusual experiences of

London visitors. The "Porcupine Man" prompted a diary note that he was "covered with small horny Bristles" a quarter of an inch in diameter and half an inch long "as thick as pins." On Monday night, November 26, he joined the assembly at the Robin Hood Tavern in Butcher Row, where the baker Caleb Jeacocke presided over a society of impromptu debaters, anyone who had paid the admission fee of sixpence having the privilege of speaking for five minutes in each debate. In Henry Fielding's satirical sketch of the Robin Hood Society, one of the subjects for debate was "whether Relidgin was of any youse to a Sosyaty."[13] The subjects on November 26 suggest a rather more intelligent effort to focus on political, ethical, and social questions of the day: "Whether it is good Policy in England to encourage the woolen Manufacture in Ireland"; "Whether it is lawful on Occasion to speak or act a Lye"; and "Whether the Institution of Charity Schools is beneficial to the Publick." Percy did not say how he reacted to the assembly or whether he joined in any of the debates. On the afternoon of November 30, doubtless through the good offices of the Earl of Sussex, he and Mrs. Perrins were admitted to St. James's Palace, where the royal family was celebrating the thirty-fourth birthday of the Dowager Princess of Wales.[14] Percy thought the princess "an exceeding fine majestic woman." The Duke of Cumberland, hero of the Battle of Culloden, he thought "excessive fat." The Prince of Wales and Prince Edward were "both fat and short."

From London Percy returned to Easton Maudit where, after breakfasting with Bennet on Sunday, December 16, he was inducted by Bennet, preached his induction sermon, dined with Steer, and then preached again in the evening. He spent that night and the next with Bennet in nearby Bozeat, reached an apparently final agreement with him to serve as curate at Easton Maudit, and then set out for Bridgnorth on the eighteenth. It was not a good time for travel. At Badby the next day he encountered such heavy rains that he sent his driver back to Easton Maudit and continued his journey in a covered van— a "carravan"—which stopped for the night at Dunchurch near Rugby. The next morning faint hearts seem to have reduced the van's twelve occupants to eight, who breakfasted at Coventry after a short run and then continued on without stopping for dinner. At one point the van was almost overturned by the floodwaters, but it managed to reach Birmingham in time for tea, and Percy went on to Bridgnorth the next day. Two days later—December 23—he was again conducting services at Astley Abbots and Tasley.[15]

One can only speculate as to why Percy chose to remain in Bridg-north as the curate of two churches rather than move to Easton Maudit as the vicar of one. Family, friends, congregations with whom he felt at ease, familiar surroundings: all were probably Bridgnorth attrac-tions. Perhaps money was an attraction, too. Although its church was much more impressive than either of his two Shropshire churches, Easton Maudit was no larger than Tasley, and even with its vicarage and glebe lands his emoluments as vicar might not have exceeded those of his two curacies. A contemporary document lists the "clear yearly value" of the Easton Maudit living as only £27/9/3.[16] One may wonder, of course, why Percy accepted a post that he did not intend to occupy; a likely explanation is that he would be prepared to occupy it at an appropriate time, and that meanwhile he was pleased to have the title of vicar and to augment his curate's income with what re-mained after he had finished paying Bennet to perform his duties at Easton Maudit.

Perhaps there was another reason for Percy to stay in Bridgnorth. He was in love, or at least thought that he was, and did not wish to leave Bridgnorth while he was savoring the pleasure of finding out. Marriage, he later confessed, was much on his mind about this time.[17] "Flavia" was the poetic name for the girl of his dreams in 1753, and, single or composite, she stirred the poet in him even if she cannot be said to have inspired him. In "A Song," dated April 2, 1753, and consisting of five eight-line stanzas and a refrain, the young lover cannot restrain his happiness as he recalls Flavia reclining "on a prim-rose Bank" and listening to his music—hearkening to his lay, to use the poem's pastoral language:

> Ye Gods! was ever maid so kind
> > Was ever Swain so gay[?]

and he bursts into his refrain:

> O the Broom, yᵉ bonny bonny broom
> > And O each conscious Dale
> Where I so oft met my dear Lass
> > The sweetest of the Vale.

Flavia makes the sun brighter, the stream more softly murmuring; and as they walk through the fields he weaves a garland for her hair.

But at the end of the fourth stanza a change is portended, and in stanza five she has left for "happier distant Shades," where she is

> The Envy of less-beauteous Maids,
>   Of ev'ry Youth the flame.

The concluding refrain saddens to "Farewell ye Broom, ye bonny bonny Broom."[18]

A pastoral so artlessly derivative and inflated may have been a mere romantic indulgence, its Eden a creation entirely of Percy's imagination. "I have known our Friend Percy . . . [to talk] of darts and wounds and Flavias when his heart has been as sound as a Roach," Robert Binnel was later to comment to James Grainger.[19] But Flavia clearly had a later existence, and even in this airy poem one of the lines suggests at least a fragile link with reality: "What pleasing Chat beguil'd the Day" records a pastime suited rather to Bridgnorth maids and men than to flower-bedecked nymphs and their adoring swains. It could well reflect the activity of a real Flavia and a romantic young curate of Astley Abbots and Tasley.

The likelihood that Percy had a real person in mind is given support by a ten-line poetic fragment originally dated April 2, 1753—as was "A Song"—and then changed to April 13. The fragment is a birthday poem in which the Morn is implored "To grace ye Day of Flavia's birth," and it seems unlikely that Percy would celebrate the birthday of someone who existed only in his imagination.[20] But however one chooses to interpret these first poems, by August 3 Flavia was unmistakably real. On that day, Percy sent her an untitled poem and its "Post-script," a total of fifteen quatrains, and he noted at the foot of his manuscript copy that the verses accompanied a present of a pair of mother-of-pearl earrings.[21] Other Flavia poems are dated September 13 and November 6, 1753, one is undated, and of course still others may have been written that did not survive. Percy's last known poetic word on the subject was an elegy of twenty-four stanzas lamenting Flavia's rejection of her "love lorn youth" which he invited Thomas Apperley to comment upon in the summer of 1755.[22]

But even if Flavia rejected Percy's attentions, she apparently retained some hold on his affections. His undated poem—"On seeing Miss *** and M^r *** running. Address'd to the latter"—would seem to be one of his last, for in it a more experienced Percy can advise another suitor, without bitterness, that overtaking Flavia will be no easy task:

> The beauteous Nymph outstrips the sweeping Air
> . . . .
> Flavia, tho' scarcely gain'd Youths earliest Dawn
> Gay as the velvet Doe that trips the Lawn
> To th' loveliest Form & gentlest heart has join'd
> Discernment's piercing Ray & Sense refin'd
> She scorns the Toys in which her Sex delight
> And nought but merit shall retard her flight.

Flavia also retained a claim upon his company. In 1755, starting his August 25 letter to Apperley after midnight, Percy reported that he would not have had to stay up so late writing if he had not spent the whole afternoon with two "lasses of my acquaintance," one of whom he had "*bepoetried*" under the Name of Flavia."[23] He and Flavia thus seem to have remained friends, but his demotion of her from garlanded nymph to "*bepoetried*" lass suggests that by the late summer of 1755 he had left the enraptured swain of "A Song" behind him.

Had Percy kept to a course that he charted in a 1752 poetic imitation, he might never have assumed his pastoral guise in the first place. Among the *jeux d'esprit* written at the expense of poet laureate Colley Cibber was the following brief epigram, attributed to Alexander Pope:

> In merry old England it once was a rule,
> The King had his Poet, and also his Fool:
> But now we're so frugal, I'd have you to know it,
> That *Cibber* can serve both for Fool and for Poet.[24]

If the epigram was Pope's, it was not one of his better efforts: colorless in language, diffuse rather than concise, and banally anticlimactic in its terminal rhyme. Percy, adapting the epigram to his own profession, avoids these faults and with a few telling strokes brings the characters of his vignette to life:

> At the Squire's long board, in the days of Queen Bess
> Sate the Fool to make sport, & the chaplain to bless.
> But frugal Sir Flint has contracted the Rule
> And Bibo's to serve both for Chaplain—and Fool.[25]

Only a few other poems from Percy's Bridgnorth period are extant. "The Disappointment," written in 1752 and revised in 1753, is a playful comment on the paradox of the beautiful Mira, who is thawed by "Fortune's chilling tempest" and frozen by "warmest sunshines." It is seriously flawed, however, by grotesque rhymes that serve no special purpose and were left standing even after the poem's revision: "Lillies" and "skill is" and "seas 'em" and "freeze 'em."[26]

The early Flavia poems followed "The Disappointment," and 1754 brought "The Mistake," dated June, "An Inscription for the Seat on Morf, occasion'd by the Ladies supping there June 22.ᵈ 1754," and possibly another sonnet. "The Mistake" reflects the same lightness of touch apparent in much of "The Disappointment"; the speaker, having mistaken Garcia successively for Venus, a Muse, and Athene, is given the correct identification by "Gay Silvio":

> 'Tis Garcia, bless'd with ev'ry Grace,
> That decks the Soul, the Voice yᵉ Face
> And yet a mortal Maid.[27]

A "Sonnet to a Lady of Indiscreet Virtue, in Imitation of Spencer" was written about 1754 and addressed to "Miss Cotton of Bridgnorth," as Percy later noted on a printed copy. It captures with some success the outgoing innocence that he predicts will subject "fair *Anna*" to censuring tongues:

> While you, fair *Anna*, innocently gay,
>   And free, and open, all reserve disdain;
> Where-ever Fancy leads, securely stray,
>   And conscious of no ill can fear no stain.[28]

Percy's final poem of the period, "A Sonnet, Occasion'd by Leaving Bath in June, 1755," was addressed to the Misses H ★★★, although subsequently the date was altered to July 1755, Bath to B–R–T–N, and the Misses H ★★★ to "Ladies."[29] Percy provided no explanation of these alterations, which artlessly permit the inference that—banished from his Garden of Eden as he depicts himself in the poem—he remained committed to the pursuit of love even if it took him as far afield as Bath and whatever place he intended by B–R–T–N.

Of these early poems—with the exception of a "Song" sent to Thomas Apperley, which will be discussed in the next chapter—only the two sonnets and the elegy were published in Percy's lifetime; and though all have been understandably forgotten, they provide some revealing glimpses into Percy's developing talents. Wit, grace, and an imaginative economy of language were not at all beyond him. He could do well when limits were set for him, as in the fourteen lines of a sonnet; he could do better still when, within prescribed limits, improving upon someone else's work posed an additional challenge, as in his imitation of the four-line epigram on Colley Cibber. When he had little or no guidance and an endless supply of quatrains or other stanza forms to draw from, he had difficulty compressing and was often pedestrian. At his worst he was embarrassingly sentimental and histrionic.

In the seven quatrains of the August 3 "Post-script," he envisions Flavia some years hence finding his gift of earrings in a neglected corner and shedding a tear for one whose

> . . . fate, alas! was too severe
> Too deeply stain'd with woe[.]

Echoes of Thomas Gray sound faintly in other Percy poems of this period, but in the "Post-script," however distorted, they are unmistakable. Percy models himself after the "Youth to Fortune and to Fame unknown" of the *Elegy Written in a Country Church Yard*, which had been published two years earlier. Gray's youth, whose humble birth "Fair Science frown'd not on" but whom Melancholy marked for her own, goes forth "at the peep of dawn." Percy too is an early morning wanderer:

> At break of Dawn he frequent stray'd
>   To swell the plaintive Song
> And oft at eve the arching Shade
>   With Flavia's name has rung[.]

> His Morn of life pass'd calm & smooth
>   Fair Hope upon him smil'd
> But early Care with rankling Tooth
>   Each blooming Joy dispoil'd.

The verses are not indebted only to Gray. In its use of alternating lines of iambic tetrameter and trimeter, the "Post-script," like the poem to which it was attached, is closer to the ballad than to Gray's

Elegy, its only modification of the ballad stanza being the rhyming of the first and third lines of each quatrain in addition to the second and fourth. The influence of ballad form is evident also in "A Song," with its recurrent use of one of the more familiar ballad refrains.

During the nineteenth and twentieth centuries an interest in ballad form could almost be expected of aspiring young poets, and even in the early eighteenth century the ancient ballads were not without admirers. But ballads were still a long way from achieving the currency given them at the end of the century. By and large the upper-class reading public associated them not with such traditional works as "Sir Patrick Spens" or "Barbara Allen" but with the hastily begotten scurrility that was hawked about London's streets in anonymous broadsides, poetic foundlings often too sickly to survive the first days of infancy. It goes without saying that ballads had held no place in Percy's Newport or Oxford studies; nor can they be found among the entries in the catalog of his boyhood library.

Thus it is quite possible that Percy's 1753 interest in ballad form was stimulated by his discovery about this time of the folio manuscript that was to furnish the basis for his 1765 *Reliques of Ancient English Poetry*. Just when he came upon this collection of old ballads, romances, and other poems has never been determined, but the most likely time was the period of his curacies at Astley Abbots and Tasley, when he was preaching in numerous Shropshire towns and cultivating his clerical and literary friendships. But family connection alone should have been sufficient to lead him to his prize. His distant cousin Mary Congreve was married to Robert Binnel, and Binnel was the nephew of Humphrey Pitt, in whose house at Shifnal, eleven miles north of Bridgnorth, the manuscript had been placed beneath a bureau in the parlor. "I saw it [there]," Percy recalled in 1769, "lying dirty on the floor . . . : being used by the Maids to light the fires."[30]

Perhaps an already developed fondness for old things prompted Percy to ask Humphrey Pitt for the manuscript. In any event, it was given to him and was thus spared any further incineration. But he was not yet in a position to exploit the manuscript's riches. Curious, but "in no Degree an Antiquary," he had little sense of its worth and contented himself with reading it, scribbling occasional notes in the margins, and even removing one or two leaves to save himself the trouble of transcribing. Other activities were simply more attractive to him at that time.

One of those activities was to extend and improve his friendships.

Robert Binnel, already a confidant, was to render important assistance in some of Percy's literary work. Through Richard Yate, Percy made the acquaintance in 1754 of the Reverend James Hervey, author of the popular *Meditations and Contemplations* and rector of Weston-Favell in Northamptonshire. Percy quickly won Hervey's esteem. "He is really an ingenious Gentleman," Hervey wrote to Yate on June 14, 1754, "has a lively Apprehension, a penetrating Judgment, as well as a large Share of Reading." Somewhat later Hervey described a letter from Percy as "fit to appear in Print": it "will do Him as much Honour as it does me."[31]

Percy conducted more extensive correspondences with Thomas Apperley of Hereford and London and with his cousin William Cleiveland of Worcester. He and Will Cleiveland were drawn together by the ties initially of family and later of profession, as Will studied for the ministry at Oxford and then succeeded his father as rector of All Saints in Worcester. Percy and Apperley, only a year apart in age, were probably brought together through Percy's distant cousin, Richard Parry Price of Brynypys in Flintshire. Apperley had been educated with Price at Brynypys. On August 8, 1752, Percy preached at Overton in Flintshire during a visit to Brynypys, which was part of Overton parish.[32] Although Percy and Cleiveland occasionally exchanged poems, and Percy even invited his cousin to collaborate with him in translating Ovid, he could arouse only limited enthusiasm for literary discussion, and by and large they concentrated in their letters on family and clerical matters.[33] These proved a strong enough bond to sustain the correspondence from 1754 until Cleiveland's death in 1794. Apperley, on the other hand, had proposed a literary correspondence in the fall of 1754, and Percy's letters to him either focus on literary subjects or become themselves literary productions prepared for Apperley's enjoyment. Apperley quickly became a close friend, a companion with whom Percy could share a book, an evening at Vauxhall Gardens, or a lottery ticket.[34] Because Percy's letters to Apperley, unlike those to Cleiveland, have survived piecemeal, and Apperley's letters to Percy have scarcely survived at all, it is impossible to determine when their rather frequent correspondence became irregular. Percy's last extant letter is dated October 14, 1775, but he probably wrote occasional letters at least until the summer of 1793, when he and Mrs. Percy stopped on their way to Ireland to visit the Apperleys at Wrexham.[35]

Most of Percy's first letter to Apperley recounts what he calls his dream after reading a speculation of Joseph Addison on flattery, and Apperley responded with a poetic imitation that Percy, in his letter of February 21, 1755, professed to find so entertaining that he had to delay a reply until he could send something "equally solid and elegant."[36] The "something" turned out to be "a few trifling Strictures on . . . a favorite Author of yours," apparently Horace. The next letter seems not to have survived, but its contents are suggested by Percy's letter of August 25, 1755, addressed to Apperley at Johnson's Court in London. He thanks Apperley for his comments on his "Poetic Trifle" (his twenty-four stanza elegy), and for procuring a number of Spanish books for him from the London bookseller Lockyer Davis: "with what I had before, I shall have enough to employ me for some time." Included among his purchases was a Portuguese grammar, which he planned to study in order to read Camoëns.[37]

Percy concluded the August 25 letter by informing Apperley that he was setting out that morning for Worcestershire to spend a week, but when he wrote again he had actually been to Gloucestershire, Flintshire, Worcestershire, "& where not?" He congratulated Apperley in his letter of September 21 on the interest he had gained at Brynypys "in every female Heart in that Neighborhood especially in those of the young & the gay!" After the visit at Brynypys, he had gone with his brother Arthur and his cousin Will Cleiveland to the "Musick Meeting" at Worcester, where he enjoyed the music of William Boyce, William Felton, Joseph Baildon, and others. He also "danc'd at the ball both nights & had frequently the honour of grasping the fairest Hand in the World, that of Lady Coventry: A lovely, vain, fantastical Creature she is."[38]

Percy's first extant letter to William Cleiveland was written from Cleiveland's own house in Worcester on March 24, 1756, Percy having traveled to Worcester to sell eight houses owned by his father in St. Swithin's parish in order to relieve his father of the lingering indebtedness from his earlier misfortunes. Cleiveland was at Oxford, and Percy announced that he was contemplating taking up his duties at Easton Maudit, where his life, like Will's, would have "something of an Academical Nature." He might, in fact, be going to Easton Maudit the next week, though only to reconnoiter.[39]

The decision to leave Bridgnorth for Easton Maudit, soon quite firm, had apparently been precipitated by the Earl of Sussex's promise of an additional living about seven miles from Easton Maudit. This was as curate to the rector of St. Mary the Virgin in Wilby, the Reverend Wolsey Johnson, who was also chaplain to the Earl of Sus-

sex. Whether or not he made the preliminary short trip to Easton
Maudit is not clear, but he was soon preparing for his departure from
Bridgnorth. He sorted through his books, by then increased to about
four hundred fifty, and either in April or on a return visit to Bridgnorth
in June he gave away or sold at cost more than half of them to friends
like Robert Binnel and William Congreve, Binnel's brother-in-law.
Among the books that he parted with were a Spanish grammar, Chaucer's works in black letter, the sermons of Bishop Burnet and Archbishop Tillotson, and the plays of Congreve, Dryden, Ben Jonson,
Otway, and Steele. Those that he kept included the works of Buckingham, Cleiveland, and Shakespeare; *Robinson Crusoe, Gulliver's
Travels,* and *Pamela*; the *Tatler, Spectator,* and *Guardian; Don Quixote*
in a 1617 Brussels edition; and the Psalms in Hebrew and English,
interleaved. He also kept Brian Hunt's *Parochial Pasturage* and Eleazar
Albin's *Natural History of English Song-Birds*, perhaps for immediate
practical use.[40]

At Easter he conducted his final service at Astley Abbots and
presumably also at Tasley. At Astley Abbots, where he perhaps felt
a stronger kinship with his congregation, he added a few personal
comments to a sermon on the love of peace. "Now I bid you a final
Adieu," he said:—

> never probably shall we meet again, till we meet face to face before
> the tremendous Judge of the Universe. . . . Be constant in your at-
> tendance on divine worship. Come not to the Temple of God with
> slackness or irreverence; or behave there inattentively or remissly.
> . . . To your Neighbours be just, be honest, be peac[e]able. . . . To
> your Superiors be respectful, be faithful, be obedient.[41]

One would hardly guess from Percy's farewell that he was going
only as far as Northamptonshire and that he would have frequent
opportunities to return to Bridgnorth to visit family and friends, but
perhaps a young clergyman saying good-bye to his first congregation
was entitled to some exaggeration. One may wonder also if his counsel
that they be faithful and obedient as well as respectful to their superiors
was not placing an unduly heavy tax on inferior social position. But
his counsel of good neighborliness was surely genuine. And as for
their behavior in church, it is interesting to see that even the bright
young Percy, like countless other clergymen, had had sufficient ex-

perience of nodding age and squirming youth to think them worthy of comment.

Five days later, on April 21, he was on his way to Easton Maudit.[42]

NOTES

1. B.L. Add. MS. 32,326, f. 23; Salop Record Office 4001/Admin/3/3.
2. Percy's manuscript sermons, with the dates and places of their delivery, have survived mainly in three Bodleian Library manuscripts: Percy d. 3–5. A few are in the collection of Kenneth Balfour, and two that were described in 1910 in the *Transactions of the Shropshire Archaeological Society* (3d ser. 10:iii) are now in the Shrewsbury School Library.
3. Bodl. MS. Percy d. 3, f. 232.
4. Osborn Collection, Yale University. Francis Colinge, perhaps John Colinge's father, signed the 1752 parish register at Astley Abbots as one of the two churchwardens.
5. Bodl. MS. Percy d. 4, f. 208.
6. Ibid., d. 3, ff. 118–39, 169–92, 280–95; d. 5, ff. 25–55, 60–79.
7. W. D. Macray, "Bishop Percy's Account of John Higgs, Incumbent of Quatford, Salop," *Notes & Queries*, 6th ser., 10(1884):341–42.
8. Both parish registers were housed a few years ago in St. Leonard's, where I viewed them. They are now in the Salop Record Office. St. Leonard's has since been closed and its parish incorporated with St. Mary's.
9. B.L. Add. MS. 32,326, f. 26. Throughout I use the modern rather than the eighteenth-century spelling, which was Easton Mauduit.
10. *The Percy Letters*, vol. 7, *The Correspondence of Thomas Percy & William Shenstone*, ed. Cleanth Brooks (New Haven: Yale Univ. Press, 1977), 46 n. 3.
11. Percy's diary is in B.L. Add. MSS. 32,336 and (after 1778) 32,337. It begins on 17 June 1753, when Percy was in Hereford to be ordained a priest, and it continues intermittently until his death, although the entries toward the end of Percy's life were made by a secretary. It consists of a series of small printed notebooks, much like today's pocket diaries, with seven rectangular spaces on the left-hand page marked with the days and dates of the week. These are generally in a half-page column with an open half-page column to the right of it for further notes and with the right-hand page lined for keeping accounts. Unfortunately the diary is fragmentary. On Percy's instructions, his daughter Barbara destroyed those parts that she saw no reason for others to examine ("Instructions," 7 June 1808, Beinecke Library, Ms. Vault File), but what she preserved provides an indispensable record of much of Percy's life.
    William S. Derham, D.D., was President of St. John's College from

1748 until his death in 1757. A number of Gowers attended Christ Church, but the "Gow'r" mentioned by Percy was probably the Reverend Foot Gower, who had matriculated at Brasenose College in 1744 and returned to Oxford in the early 1750s to study medicine. He was awarded the B.Med. in 1755 and the D.Med. in 1757. Percy's 1761 diary records a supper with Dr. Gower on 22 May and a visit to Vauxhall on 6 June. "Brooke" was probably John Brooke of Shifnal in Shropshire, who matriculated at Wadham College in 1749 and was awarded the B.A. in 1752 and the M.A. in 1755.

12. Mary Perrins was the daughter of Anthony Percy, the brother of Thomas's grandfather Arthur Percy.

13. Henry Fielding, *The Covent-Garden Journal*, ed. Gerard Edward Jensen (New Haven: Yale Univ. Press, 1965), 1:181. The quotation is from No. 8, dated 28 Jan. 1752.

14. Diary; *Public Advertiser*, 30 Nov. 1753; *Daily Advertiser*, 3 Dec. 1753.

15. Bodl. MS. Percy d. 3, f. 1.

16. The listing for Easton Maudit is in Percy's library, now at the Queen's University of Belfast.

17. B.L. Add. MS. 32,333, f. 7 (Letter to William Cleiveland, 25 Aug. 1756).

18. Huntington Library MS. HM 216.

19. Sotheby's Sale Catalogue, 13 Dec. 1977, no. 338 (Letter Robert Binnel to James Grainger).

20. Huntington Library MS. HM 216. Percy's eleven-day correction—from 2 April to 13 April—brings to mind England's shift from the Julian to the Gregorian calendar on 2 September 1752, when England made up the eleven days it had fallen behind the Continent. In 1753, the first full year of the new calendar, Flavia and Percy would still naturally have thought of her birthday as 2 April—if that indeed was her birthday under the Julian calendar—when in fact it had become appropriate to celebrate it on 13 April.

21. Huntington Library MS. HM 216.

22. The 13 September poem is in the Huntington Library (HM 216) and the 6 November poem in the Hyde Collection. The undated poem is in the Houghton Library (Percy MS. bMS Eng 893 [260]). The elegy is first mentioned in Percy's letter to Thomas Apperley of 25 August 1755 (Hyde). In 1757 William Shenstone sent the elegy to Robert Dodsley, who published it as "Cynthia, an Elegiac Poem" in his *Collection of Poems* (London, 1758), 6:234–39 (Letter to Apperley, 20 Sept. 1757, Berg Collection, New York Public Library). Percy's manuscript copy of the elegy is in the Folger Shakespeare Library (Y.c. 1452 [19]).

23. Hyde Collection.

24. Alexander Pope, *Minor Poems*, ed. Norman Ault and John Butt (London: Methuen, 1954), 302.

25. *Shenstone's Miscellany 1759–1763*, ed. Ian A. Gordon (Oxford: Clarendon Press, 1952), 48.

26. Ibid., 53–54, 137–38.

27. "An Inscription . . . " and "The Mistake" exist in manuscript at the end of the second volume of Percy's diary. (B.L. Add. MS. 32,337, ff. 201 and 206). The Forest of Morf was just east of Bridgnorth. The Houghton Library has a fragmentary poem, "Shakenhurst Woods," which was probably also written during this period.

28. *Universal Visiter* (May 1756), 240; Anna Williams, *Miscellanies in Prose and Verse* (London, 1766), 3. Percy's copy of the *Miscellanies*, with his notations, is at the Queen's University of Belfast. I have been unable to identify Anna Cotton.

29. *Universal Visiter* (July 1756), 330–31; *Grand Magazine of Universal Intelligence* (March 1758), 145.

30. B.L. Add. MS. 27,879, f. 1; *Bishop Percy's Folio Manuscript*, ed. John W. Hales and Frederick J. Furnivall (London: 1867–68), 1:lxxiv. Percy was the great grandson of William Bankes and Mary Taylor; Mary Congreve was the granddaughter of Mary Taylor and her second husband Humphrey Grenowes (B.L. Add. MS. 32,326, f. 25).

    In his *Antiquities of Bridgnorth* ([Bridgnorth, 1856], 240), the Reverend G. Bellett noted that he received a letter from H. E. Boyd, rector of Dromore and former secretary to Bishop Percy, informing him that Percy had acquired the folio manuscript while he was living in Bridgnorth.

31. *A Collection of the Letters of the Late Reverend James Hervey* (London, 1760), 2:121, 193. Although designated in the text only as Mr. P———, Percy provided the identifications in his copy, now at the Queen's University of Belfast.

32. B.L. Add. MS. 32,333, f. 54 (Letter Percy to Cleiveland, 31 Jan. 1770); Bodl. MS. Percy d. 3, f. 19. Richard Price's mother, born Alice Cleiveland, was the granddaughter of Joseph Cleiveland, brother of the poet John Cleiveland. Percy and William Cleiveland were great grandsons of the Reverend William Cleiveland, brother of Joseph and John.

33. The letters are in B.L. Add. MS. 32,333.

34. Letter to Apperley, 17 March 1756 (Hyde Collection).

35. Percy's letter of 14 October 1775, is in the National Library of Wales (MS. 4955 D). An 8 July 1798 letter, with which Apperley introduced his son—attached to the Corps of Ancient Britons—to Percy suggests that their correspondence had been discontinued for some time (collection of Kenneth Balfour).

36. Percy's first letter in the correspondence is dated 9 December 1754 (Robert Taylor Collection, Princeton University). The letter of 21 February 1755 is in the Folger Shakespeare Library (Art, Vol. a9, opp. p. 199). Perhaps

the speculation on flattery was in *Spectator* 460, which was by Richard Steele rather than Joseph Addison.

37. *The Percy Letters*, vol. 1, *The Correspondence of Thomas Percy & Edmond Malone*, ed. Arthur Tillotson (Baton Rouge: Louisiana State Univ. Press, 1944), 192. The 25 August letter is in the Hyde Collection.

38. Letter to Apperley, 21 Sept. 1755 (Bodl. MS. Eng. Lett. d. 219, ff. 23–24).

39. B.L. Add. MSS. 32,326, f. 35; 32,333, ff. 2–3.

40. Bodl. MS. Percy c. 9, ff. 2–18. Other purchasers included Bryan Bromwich, William White, and Mr. Wright and Dr. Steuart, whose first names Percy did not record. Wright, whom Percy was to see occasionally in London, may have been Paul Wright, in later years a fellow member of the Society of Antiquaries.

41. Collection of Kenneth Balfour ("Ecclesiastical papers").

42. B.L. Add. MS. 32,326, f. 26.

CHAPTER III

Easton Maudit:
1756–1759

AFTER A STOP at Worcester, Percy reached Easton Maudit at noon on Saturday, April 24, expecting to take up his duties as vicar of Easton Maudit and curate to Wolsey Johnson at Wilby. To his surprise he discovered that Johnson had died on April 21, leaving the hoped-for curacy at the disposal of the next and as yet unnamed rector. Percy's disappointment must have been intense. But aware that the Earl of Sussex, who could bestow the rectorate as he wished, had promised the first vacancy to one of his chaplains before becoming acquainted with Percy, he set out for London a day or two later to ask the Earl to obtain the curacy for him once again.[1]

He had been given a standing invitation to stay at the Earl's house when he was in London, and thus went directly to Pall Mall, where the Earl was in residence to attend the session of Parliament and to discharge whatever duties fell to him as Master of the Bedchamber to the Prince of Wales, the future George III. Fortunately for Percy, the Earl was a generous and honorable patron who was plainly dismayed that his commitment to his chaplain precluded his granting the promised curacy. He received Percy "with the most particular friendship" and during the week of Percy's visit took him frequently to the House of Lords and, with a tacit acknowledgment of his own powers of persuasion, promised to secure him the curacy, at least. At the end of the week, with nothing to report, he asked Percy to return in a fortnight after taking care of his clerical duties at Easton Maudit. Percy was accordingly at Pall Mall again on May 17, but by the end of a two-week visit had still heard nothing about the curacy. The Earl appointed him his chaplain on May 28, however, and presented him with the scarf appropriate to that office.[2]

On May 30 Percy was again at Easton Maudit, looking back

fondly upon the pleasures of his London visit but also enjoying the Northamptonshire village that he had served as vicar for three years without coming to know. Writing to Thomas Apperley at ten in the evening of June 2, he imagined his friend returning from the pleasure gardens at Vauxhall, "where you have been giving every Sense it's most exquisite Feast." But he did not envy him. He himself had just been strolling through the woods as fancy led him, and for over an hour had been listening to a nightingale "lavishing forth such strains of Harmony, as . . . the softest Squeakers of the Opera never came up to." With wood pigeons, a tinkling rill, and a distant curfew bell as accompaniment—and now and then a hare or doe to stare at him— he had no need for Vauxhall's "Delicious Viands, & still more delicious Damsels." Instead he could let his imagination form "a romance as full of wild unaccountable Adventures, & fairy Scenes, as any Composition out of Nature, wch the last Romance-writing Age ever produc'd."[3]

Percy officiated at a baptism on June 20 and a burial on June 27, and shortly thereafter left for Bridgnorth to pack up his books and take a final leave of family and friends. He prolonged his leave-taking until mid-July, surprised that during all that time he had seen no notice in the newspapers about the Wilby living. On his return trip to Easton Maudit he called at Brandon in Warwickshire, the seat of the Viscountess of Longueville, grandmother of the Earl of Sussex, who, like the Earl, seems to have become a steady friend after Percy's appointment as vicar in the autumn of 1753. The Earl himself arrived at Brandon on July 19 and on the next day gave Percy the unexpected but welcome news that he planned to make him rector of Wilby. It had taken him all this time, he explained, to prevail upon the other clergyman to relinquish his claim to the living and put off his expectations somewhat longer. Apparently eager to implement his decision, he drove Percy to Coventry the next morning to secure the necessary stamp for the presentation but found none available. After their return to Brandon, the Earl spent the better part of two days entertaining Percy and other guests at dinner, showing Percy the ruins of Brandon Castle, and escorting him to Lord Craven's estate at Combe Abbey, where Percy enjoyed the "many fine Pictures" by Titian, Holbein, Rembrandt, Rubens, Vandyke, and others.

Percy, of course, was elated by the Earl's announcement, and he immediately sent off letters to his brother Arthur and a number of friends, including one whom he identified in his diary only as "Miss

A." For Will Cleiveland he provided a full account of his spring and summer adventures, with the further information that the Wilby living, which he would hold concurrently with his vicarage, was usually estimated at about £200 a year. "What Reason have I to bless Providence," he exclaimed, "& to be thankful for this ample, this early Provision of me?—So much beyond my Expectations, Hopes, or Merit?"[4]

The Earl's gift of the rectorate did not complete Percy's task of establishing himself in Northamptonshire. On July 30, the morning after he wrote to Will Cleiveland, he met the Earl by arrangement on the London road, and they traveled to town together for Percy to file the required nomination, presentation, and testimonials and to seek a dispensation to hold the two livings simultaneously. For the dispensation he was obliged to sit for an examination consisting of three questions written out for him in Latin by Dr. Nathaniel Foster, Fellow of Corpus Christi College, Oxford: What is the most forceful argument to prove the divine authority of the Scriptures? What is the Catholic Church? Should the goods of Christians be held in common in accordance with law and title? Presumably Dr. Foster was satisfied with Percy's answers, for the dispensation was granted by the Crown on August 10, and Percy was able to travel to Wilby to take possession of the living and preach the induction sermon on August 22.[5] But still other formalities compelled his prompt return to London, his fourth such trip of the four-month period. "I am heartily weary of both the Trouble and Expence," he wrote to Will Cleiveland from Pall Mall on August 25. "The Ecclesiastical Leeches have almost suck'd me dry; they having already drain'd my Pockets of near 50 Pounds."[6]

Vexing and expensive though his long wait had been, Percy's limited diary entries for the period from April to September reveal that he managed in his four visits to sample London's attractions much as in his first visit in 1753. No doubt living with the Earl of Sussex in Pall Mall imposed some constraints upon him, but during most of his seven weeks in London he seems to have been free to come and go as he pleased. He dined on at least four afternoons with his cousin Mary Perrins and on May 25 went to Sadler's Wells with her son-in-law Richard Rolt, one of the editors of the *Universal Visiter*, to whom he gave two of his sonnets. Featured at Sadler's Wells was "the amazing Equilibrist Signora Catherina."[7] He saw his friend Apperley on several occasions and renewed his acquaintance with George Durant and the Woodingtons. On August 27 he visited Bethlehem Hospital, the asylum in Moorfields better known as Bedlam, but did not record his impressions. By sheer chance on August 23 he rode to London in the stagecoach with George Faulkner, Jonathan Swift's Dublin printer, who entertained him with anecdotes of Swift. His fondness for the theater took him to Drury Lane on May 19 to see David Garrick in *King Lear* and on May 26 to Covent Garden, where Peg Woffington was closing the theater's 1755–56 season in George Farquhar's *Constant Couple*. He patronized the Smyrna, the Grecian, and other coffee houses, and visited the rotunda at Ranelagh and the gardens at Vauxhall.

Some of his activities reflect his status as the guest and chaplain of a court favorite. On May 22 he accompanied the Earl of Sussex to a performance of Giovanni Battista Lampugnani's opera *Siroë* at the King's Theater. Four days earlier he was at Westminster in the midst of the excitement as George II, at Kensington Palace, signed a declaration of war against France, the start of what was to be known in England as the Seven Years' War and, in America, as the French and Indian War.[8] I "saw it all," Percy confided to his diary. Perhaps the Earl also introduced him to Richard Backwell, member of Parliament for Northampton, with whom Percy had dinner on the same day. On Sunday morning, August 1, he attended services in the chapel at Kensington Palace dressed in his gown and cassock, and afterwards had the pleasure of seeing the royal family in the drawing room.

Attendance at a private gathering in the King's drawing room was a fairy-tale adventure for a young suppliant seeking only a dispensation to hold two livings in an obscure corner of England's midlands. But a seven-weeks' welcome in an earl's house in Pall Mall must have seemed quite beyond the reach of Mr. Adamson's curate, a stroke of good fortune, or providence, which even a romantic imagination fired by *Extraordinary Adventures, Unparallel'd Varieties,* and *Wonderful Prodigies* could scarcely have dreamed of. If Percy had learned early to conciliate the favor of those he conversed with, he had also developed qualities that made his attentions acceptable—a convivial nature, a quick mind, an infectious enthusiasm, a fund of information and anecdote, a readiness to be of service—and raised him above the station of a mere seeker of favors. The Earl of Sussex, only two years Percy's senior, responded by offering him not just his patronage, but his friendship as well.

Percy, obviously, was not above seeking favors. In an age in which appointment and advancement depended largely upon patronage, it was assumed that the great could always supply something—influence if not actual preferment—that might further one's objectives, and no stigma was attached to seeking it for one's self or one's relatives or friends. True to the system, Percy planned to speak up not just for himself but for at least one of his brothers as well. Both were among his London companions in the spring and summer of 1756; Arthur arrived in London on May 27, and Anthony and Thomas were together frequently after Thomas's return on August 23 for his final trip of the summer. But without waiting for Percy to assume the initiative, the Earl of Sussex explored with him the likely prospects for the twenty-two-year-old Arthur, who had been trained for business but was leaning toward a military career; and on the day after Percy's return to London in August the Earl announced that he had secured a commission for Arthur in the 37th Company of marines.[9] He apparently said nothing about Anthony, whom Percy had probably brought to London to be introduced as a candidate for preferment once Arthur's needs had been taken care of. Anthony, a shadowy figure and perhaps something of a ne'er-do-well, was to prove more difficult to assist.

Percy returned to Easton Maudit early in September with a gratifying summer behind him and excellent prospects ahead. No longer a curate of two churches but a vicar of one and rector of another, he had fulfilled at age twenty-seven the ambition of most young clergymen of his time, a secure place with an income adequate for his needs. His admired patron—his London host—was now his Easton Maudit neighbor, and with his customary generosity the Earl of Sussex placed his library at Percy's disposal and seems to have reserved a room for him in the manor house while the vicarage underwent repairs and renovation. "My Lord & some very agreable [sic] young People of distinction are down here," Percy wrote to Will Cleiveland on October 14, 1756, and "they do me the honour to confine me altogether to their Company."[10] He also treasured the connection with Lady Longueville, who had grown up in the reign of Charles II and could draw upon her memories of the Restoration court for anecdotes in which Percy took special delight.[11]

For scholarly company Percy could walk or ride the mile and a half to Yardley Hastings, where Edward Lye, the editor of Junius's *Etymologicum Anglicanum* and the Gothic Gospels, was rector. The elderly Lye, whom Percy had known before his move from Bridgnorth, seems to have taken a fatherly interest in his new neighbor, whom he accompanied on his May 1756 trip to London and inducted into his Wilby living on August 22.[12] Percy responded with more than filial respect. Lye, he wrote Apperley on March 17, 1756, was a "Prodigy of Learning": besides Latin and Greek, in which he was a "complete Critick," he had a general acquaintance with the Near Eastern languages and a more precise acquaintance with the modern European languages and Irish and Welsh. But his most perfect knowledge was of the northern languages, particularly the Teutonic, of which, Percy noted, "He has told me himself he understands the ancient Gothic, Saxon, Islandic, High Dutch, Low Dutch, Danish, Swedish—& what not?" "After all this," Percy added, "will you not wonder when I tell you that he . . . [wears] the plainest Habit . . . [and is] ready to trot or walk half a dozen Mile upon a Moment's Warning to pray by an Old Woman for any neighbouring Curate."[13]

By this time Percy was himself a published author, the "Sonnet to a Lady" having been printed by Richard Rolt in the May issue of the *Universal Visiter* and the "Sonnet Occasion'd by Leaving Bath" in the July issue.[14] The prospect of further writing attracted him, and limited church duties permitted him as much free time for literary and other pleasures as he had enjoyed in Bridgnorth. During the long wait in London, Dr. Steuart of Wolverhampton had introduced him to the Scottish poet and physician James Grainger, who was five years Percy's senior, and in early October he wrote to Grainger to propose a literary correspondence such as Thomas Apperley had proposed to him in 1754.[15] Even marriage seemed no longer essential to his happiness, as he informed the recently ordained William Cleiveland on August 25 before he returned to Easton Maudit from London:

> To tell you the truth the Life I lead at present is so very agreable, & so suited to my Tast [*sic*]; that I am not quite convinc'd, it will receive any Improvem.! from Matrimony:—At present my Time is pretty equally divided between Books & Pleasure: I enjoy as much of the company of the Fair Sex, as serves to brighten up & throw a Gaiety upon Life: without being pester'd with too much Care: I am near enough to London to go up at any Time in a Day, & yet so far from it as not to feel the Inconvenience of its Neighbourhood:—When I am in a studious fit, I can bury myself in books without fear of Interruption: When in a gay Mood, I can gallant it among the Ladies. . . . Do you in your Next tell me what Accession of Happiness c.? be gain'd by Matrimony.[16]

He had not changed his view of the bachelor's life when he wrote to Will again on October 14. That very night, he reported, he was to attend a "grand Ball & Assembly" eight miles away at Newport Pagnell, where all the nobility and gentry of the neighborhood would gather, and he was "already engaged to dance with a New-married Lady of s[ome] distinction." This was by his own choice, he added, for having seen few of the young women in that area, he thought it desirable to keep apart from them for the present and use the occasion for the "more general Survey" which would facilitate his choice the next time. He was given to expect "a fine Collection of Belles" at Newport Pagnell, "and how my Heart will escape among them, heaven knows, at present it is pretty sound & whole."[17]

During the summer he had discarded the spelling "Piercy" in favor of the more illustrious "Percy," a decision hastened perhaps by his association with the Earl of Sussex and his new circle of fashionable Midland friends. By his own account, his March 1756 trip to Worcester to sell his father's properties had provided him with the opportunity to inquire into old city registers, where he found the name written without the "i." He noted also that his best informed Worcester relations had retained the more familiar spelling, and that those who added the "i" spelled the name in various ways: not just Piercy, as his immediate family had done, but Peircy, Piercey, or "still more corruptly." He determined as a result to adopt what seemed to him the "most ancient and correct Spelling" and in August entered his name as Thomas Percy in all the official documents concerned with his Wilby appointment.[18]

Sometime in the summer of 1756 occurred an event of great consequence to Percy's life: Grainger's introduction of him to Samuel Johnson. Percy dated it explicitly in that year,[19] and no evidence exists of another visit to London after his return to Easton Maudit in early September. Already acclaimed as the author of *The Life of Richard Savage, The Vanity of Human Wishes,* and *The Rambler,* Johnson had achieved a unique eminence with the publication of the *Dictionary of the English Language* in 1755; and on June 2, 1756, he had followed up his success with proposals for an edition of Shakespeare's plays. Possibly Percy volunteered his assistance from the beginning, but in any event he was soon to be at work collecting subscriptions for the edition among his Northamptonshire and Shropshire friends.[20] He also visited the house in Gough Square where the widower Johnson resided with the blind poetess Anna Williams, the young black servant Frank Barber, and a maidservant who, Percy later recalled, had lost her nose to the ravages of venereal disease.[21]

In mid-autumn a gloom was cast over Percy's idyllic life by news of the death of his brother Arthur, who had contracted a fever only a few days after joining his company of marines at Portsmouth and had died on October 24. An obvious favorite of his older brother, Arthur had also endeared himself to the Earl of Sussex. Writing from Bridgnorth, where he had gone to console his parents, Percy informed Will Cleiveland on November 30 that during the summer the Earl had walked with Arthur daily in St. James's Park and elsewhere, and had undertaken to fit him for his new position by introducing him into the best company and personally commending him to his superior officers. Percy himself, among other assistance, had made Arthur a "compleat Master of Geography," and Mrs. Price of Brynypys had contributed fifty of the nearly £100 required for Arthur's equipment and instruction. By August 26 Arthur was able to demonstrate his newly acquired skill in fencing to Percy and George Durant. Reviewing Arthur's general progress during his two months in London, Percy ventured the opinion that "there never was a young fellow so much improved"; yet, for all the attention lavished on him, Arthur preserved his "genuine Modesty & unaffected Simplicity of Manners."[22]

By the time of Arthur's death, Percy's acquaintance with James Grainger was prospering. A down-to-earth man, Grainger insisted that they observe no ceremony in the correspondence that Percy proposed to him; "there can be no pleasure where correspondents stand upon punctilios," he wrote on October 22 in belated reply to Percy's initial letter. If Percy wishes to trust him with his literary work, he may depend upon Grainger's sincerity, however much he may question his judgment. In return he expects "a cessation of compliments, and as frequent letters as you think proper."[23]

The October 22 letter also contains the first indication that Grainger had invited Percy to contribute to the translation of the Latin poet Tibullus's elegies that he was preparing for the publisher Andrew Millar. Grainger later acknowledged publicly that he had lost his own translation of Tibullus's first elegy, and it seems likely that he turned to Percy for a replacement both to avoid the tedium of doing the work over and to encourage a new young friend whose talents promised to match his enthusiasm. Percy's favorite among the Latin poets was Ovid, whose *Epistles* he may have begun translating while he was still a curate in Shropshire, and in time he was to assist Grainger further by translating Ovid's elegy on Tibullus for the projected edition. In the months following their initial exchange of letters, Percy read proofs of the edition, suggested changes in Grainger's translations, and also interested Robert Binnel in supplying notes that Grainger generously added to his own. When Percy wrote to Thomas Apperley on January 16, 1757, he was pleased to report that the Tibullus edition had the approval of Samuel Johnson. He confessed also, with a flourish characteristic of his letters to Apperley, that this first experience of writing for the public induced "Palpitations" and "pannicks" whenever he thought of the risk he would be running from "Coffee-house Critticks, Young Templars, Oxford Smarts, Bucks, Bloods, Magazines & Reviews."[24]

Perhaps Johnson's endorsement, coupled with the news from Grainger in a March 30 letter that Johnson and Miss Williams had asked for him "very kindly," was all the antidote required for Percy's palpitations and panics.[25] But another ailment proved more troublesome. "A weakness in my Eyes . . . has teis'd me for above a Week past," he wrote to a friend—probably Robert Binnel—on March 5.[26] Grainger, to whom he must have written a week or two later, responded on March 24 by recommending an eye ointment, eyedrops, and a laxative. In his next letter he assured Percy that there was no reason to fear blindness or any radical deterioration of the eyes. He himself had once experienced the same "floating atoms" but had recovered with the help of a ten-part course that he now laid out for his friend.[27]

No doubt the first steps in Grainger's course would have sufficed: reduce strain on the eyes by studying as little as possible, and never by candlelight; shade them with green silk both indoors and out; and go to bed by eleven. Perhaps Grainger's eyewash and ointment were harmless, though one wonders if the camphor prescribed in both would not have made them more abrasive than soothing; Percy, in fact, complained that the ointment had aggravated rather than relieved his condition. The rest of Grainger's prescription seem mere straws, a gathering that suggests the desperation of eighteenth-century medical ignorance: a weekly laxative; the avoidance of highly seasoned foods, malt liquors, and tea; cutting an issue (a "seton") in the neck; shaving the head close and bathing it night and morning in cold water; and taking a pinch of snuff a half hour before bedtime. "The more it makes you sneeze, and opens your head," advised Grainger, "the better."

Grainger's elaborate and probably unique course seems to have had no immediate beneficial effect, for Percy's eye problem persisted at least until April 12, 1757, when Grainger suggested further remedies. It is to be hoped that, by then, Percy had discovered a Chinese apothegm that he inserted in his edition of the novel *Hau Kiou Choaan* in 1761: "Whosoever hath sore eyes will see clearly in ten days, if he let them alone to cure themselves."[28] How much work he accomplished during this period of distress remains a question. He informed Will Cleiveland on March 24 that, after trying to carry on his work as usual, he had at last been forced to give up reading almost totally— a particular loss, since, in the absence of the Earl of Sussex, there was not a "Conversable Soul in the Parish."[29] He preached at Mears Ashby, near Wilby, on March 6, the day after his first surviving letter reporting his disability, perhaps consciously choosing a sermon he had preached a dozen times before to avoid the necessity of close attention to his manuscript.[30] But a severe strain must have been placed on his eyes by his revision of passages in Grainger's translations of Tibullus's Elegies 5, 8, and 9 on the evening of March 23, when he would have been forced to work by candle or lamplight. Strangely enough, he did not mention his eyes when he sent off his proposed revisions to Grainger on March 24, and in his letter to Will Cleiveland on the same day he actually pronounced them somewhat better, though still "very weak & infirm."[31]

"Half-blind" as he was, he turned from books and study to the garden at the vicarage, which he was still waiting to move into. Overgrown with weeds, nettles, and briars, its fences penetrated by "Squadrons of Hogs & other paultry & noxious Animals," the garden seemed to Percy "no bad Emblem of a certain larger tract of ye Globe," and he responded"like a second Mr Pitt" to the challenge of reforming all abuses. He would count upon dogs to repulse any further invasions. He himself removed the weeds from the terraces and resolved to plant wildflowers along the banks of a narrow stream at the bottom of a gentle slope in the meadow beyond the terraces. He welcomed both the shelter afforded the garden by the Earl of Sussex's "stately Groves" and the "uninterrupted Gleam of Warmth" from the south, which he looked to for its benign influence upon some forty fruit trees, a gift from one of the Earl's friends. In mid-March he spent a week planting the trees along his walls, an activity doubtless all the more enjoyable because it so closely paralleled the bucolic verses of Tibullus that he was translating for Grainger into his favorite elegiac stanza form, the quatrain popularized by Thomas Gray's *Elegy:*

> My tender Vines I'll plant with early Care,
>   And choicest Apples, with a skilful Hand;
> Nor blush, a Rustic, oft to guide the Share,
>   Or goad the tardy Ox along the Land.[32]

When he wrote to Will Cleiveland again on June 25, he had apparently moved into the vicarage and was enjoying the relative independence of a single and not overburdened country parson. In early May he joined James Hervey at Weston-Favell at a family dinner. On May 19 he made his first perambulation of the parish, accompanied by some forty-five men and boys, all of them no doubt delighted with this convivial reassertion of their parish bounds. Along the way they were met by representatives of neighboring parishes, including the Reverend Samuel Edwards, who had replaced Thomas Gery Bennet as curate of Bozeat.[33] In June he traveled to London to attend the Earl of Sussex. His income, he informed his cousin, was sufficient for him to keep a tolerably good horse and a little boy in a livery, to buy books, and to enjoy an occasional party of pleasure. He was also enjoying the attentions of the young women of the neighborhood. Just the week before, some of them had come into the fields to help him make hay after he had mowed his "little Vicarage-Close," and together they sat down to drink tea and chatted "upon no other velvet Couch than a soft & fragrant Hay-Cock, with the Canopy of a spreading Ash."

Was marriage on his mind? Yes, he acknowledged to Will, but he was no closer to it than he had been a year before and in no haste. He held the most respectful views of marriage, but considered that one could not enter with too much caution into a state from which the only deliverance was death. Thus, unless a change should be much for the better, he would choose to remain as he was: "I am affraid I sh.^d not be content to be but moderately happy in my Choice."[34]

His choice was for one

> possess'd with a sweetness of Temper able to soften the bitter Cares of Life, with a Mind properly cultivated to render her not undelighted with the Conversation of a Book-worm: & with such a moderate Knowledge of the World & Share of good breeding, as to do the Honours of my little Table with a become.^g Ease & dignity, & when my Noble Patron or any of his Friends honour my humble Roof with their Presence, they may meet with no aukard [sic] or unpolite Reception: . . . [and] with such a portion of the Graces of

Person, as may secure my heart from all fear of disgust, & such a Share of the Gifts of Fortune as may prevent our softer Hours from being imbitter'd by apprehensions of future distress to ourselves or those as dear to us.

While he awaits this millennium, he concluded, he contrives to live pleasantly enough for a *"batchelor forlorn."*

Perhaps an extended trip in the late summer of 1757 was not unrelated to the hoped-for millennium. After conducting the service on August 7, Percy left Easton Maudit for Bridgnorth, where he arrived in time to preach the next Sunday's sermon at St. Leonard's.[35] A week or two later he continued on to Brynypys in Flintshire, where he participated in the festival of the "Overton Wakes" and helped to celebrate the birthday of Miss Fletcher at Guernhayled, the estate next to that of his cousins the Prices. His partner for two balls, he informed Apperley in a letter dated September 20, was a good dancer, but not handsome enough to warrant special notice. At the Guernhayled ball, nonetheless, he danced until five in the morning and, still flush with energy, rode horseback for nearly forty miles after all the others had gone home to bed.[36]

Close to home again, and in his capacity as chaplain to the Earl of Sussex, he enjoyed mingling with "Gentlemen & Ladies of the prime Distinction" at the Newport Pagnell races, held during the week of September 11. Two horses ran a close race on the first day, he reported to Apperley, but in the field of eight on the second day there was no contest: the winner beat the others *"all Hollow."* This is to show you, he joked to Apperley, "that I do not live in a Sporting Country; without picking up some Arcana of the Science." At Newport Pagnell he also attended another two balls, where the "principal Beauty," Lord Howe's daughter, was toasted constantly by the bachelor Earl of Sussex.

Not without a taste for gambling, Percy asked Apperley to buy him a ticket in the lottery then being drawn in London and send it to him by the first post. It was "for a very pretty Girl of my Acquaintance, to whom I heartily wish the £10,000," and he would assume, whatever the price, that Apperley had purchased it as cheaply as he could. One can only speculate on the identity of the very pretty girl who merited such special notice. If she was Anne Gutteridge of Desborough in Northamptonshire, Percy's millennium was already in sight.

The jaunt west had literary rewards also. Near Halesowen in Shropshire he stopped to visit the poet William Shenstone at the Leasowes, Shenstone's garden showpiece of brook, cascade, ruined priory, copses, and trim enclosures looking out on the Wrekin, Shropshire's most famous landmark some thirty miles away. After writing a description of the Leasowes in 1753, Percy continued over the years to admire Shenstone's steady improvements to his estate, and the two kept up at least a casual acquaintance. In 1757 they became much closer friends. Some time before Percy's 1757 visit, copies of Percy's elegy on Flavia and a "Song" had come to Shenstone's hands, doubtless through Robert Binnel, and Shenstone had forwarded them to the publisher Robert Dodsley for use in a future miscellany. During the visit, Shenstone—fifteen years Percy's senior— offered to correct other poems that Percy had brought with him, and he lent Percy a copy of Thomas Gray's *Odes*, which Horace Walpole had recently published at Strawberry Hill. As he informed Apperley in his September 20 letter, Percy found "The Bard," his favorite of the two odes in the volume, "wonderfully romantic" and one of the most sublime poems ever written, although he acknowledged that it had taken him several readings to appreciate it.

In the early fall Percy was in close attendance on the Earl of Sussex, who had returned to Easton Maudit for the hunting season, and in November he was back in London, lodged once again in the Earl's Pall Mall residence.[37] He called on Johnson at Gough Square frequently and was surprised that Johnson remained hopeful of seeing his edition of Shakespeare published before Easter when he had not yet completed the second volume. At Pall Mall he received Shenstone's recommended changes in the verses he had left at the Leasowes, and he responded appreciatively on November 24, though not with total acquiescence: "You will . . . make allowances for the foolish Fondness of Scriblers, if you should find I have now and then ventur'd to retain the old Reading, in Defiance of your superior Judgment."

Percy's most important announcement in the letter was that he possessed "a very curious old MS Collection of ancient Ballads" and that Johnson, to whom he had shown it, desired to see it printed. Perhaps as a first step in carrying out Johnson's desires, he asked Shenstone to send him his copy of the Scottish ballad "Gil Morrice," which Shenstone had read to him during his summer visit to the Leasowes. He wished to collate it with the ballad "Child Maurice" in his folio manuscript.[38]

Shenstone's curiosity was piqued. He sent Percy "Gil Morrice" on January 4, 1758, with the comment that nothing pleased him more than the "simplicity of style and sentiment" of the old ballads. The only thing that could increase his pleasure would be to peruse Percy's ballads in his company at the Leasowes: "pray do not think of *publishing* them, until you have *given* me that opportunity."[39]

Percy wrote his reply on January 9, but did not post it until January 15. He was astonished, he said, by the differences between Shenstone's copy of "Gil Morrice" and his own of "Child Maurice." Scarcely two lines were alike, and even the names were different— John Stewart in his ballad and Lord Barnard in Shenstone's—and his was "in general but a poor imperfect Fragment" compared with Shenstone's. But he would go no further into particulars, since he would be showing the whole collection to Shenstone as soon as he could.

"If I regarded only my own private satisfaction," he added, "I should by no means be eager to render my Collection cheap by publication." It was Johnson who extorted a promise of publication from him: he said he would "assist me in selecting the most valuable pieces and in revising the Text of those he selected: Nay further, if I would leave a blank Page between every two that I transcribed, he would furnish it out with proper Notes, etc. etc." Edward Lye, moreover, had promised assistance in compiling a glossary and explaining obsolete phrases. All these together, in short, "were such inviting Inducements as I knew not how to resist: advantages, which I could never hope to have hereafter." Nevertheless, he would not be in a hurry to start upon his task; it was agreed that he would await a "Summons" from Johnson, who had his hands full with his edition of Shakespeare. He himself was still preoccupied with Tibullus, and he enclosed his translation of Ovid's elegy on Tibullus with a request for Shenstone's corrections. He also enclosed the fragmentary poem "Gentle Heardsman" from his folio manuscript "as a Specimen of what it can produce."

A postscript explains Percy's delay in posting the letter. The Earl of Sussex, only two years Percy's senior, had died of a fever in London on January 8, "a Death . . . truly afflicting to all that knew him: but especially to myself, to whom he was the noblest of Patrons and truest of Friends." Percy had good reason to grieve. He and Lord Sussex had been drawn to each other from their first meeting, and the Earl seems to have spared no effort to make Percy's position comfortable and pleasant, to assist his family, to encourage his studies, and to improve his prospects in the church. At times he seemed more a companion than a patron: "In him I found a friend," Percy wrote in his diary: "& (tho' his equal in Age) a Father . . . to whom I could unbosom all my secrets: who was my best Advisor & director."

James Grainger, sensing the depth of Percy's sorrow, urged him to alleviate it by celebrating the Earl's virtues in an elegy. Percy welcomed the suggestion and, working rather slowly, completed a seventy-eight line "Ode on the Death of Augustus, Earl of Sussex," which he dated August 28 but was still revising in November with the help of suggestions from Shenstone.[40] By summer, understandably, his grief had been much assuaged, and he could turn from his mournful strains to a final section of four stanzas in which he commended the new earl and his countess for improvements to the manor house that their predecessor had lived too briefly to accomplish:

> See the future Plan they draw!
>   Taste & elegance attend,
> Each charm to heighten, veil each flaw,
>   Neatness, beauty, grace to lend.
> *Art* brings the Level and the Line,
> While nature prompts & guides the whole Design.

The "Ode" was not published in Percy's lifetime, but first appeared in 1952 in *Shenstone's Miscellany*, a collection of poems compiled by Shenstone which Percy fell heir to and edited, but apparently made no effort to publish.[41]

The Earl's body was brought back to Easton Maudit and laid to rest in the northeast corner of the church among the Earl's Yelverton ancestors. The successor to the title was the Earl's younger brother, Henry Yelverton, a soldier by profession with whom Percy never formed a relationship of the kind that he had found so attractive in his first year and a half at Easton Maudit. The Earl made Percy his chaplain on February 18, 1758, however, and continued to give him access to the manor house library, and there is no evidence that Percy ever complained of ill treatment or indifference.[42] Grainger, in fact, expressed his satisfaction in February 1758 that Percy was on such good terms with his new patron: "In truth, if he is a man of sense and politeness, I never doubted of your acquiring his esteem."[43]

Percy's literary projects were beginning to multiply at the time of the Earl's death. In February Grainger informed him that the printer

William Strahan and others were about to launch a new periodical and were eager to print his "Scotch Song." "Shall I let them have it?" Grainger asked.[44] The Scotch Song was the original version of the English "Song" awaiting publication in Dodsley's *Collection of Poems*, and Percy—perhaps not wishing to offend Dodsley—responded to Grainger's question with twelve verses in Latin, which the newly launched *Grand Magazine* published in its February issue.[45] Grainger was also trying to interest Ralph Griffiths in publishing the Chinese novel *Hau Kiou Choaan*, a manuscript translation of which Percy had borrowed from Captain James Wilkinson of Bugbrooke in Northamptonshire and proposed to revise and edit. In March Dodsley published *A Collection of Poems in Six Volumes*, containing Percy's "Song" and "Cynthia, an Elegiac Poem" in its final volume.[46]

The second of these was Percy's 1755 elegy on Flavia, her name changed by Dodsley without Percy's authorization. The first was to become Percy's best known and best liked poem. It was later acclaimed by Robert Burns as "perhaps, the most beautiful Ballad in the English language," and both versions were set to music, the Scottish by Joseph Baildon and the English by Thomas Carter.[47] It has also been prized as Percy's tribute to his own wife-to-be, who is personified in the Scottish version as Annie and in the English as Nancy. In four eight-line stanzas, all of which begin with similar and end with identical lines, the speaker submits his loved one to a series of questions. He asks in the first stanza if she can give up the pleasures of the town for the humble life she must lead with him.

> O Nancy, wilt thou go with me,
>   Nor sigh to leave the flaunting town:
> Can silent glens have charms for thee,
>   The lowly cot and russet gown?
> No longer dress'd in silken sheen,
>   No longer deck'd with jewels rare,
> Say can'st thou quit each courtly scene,
> Where thou wert fairest of the fair?

In successive stanzas he asks if she can endure "the parching ray" and "wintry wind" without looking back wistfully upon her comfortable early life; if she is ready to assume "the nurse's care" when "disease or pain befal" her swain; and if she will still be pleased with her choice when he is dead:

And wilt thou o'er his breathless clay
　　Strew flow'rs, and drop the tender tear,
Nor *then* regret those scenes so gay,
　　Where thou wert fairest of the fair?

Two and a half years earlier, when he wrote to Thomas Apperley on August 25, 1755, Percy had noted that in his next letter he might send an "Imitation of the Scotch Mann.ʳ in a Song, wᶜʰ. I compos'd lately for a friend of mine to set to Musick." In the next letter, written on September 21, 1755, he enclosed the "sonnet" that Apperley had expressed a desire to see, and he invited him to criticize it "with the utmost freedom of severity." It had already been shown to Richard Hurd, "one of the most celebrated Criticks in the Kingdom," whose advice Percy had accepted at only one point. The poem, Percy continued, "is meant as a sort of Test of female Love: There is a kind of Gradation intended in it." In stanza 1, the loved one is "expected to quit her Splendour &c. . . . Ask yᵉ Ladies if it is not monstrously unnatural."[48]

Percy's description in the two 1755 letters fits the "Song" of Dodsley's 1758 *Collection* exactly, even to the word *sonnet*, which at that time was still occasionally applied to any short love poem. The "Song" was written originally in the Scottish manner and was plainly intended as a test of female love, with the test moving in gradations from the first stanza to the last. In the first the loved one is expected to give up silken sheen and jewels—splendor indeed—and in the last she must be prepared to give up her lover himself. Perhaps even in Percy's time most women would have looked upon such a test as "monstrously unnatural."

Inevitably the two 1755 letters to Apperley lead one to question the traditional view that the "Song" was written for Anne Gutteridge, Percy's wife-to-be, who holds a manuscript copy of it in her only known portrait. In September 1755, when the "Song" had already undergone Richard Hurd's scrutiny, Percy had probably not made Anne's acquaintance. His pursuit of Flavia, as we have seen, had ended in disappointment, and he had been able to spend the afternoon of August 25, 1755, with Flavia and another feminine friend without any rekindling of his former passion. There is no indication, however, that Flavia had been replaced by anyone else in his affections. On June 25, 1756, he had informed Will Cleiveland that he was no closer to marriage than he had been a year before and was in no hurry. Two months later he expressed doubts to Will that marriage could improve his idyllic life at Easton Maudit, and on October 14, 1756, he was sizing up his prospects among the unmarried women at the Newport Pagnell ball and assembly. Not until the autumn of 1757, when he returned to Easton Maudit from Shropshire, Flintshire, and the Newport Pagnell races, did he indicate to any of his friends, and then only to Apperley, that a pretty girl had inspired him to try the only way he knew to provide her with a fortune of £10,000. By that time Shenstone had already forwarded the "Song" to Robert Dodsley.

Whatever his disclaimers, of course, marriage was seldom out of Percy's mind in these early years at Easton Maudit, but with the experience of one disappointment to guide him he could see more clearly how to avoid another. The "unnatural" test of the "Song" and the portrait of the ideal wife that he sketched for Will Cleiveland were useful safeguards, the moat and drawbridge of a not impregnable Percy castle. Flavia, one can guess, was not the model for Percy's portrait, which he would hardly have drawn to the measure of a lost love. For all that is known of her, she might have dismissed his test as "monstrously unnatural." The portrait and "Song" were simply expressions of an ideal not yet realized; and thus, when the woman of his dreams at last appeared, Percy could reasonably permit the impression that she was, in fact, the subject of his poem. Actually, by the time the poem was published in March 1758, the ideal was becoming excitingly real and was drawing his thoughts steadily away from the misfortune of the Earl of Sussex's death.

In 1757 Samuel Edwards was appointed curate to Ralph Barlow, vicar of Bozeat, a village about a mile down the road from Easton Maudit. Edwards had married Mary Gutteridge of Desborough on March 1, 1756; and in all likelihood these near neighbors introduced Percy in 1757 to Mary's younger sister Anne, who had remained with her mother in Desborough, some twenty miles away, since the death of her father on January 22, 1757.[49] Percy's diary for 1757 has not survived, and the 1756 diary, containing entries from May to October, mentions neither Mr. and Mrs. Edwards nor Anne Gutteridge. But two entries in the diary for January 1758 seem to show Percy in the midst of a new courtship.

The Edwards's first child, Susanna Whithorne, was born on September 18, 1757, but lived for only four months and was buried at Bozeat on January 19, 1758. On that day Percy recorded in his diary that he went to Bozeat "to bury M! Edw^{ds} little Child." It was a day of freezing temperatures, and, instead of returning to Easton Maudit after the funeral, he stayed the night. But Percy had more than the weather to detain him at Bozeat. On the next day, his diary reveals, he read some of James Thomson's *Winter* "along with Miss G."—that is, Anne Gutteridge, who had doubtless come to Bozeat also to attend the funeral, as well as to console her sister and brother-in-law. Perhaps this was Percy's and Anne's first meeting; but reading poetry together, even Thomson's *Winter* at a time of "violent Frost," was an unlikely pastime for a young man and woman of recent acquaintance, and it seems a reasonable conclusion that the courtship had had some time to mature.

By March their courtship was full-blown. In that month Percy visited Shropshire and Worcester, and at Worcester he ran into a storm that might under normal circumstances have held him in the comfort and security of the rectory at All Saints, where Will Cleiveland had succeeded his recently deceased father as rector. But "Miss G." was not at Worcester, and on March 24 he fled impetuously into the night, driven by a passion that was soon to find expression in one of the best of his poems:

> Deep howls the storm with chilling blast
>   Fast falls the snow and rain
> Down rush the floods with headlong haste
>   And deluge all the plain.
>
> Yet all in vain the tempest roars
>   And whirls the drifted snow
> In vain the torrents scorn the shores
>   To Delia I must go.
>
> . . . .
>
> Love bids atchieve the hardy Deed
>   And act the wonderous part
> He wings the foot with eagle-speed
>   And lends the Lion-heart
>
> Then led by thee, all-powerful boy
>   I'll dare this hideous night.
> Thy Dart shall guard me from annoy
>   Thy torch, my Footsteps light.
>
> The chearfull blaze, the social hour,
>   The Friend—all plead in vain

Love calls—I brave each adverse pow'r
  Of Peril and of Pain.

Percy sent copies of the poem to Will Cleiveland, Shenstone, Grainger, and Apperley, but he seems to have made no effort to have it published.[50]

Cleiveland's and Apperley's reactions are not known, but Shenstone approved sufficiently to retain the poem for his projected miscellany, and Grainger was plainly delighted. "Your poem pleases me," he wrote to Percy on April 14. "And so, my friend, I find you have got it. . . . None of your social turn would desert your beloved companion, and brave the elements, without some very valuable consideration in view, and what that consideration should be, I, who have read Tibullus, can be at no loss to guess." What was her name, Grainger asked, and how far had Percy progressed in her affections? And wasn't hers "the pretty Italian hand" that he had noticed on the backs of some of Percy's letters? He himself, he confessed, had come close to signing marriage articles not long ago, but had withdrawn because of his parents' objections; "if I feel much uneasiness now, it is chiefly on account of the sweet girl of whom I must no longer think as a partner for life."[51]

The intimacy of Grainger's letter marks him as the closest of Percy's confidants at this time, and he was never to lose his interest in the welfare of Percy's heart, health, and pen. From marriage he went on in the April 14 letter to the subject of smallpox inoculation, about which Percy had apparently inquired in the letter that accompanied his poem. Never trust a country surgeon with inoculation, Grainger advised. A short time later he encouraged Percy to send him his translation of Ovid's epistle "Penelope to Ulysses" so that he could show it as a sample to the publisher Andrew Millar, who, he assured Percy, paid better for poetry than other publishers. Johnson, he wrote on May 30, "thinks you may get fifty pieces" for Ovid's *Epistles*. He tried to interest Ralph Griffiths in publishing Percy's edition of *Hau Kiou Choaan*, and, after Griffiths rejected the manuscript on June 24, commended it to John Hawkesworth. He praised Percy's translation of Ovid's elegy on Tibullus, with which he planned to introduce his edition of Tibullus's elegies, and yielded to Percy's entreaties that he print Ovid's Latin alongside the translation. He negotiated with a sea captain to find a place for a young boy whom Percy had asked him to assist, and he passed on the subscription money that Percy had collected for Johnson's edition of Shakespeare.[52]

In May Grainger sent Percy further advice on inoculation and congratulated him on having found "a young lady so every way agreeable" to him. If Percy had not done so earlier, he probably submitted to a smallpox inoculation himself at this time. A prayer that he composed for Anne Gutteridge suggests, however, that the advice he requested from Grainger was intended to prepare Anne for inoculation, a dangerous and frightening ordeal in the days before Edward Jenner's discovery of a beneficent vaccine in 1796: "O strengthen and support me during this alarming trial; soften the pains, and abate the violence of the disorder." By the end of May, Anne's ordeal was concluded, and Grainger in his letter of May 30 rejoiced with Percy "on the recovery of your favourite." Three years later, when Griffiths published the prayer in the May 1761 issue of *The Library*, Percy prefaced it with an unsigned note expressing the hope that the prayer would help to remove "the scruples of many well-meaning, but weak people, who look upon inoculation as an impious practice."[53]

In early May 1758, Percy was called to Bridgnorth because of the serious illness of his father, but, with his father recovering, he rode fifty-six of the eighty miles on Saturday, May 13, to be back at Easton Maudit in time for the Sunday service. Writing to Will Cleiveland on May 18, he turned quickly to the subject of marriage:

> Let me now inquire how the Rector of All-Saints goes on: whether I am soon to congratulate him upon a happy Nuptials!—From the Knowledge I have of my friends gentle Turn & fondness for domestic Pleasures, I fancy that will be the Case eir [*sic*] long:—You have already I doubt not been looking out: send me a description of your Choice: perhaps in another Letter I may return the Compliment.[54]

With the letter he enclosed his "Verses on Leaving **** in a Tempestuous Night," an eloquent expression of the condition of his own heart.

Three days later he assured Apperley in a letter that he would let him know when he had a prospect of marriage; he was now bound for that port but was not certain to arrive soon.[55] The delay seems not to have resulted from any lack of inclination on either Percy's or

Anne's part. The ordeal of inoculation had doubtless brought them closer together, and another ordeal in the summer of 1758, the third of his providential escapes, must have strengthened their attachment even if it did not precipitate their marriage.

Walking one evening in the fields near Anne's mother's house in Desborough, Anne and Percy came upon an enclosure in which a bull was bellowing and tearing up the ground with his horns. They had planned to cross the enclosure; but, understandably frightened, they skirted it along a grassy lane, only to find the bull moving toward them, with his rage apparently much increased. What if he should come through the hedge to us? they asked each other, and at almost the same moment the bull charged in their direction. Anne "took to her heels," and Percy recalled that he too would have run if he had been alone or if he had perceived a chance of their escaping together. Instead—remembering having read that "all Animals are affraid of the Voice of Man"—he brandished his cane and, with a menacing shout, charged at the bull. For a moment the bull continued toward him, but as Percy closed in, he "suddenly turned tail and ran off." Emboldened by his success, Percy, instead of withdrawing, continued his pursuit in the hope of giving the bull a good rap with his cane, "to impress him with the more terror." But, outrun by the bull, he returned to his companion, whose fear had taken her some distance before she discovered that Percy was not with her. Afterwards, he wrote, "I saw her home in perfect Safety."[56]

Noting the strength of Percy's attachment, Grainger urged him to postpone the marriage no longer. Why delay the happiness of marriage until the spring? he asked in a letter dated October 18. Make Anne yours as soon as her uncle consents. In the same letter Grainger announced that his friend John Bourryau, to whom he was dedicating his edition of Tibullus, had offered to settle £200 a year on him if he would accompany him on his travels, and he would thus be leaving England for the West Indies in the spring.[57] Meanwhile he continued to encourage Percy's own efforts, particularly his translation of Ovid's *Epistles*, about which he spoke to Andrew Millar and Robert Dodsley in the hope that they might publish it jointly.[58] For all Grainger's efforts, the translation remained in manuscript, perhaps because the publication of a translation by Stephen Barrett in January 1759 discouraged both publishers.

Grainger's edition of Tibullus, its publisher already secured, was released toward the end of 1758 and promptly came under attack by

Tobias Smollett, by then well known for his novels *Roderick Random* and *Peregrine Pickle* and other works. In a seven-page article in the December *Critical Review*, Smollett questioned the wisdom of translating Tibullus into heroic couplets, ridiculed a number of Grainger's specific translations, and dismissed the notes—many of them supplied by Percy's friend Robert Binnel—as "a huge farrago of learned lumber, jumbled together to very little purpose." He also found very little in Grainger's introductory life of Tibullus "to inform, interest, or amuse the reader," although he praised Percy's translation of Ovid's elegy on Tibullus, with which Grainger concluded the life. He singled out for praise as well the few other poems written in the "alternate" stanza of Gray's *Elegy*, the chief of which was Percy's translation of Tibullus's Elegy I.[59]

No doubt Percy was embarrassed to be compared so favorably to his good friend and benefactor, but Grainger was angered by the review, convinced, as he wrote Percy on January 10, that Smollett had written out of "a personal pique to me." He replied in a rather abusive twenty-five-page pamphlet entitled *A Letter to Tobias Smollet, M.D. Occasioned by His Criticism upon a Late Translation of Tibullus*— a rash act which succeeded only in drawing a withering fire from Smollett in the February *Critical Review*. "I am in pain" for Grainger, Percy wrote to Shenstone on February 4 before the February *Critical Review* appeared, and his pain must have intensified as he saw his friend besieged unmercifully through another eighteen pages.[60]

On December 2, 1758, Percy experienced the fourth of the "singular Instances of Divine Mercy" by which his life was preserved. In Wellingborough, perhaps after a shooting party, he entered a brazier's shop with a loaded pistol in his greatcoat pocket, carelessly placed there, he later acknowledged, to be carried back to Easton Maudit. As he was making a small purchase, the pistol suddenly went off, sending the bullet upward toward his left armpit only two inches from his heart. Had it struck the aorta, Percy noted, he would have bled to death. Fortunately, it was obstructed by one or two handkerchiefs in the pocket and by the folds of his undercoat and greatcoat, so that he felt no immediate pain and was even unaware that the bullet had touched him until he found his arm contracted and his hand drawn to his shoulder. Actually the bullet had reached all the way to the armpit without breaking the skin, although in scorching the skin it left a painful contusion which required the attention of a surgeon for some time afterward.

Perhaps most men who, on three different occasions, had come close to suffering serious and even fatal injury from the careless handling of a firearm would have given up shooting in favor of a less hazardous sport. But Percy was not deterred. Two months after the Wellingborough incident— on February 8, 1759—he went to Strixton enclosure with Samuel Edwards and John Ward, a tenant of the Earl of Sussex, and had "a very fine shoot" during which he killed two hares.[61]

The record of Percy's clerical activity during this period is also scanty, his diary for 1758 being almost totally lost and his extant sermons recording only one engagement between May 28, 1758, when he preached at Easton Maudit, and February 11, 1759, when he preached at Easton Maudit and nearby Grendon.[62] In a letter written on July 20, 1758, Ambrose Isted, justice of the peace and lord of the manor at Ecton, near Northampton, requested a sermon at All Saints in Northampton for the benefit of the sick and lame at the county hospital, and on September 22 Percy preached what appears to have been an original sermon based on John 13:13–14:

> The Heart that is not dispos'd to mourn with those that mourn, is casting off it's alliance with Flesh & Blood. . . . If there are any amongst my Hearers this day that are thus dead to all moral feeling, which from this attendance here I can hardly suppose, or religious Motives; let me endeavour to quicken them wth a few very plain Words . . . that those who refuse to minister to the least of his [*sic*] Brethren, to cloath the naked, to give meat to the hungry, and to visit the sick & the afflicted shall go away into everlasting Punishment; But the righteous, the merciful and the tender-hearted shall go into Life eternal.[63]

The record of Percy's literary activity in this period, mirrored, as has been seen, in his correspondence with Grainger and, to a lesser extent, Shenstone, is by no means scanty. A serious illness contracted by Shenstone interrupted their correspondence between January and October of 1758, but Percy visited the Leasowes after the end of the year. And in February 1759 he sent Shenstone his translation of the epistle "Penelope to Ulysses," with a request that he compare it with the original and suggest revisions. As an inducement to "this friendly office," he added transcriptions of a number of ballads from the folio manuscript. He was not discouraged, he wrote Shenstone on February 4, by the publication of Barrett's translation of Ovid, and he proceeded to translate part of the epistle "Briseis to Achilles" on February 10 and resumed work on it on February 15.[64]

His major literary effort was related to the seventeenth-century Chinese novel *Hau Kiou Choaan*. On February 5 he finished revising the novel's first book, one of three translated into English in 1719 by James Wilkinson, a representative of the East India Company in Canton who was an uncle of the Captain Wilkinson from whom Percy had borrowed the manuscript in February 1758. On February 6 he reread all three of the books in English, along with the concluding fourth part, which had been translated into Portuguese by an unknown person, possibly James Wilkinson's tutor or one of his fellow students of the Chinese language.[65] Although he had borrowed a copy of the Chinese original from Captain Wilkinson, Percy did not himself know Chinese and could only hope to compensate for his predecessor's and his own inadequacies by intelligent revision and translation of the Wilkinson manuscript and by a series of annotations intended to illuminate the manners of the Chinese upper classes in the seventeenth century.

On February 13 he began revising the second book of *Hau Kiou Choaan*, and on Sunday, February 18, he received a letter from Grainger informing him that Dodsley thought well of the novel and that Grainger that week would be showing Dodsley the specimen that Percy had given him. Let me know what you expect for your labor, Grainger added.[66] There was no occasion for Percy to reply. On Monday morning he set out from Easton Maudit, spent the night at Barnet, and reached London on Tuesday in time to have breakfast with his aunt Betty Nott, who was visiting Percy's great uncle Anthony Nott— "a Gentleman of easy Fortune"[67]—and his wife.

Anxious though Percy must have been to conclude an arrangement with Dodsley, his negotiations about *Hau Kiou Choaan* provided him with only one of many literary satisfactions during a stay of nearly three weeks in London. Could Percy not spare ten days in London before Bourryau and he went abroad in June? Grainger had asked in his letter of January 10, and Percy's diary shows him in the company of Grainger more frequently than with any other of his numerous London friends and relations except the Notts, with whom he seems to have stayed. He breakfasted with Grainger on the morning after his arrival, and in a visit to him that evening was introduced to Oliver Goldsmith, then an unheralded author only recently arrived in London from his travels on the Continent. Percy called on Grainger again after

attending services at St. Mary le Bow on February 25. The next day
he was at Dodsley's in Pall Mall reading to him from *Hau Kiou Choaan*,
apparently for the first time. He breakfasted with Grainger again on
February 27 and March 1 and saw him again on March 2, 3, 7, and
8. On the third they had tea with the American-born novelist and
poet Charlotte Lennox. He was in Johnson's company almost as frequently, and perhaps during this trip he first suggested that Johnson
pay him a visit at Easton Maudit.[68] He and Johnson dined at a tavern
together on February 21, and on March 1 Percy became one of the
select group that Johnson took with him on occasion to have tea with
Miss Williams, who was then living by herself. On March 2 he called
on Johnson again, and on the fifth he spent the entire day with Johnson
and Miss Williams—probably the occasion when Johnson boasted, as
Percy later reported to Shenstone, that he "had not been guilty of a
Parenthesis these twenty years."[69] Sometime on the fifth they were
joined by Dodsley and the Italian scholar Giuseppe Baretti, and once
again Percy read from his novel. Three days later Dodsley rewarded
his efforts with a payment of £25 and a contract to publish *Hau Kiou
Choaan*.

Goldsmith may also have helped to bring Dodsley to a favorable
decision. His own *Enquiry into the Present State of Polite Learning in
Europe* was shortly to be published by Dodsley, and on February 26,
after Percy's first reading of *Hau Kiou Choaan*, Goldsmith accompanied
him on an evening visit to Dodsley. The Percy-Goldsmith friendship,
in any event, was developing rapidly. On March 3 Percy spent the
morning at Goldsmith's quarters in Green Arbour Court, where Goldsmith was at work on the *Enquiry*. I found him, Percy wrote in the
biography with which he introduced Goldsmith's *Miscellaneous Works*
in 1801,

> in a wretched dirty room, in which there was but one chair, and
> when he, from civility, offered it to his visitant [Percy], himself
> was obliged to sit in the window. While they were conversing,
> some one gently rapped at the door, and being desired to come in,
> a poor ragged little girl of very decent behaviour, entered, who,
> dropping a curtsie, said, "My mamma sends her compliments, and
> begs the favour of you to lend her a chamber-pot full of coals."[70]

Percy was back at Goldsmith's quarters on March 6.

However successful Percy's London visit was from a literary

standpoint, a number of entries in the diary suggest that its objective was not solely to further his literary ambitions. On the day before he left for London he had tea with Samuel Edwards in the morning and with Edward Lye in the afternoon—the two persons who, aside from his bride and himself, were to play the principal roles in his marriage ceremony. During his London stay he corresponded with Anne Gutteridge's brother William, to whom he wrote on March 3 and 8 and from whom he received a letter on March 7. And on March 8 he went to Chelsea to have dinner and tea with a Mr. Hill, perhaps the uncle whose permission for Anne to marry was all that, in Grainger's view, was needed to open the way for the marriage. The maiden name of Anne's mother was Anne Hill. Percy was later to receive regular dividends from an annuity established for him by William Gutteridge and George Hill,[71] and the conjunction of the Gutteridge and Hill names at this critical point in his courtship points convincingly to an activity related to the impending marriage. Perhaps Percy's February 19 trip to London was precipitated by the receipt of Grainger's letter the day before, but, pleased as he was to find a publisher for *Hau Kiou Choaan*, the most important accomplishment of his visit would seem to have been the removal of the remaining obstacles to his marriage with Anne Gutteridge.

His success climaxed a nearly three-week expedition that he could look back upon with extraordinary satisfaction. He had secured his first contract for a book. He had been welcomed by Johnson and Miss Williams and enjoyed the frequent companionship of James Grainger. He had spent the evening of February 28 with Thomas Apperley and breakfasted with him on March 9. He had seen the poet Mark Akenside, author of *The Pleasures of Imagination*, and had struck up a friendship with Oliver Goldsmith that he was to prize for the rest of his life. He had been much in the company of his relations the Notts and the Perrinses, and of George Haslewood, a tailor and perhaps also a relation, whom he described to Thomas Apperley as "a very honest man and very good workman."[72] He had indulged his fondness for the theater by attending a performance of *Cymbeline* with Frank Perrins on his first evening in town, and of Congreve's *Double Dealer* with his Aunt Betty and Mr. and Mrs. Nott on March 6. On March 9 he escorted the Notts' daughter to the British Museum, where they stayed for three hours. He attended two auctions, dined on lobster at the Union Coffee House, visited other coffee houses and inns, saw a live crocodile, and attended services at St. Paul's, Lincoln's Inn Chapel, and Temple Church, in addition to St. Mary le Bow. His only apparent misfortune was the loss on March 7 of a bank draft for £25, on which he promptly stopped payment at Drummond's Bank in Charing Cross.

On March 9, the day before his return to Easton Maudit, Percy recorded that he "took leave of Friends every where." Doubtless they were all cordial good-byes, but none could have been warmer or sadder than that with James Grainger, who would soon be on his way to St. Kitts with John Bourryau. The nearer his departure approached, Grainger wrote Percy on March 31, the more depressed he became. On April 9, only half an hour before setting out for Portsmouth, Grainger wrote again to encourage Percy to continue working on Ovid's *Epistles* and to wish Percy and Anne a happy marriage. Remember, he said, that "I am to stand godfather to a young Percy."[73]

In his own last letter to Grainger, written on April 2, Percy reported that he had translated five of Ovid's twenty-one epistles and promised to send Grainger copies of any works that he published. He also asked for copies of Grainger's poems and appointed him his literary executor. "I will not afflict my Heart with so painful a Thought," he wrote, "as to suppose we shall never meet again: but . . . I shall ever look back upon the Hours I have spent in conversing or corresponding with you, among the most pleasing of my Life." "Well, my Friend," he concluded, "you are imbarking on the wide Atlantic: I am launching on the Sea of Matrimony:— May we both have gentle Gales, smooth Seas & every requisite to a happy Voyage. . . . When we meet again it will be a happy hour."[74]

In a postscript Percy noted that all the legal preliminaries of the marriage had been concluded except for an agreement upon the trustees of the settlement. Had Grainger not been leaving England, he believed he would have entreated him to serve on his behalf. As for the dowry, Percy later informed Will Cleiveland that Anne brought him £2000, more than half of which he received at the time of the settlement. Of the total sum, £500 plus some interest came from the will of Anne's father, Bartin Gutteridge, who had stipulated that she should receive £200 on her marriage and £100 in each of the next three years. Some additional money probably came from Anne's inheritance from her half-brother, also named Bartin, who had died just a few months earlier on January 7, 1759. The younger Bartin, rector of

Thorpe Malsor in Northamptonshire, left her £200 and designated her, her brother William, and her sister Mary as residuary legatees and joint executors.[75]

The question of trustees must have been resolved fairly promptly, for April 24, when Percy would celebrate his thirtieth birthday, was chosen as the wedding day. Anne had turned twenty-eight on January 28. On Sunday, April 22, Percy administered the communion at Wilby in the morning and conducted the service at Easton Maudit in the evening. In the afternoon Edward Lye and Samuel Edwards came to tea, and a servant hand-delivered Percy a letter from Anne. On the next morning he was with his workmen, who were repairing the somewhat "ruinous" vicarage but would not have it ready for the newly married couple's occupancy for some weeks. After dinner he set out for Desborough, where he arrived shortly before Lye and Edwards.

The service was performed on the morning of April 24 at Desborough Church, near Rothwell, with Edwards officiating and Lye acting in the place of Anne's father. Although others were probably present—Anne's mother, for example—the only other witness Percy made a note of was Anne's brother William. No grand celebration followed the wedding, but Percy, who disliked the taste of wine, yielded to custom and drank the first full glass of his life. "And so," he wrote, "I happily married the loveliest and best of Women."[76]

NOTES

Information on baptisms, marriages, and burials is taken from the parish register, now in the Northamptonshire Record Office.

1. B.L. Add. MS. 32,333, f. 4 (Letter to Cleiveland, 29 July 1756). Much of the account that follows is taken from this letter. Johnson's death date is from *Alumni Cantabrigienses*.
2. The diary has 28 May. In B.L. Add. MS. 32,326 (f. 26) Percy recorded the date as 26 May.
3. Hyde Collection.
4. B.L. Add. MS. 32,333, f. 5 (Letter 29 July 1756).
5. B.L. Add. MS. 32,326, f. 27. The manuscript of the examination is in Special Collections, Florida State University.
6. B.L. Add. MS. 32,333, f. 6.
7. *Public Advertiser*, 25 May 1756.
8. Ibid., 19 May 1756.

9. A comparatively full diary record has survived for May and August 1756.

10. B.L. Add. MS. 32,333, f. 8.

11. *Notes & Queries*, 2d ser., 11(1861):162–63; Vincent Ogburn, "Further Notes on Thomas Percy," *PMLA* 51(1936):449.

12. B.L. Add. MS. 32,326, f. 27.

13. Hyde Collection.

14. *Universal Visiter* (May 1756), 240; (July 1756), 330–31.

15. *Illustrations of the Literary History of the Eighteenth Century*, ed. John Nichols and John Bowyer Nichols (London, 1817–58), 7:240–41 (Letter Grainger to Percy, 22 Oct. 1756); 266 (Letter Grainger to Percy, 18 Oct. 1758)—referred to hereafter as *Lit. Illus.* Dr. Steuart (or Stuart) purchased some of Percy's books before the move from Bridgnorth to Easton Maudit.

16. B.L. Add. MS. 32,333, f. 7.

17. Ibid., ff. 8–9.

18. B.L. Add. MS. 32,326, f. 35. In B.L. Add. MS. 32,327, ff. 183–84, Percy listed thirty-one spellings of the name.

19. Bodl. MS. Percy d. 11, f. 13; Robert Anderson, *The Life of Samuel Johnson, LL.D.*, 3d ed. (London, 1815), 285n.

20. Percy sent subscription money through Grainger, as some of the Grainger letters show.

21. Bodl. MS. Percy d. 11, f. 13.

22. B.L. Add. MSS. 32,333, ff. 10–11; 32,327, f. 171.

23. *Lit. Illus.*, 7:240–41.

24. Hyde Collection.

25. *Lit. Illus.*, 7:246.

26. Osborn Collection, Yale University.

27. Bodl. MS. Percy c. 10, f. 1 (Letter Grainger to Percy, 24 March 1757); *Lit. Illus.*, 7:244–46 (Undated letter Grainger to Percy, probably written about 27 March 1757).

28. Bodl. MS. Percy c. 10, f. 5; *Hau Kiou Choaan* (London, 1761), 3:258.

29. B.L. Add. MS. 32,333, f. 12.

30. Bodl. MS. Percy d. 3, f. 92.

31. *Lit. Illus.*, 7:242–44; B.L. Add. MS. 32,333, f. 12.

32. Osborn Collection, Yale University (Letter 5 March 1757, probably to Robert Binnel); B.L. Add. MS. 32,333, f. 13 (Letter Percy to Cleiveland, 24 March 1757). James Grainger, *A Poetical Translation of the Elegies of Tibullus* (London, 1759), Elegy I, 13–16.

33. B.L. Add. MS. 32,333, ff. 15–16. *A Collection of the Letters of the Late Reverend James Hervey* (London, 1760), 2:422. The perambulation is recorded in the Easton Maudit parish register (Northamptonshire Record Office).

34. B.L. Add. MS. 32,333, ff. 15–16. Mr. B——— used almost the same

words in Samuel Richardson's *Pamela*, published in 1740: "I could not have been contented to have been but *moderately happy* in a wife" (London and New York: Everyman's Library, 1969), 1:405.

35. Bodl. MSS. Percy d. 3, f. 242; d. 4, f. 30.

36. Berg Collection, New York Public Library. Most of the information about Percy's August–September travels is derived from the same letter. Some is from *The Percy Letters*, 7:4 and 46n. Miss Fletcher was probably Mary Fletcher, sister of Philip Lloyd Fletcher (information supplied by National Library of Wales).

37. B.L. Add. MS. 32,333, ff. 17–18 (Letter Percy to Cleiveland, 24 Dec. 1757).

38. *The Percy Letters*, 7:1–3. The plot of John Home's *Douglas*, which was produced in Edinburgh in 1756 and London in 1757, was based on "Gil Morrice."

39. Ibid., 5; Percy's reply of 9 January is on 9–13.

40. *Lit. Illus.*, 7:247 (Letter Grainger to Percy, Feb. 1758). *The Percy Letters*, 7:16 (Letter Shenstone to Percy, 29? Nov. 1758).

41. *Shenstone's Miscellany*, 57–60.

42. B.L. Add. MS. 32,327, f. 172.

43. *Lit. Illus.*, 7:250 (Letter dated only [Feb. 1758]).

44. Ibid., 247.

45. *The Grand Magazine of Universal Intelligence* (Feb. 1758), 96.

46. *A Collection of Poems in Six Volumes, by Several Hands* (London, 1758), 6:233–39. I have taken the text from this work.

47. *The Letters of Robert Burns*, ed. J. Delancey Ferguson (Oxford: Clarendon Press, 1931), 2:126. For the Scottish text of the "Song," the original of which is in the Houghton Library, see George Lyman Kittredge, "Percy and His Nancy," *The Manly Anniversary Studies in Language and Literature* (Chicago: Univ. of Chicago Press, 1923), 212–13. Joseph Baildon's setting of the "Song" was published in James Johnson's *Scots Musical Museum* (Edinburgh, 1787), 1:33. Thomas Carter is said to have set the English version to music in 1770; it can be seen in William Stenhouse's *Illustrations of the Lyric Poetry and Music of Scotland* (Edinburgh, 1853), 29–31.

In a memorandum in the collection of Kenneth Balfour, Sir Ernest Clarke stated that an earlier setting of the "Song" was made by William Jackson of Exeter and is No. 9 in Jackson's second set of four series (1767?). I have not seen this setting, which is said to be for two violins, viola, and bass.

48. Hyde Collection. Bodl. MS. Eng. Lett., d. 219, f. 24. The friend who set the "Song" to music was Robert Shenton, one of Percy's Christ Church classmates (Identification by Percy's daughter Barbara [Beinecke Library, Ms. Vault File]).

49. B.L. Add. MS. 32,326, f. 26. Edwards also assisted Percy as curate at Wilby in 1757 (Parish Register, 29 May and 11 Oct. 1757 [Northamptonshire Record Office]).

50. The text but not the date of the poem is taken from *Shenstone's Miscellany*, 8–9. The *Miscellany* gives the date as 22 March, whereas Percy gave it as 24 March in both his 10 May letter to Apperley (Osborn Collection, Yale University) and his 18 May letter to Cleiveland (B.L. Add. MS. 32,333, f. 19).

51. *Lit. Illus.*, 7:252–53.

52. Ibid., 249–51; 253–58. Griffiths's rejection letter is in the Hyde Collection.

53. *Lit. Illus.*, 7:253, 255, and 258 (Letters n.d. and 13 and 30 May, 1758). *The Library* (May 1761), 93–95. The ordeal of inoculation consisted in a long preparatory period of purging and bleeding and then the infection of the person with matter from an active smallpox pustule. Some persons contracted smallpox and died, perhaps as much from being weakened by the purging and bleeding as from the inoculation itself.

54. B.L. Add. MS. 32,333, f. 19.

55. Bodl. MS. Eng. Lett. d. 219, f. 25.

56. B.L. Add. MS. 32,323, f. 32. Perhaps Percy remembered one of the last episodes in *Robinson Crusoe*, when the wolves are frightened away by shouts.

57. *Lit. Illus.*, 7:266–67.

58. Ibid., 269 (Letter Grainger to Percy, 17 Feb. 1759).

59. *Critical Review* (Dec. 1758), 475–82.

60. *Lit. Illus.*, 7:268; *Critical Review* (Feb. 1759), 141–48; *The Percy Letters*, 7:23.

61. B.L. Add. MS. 32,326, f. 31; Diary; "The Inventory of the Tythe Rents," ff. 298–300 (Muniments Room, Christ Church).

62. Bodl. MSS. Percy d. 3, f. 280; d. 4, f. 70.

63. Ibid., d. 4, ff. 155–77. Alnwick Castle MS. 93A/27.

64. *The Percy Letters*, 7:17, 20, 22.

65. Ch'en Shou-Yi, "Thomas Percy and His Chinese Studies," *Chinese Social and Political Science Review*, 20(July 1936):216.

66. *Lit. Illus.*, 7:269–70 (Letter Grainger to Percy, 17 Feb. 1759).

67. *The Percy Letters*, vol. 2, *The Correspondence of Thomas Percy & Richard Farmer*, ed. Cleanth Brooks (Baton Rouge: Louisiana State Univ. Press, 1946), 158 (Letter, Percy to Farmer, 16 Nov. 1772).

68. Percy informed Shenstone on 22 May 1761 that Johnson had been resolving to visit him for two years (*The Percy Letters*, 7:98).

69. *The Percy Letters*, 7:58 (Letter Percy to Shenstone, 12 March 1760). Percy does not seem to have visited London again in 1759 or in 1760.

70. *The Miscellaneous Works of Oliver Goldsmith, M.D.* (London, 1801), 1:61.

71. Percy Ledger, Goslings Bank.

72. Bodl. MS. Eng. Lett. d. 219, ff. 23–24 (Letter Percy to Apperley, 21 Sept. 1755). The Haslewoods were a well-known Bridgnorth family. Percy's godmother, his mother's sister Mary, was married to James Haslewood; and Thomas Haslewood, who had entered the Bridgnorth Free School at the same time as Percy, was probably the Mr. Haslewood Percy described as his attorney in a fragmentary note preserved in the Northamptonshire Record Office (Sotheby Ecton Coll., Box X 1079 E(s)1211, f. 68); B.L. Add. MS. 34,756, f. 43 (Letter Percy to J. D. Haslewood, 10 Sept. 1810).

Percy's diary reveals that he received a letter from "Haslew.ᵈ" on 5 February, called at "Mr. Haslew.ᵈˢ" immediately after breakfast following his arrival in London on 20 February, had tea at "Geo. Haslew.ᵈˢ" on 28 February, breakfasted there on 3 March, and stopped there for a visit on 7 March. A letter and four visits, including breakfast and tea, suggest that Percy had more on his mind when he visited George Haslewood than being measured for a new wardrobe. An attorney would have been of particular assistance to him when he was seeking agreement upon the terms of a marriage settlement, and it seems possible that he was also meeting with Thomas Haslewood during these calls to a tailor with the same surname. The possibility is given some further support by the fact that Percy visited Haslewood both before he wrote to William Gutteridge and after he received Gutteridge's reply, and before he went to Chelsea to see Mr. Hill.

73. *Lit. Illus.*, 7:270–71.

74. Special Collections, Florida State University. Percy's translations of the five Ovid epistles are in Bodl. MS. Percy e. 6, ff. 1–106. Copies of the epistles "Penelope to Ulysses" and "Oenone to Paris" are also in the Huntington Library, MS. HM 216 (59–65).

75. B.L. Add. MS. 32,333, f. 21 (Letter Percy to Cleiveland, 4 June 1759). The will of the senior Bartin Gutteridge, who was lord of the manor at Desborough, is in the Public Record Office (Prob. 11/932–33/346). For the younger Bartin's, see Henry Isham Longden, *Northamptonshire and Rutland Clergy from 1500* (Northampton: Archer and Goodman, 1938–43), vol. 6.

76. B.L. Add. MSS. 32,326, f. 27; 32,327, f. 173; Diary, 17 March 1766.

CHAPTER IV

A London Quest:

1759–1761

THE FIRST WEEKS of Thomas and Anne Percy's married life, happy though they must have been, did not go totally undisturbed. For all his labors, the vicarage was still not ready for occupancy when Percy wrote to Will Cleiveland on June 4, and apparently Anne remained in Desborough after their honeymoon while he returned to his quarters in the Earl of Sussex's manor house.[1] He was back preaching at Easton Maudit on May 6, twelve days after the wedding.[2] No doubt he found frequent opportunities to travel the twenty miles to Desborough, even though, as he wrote to Shenstone on August 9, attention to economy required him to be constantly with the workmen, who settled on the house like "Locusts." Not until the last week of July had the work progressed sufficiently for him and Anne to move in.[3]

The vicarage repairs were not their only problem. Anthony Percy had become involved in unidentified "difficulties," serious enough to upset his older brother, and even more afflicting to the Percy parents, who were on the scene in Bridgnorth. Anne, Percy informed Will Cleiveland, had done everything she could to console and calm him, and on her own initiative had undertaken to comfort his father by a series of letters, in which she displayed "a Temper of the most angelick Kind." In spite of their seriousness, he remained hopeful that Anthony's difficulties would still be resolved satisfactorily, and the absence of any further reference to them suggests that his hope may have been realized.

By October 20, when he wrote Will again, Percy could provide a brighter account of his married state. For him and Anne, each day brought a round of quiet enjoyments: "we eat together, walk together, when weary sit down & chat together, & sometimes read together."

His pen, though not totally idle, had altered its course: instead of sonnets to Amaryllis, it traveled "the more humble track of domestic Memorandums" and had been so worn down "with Items of Bakers & Butchers Bills" that he doubted whether it could fashion a rebus or an acrostic. He could not say that he, like Parson Adams in Fielding's *Joseph Andrews*, ever lamented his wife's inability to understand Greek, but he fancied that she could wish him a better judge of the domestic "Excellences, in which I believe she appears to advantage." Still, he was trying, and had already mastered most of "the terms of art" employed in making a pudding or a cheesecake.[4] He had also begun to keep bees and, in a letter of August 9, invited Shenstone to provide an appropriate inscription for a glass beehive.[5]

Anne and Thomas had hoped to accept an invitation from Shenstone to visit him at the Leasowes, but by August Anne was pregnant and they concluded that any extended trip would have to be postponed for another year. Instead, Percy urged his friend to join them at Easton Maudit, and he held up as attractions his folio manuscript of ballads and romances and a smaller collection of old Spanish ballads, one of which he enclosed in his own translation. In reply, Shenstone acknowledged the temptation and commended Percy's translation, but ruled out a visit that year as impracticable. He seemed to have "neglected civilities and broken engagements" in every county around him, he confessed, and owed just about everyone a visit, a letter, or money.[6]

Will Cleiveland was to remain Percy's closest confidant on family matters, but with James Grainger far off in St. Kitts Percy turned more and more to Shenstone for literary advice and companionship. In a June 6 letter—his first after the Percy marriage—Shenstone announced that he had "retouch'd" "Gentle Heardsman," the ancient ballad that Percy had transcribed from his folio manuscript and sent to him with his letter of January 9, 1758. Like Shenstone, Percy himself had written new stanzas to replace the three that were missing from the middle of the poem; and their efforts, though performed separately and at a distance, set in motion a process of revision that was to transform a number of the ballads in Percy's collection and become in time the most controversial of his editorial practices. But there was no controversy between Percy and Shenstone in the spring and summer of 1759. In the same letter Shenstone announced that he had also retouched the ballad "Edom o'Gordon," which had been published in Glasgow in 1755, and on August 9 Percy asked, with obvious interest, to be shown Shenstone's "Improvements" to both poems.[7]

In the June 6 letter, Shenstone informed Percy that a gift he had left at the Leasowes for Shenstone's friend and neighbor, John Scott Hylton, had become the occasion of an elaborate hoax. The gift, a tobacco stopper purchased by Percy in January at Mr. Moody's toy-shop in Birmingham, consisted of a head of Shakespeare reputedly carved from the wood of a mulberry tree that Shakespeare had planted at Stratford. Shenstone forwarded the tobacco stopper to Hylton, a collector of curios, with a January 26 letter from Percy, and he followed them the next day with a forged letter in which "Moody" offered to join Hylton in purchasing the whole tree. He also succeeded in intercepting Hylton's reply containing a request for only enough of the tree to make him a cup. In a second forged letter, "Moody" reported that he had purchased the tree and was having the cup carved with vignettes in bas-relief, including one of Shakespeare planting the tree while Moody shows it to Hylton. "The Cup is now in my Bureau," Shenstone chortled to Percy—"with the Figures well-enough executed." Shenstone added that Percy must help him in making up a list of curios, since Hylton had been told of a Moody acquaintance in Nottingham ready to part with a large collection to help him support his ten children.[8]

Percy entered into the fun. Shenstone had begun the list with two items: a memento of the legendary Thomas Parr, who was said to have been 152 when he died in 1635—a spoon with which Parr had drunk buttermilk; and a cravat of the kind worn by King William III. To these, Percy offered on August 9, 1759, to add a brass Dutch counter green enough with age to pass for a coin of a Ptolemy or a Syrian king; a snuff box made of a snail shell rescued from the "sordid Company" of a nutmeg grater and a thimble in an old woman's pocket; and a lion of ancient red potter's ware, no less valuable for having lost half its backside, like the old woman in *Candide*. Seven months later, with Shenstone continuing to press for contributions, he suggested a few more, including "a Hat made for the People who have no Heads." At some point Percy apparently tied up his curiosities and sent them to Hylton, not with a view to furthering Shenstone's hoax, but simply as a joke that he thought Hylton would enjoy. Hylton later acknowledged that they were too absurd for him to take them seriously.[9]

Diverting though he found Shenstone's "tobacco-stopper plot," Percy hoped that Hylton would not be offended by his having been the innocent cause of it. But Hylton did take offense when he visited Birmingham and Stratford in April 1760 and discovered that he had been the victim of a hoax. In an indignant letter of July 1760 he accused Percy of participating in the plot, and he demanded an explanation: "You should have been a little more cautious, and known more of my Tast(e), than to join any one, in an imposition of the kind that you were concerned in with M.ʳ Shenstone against me."[10]

Percy responded, as he informed Shenstone on July 29, by clarifying his role in the "Adventure," which he urged Hylton to accept as "a pleasant Jest" and be the first to laugh at. "He is a very good natured obliging Man," Percy commented to Shenstone, "and I should be sorry to have him rendered unhappy." Percy's advice, sound as it was, probably had little effect, but his letter achieved at least part of its purpose. Although Hylton may never have been fully reconciled to Shenstone, he apologized to Percy for having considered him part of the conspiracy; "*I hope* you will . . . believe," he wrote to him on August 20, "that the same Heart which was heated by resentment, now glows with as warm an Opinion of the Veracity and Honour of M.ʳ Percy as usual."[11]

Percy visited Shenstone again in May 1760, but by and large the demands and attractions of Easton Maudit kept him at home during the year and a half following his marriage. He conducted services regularly at Easton Maudit and Wilby and occasionally substituted for neighboring clergymen, as he did for Edward Lye at Yardley Hastings on November 11, 1759.[12] Assuring the comfort of the sixteenth-century thatched vicarage must have required considerable imagination and expense, for with two good-sized parlors and a kitchen on the ground floor and several bedrooms upstairs—two of them "really capital," as Percy's successor Robert Nares later described them[13]—the decisions to be reached on furnishings and decorations would have been numerous. No doubt Percy's earlier devotion to the garden was bringing its rewards as the forty fruit trees matured, a harvest for both eye and taste. In late June the glebe lands summoned him, scythe in hand, to secure the hay; but even in travail Percy and Anne could look with pleasure toward the Earl of Sussex's spreading estate and manor house, enjoy the wildflowers along the brook behind the garden, or admire the tall spire of the Church of St. Peter and St. Paul just across the road from them. It is not surprising to find Percy, in August 1760, describing himself as the happiest of men.[14]

Much of Percy's happiness, like Anne's, grew out of the birth of their first child on March 18, 1760, a daughter named Anne Cleiveland in honor of her mother and of Percy's grandmother's family.[15] The infant Anne was baptized in the church on April 24, the anniversary of Percy's birth and of his and Anne's marriage, and the godmothers were the elder Mrs. Price of Brynypys, who had been born a Cleiveland, and Anne Gutteridge, young Anne's maternal grandmother. The godfather was Richard Backwell, member of Parliament for Northampton.[16]

Both mother and daughter progressed, and on September 2 Percy could report to Will Cleiveland that the infant Anne was "almost ready to get upon her legs." All three Percys remained well, in fact, during a year that Percy could only look upon as "remarkably unhealthy." Both of his parents became sick in the spring, and his mother, chronically ill with consumption, died at Bridgnorth on May 21 while he was visiting Shenstone at the Leasowes. The night before she died, Percy wrote in his family memoirs, his father had gone to bed before her in a separate room, and, near death though she was, she took him a glass of wine with her own hands. It was the last time his father saw her alive.[17]

Percy's scholarly work was not neglected, of course, although his time for it was more limited than it had been before his marriage. With a contract in hand for a translation of the seventeenth-century Chinese novel Hau Kiou Choaan, he could turn his pen from bakers' and butchers' bills to the more alluring adventures of Shuey-ping-sin as she matched her wits against those of the malicious Kwo-khé-tzu, a suitor less attractive than Mr. B in Samuel Richardson's Pamela, but much more persistent. By August 5, 1759—the last indication in the diary of his progress—Percy had returned a number of half sheets of proof to Dodsley, and presumably he continued to work steadily at the book until its publication in late 1761.

The translation was a pioneering project designed to take advantage of the cult of chinoiserie which had begun in England in the seventeenth century and reached its height in the middle of the eighteenth, with public attention focused largely on such useful and attractive articles as furniture, porcelain, textiles, and wallpaper. Chinese literature was virtually unknown, and no Chinese novel had ever been published in England. Limited by his total ignorance of the Chinese language, Percy had no alternative but to work from the manuscripts of James Wilkinson's translation of the first three volumes and the anonymous Portuguese translation of the fourth, the accuracy of which he could not determine with any certainty. He acknowledged that, judged by the "laws of European criticism," the novel was open to many objections. But he came to the conclusion that, whatever its shortcomings, it provided a more faithful picture of Chinese manners than could be found in histories or travel books, just as a page of Henry Fielding, or one or two other modern writers, conveyed "a truer notion of the genius and spirit of the English . . . than . . . whole volumes of *Present States of England,* or *French Letters concerning the English Nation.*"[18]

Impelled by this conviction, and aware that many exotic customs, habits of thought, and modes of expression would require explanation, he abandoned his original intention of inserting as few notes as possible and, with a scholar's thoroughness, ransacked as many volumes on China as his publisher Dodsley and the Earl of Sussex's library could supply. From these he drew a vast array of notes, some of them reflecting the prejudices of the merchants and missionaries who brought back accounts of China, but many of them almost as interesting as the narrative they were intended to illuminate. "There is nothing for which the Chinese have higher veneration than their ceremonies," he writes; "these are looked upon by them as essential to the good order and peace of the state. The common salutations, visits, presents, feasts, &c. &c. being rather so many standing laws than fashions introduced by custom. Among their books upon this subject, there is one that prescribes upwards of 3000 rules of civility." The Chinese reputation for cheating draws a more critical note, though seasoned with some admiration:

> The *Chinese* are such subtle and exquisite cheats, that were money to pass among them by tale, as in other countries, it would give birth to continual adulterations. For the same reason, when the *Chinese* transport these . . . [pieces of gold] into other countries, the merchants cut them through the middle, not daring to trust that crafty people, who have a method of stuffing these pieces, insomuch that withinside shall be sometimes found a third part of copper or silver.[19]

To the novel and its annotations Percy added a seventy-five-page section of "Chinese Proverbs and Apothegms," "The Argument or Story of a Chinese Play Acted at Canton, in the Year MDCCXIX," and sixty pages of "Fragments of Chinese Poetry: with a Dissertation." He adapted the "Argument" from the English of James Wilkinson and translated the proverbs, apothegms, and poems mostly from French translations by Pierre du Halde, whose *Description of the Empire of China and Chinese-Tartary* was his primary authority.

Shenstone, who was unacquainted with *Hau Kiou Choaan*, was skeptical of Percy's project. Is it possible, he asked on February 15, 1760, that you are imagining something more extraordinary in this work than the public is likely to discover? Percy did not reply to the question, and on August 11 of the same year Shenstone reported that Dodsley, who was then his guest at the Leasowes, "seems to entertain no doubt that your Chinese novel will excite Curiosity."[20]

Another pioneering project of the period was inspired by the success of the Erse fragments collected by James Macpherson and published at Edinburgh in June 1760, under the title *Fragments of Ancient Poetry Collected in the Highlands of Scotland*.[21] Most of the Icelandic poetry known in Britain—celebrations of battle like "The Dying Ode of Regner Lodbrog" or "The Ransome of Egill the Scald"—was accessible only in the original or in Latin, French, or Swedish translations. Through his association with Edward Lye, Percy had learned the runic letters on February 3, 1759,[22] and, with Lye's knowledge of the northern languages and civilizations to draw upon, he decided to translate a few pieces of Icelandic poetry and edit them in a brief volume. Helpful also was Paul Henri Mallet's *Introduction à l'Histoire de Dannemarc*, a translation of which he was to undertake a few years later. In September 1760, he informed Shenstone of his proposed collection and sent him one of his translations: "You will probably be disgusted to see it so incumbered with Notes," he remarked, but he thought that the poem would be unintelligible without them. He also added a few shorter fragments and asked for Shenstone's opinion on the desirability of printing the Icelandic originals.[23]

Shenstone replied promptly. There was something good in the poem, he acknowledged, but the "absolute *Necessity* of Notes, will be the Rock that you may chance to split upon." Keep the notes as short as possible, he advised, and place them either at the end of each piece or in a glossary; perhaps a short preface would preclude the need for many of them. As for the translation, it should be in "a kind of *flowing* yet *pompous Prose.*" The originals should be omitted, as should the shorter fragments if there is the slightest need for explanatory notes.[24]

Percy accepted most of Shenstone's advice. A general preface and an introduction to each poem permitted him to dispense with a glossary and all but a few notes, and his translations reflect an attempt to follow Shenstone's prescription of a flowing yet pompous prose. "The leader of the people," we read in "The Funeral Song of Hacon,"

> had just before cast aside his armour; he had put off his coat of mail: he had thrown them down in the field a little before the beginning of battle. He was playing with the sons of renowned men, when he was called forth to defend his kingdom. The gallant king now stood under his golden helmet.
>   Then the sword in the king's hand cut the coverings of brass, as easily as if it had been brandished in water. The javelins clashed together: the shields were broken: the arms resounded on the sculls of men.

He departed from Shenstone's advice only through his inclusion of the Icelandic originals of his five poems and of two fragments cited in his comments about the poems. As he noted in his preface, the translator of the Erse fragments, by failing to produce the originals, had encouraged the belief that he was their author rather than merely the translator. James Grainger, a native Scot, saw still another reason to be skeptical: "Depend upon it," he wrote from St. Kitts on January 16, 1761, "the 'Fragments' are not translated from the Erse; there is not one local or appropriated image in the whole." Percy would have heard similar doubts from Samuel Johnson, and he wisely took this way of forestalling any question about the authenticity of his own collection.[25]

Other projects of varying importance helped to occupy Percy's time in 1760 and early 1761. On January 7, 1760, Shenstone suggested that he translate a French song but was not pleased with the result: "The translation will not do, either in point of metre, or expression."[26] Dodsley's publication in February 1761 of *Select Fables of Esop*—including a section of original fables—inspired Percy to attempt four fables of his own, which he appended to a copy of the book and addressed to Anne Isted, the wife of Ambrose Isted, at Ecton: "The best of mothers and of wives." Unfortunately they are rather too remote from reality to carry much conviction. In "The Nightingale and the Rose," for example, the nightingale woos the rose each evening and is constantly rebuffed; when he decides to woo her at noon, he discovers a painted butterfly enjoying the charms that he has been denied and is promptly cured of his passion. "Those Ladies that are fond of the admiration of fops," goes Percy's moral, "will be shunned and forsaken by men of sense"—a sentiment closer in spirit to Restoration comedy than to Aesopian fable.[27]

Far more substantial, at least as Percy contemplated it, was a project related to *Don Quixote*, which he described as his favorite book. In ordering a number of old Spanish romances from a catalog of the London bookseller Lockyer Davis, Percy proposed a key to the satire in *Don Quixote* in the form of explanatory notes, which he thought would fill two volumes. "The Intention of *Cervantes*," he wrote to Davis in an undated letter probably of early or mid-March, 1761,

> the great Design of his Work, was to laugh at & expose the absurdities of the Old favorite Romances of that age: and accordingly in almost every line, there is an allusion to one or other of them: ... [but not] one reader in five hundred has ever seen a line in any of those books: and consequently all the fine ridicule of *Cervantes* must be lost upon them.

He had been collecting the romances since he first read *Don Quixote* in the original Spanish, he reported, and perhaps he could go a step further and use them, not just for explanatory notes, but for a new and improved edition of an English translation, preferably that of Thomas Shelton.[28]

Although less enthusiastic than Percy, Davis expressed interest in the proposal when he replied on March 20, 1761;[29] and on April 5, having received nine books priced by Davis at £10/13/0, Percy suggested an arrangement whereby Davis would have the first refusal of his project and Percy would pay for the books only if he entered into an agreement with another bookseller, or if the project was given up and he failed to return them in good condition.[30] It is not known how Davis responded to this letter, and no agreement between him and Percy has come to light.

Four other projects, though not mentioned in Percy's correspondence of this period, were certainly under consideration if not actively under way. During his reading for *Hau Kiou Choaan*, Percy had assembled a number of comparatively short pieces relating to China, one of which—Frère Attiret's "Description of the Emperor of China's Garden and Pleasure-Houses near Peking"—he alluded to in his letter to Shenstone of April 13, 1760. These he planned to bring together in a separate publication. He also planned another collection which seems to have been a by-product of *Hau Kiou Choaan*. In reading du Halde, he came upon the Chinese story of the faithless widow Lady Tien, and in time he joined it with others exemplifying the frailty of widows, the classic tale of which was Petronius's *Ephesian Matron*. Finally, he must also have been contemplating an edition and new translation of *The Song of Solomon* and an edition of the works of George Villiers, Duke of Buckingham.

Percy's major decision was to turn to his old ballads in earnest and to the possibility of publication that Johnson had urged upon him in 1757. He abandoned fairly early the idea of publishing the whole of his folio manuscript or of confining himself exclusively to the poems contained in it. Their quality was uneven, and too many of them had been mutilated when Humphrey Pitt's maids ripped out pages or parts of pages to light his parlor fire. And as Percy's knowledge of balladry increased, he came to see that the long romances of the manuscript probably belonged in a collection by themselves, and that a ballad collection would gain in variety and interest if it were opened to numerous poems not to be found in his manuscript.

From the moment of his decision he worked closely with Shenstone. In late August or September 1760 he visited the Leasowes, encouraged perhaps by Shenstone's announcement in his August 11 letter that Robert Dodsley was spending two months at the Leasowes to correct the edition of Aesop's fables.[31] Exactly what Percy and Shenstone discussed during the visit is not apparent, but Percy seems to have raised some basic questions about editorial practice and brought out his folio manuscript for Shenstone to evaluate individual poems. Shenstone's letter of October 1, his first to follow Percy's visit, doubtless reflects the questions uppermost in Percy's mind, and it is filled with advice that Percy was to take into account as he proceeded with the extraordinarily complex task of assembling and editing his collection. Never put two long poems together, Shenstone counseled. Restrict the publication to two volumes, though three will be acceptable if they can all be filled "properly." "*Improvements*" to the poems will not be objectionable unless they clearly "*contradict Antiquity.*" Only alterations of a line or more—not of just a word or two—need be cited, perhaps by the use of italic type: "It will have the appearance of a modern *Toe* or *Finger*, which is *allowably* added to the best old Statues: And I think I should always let the Publick imagine, that these were owing to Gaps, rather than to *faulty Passages*."[32]

In his October 1 letter Shenstone also explained his system for rating the poems that Percy had left at the Leasowes or had sent to him; a + for the least approbation, a ⫫ for the next, and a ⫪ for the highest. He would try to return the parcels at hand within a week or two with his judgments, and would be pleased if Percy, placing the poems in his preferred order, would transcribe those that he found acceptable in a large notebook and let him reconsider them all together before he sent them off to the press.

During his visit to the Leasowes, Percy must also have discussed the possibility of publication with Robert Dodsley, who, as Percy later noted, "had never much opinion of the work."[33] But on October 4, while Dodsley was still at the Leasowes, Samuel Johnson wrote to say that Percy's friend—doubtless Thomas Apperley, who had carried messages earlier from Percy to Johnson—had called on him with an offer from Dodsley's brother James "which I think moderately good, that is, not so good as might be hoped, nor so bad as might be feared." On the whole, added Johnson, "I would not have you reject the offer as it is, for I know not who will make a better."[34]

Percy's fortunes were to turn more than once before an agreement could be reached. On November 27, he informed Shenstone that he had broken off negotiations with Dodsley: "James Dodsley is generous enough and offered me terms that would have repaid my Labour." But I suppose, Percy continued, that his brother has "persuaded him to desist." He was now negotiating with another bookseller.[35]

The other bookseller was Andrew Millar, whom Grainger had once commended to Percy as a likely publisher of his translation of Ovid's *Epistles*. Once again Johnson was Percy's intermediary: "I went this morning to Mr. Millar," he wrote to Percy on November 29, "and found him very well disposed to your project. I told him the price of 3 vols was an hundred guineas, to which he made no objection . . . You will know from his own Letter, which he promised me to write to night."[36]

It is not known whether Millar sent the promised letter, or to what extent Percy and his friends conducted further negotiations with prospective publishers during the six months that followed Johnson's letter. On April 24, 1761, Shenstone wrote to say that he had marked the ballads in the three-volume *Collection of Old Ballads* of 1723–25, but could not properly recommend any of them until he was better acquainted with Percy's plans. Did Percy make a distinction between a ballad and a song and confine himself to the former? he asked. To the "common people," he believed, a song becomes a ballad as it grows in years; he himself considered a ballad to contain "some little story, either real or invented"—but he realized that his definition might be too narrow. And if Percy were to admit songs into the collection, what time period would he limit himself to? What about "old renowned songs" remembered for their tunes but with little or no merit? Would Percy put the Scottish poems in a separate volume with a glossary, which many "will too much require"?[37]

Shenstone closed the letter by inviting Percy to a conference at the Leasowes to settle these and other questions "when you have dispatched your other publications." As Shenstone seems to have been aware, Percy was concentrating for the moment on traveling to London to seek contracts for a number of his projects. On April 13 he applied for admission to the reading room of the British Museum for a two–month period, and the application was approved on April 24.[38] On Monday, May 18, he sent his portmanteau to Newport Pagnell, though he himself remained in the vicarage all day reading five plays. He set out the next morning before breakfast, caught the berlin at Newport Pagnell, and by seven in the evening reached Mr. Backwell's, where he spent the night and perhaps much of his London visit.[39] Wasting no time, he called on Dodsley the following morning and then, over dinner, had what he described to Shenstone as a "council of war" with Johnson to consider the questions Shenstone had raised about the ballad project, and probably to discuss the lingering problem of coming to terms with a publisher. Later that afternoon Johnson and Percy joined Miss Williams at tea.

The next two days were critical. On Thursday he met with Dodsley once again and reached agreements for publishing his *Song of Solomon* and *Five Pieces of Runic Poetry*.[40] His sample for the latter was his translation of "The Incantation of Hervor," which the *Lady's Magazine* published in its June issue. He then called on Andrew Millar, perhaps to lay before him the decisions reached in his council of war with Johnson. On Friday, May 22, he held a further meeting with Dodsley, and this time he concluded the negotiations that were the primary objective of his trip. "Sold Dodsley my Old Ballads," he noted tersely in his diary.

He wrote to Shenstone the same day: Dodsley "has thought better of the scheme, and has come up to my terms: which M.ʳ Millar would indeed have done as to money, but he wanted to lay me under some difficulties about the execution that prevented us from coming to an agreement." The agreement, out of deference to Shenstone, was for two volumes, but a third volume might be added if its quality could be made equal to that of the first two. Under no condition would there be a fourth. For two volumes Percy would receive £70; for three volumes, a hundred guineas. "You see," Percy commented, "I shall give up near [£]40 by dropping a third Volume to oblige you: but I assure you I shall do it with the greatest pleasure to obtain the approbation of so valuable a Friend and so excellent a Judge."

The meeting with Johnson had also produced answers to most of Shenstone's questions. The collection would be "promiscuous"— not confined to any one sort of poem or to a rigid order—but so distributed that the poems would if possible illustrate each other and preclude the reader's becoming tired: "I shall not easily suffer two long ditties to come together," Percy wrote, "nor permit a long series of Love Songs to remain undivided." The best ancient Scottish poems would be admitted. And as for the time frame, he would not readily admit anything written since the Restoration, but he would not totally exclude a few good later poems, English or Scottish, written in imitation of the earlier ballads.[41]

Three contracts in two days were an extraordinary achievement, even for a scholar as conscientious and energetic as Thomas Percy. But Percy was not finished. He had caught Robert Dodsley in a generous mood, and the next morning he returned to conclude agreements for his miscellaneous Chinese pieces and his "3 Matrons," the collection of stories about the frailty of widows.[42] He also accompanied Dodsley to the printing shop of John Hughes, probably to look into the progress of Hau Kiou Choaan, but perhaps also to discuss his projected work. He may, in addition, have been continuing his negotiations with Lockyer Davis on Don Quixote or discussing a proposal for the Key to the New Testament, which Davis was to publish in 1766, since he called on Davis on May 25 and again on June 4.

Percy's 1761 London visit was his first in the two years since his marriage, and he made the best of it in other ways as well. He went with Edward Lye to the Society of Antiquaries on May 22 and visited it again on June 6. On May 26 he began reading in the British Museum, to which he returned on June 2 and 4. He would have returned on the third also, but a piece of string got in his eye and irritated it. His time in the museum brought him not merely the rewards of research, but also the friendship of Thomas Astle, who was compiling an index of the museum's catalog of Harleian manuscripts, an invaluable resource for Percy's study of ancient poetry. On June 5 he dined and spent the rest of the day with the scholar Edward Capell, whose collection of poetry entitled *Prolusions* had been called to his attention by Shenstone on August 11, 1760.[43]

On the evening of May 22 he went to Drury Lane Theatre, where David Garrick was performing the role of John Bayes in Buckingham's *Rehearsal*, and he noted in his diary that he had spent three shillings for a ticket and 2/3 for oranges and a coffee house—a modest celebration for one who earlier the same day had concluded months of negotiations for a major collection of poetry. He had supper after the performance with his Oxford friend, Dr. Gower.[44] On June 1 he was back at Drury Lane to see Garrick, Kitty Clive, and Hannah Pritchard in George Colman's *The Jealous Wife*. For lighter amusement he visited Spring Gardens with Oliver Goldsmith on May 25, spent a shilling to view Mrs. Salmon's waxworks on May 28, and observed the illuminations for the King's birthday on June 4. On June 6 he was at Vauxhall, again in the company of Dr. Gower.

He was with old friends a good part of his time: Goldsmith and Thomas Apperley on at least four occasions each and Johnson on at least seven.[45] Surprisingly, Johnson and Goldsmith—near neighbors in London—had not yet formed the friendship that was to be commemorated years later in Boswell's *Life of Johnson*. Percy seems to have brought them together for the first time on May 31, when, as he noted in his diary, he spent the "Ev^g at Goldsmith's with much Company." The evening's event was a supper, to which many "literary men" had been invited; and Percy was asked to call for Johnson and escort him from Inner Temple Lane, where Johnson was living, to Goldsmith's lodgings in Wine Office Court. As they walked together, Percy recalled in his life of Goldsmith, he

> was much struck with the studied neatness of Johnson's dress: he had on a new suit of cloaths, a new wig nicely powdered, and every thing about him so perfectly dissimilar from his usual habits and appearance, that his companion could not help inquiring the cause of this singular transformation. "Why, sir," said Johnson, "I hear that Goldsmith, who is a very great sloven, justifies his disregard of cleanliness and decency, by quoting my practice, and I am desirous this night to show him a better example."[46]

Perhaps one of the literary men present that evening was David Garrick, with whom Percy met a number of times during his visit to London. On May 27 he had breakfast with Garrick at Drury Lane Theatre during a rehearsal for a May 28 performance of *King Lear*, and he called upon him again on May 29 and May 30. It is not impossible that he had already met Garrick through Johnson during an earlier London visit. But in 1761 Percy had a compelling scholarly reason to seek out his acquaintance. The five plays that Percy read on May 18, just before his departure for London; his evening at Drury Lane seeing Buckingham's *Rehearsal*; and his cultivation of Garrick— all seem to be of a piece in the light of one final accomplishment of Percy's London visit. On June 12 he signed a contract with the bookseller Jacob Tonson to edit, in two volumes, the works of George Villiers, second Duke of Buckingham, whose major achievement was *The Rehearsal*, a satirical comedy first produced in 1771 and aimed at the plays of the early Restoration period.[47]

In all likelihood Percy on May 18 was reading early Restoration plays in anticipation of his negotiations with Tonson. Meeting with Garrick would also have been very much to the same purpose, for Garrick was known to have assembled the most comprehensive collection of English plays available, and Percy saw the need to secure it for his own use. With its help he could make a revision of the "Key to *The Rehearsal*," first published in the 1704 edition of Buckingham's works, a true showpiece of his own edition. It was indispensable, in short, if Percy was to go beyond the earlier key and identify additional passages in the Restoration plays that were likely targets of Buckingham's satire.

His discussions with Garrick succeeded as he wished: within a few months Garrick was to turn over at least nine volumes of old plays to Jacob Tonson to be forwarded to Easton Maudit.[48] So Percy returned to his vicarage in mid-June with six contracts in his portmanteau and a veritable Everest of work ahead of him.

NOTES

1. B.L. Add. MS. 32,333, ff. 21–22.
2. Bodl. MS. Percy d. 4, f. 37.
3. *The Percy Letters*, 7:31.
4. B.L. Add. MS. 32,333, ff. 23–24.
5. *The Percy Letters*, 7:34.
6. Ibid., 31, 37 (Letters 9 Aug. and 3 Oct.).

7. Ibid., 12, 25–26, 32; *Shenstone's Miscellany*, 154–55.

8. *The Percy Letters*, 7:28–29.

9. Ibid., 29, 35–36, 57, 196. Pages 198–99 provide evidence that the tree may, in fact, have come from Shakespeare's garden in Stratford.

10. Ibid., 194–95.

11. Ibid., 63, 195–96, 197.

12. Bodl. MS. Percy d. 3, f. 18.

13. Letter Robert Nares to the future Mrs. Nares, 23 June 1782, seen at the Old Vicarage, Easton Maudit. The letter has been printed in Anne Baker, "The Old Vicarage Easton Maudit: The Home of Mr. and Mrs. Eric Brook," *Northamptonshire & Bedfordshire Life* (Jan. 1978), 18.

14. Bodl. MS. Percy c. 1, f. 7 (Draft of a letter to William Cleiveland, 11 Aug. 1760).

15. B.L. Add. MS. 32,333, f. 25 (Letter Percy to William Cleiveland, 2 Sept. 1760).

16. B.L. Add. MS. 32,326, f. 27.

17. B.L. Add. MSS. 32,333, f. 25; 32,326, f. 23. Bodl. MS. Percy c. 1, f. 8.

18. *Hau Kiou Choaan* (London, 1761), 1:xii, xvii.

19. Ibid., 4:110; 1:141–2. The list of books consulted by Percy is at 1:xxix–xxxi.

20. *The Percy Letters*, 7:51, 67.

21. *Five Pieces of Runic Poetry* (London, 1763), [vi].

22. Percy recorded this fact on a card inserted in vol. 1 of William Shaw's *Earse Dictionary*, now at the Queen's University of Belfast.

23. *The Percy Letters*, 7:70–71. Mallet's book was published in Copenhagen in two volumes in 1755 and 1756. A second edition was published in Geneva in 1763. Percy seems to have considered including some Icelandic verse in the *Reliques* (Margaret M. Smith, "Thomas Percy, William Shenstone, *Five Pieces of Runic Poetry*, and the *Reliques*" [*Bodleian Library Record*, Vol. 12, No. 6 (April 1988), 471–77]).

24. *The Percy Letters*, 7:74 (Letter 1 Oct. 1760).

25. *Five Pieces of Runic Poetry*, [vi], 64–65; *Lit. Illus.*, 7:275.

26. *The Percy Letters*, 7:46, 49 (Letter 5 Feb. 1760).

27. *Select Fables of Esop and Other Fabulists* (Birmingham; 1761). I am indebted to Mr. Arthur Houghton for the opportunity to see this copy of the *Fables*.

28. *Ancient Songs Chiefly on Moorish Subjects*, x–xiii. Percy's letter is printed from two drafts in the Bodleian Library (MS. Percy c. 2, ff. 235–40).

29. Boston Public Library MS. Eng. 154 (1).

30. Osborn Collection, Yale University. Davis sent his bill with a letter dated 28 March 1761 (Boston Public Library MS. Eng. 154 [2]).

31. *The Percy Letters*, 7:67. John Baskerville was printing the *Fables* in Birmingham.
32. Ibid., 73.
33. Ibid., 79 (Letter Percy to Shenstone, 27 Nov. 1760).
34. *The Letters of Samuel Johnson*, ed. R. W. Chapman (Oxford: Clarendon Press, 1952), 1:128. Percy thanked Apperley in a letter of 28 February 1760 for his frequent visits to Johnson's lodgings on his behalf (Hyde Collection).
35. *The Percy Letters*, 7:79.
36. *The Letters of Samuel Johnson*, 1:130.
37. *The Percy Letters*, 7:94–95. Percy's indebtedness to the *Collection of Old Ballads* is examined by Stephen Vartin in "Thomas Percy's *Reliques*: Its Structure and Organization," Ph.D. diss., New York University, 1972.
38. B.L. Add. MS. 45,867, B. 40 and A. 28.
39. Backwell was no longer a member of Parliament, having lost his seat in the elections following the accession of George III in 1760. Percy's diary shows that he dined with Backwell on at least five of the days during his London visit.
40. Under the contracts Percy was to receive ten guineas for each work (Bodl. MS. Eng. Lett. d. 59, f. 8).
41. *The Percy Letters*, 7:96–97.
42. Percy noted all five of the agreements in his diary. The contract for his *Chinese Miscellanies*, as it was initially entitled, called for James Dodsley to pay Percy twenty-one guineas "on demand" (Osborn Collection, Yale University).
43. *The Percy Letters*, 7:68. Percy also visited various relations, including the Perrinses, with whom he may have lodged for part of his stay.
44. See pp. 16 and 29 n. 11.
45. The diary breaks off after 7 June.
46. *The Miscellaneous Works of Oliver Goldsmith, M.D.*, 1:62–63.
47. *Lit. Illus.*, 6:556–57; B.L. Add. MS. 38,728, f. 167. Percy's interest in Buckingham had probably been aroused by Lady Longueville.
48. Folger Shakespeare Library w. b. 475, p. 96 (Letter Tonson to Percy, 10 Oct. 1761). Among Garrick's plays was a copy of *The Rehearsal* with notes by the early eighteenth-century scholar Lewis Theobald (George Winchester Stone and George M. Kahrl, *David Garrick: A Critical Biography* [Carbondale and Edwardsville: Southern Illinois Univ. Press, 1979], 186).

CHAPTER V

A Scholar's Life:
1761–1764

O F ALL PERCY'S projects, the collection of ancient poems—
Percy's *Reliques*, as it came familiarly to be known—had
required the closest attention in the months preceding his
trip to London, and it was to prove even more demanding in the
months that followed. Not content to include only the readily accessible pieces in his folio manuscript and elsewhere, Percy resolved to
search every corner of Britain for treasures that might have eluded the
more casual efforts of earlier editors. Even before he concluded his agreement with Dodsley on May 22, 1761, he was in touch with Richard
Farmer of Emmanuel College and Edward Blakeway of Magdalene
College, who gave him some account of the older poems in the Cambridge University libraries.[1] In London Edward Capell provided assistance, and Thomas Astle, through his knowledge of the British
Museum manuscripts, appeared an even more promising resource for
the future. On May 28, while still in London, Percy introduced himself by letter to Thomas Warton, Professor of Poetry at Oxford, whose
Observations on the Faerie Queene (1754) was shortly to be republished
by Dodsley in a revised edition.[2]

To correct Warton's apparent impression that the Arthurian
knights and stories were inventions of Sir Thomas Malory in his *Morte
Darthur*, Percy called his attention to numerous Arthurian ballads that
antedated even Chaucer. Many "passages in our ancient English Poets
may be illustrated from these Old Ballads," he commented, and he
enclosed copies of "The Boy and the Mantle" and the fragmentary
"Marriage of Sir Gawaine," transcribed from his folio manuscript, to
demonstrate what he believed to be Spenser's indebtedness to the first
and Chaucer's to the second. He himself, he informed Warton, was
about to edit the best of the old ballads in his manuscript and in the

university libraries. Would Warton tell him, he asked, what materials could be seen in the Oxford libraries and whether or not they were worth the trouble and expense of a journey to Oxford?

Warton, suffering from a dislocated shoulder, did not reply until June 19, when he expressed appreciation for the old ballads and offered Percy his assistance in any of his projects. For the moment most of the assistance was in the other direction. Percy was back promptly with two letters containing detailed information about alliterative verse, Shakespeare's ballad sources, and Chaucer's burlesquing of the old romances, much of which Warton incorporated into his revised edition of the *Observations* or made use of later in his *History of English Poetry*.[3]

Although Percy had assured Shenstone only six days earlier that he would be content with two volumes, he announced to Warton in his May 28 letter that his design was to present his collection in three. Obviously he felt confident that he would discover enough first-rate material to justify a third volume and to satisfy Shenstone's doubts, as in fact he was later to do. His confidence extended even to the likelihood of early publication, which, with some hesitation, he set for the coming winter.[4] But, with Shenstone and highly qualified university scholars to support him, it is not surprising that he would underestimate the task he was undertaking.

How much additional help he expected from Samuel Johnson in these days of his first enthusiasm is not clear. Preoccupied as Johnson was with editing Shakespeare, Percy was probably pleased simply to be able to call upon him for advice and encouragement, or for another "council of war" when critical decisions had to be reached. It is not apparent that he ever acted upon Johnson's 1758 suggestion that he provide an interleaved text for Johnson to annotate, or that Johnson renewed the suggestion. Perhaps Percy's fondest hope was that John-son would honor him with a visit to Easton Maudit. He talks of making a trip to the Leasowes, Percy wrote to Shenstone on May 22, 1761, "but this you must not much depend on, he is no more formed for long Journeys than a Tortoise: 'Tis two years that he has been resolving to come and see me, who consider myself, as in the neigh-bourhood of London."[5]

No doubt the vicarage would have been ready to receive such a distinguished guest whenever he could be drawn away from the "full tide of human existence" that held him close to London's Charing Cross. Easton Maudit, of course, had nothing comparable, but it could offer hospitality, a convivial host and hostess, literary talk, and a household managed with quiet efficiency by Anne Percy, who clearly fitted the portrait of the ideal wife that Percy had drawn for Will Cleiveland in June of 1757.[6] The Percys' later friend Joseph Cradock, turning to Nicholas Rowe's *Jane Shore* for words to describe her, remembered her in his *Memoirs* as

> without one jarring atom form'd,
> And gentleness and joy made up her being.[7]

But the early summer of 1761, when the Percys were expecting their second child, was not an opportune time for a Johnson visit. On August 3 another daughter was born at the vicarage and was named Barbara in honor of the nonagenarian Barbara, Viscountess Longueville, who was to be one of young Barbara's godmothers.[8] Johnson's visit would have to be put off, at least for a few months.

In the summer of 1761 Percy extended his scholarly connections into Wales. English interest in early Welsh literature had been stimulated by recent works like Thomas Gray's "The Bard" and William Mason's play *Caractacus*, and Percy, curious about all early literatures, was drawn irresistibly into the effort to reclaim the works of the ancient Welsh bards. About a year earlier he had approached Rice Williams, a Welsh friend of Shenstone and Robert Binnel who was rector of Weston-under-Lizard in Staffordshire, in the hope that Williams could introduce him to a scholar learned in the Welsh language and literature. But Williams had little knowledge of Welsh poetry and scholarship. For some months, however, he and Percy corresponded about the possibility of jointly editing a collection of Welsh proverbs; and in June 1761, with the help of another Welsh clergyman, Williams was able to refer Percy to the scholar and poet Evan Evans. A letter written by Percy to Evans on July 21 was enclosed by Williams in one of his own letters, recommending Percy as "inquisitive and indefatigable, with a good share of taste, Judgement and poetic Genius."[9]

In his letter Percy expressed dismay that the Welsh seemed so much less interested in their literature and antiquities than the Scots, and he urged Evans to continue translating the odes of the ancient Welsh bards and to give "a select collection" of them to the world. "I may modestly pretend," he wrote, "to have some credit with the Booksellers, and with M.ͬ Dodsley in particular, who is my intimate friend; I shall be very happy to do you any good offices with him."

Percy added that he had "prevailed on a friend" to translate some of the ancient runic poetry, that Edward Lye was rescuing some Saxon poetry from oblivion, and that he himself planned to translate some pieces of ancient Spanish poetry. With all this "attention to ancient and foreign Poetry, it would be pity to have that of the ancient Britons forgot." If Evans would give him an account of his labors, he would "communicate them to several eminent *Literati* of my acquaintance, and to mention one in particular, M! Johnson, the Author of the *Rambler, Dictionary*, &c., who will, I am sure, be glad to recommend your work, and to give you any advice for the most advantageous disposal of it."[10]

Two such names as Dodsley and Johnson could hardly go unnoticed, but when Evans replied on August 8 he displayed more interest in Percy's scholarly credentials than his literary connections. In particular he joined Percy in deploring the Welsh neglect of their literature and antiquities: "There are very few persons in Wales that understand anything of . . . [the early bards] or heed them in this age, nor indeed much ever since Queen Elizabeth's time when the [professional order of Welsh poets] was extinct. So that in one century more their valuable works will be in the utmost danger of being entirely lost." He also enclosed his translation of an early ode and expressed his intention of completing a collection of translations and introducing it with a short Latin dissertation on the Welsh bards from the sixth to the sixteenth century. If his work progressed, he would be pleased to have Percy recommend him to Dodsley, but he was afraid that he could produce nothing to merit the attention of Johnson and the other *literati* of Percy's acquaintance.[11]

The connection with Evans was plainly satisfying to Percy, who welcomed the opportunity to sharpen his critical judgment in his exchanges with this most eminent of Welsh scholars. In his letter to Evans of October 15, 1761, for example, his carefully drawn distinction between what he called epic poetry's delight in circumstance and the ode's neglect of it was worthy of publication, a brief essay such as a latter-day Addison or Steele might have been happy to accept from a correspondent.[12] Unfortunately Evans's knowledge of English literature was limited, and from early Welsh literature he could promise nothing comparable to the ballads that were the standard fare of Percy's collection. But he was an indispensable resource on traditions and beliefs common to England and Wales, such as the Arthurian legend and the lore of fairies, and he constantly encouraged Percy in his work even when he could provide no special help. His most significant assistance was to come when Percy turned to his translation of Paul Henri Mallet's *Introduction à l'Histoire de Dannemarc.*

For help in building his collection of poems Percy knew that he would have to continue looking elsewhere, particularly to Scotland, where the border wars and innumerable other events had been celebrated in verse, much of which was little known. He had been pleased when Shenstone, in a letter of July 5, 1761, offered to enlist the aid of a "a very good Friend in Scotland, who has a taste for Vertu and for Antiquity."[13] The friend was John McGowan, an Edinburgh solicitor and a member of the Society of Antiquaries. Percy accepted the offer and reported to Shenstone that he had "settled a correspondence in the very heart of Wales, and another in the Wilds of Staffordshire and Derbyshire." He intended also to write to a friend in Ireland and would not fail to mention "our scheme" to Grainger in the West Indies; "thus shall we ransack the whole British Empire."[14]

Percy's friend in Ireland, whoever he was, apparently turned up nothing that could be put to use. As for the West Indies, Grainger reported a total lack of success: "nobody can tell me any thing of the Charibbean poetry," he wrote on July 25, 1762; "indeed, from what I have seen of these savages, I have no curiosity to know ought of their compositions." His inquiries about the North American Indians brought the same result.[15] With Scotland, of course, Percy fared much better, although Shenstone, a chronic procrastinator, did not write to McGowan for almost three months, and it was another two years before Percy received the help from McGowan he was counting on.

In England he was making steady progress. The London printer William Dicey, "the greatest printer of Ballads in the kingdom," gave him over eighty pieces that he had not seen before and promised him copies of all his old stock ballads.[16] In the old plays lent to him by David Garrick he found numerous "scarce pieces of ancient poetry."[17] Thomas Astle came up with a number of materials, including an unidentified collection of "Old Songs and Sonnets," which, Percy assured Astle on July 19, 1761, greatly enriched his collection. "I am content to perform the office of scavenger for the public," Percy added, "and as Virgil found *Gold* among the *Dung* of *Ennius*, from all this learned Lumber I hope to extract something that shall please the most delicate and correct Taste." Astle sent further materials that Percy acknowledged in letters of January 14 and 31, 1762.[18]

With numerous contracts to fulfill, Percy could not, of course, devote his free time solely to his collection of poetry. On June 29, 1761, as he noted in his diary, he began to translate *The Little Orphan of China* for his "Chinese Miscellanies," using as his text a French translation by Pierre du Halde. On the same day he read a play of Thomas Shadwell, probably as part of his research for the new key with which he hoped to release the secrets of Buckingham's *Rehearsal* that had resisted earlier inquiry. A summer and fall of intensive reading followed as the publisher Jacob Tonson kept him supplied with Garrick's old plays.[19] *Hau Kiou Choaan* was moving steadily through the press, and Percy's "3 Matrons" were probably already admitting the company that in time was to double their membership. As though all this activity was not sufficient for a clergyman with two churches, a chaplaincy, and a house and family to look after, Percy was also in correspondence with Ralph Griffiths, who had solicited contributions for a new periodical, *The Library*. In the May 1761 issue Griffiths published the prayer composed by Percy for Anne when she was preparing for her smallpox inoculation in 1758, but the magazine expired before he could publish a Percy article on "Popish Relics" and a burlesque on a country schoolmaster, the first of which Griffiths's assistant carelessly left in a bureau drawer in the country.[20]

On August 17 Percy set out for Cambridge, which he reached in the evening after dining at Huntingdon with Owen Manning, author of *The History of Surrey* and a close friend of Edward Lye. His Cambridge hosts during a visit of more than two weeks were Richard Farmer and Edward Blakeway, and his primary purpose was to examine the extensive collection of broadside ballads bequeathed to Magdalene College by Samuel Pepys. The five volumes of Pepys ballads, with their nucleus in an earlier collection by John Selden, held for Percy the attractions of quantity, uniqueness, and antiquity, the last of these graphically exemplified in the predominance of black-letter ballads—a visual separation from the later street ballads in which Percy took little interest and from which he constantly sought to dissociate his own compilation.

Percy stayed at Emmanuel College, where Farmer apparently found a room for him and where they were joined on the first evening by James Devey, another fellow of the college. After breakfasting with Farmer the next morning, he visited the university library and later had tea at Magdalene College with Blakeway, who had made arrangements for him to consult the Pepys collection. With six amanuenses to assist him, he began the laborious task of transcribing ballads on Wednesday, August 19, and he interrupted his daily routine only on Sunday the twenty-third, when he attended church at St. Mary's in the morning and evening, wrote letters to Edward Lye and Samuel Edwards, and spent the rest of the evening at Emmanuel.[21]

By the following Sunday he had finished transcribing and was ready to enter more fully into the Cambridge society than his rigorous schedule of the first two weeks had permitted. On Tuesday evening, September 1, he entertained guests in his own room; on Wednesday evening he joined a group at the lodging of Henry Hubbard, one of the older Emmanuel fellows; and on Thursday evening he was with another group at Blakeway's. Perhaps his chief gratification of these last days was making the acquaintance of Thomas Gray, whose poetry he had imitated and much admired. They met in the university library, and Gray, who was projecting a history of English poetry, invited him to tea at Pembroke College on September 1. Percy took with him either his folio manuscript or transcriptions made from it, along with Evan Evans's August 8 letter, in which Evans had inquired about a note in Gray's "The Bard." Probably they discussed Icelandic poetry, in which both were interested; and Gray showed Percy an early version of James Macpherson's translation of the Erse fragments, from which, Percy later told Shenstone, it was apparent that Macpherson had exercised considerable freedom in adapting the translation for the public.[22] He saw Gray again in the university library on the morning of September 3, but recorded no details of the meeting.

Perhaps during the visit Percy and some of his friends discussed the desirability of proposing to the prime minister that Samuel Johnson be granted a pension by the government. On November 15, 1761, an unsigned letter in Blakeway's handwriting was sent from Cambridge to the Earl of Bute recommending a pension of £200 to £300 as a reward to Johnson for "immortalizing" the English language in his *Dictionary* and promoting religion and morality in all his works. According to the letter, however, its author was not writing in his own hand and had no personal knowledge of Johnson, thus eliminating both Blakeway and Percy as possible authors. Who the author was can only be guessed at, although Farmer, as Percy's only other close Cambridge friend, seems a likely candidate. But the inspiration for the letter probably came from Percy, who in 1761 had particular reason to feel grateful to Johnson, with whose help he had secured his numerous contracts with Robert and James Dodsley. A subsequent letter

from Blakeway congratulating Percy on Johnson's pension seems tac-
itly to acknowledge his role in this anonymous effort.[23]

Percy left for home after breakfast on Saturday, September 5,
stopping once again at Huntingdon, and the next day he was back in
the routine of conducting services at Easton Maudit and Wilby. The
Cambridge trip, which had cost him £10, had been a fruitful one, and
he was quick to share his experiences with Edward Lye and Richard
Backwell, whom he visited on Monday. On the next day he was off
to Hinwick to dine and play chess with John Orlebar, lord of the
manor and one of the commissioners of excise; and on Thursday he
dined and had tea with Ambrose Isted at Ecton. How much of his
Cambridge visit he shared with Johnson is not known, but he must
have written to him during the week of September 6. Young Barbara
Percy's baptism had been set for September 22, the day of George
III's coronation, and Percy, eager to bring Johnson to Easton Maudit,
invited him to join the Percy family for the double celebration on that
day. But Johnson was not ready, at least on that occasion, to be drawn
to rural Northamptonshire. "The kindness of your invitation," he
replied on September 12,

> would tempt one to leave pomp and tumult behind, and hasten to
> your retreat, however as I cannot perhaps see another coronation
> so conveniently as this, and I may see many young Percies, I beg
> your pardon for staying till this great ceremony is over after which
> I purpose to pass some time with you, though I cannot flatter myself
> that I can even then long enjoy the pleasure which your company
> always gives me, and which is likewise expected from that of Mrs.
> Percy.[24]

On October 15 Percy wrote to inform Evans of his visit with
Gray, and, while expressing pleasure in Evans's intention to prepare
a Latin version of early Welsh poems, he urged him at the same time
to publish "a liberal English Translation."[25] Eleven days later, taking
with him some of his own poetic treasures, he set out for the Leasowes
by way of Brandon, where he had dinner, spent the night, and conversed at length with Lady Longueville, perhaps about some of his
many questions concerning the Duke of Buckingham and the Restoration court. He reached the Leasowes in time for dinner on the
twenty-seventh, showed Shenstone his runic fragments, and on the

next day brought out his folio manuscript. It was his first opportunity since the spring to discuss at leisure some of the complex problems presented by his poems, many of which were incomplete or obscured by archaic language. As his study of the Pepys ballads confirmed, many also existed in multiple and sometimes very different versions, among which difficult choices had to be made. He spent much of the twenty-ninth revising some of the ballads, but also took time to show Shenstone his translation of *The Song of Solomon*. He left after dinner on the thirtieth for Birmingham, where his brother Anthony joined him for the night, and they went on to Easton Maudit together the next day.

Percy's diary for the next fourteen months has not survived, but many of his activities can be pieced together from his letters and other sources. On November 14 his first book, *Hau Kiou Choaan*; or, *the Pleasing History*, made its appearance in four small volumes, with no indication of Percy's role in it on the title page or in the dedication to the Countess of Sussex, which was signed only "The Editor." Dodsley had delayed publication until Parliament reconvened in the fall of 1761, but the delay provided no assurance of a favorable reception.[26] "Curious, tho' not very entertaining," was the best that the *British Magazine* could say of it, and the *Critical Review* dismissed *the Pleasing History* as "the most *unpleasing* performance which we have perused for some months past." Only Ralph Griffiths, who had once rejected the manuscript, had some kind words, though these were more for Percy's editing than for the story of Shuey-ping-sin and her tireless pursuer: "Readers," Griffiths wrote in the *Monthly Review*, "will think themselves very much obliged to . . . [the editor] for the entertainment they will meet with in these curious annotations, which . . . contain a great variety of useful and entertaining particulars."[27]

Shenstone had expressed a similar view after reading an advance copy that Percy had Dodsley send to him in late June or early July. But Shenstone's chief reaction was to the vast number of misprints and to Percy's solicitousness to see that no error went uncorrected and no omission unrepaired. Like confessionals in which Percy poured out all his sins at once, each volume contained pages of "Additions and Corrections" or lists of "Errata" and two contained both; and the "Collection of Chinese Proverbs and Apothegms" in volume three was followed by lists of "Proverbs Omitted," Proverbs Corrected," and "Parallels Omitted." Do not "affix anything *more* of *this nature*" to the book, Shenstone grumbled when he wrote to Percy early in December.[28]

Dodsley had printed a thousand copies of *Hau Kiou Choaan* in the hope that it would catch the current fancy for things Chinese, but, with so little enthusiasm even from a close friend like Shenstone, it is not surprising that numerous copies remained unsold a dozen years later.[29] In 1774 James Dodsley, who succeeded to the business after his brother's death in 1764, reissued the unsold copies with a slightly revised dedication and an "Advertisement" responding to doubts raised about the authenticity of the Chinese original and the translation.[30] In spite of the disappointing English sale, the book was translated into French and German in 1766 and into Dutch a year later.

In his December letter Shenstone argued his case once again for a two-volume edition of the ballads: with three volumes to fill, he concluded, Percy would more readily be imposed upon by antiquity "in the Garb of merit" than he would with two. "Percy is a man of learning, taste, and indefatigable industry," Shenstone had written to John McGowan on September 24. "I am only afraid that his fondness for antiquity should tempt him to admit pieces that have no other sort of merit." His advice to Percy was to hold off on poems like "The Battle of Otterbourne" until he saw how the public responded to the first two volumes. Shenstone perceived a problem also in Percy's proposal to print the oldest poems first, since all the more irregular and obscure poems would thus be thrown together. Why not group them according to "areas of 20, 40 or 50 years?" he asked.

Acting upon this and a later Shenstone suggestion, Percy divided each volume into three parts, with the poems of each part arranged largely in chronological order.[31] But he found it difficult to think of fewer than three volumes for the edition. Perhaps he was preparing for three solely to have the third in readiness if the first two should be favorably received. It seems likely, however, that his initial table of contents, probably drawn up in the late fall of 1761, was intended also to win Shenstone over to the virtues of his own plan. Volume 3 to be sure, was to open with "The Battle of Otterbourne," perhaps out of respect for Shenstone's advice. But Percy probably found more merit in the poem than Shenstone was willing to acknowledge; and he continued through the third volume with "Chevy-Chase," several other ballads of the Northumberland Percys, and such popular ballads as "King Estmere," "Barbara Allan," and "The Children of the

Wood"—poems, in short, of considerable variety, ranking in quality with those of his first two volumes.[32]

Much as there remained to do, Percy began preparing copy of the first volume for the press, and on February 28, 1762, he was able to send Thomas Warton the first proof sheet, containing "The Boy and the Mantle" and part of "The Marriage of Sir Gawaine," which Percy had attempted to restore from the fragmented copy in his folio manuscript.[33] Throughout the year the poems for the first volume moved steadily though slowly through the press while Percy consulted with Shenstone, Farmer, Warton, and others about poems for the later volumes. Warton, whom Percy called "of infinite service," checked on materials at Oxford for both the collection of poems and the edition of Buckingham and promised to send transcriptions of the poems in an Ashmolean manuscript.[34] Farmer provided similar assistance and even supplied books from the Cambridge University library, including early editions of *Tottel's Miscellany* and Shakespeare's plays, but he demurred when Percy asked him to send the manuscripts of "Guy of Warwick" and other early poems. "I am not a little pleased," he wrote on August 28, 1762, "when you set me about any business, which it is in my power to perform; & equally sorry when I am disappointed but how ye Duce came you to imagine, y^t such *valuable* M.S.S. as you speak of, could be got out of our University Library? I dare not own y^t I send any of y^e *printed* Books out of Town, which now & then brings me into ridiculous circumstances."[35]

Shenstone continued to send his evaluations of poems from earlier collections such as *The Hive* and *The Tea-Table Miscellany* and to caution Percy against too great a partiality for antiquity, though to what extent he exercised a "rejecting Power" that Percy offered him is not clear: "an *Over* proportion of *this Kind* of *Ballast*, will sink your vessel to the Bottom of the Sea," he prophesied on May 16, 1762. By that date, nonetheless, he had become reconciled to the idea of three volumes, though he expressed the hope that Percy would keep each of them well under three hundred pages.[36]

Other projects progressed also, and new projects sprang up in Percy's mind like wildflowers, some of them to enjoy only a few moments in the sun. By February he had collected most of the old Spanish romances satirized in *Don Quixote* for his projected new edition. He hoped "to rake together in one volume" everything relating to Kenilworth and to publish "all the Old didactic tracts on Poetry" and "some curious old military instructions."[37] On August 14 he proposed to Evans a scheme for *"Specimens of the ancient Poetry of different Nations"* to include two Welsh odes translated by Evans into English, the Chinese poetry published in *Hau Kiou Choaan*, James Macpherson's Erse fragments, his own *Five Pieces of Runic Poetry* still in the press, and *The Song of Solomon*, which Percy—probably unwilling to claim too much for himself—informed Evans he had "set a friend to translate... afresh from the Hebrew." He himself, he added, had specimens of East Indian, Peruvian, Lapland, Greenland, and Saxon poetry.[38] He continued reading plays for his new key to Buckingham's *Rehearsal*, and he introduced himself to Sir David Dalrymple, a literary scholar and a member of the Scottish Faculty of Advocates, who had commended Jacob Tonson on the proposed Buckingham edition. Writing to Dalrymple on November 10, 1762, Percy noted that he had read every play in David Garrick's collection published between 1660 and 1672, the year *The Rehearsal* was published, a number not much short of two hundred.[39] As it turned out, Dalrymple proved to be the Scottish source Percy had been seeking in his effort to ransack the British Empire. He confessed to little knowledge of the English stage, but he had done some ballad editing for the publisher Foulis in Glasgow, and he was far more communicative than John McGowan, whom Percy still had not heard from. It was he, in fact, who introduced the subject of the ballads in their correspondence by asking, in his reply to Percy's first letter, about Percy's progress with his collection of poems and mentioning that he had given several poems to McGowan for Percy's use and had continued to look for others.[40]

The year 1762 saw the publication of two of Percy's books, *The Matrons* on May 28 and *Miscellaneous Pieces Relating to the Chinese* on December 13, which were alike in a number of respects. Anonymous and largely unpretentious volumes, neither contained much original work. In the *Miscellaneous Pieces*, dedicated to Lady Longueville, Percy gathered up various strands of his research for *Hau Kiou Choaan*, including such essays as J. L. deMosheim's "Authentic Memoirs of the Christian Church in China," William Chambers's "Of the Art of Laying out Gardens among the Chinese," and Richard Hurd's "On the Chinese Drama." *The Matrons*, dedicated to "the Matrons of Great Britain and Ireland," also had ties with *Hau Kiou Choaan* through its story "The Chinese Matron," as well as with Percy's Buckingham project through "The French Matron," reprinted from a published letter of Sir George Etherege to the Duke of Buckingham. Another of its six stories of feminine frailty, "The Roman Matron," was drawn from *The Seven Wise Maisters of Rome*, one of the black-letter books in Percy's boyhood library.

Percy translated anew Petronius's classic tale of the Ephesian matron and, from the French of du Halde, adapted the story of the Chinese matron, which Goldsmith had made the subject of Letter XVIII in his *Citizen of the World*; except for brief introductions to the tales, however, little else beside the dedication was his own. In the *Miscellaneous Pieces* his contributions were somewhat more substantial: a preface and a noteworthy "Dissertation on the Language and Characters of the Chinese," which was justly singled out for praise by both the *Monthly* and the *Critical Review*.[41]

Both books required some apology, *The Matrons* in the work itself and the *Miscellaneous Pieces* shortly after publication. A succession of widows false to their vows of fidelity to their dead husbands could hardly have gained Percy a following among women: "monstrously unnatural," they might have thought it, as Percy assumed they would think the demands upon Nancy, "fairest of the fair," in his "Song."[42] In his "dedication" he assured them, perhaps not altogether facetiously, that the stories should really be read in praise of women, since to bring his six together he had been forced "to ransack the mouldy volumes of Antiquity, and to take a voyage as far as China."[43] As for the *Miscellaneous Pieces*, having reprinted, without permission, a Richard Hurd essay that he knew Hurd to be dissatisfied with, Percy asked Farmer to convey a set of the work to Hurd "by way of atonement." "I thought he wou'd be more likely to forgive the thing when done," he commented to Farmer, "than to give his consent in form if it was previously solicited."[44] He also had reason to regret his hasty acceptance, in his preface, of a reported discovery by Turberville Needham, an English Jesuit living in Italy, that the Chinese characters had been derived from Egyptian hieroglyphics. Needham's fiction was exposed promptly, but not in time for Percy to revise his preface.[45]

Neither book made much impression on Percy's contemporaries, and both are seen infrequently today. Much more widely disseminated was a poem that he wrote to introduce the ninth edition of Sir James Stonhouse's *Friendly Advice to a Patient*, in place of one by Moses Browne which had embarrassed Stonhouse with its praise of him as a "Great and good man! by Heaven blest." "I am far from being great," Stonhouse, the founder of the Northampton Infirmary, wrote to Percy on August 5, 1762, "& not very good I can tell you."[46] In his nine six-line stanzas, Percy directed his praise rather to the medical profession and Stonhouse's pamphlet than to Stonhouse himself:

> . . . while Medicine makes the Body whole,
> This little Tract affords Prescriptions for the Soul.

The ninth edition was distributed in quantity by the Society for Promoting Christian Knowledge, and Percy's poem was reprinted in both the *Scots* and the *Gentleman's* magazines for November 1762. Superior though it was to Moses Browne's, it is less interesting than the exchange of letters before publication by Percy and Stonhouse, who had sought the reactions of some of his friends to Percy's poem. When one of them declared the last line of the poem "not grammar," objected to the use of the word "say" three times in four stanzas, and suggested that "little" in the line "That make him loath Life's little Span" be changed to "scanty" to avoid the alliteration, Percy responded to Stonhouse with some asperity:

> You say "Nixon pronounces the last line *not* grammar." If he does, I pronounce him hasty and inconsiderate. He forgets that *true poetry* delights in bold figures, and loves to drop an obvious word for the imagination to supply . . . .
>
> Remember, that a graceful negligence, if accompanied with beauty, is in poetry, infinitely preferable to a tame and faultless insipidity. This *alone* is high treason ag.st the muses. Was I to make all the alterations recommended in your friends papers, and adopt all the corrections there proposed, I should drain my small poem of whatever little spirit it chances to be possest of.

"What think you of *life's scanty span*?" Percy asked. There's "a fine hissing dissonant cluster of consonants," and all to avoid the alliteration, which "was here studied, and is a beauty." The same critic, he added, "counts over his fingers how often a word or a letter has been used in the poem. . . . A fine mechanical way of wit!"[47]

Percy made one or two minor changes in the poem, but it remained virtually as it was when Stonhouse circulated it to his friends. Much pleased with its reception, Stonhouse reported to Percy on November 6 that everyone thought his stanzas elegant, and he went on to urge Percy to devote the coming winter evenings to revising a seventeenth-century pamphlet entitled *The Comforts of Having Many Children:* "What gets a poor Cottager y.e Favour of his Squire?—a

Large Family of children. . . . What often reforms a Spendthrift? his children."[48] Percy seems not to have risen to Stonhouse's challenge.

Percy's correspondence gives no indication that he informed Grainger and Shenstone of his exchange with Dr. Stonhouse, but doubtless both would have relished his spirited dismissal of criticism he quite properly labeled "mechanical." To judge from his role in the tobacco-stopper plot against Hylton, Shenstone would have welcomed a second round of such letters, but any further response from Nixon seems to have been precluded by Stonhouse's ready acceptance of Percy's judgment. Even trivial intellectual fun was almost a stock-in-trade with Shenstone. On February 3, 1762, he announced that he was making a set of boxes to appear on the outside like books, and he invited Percy to suggest titles "in lieu of what *these books* may want *within*." The titles could be Puritanical: "a new round to Jacob's Ladder"; quaint and antiquated: "a tragedie of pleasaunte thinges"; or nothing: "Dutch Wit" or "French Probity." Percy, who enjoyed Shenstone's games, submitted more than a dozen titles, including "Court sincerity," "a cordial dram for a drooping saint," "a mouse-trap for a nibbling sinner," and "a box of pills for the whore of Babylon."[49]

Grainger, married and the father of a young daughter, had settled happily into his medical practice in St. Kitts but had not lost his poetic interests. He informed Percy in a letter of June 5 that he had completed, "at least for the present," his "Cane Piece," a long Virgilian Georgic composed for the most part during his rides about the island to visit his patients. He was now sending it for Percy to peruse "with the utmost attention" and to polish "with the utmost exactness" if he thought that its publication would establish Grainger's fame as a poet. He hoped that Shenstone and Binnel would give it the same scrutiny. "I know your regard for me inclines you to think well of every thing I write," he added in a letter of July 25; "I must, therefore, entreat you to communicate the whole to Mr. Shenstone, as he knows me less, and must be more dispassionate."[50] In his June 5 letter Grainger also reported that he had found a position for Percy's brother Anthony with the most eminent merchant in St. Kitts, and he expressed regret that Anthony had abandoned the idea of seeking his fortune in the West Indies.

The spring of 1762 brought an epidemic of influenza to England, and both Percy in Easton Maudit and Farmer in Cambridge were stricken with it.[51] Percy also suffered a severe second attack in late

May or early June, and he had still not recovered on June 17, when he wrote to Shenstone that continual headaches and a low fever were making him unfit for work and spoiling his taste for life's "refined amusements." A few weeks later, however, he was able to entertain Edward Blakeway, who spent three days at Easton Maudit.

"I most heartily congratulate you upon your friend M.ʳ Johnson's honourable pension," Blakeway wrote to Percy on July 31, twelve days after the government had awarded Johnson a pension of £300— "I have not lately seen a piece of news that has given me so much pleasure." It was, of course, natural for Blakeway to assume that the letter he had penned on November 15 had played some part in the government's decision, but unfortunately no evidence has been found to support such an assumption. With numerous political considerations to take into account, as well as Johnson's preeminent position among English writers, it is hardly likely that the Earl of Bute would have paid much attention to a letter from an unknown and unknowable Johnson admirer.[52] But perhaps those responsible for the letter merit some recognition for their effort in behalf of one of the eighteenth century's best known and most deserved pensions.

In May Shenstone informed Percy that he was seeking a place in his shrubbery to inscribe a seat to him, just as he was for two "Prime Friends," Richard Jago, a former schoolmate, and Richard Graves, a classmate at Oxford's Pembroke College. The truest pleasure of his garden walks, Shenstone wrote, was the pleasure they gave to a friend; "Should *you* come over and be delighted here, the Pleasure would be increased an hundred-fold."[53] Percy accepted the invitation for both Anne and himself, but it was September 13 before they could get away for what proved to be an agreeable change of scene for them both. Anne, who had not been in very good health for months, was much improved, "thanks to the pure air" of Shenstone's "Elizium." Percy wandered about the walks with Jago, and together they undertook a description of the Leasowes that was doubtless more elaborate and affectionate than Percy's first such attempt in the early days of his acquaintance with Shenstone.[54] Although no details of their conversations remain, Percy and Shenstone must have spent much of the time discussing Percy's collection of poems and other projects, as well as an edition of Shenstone's works that Shenstone, with Percy's encouragement, was preparing.

The year ended uneventfully, as it had begun. But 1763 served notice from the beginning that it would be different. It came in on a winter that Percy called the worst since 1739, and, with Anne nearing the end of her third pregnancy, its ravages must have been felt keenly in the Percy household.[55] During a week of constant frost in mid-January, the maids, including the children's nursemaid, Mary Langley, required the attendance of Mr. Clarke, an otherwise unidentified medical practitioner. Nearby, the Earl of Sussex's manor house nearly caught fire on the evening of January 21. On January 23 the much revered Lady Longueville, just a few years short of a hundred, died at Brandon. "I have lost an excellent Chronicle and valuable friend," Percy lamented to Farmer;[56] and in the parish register he described her as "the wonder of her time . . . who left a most noble character." She was buried in the church at Easton Maudit on February 10.

On February 7 the Percy's third child was born, a boy whom they named Henry after the Earl of Sussex, one of his godfathers.[57] But their pleasure in the arrival of a son was interrupted a few days later with the news that Shenstone, only recently turned forty-eight, had died at the Leasowes on February 11 after a fever of eleven days. For Percy the loss was inestimable. For five years Shenstone had encouraged and assisted his work with the ballads, and Percy, who scarcely made a decision without consulting him, had come to look upon him more as a coeditor than an advisor. He was also a warm friend—"one of the most elegant and amiable of men," Percy wrote to Farmer on February 27, "and his tender writings were but the counterpart of his heart, which was one of the best that ever animated a human body."[58] Shenstone never completed his tribute to Percy, the seat in his garden to be inscribed with Percy's name. Percy's tribute to Shenstone was to join with Jago and Robert Dodsley to complete the description of the Leasowes, which Dodsley published in 1764 in his edition of Shenstone's works.[59] By the summer of 1763 Percy had also resolved to dedicate the still untitled collection of poems to Shenstone's memory.[60]

The severe weather continued in February. The snow fell heavily on the fourteenth, although Percy managed to get in a morning walk, but the next day conditions were so bad that he did not leave the house. On the sixteenth, which was Ash Wednesday, a thaw assisted by rain made walking treacherous—"a time of a great flood," Percy noted in the parish register—and few of his parishioners attended the church service. On that day the Earl of Sussex's groom, William Thompson, was drowned in the brook below Grendon field as he was returning with letters from the Castle Ashby post office. On Thursday

Percy had dinner and spent the evening with Lord Sussex, whom he visited again on Friday evening. With the weather clearing and the floods receding, life in Easton Maudit was resuming its normal pattern. Percy and a Mr. Bateman even went shooting near Hinwick on the nineteenth.

Young Henry Percy was baptized privately on March 7 but was not received in the church until April 24, the anniversary of Percy's birth and of his and Anne's marriage.[61] On March 10 Percy was at Cambridge, and in the latter part of March he journeyed to London, where he conferred with his publishers, received from Dodsley a total of £131/13/10½ for three of his works, and checked on the progress of his poems and the Buckingham edition; but he came down with a cold during his visit and was unable to accomplish all that he had set out to do.[62] He regretted particularly having to miss seeing Thomas Birch, a scholar of varied interests who was providing information for the Buckingham edition. He had hoped to present Birch and Lord Hardwicke, who had also expressed interest, with printed copies of the new key to *The Rehearsal*, but the printer was behind schedule and did not have them ready.[63]

Percy's London trip was timed so that he was on hand for the long overdue publication of *Five Pieces of Runic Poetry* on April 2. His major accomplishment was to contract with Jacob Tonson for an edition of the Earl of Surrey's poems, in anticipation of which he had for some time been seeking out the early editions of *Tottel's Miscellany*, where both Surrey's and Thomas Wyatt's poems had been published in 1557. He must also have discussed with Tonson a proposal to reprint the essays of Addison and Steele, for on April 23 Tonson sent him copies of the original editions of the *Spectator* and *Guardian* and duodecimo sets of the *Tatler*, *Spectator*, and *Guardian*. Tonson's parcel also included books from Apperley and five volumes of plays from David Garrick.[64]

Percy spent the mornings of March 28 to 31 in the British Museum but noted that Thomas Astle, to whom he looked for assistance with the manuscripts, was very ill on the twenty-ninth and "still poorly" on the thirty-first. He entertained Apperley at breakfast on the twenty-ninth and at Apperley's that afternoon met the classical scholar Samuel Dyer, who had been a member of Johnson's Ivy Lane Club. On the thirty-first he spent the evening at Dyer's. The incomplete diary entries of the trip give no indication that he saw Johnson, but he visited Miss Williams on the evenings of the twenty-ninth and the thirtieth, and it is unlikely that he would have overlooked the opportunity to inform Johnson of his literary progress and to renew his invitation for a visit to Easton Maudit. Perhaps he called on Johnson when, as he noted, he took leave of all his friends on April 1. On Saturday, April 2— probably carrying copies of *Five Pieces of Runic Poetry* to give to friends—he returned to the vicarage in time to conduct the Easter services at Easton Maudit and Wilby the next day.[65] On the seventh he rode again to Wilby, where he met with his parishioners, accepted a half-year's tithes, and made a new agreement, though on what terms he did not record.[66]

On April 10 he suffered another severe loss in the death of his friend Robert Binnel of Newport. Binnel, described by Percy as "the most accomplished scholar" he had ever known, had supplied him with numerous notes for the edition of *The Song of Solomon* contracted for with Dodsley on May 21, 1761, and perhaps it was a feeling of obligation to Binnel that sent him back to *The Song of Solomon* almost immediately after he received the news of his death. On April 19 he was busy collecting notes for the edition, and then, after a day of visitors, including Edward Lye, Owen Manning, and Percy's neighbor Joseph Steer, he devoted the next two days to it. Probably about this time he also asked Farmer to send him books to help him complete his annotation, for on May 14 he thanked Farmer for the "noble sortment" he had chosen. He enclosed a printed copy of his translation of *The Song of Solomon*, noting that the rest of the book was yet to be printed.[67]

Percy had been drawn to *The Song of Solomon* as "one of the most beautiful pastorals in the world," and he hoped to rescue it from the "obscurity and confusion" created by commentators who, in probing its allegorical meaning, had lost sight of its "literal sense." The "whole poem has a pastoral air," he wrote in his introduction, although, he noted later, it is neither a "pure pastoral" nor a "regular nuptial song."[68] Following the lead of the French critic Bossuet, he treated it as a dramatic eclogue in seven parts, one for each day of a "nuptial solemnity," with each verse spoken by the bridegroom, the spouse, the companions of the bridegroom, or the virgins attending the spouse.

Another of Percy's friends, James Grainger, had come close to dying late in 1762 and, concerned that nothing to harm his reputation be published, had left instructions for all his poetry to be sent to Percy. "I had rather not be talked about hereafter, than talked of as an indifferent poet," he wrote on April 18, 1763. He was distressed, how-ever, to have had no word from Percy in over fourteen months, a gap that he thought attributable to the French seizure of an English packet boat some seven months before. He did know that Percy had received the four books of his "cane piece," which his wife's brother-in-law had taken to England with him.[69]

Percy could not help wondering if there was "something omi-nous" in Grainger's poem. Shenstone was to have revised it, and he died. Then it was sent to Binnel for the same purpose, and he died. Did Farmer think, he asked on June 16, that Richard Hurd might be prevailed on to look it over? "I am solicitous for his fame, and would have this poem rendered a standard and classical work."[70]

Whether or not Hurd assisted with the poem is not apparent. In the end the major work fell to Percy, though he did not accomplish it until late in the year, after Grainger surprised him by returning to Britain to attend to family business in Scotland. Meanwhile there was much else to occupy Percy's time. On June 26 John Scott Hylton sent him the manuscript of "Shenstone's Miscellany," Shenstone's collec-tion of poems largely by his friends, including Percy, which Percy edited with considerable care but never had published.[71] He corre-sponded with Andrew Millar and John Newbery about publishing his translation of Mallet's *Introduction à l'Histoire de Dannemarc*, which, in his *Five Pieces of Runic Poetry*, he reported "in great forwardness," although his diary indicates that he did not begin the actual translation until November 21.[72] Sometime in 1763 he probably began writing *A Key to the New Testament* for the publisher Lockyer Davis. From Thomas Birch he borrowed an interleaved copy of Gerard Langbaine's 1691 *Account of the English Dramatick Poets* with copious manuscript notes by the antiquary William Oldys, and proceeded to transcribe Oldys's notes into his own copy and supplement them with notes of his own.[73]

Although a minor example, Percy's close attention to Langbaine, whose book contained information useful for the *Reliques* and the Buckingham and Surrey editions, typifies his care to overlook nothing that might prove helpful to him. His network of correspondents per-mitted him to reach out to all parts of Britain for poems suitable for his collection. By October 1763 he had acquired all five editions of *The Rehearsal* published in Buckingham's lifetime and needed only one more Restoration play to complete his new key. And by the year 1767 his search for the early editions of *Tottel's Miscellany* was to lead him to six editions published between 1557 and 1587, some of which appear to have survived in only one or two copies.[74]

Inevitably his collection of poems remained his major literary preoccupation, and he was delighted on August 30, when, after almost despairing of them, he received four Scottish ballads from John McGowan, three of which he considered of first merit.[75] He quickly found room for one of the ballads, "Lord Thomas and Fair Annet," in his second volume, where it joined such Scottish stalwarts as "The Bonny Earl of Murray" and "Young Waters." The other three cannot be certainly identified. Early in his third volume he inserted three Scottish ballads, the first of which, "The Jew's Daughter," probably came from McGowan. The second, "Edward, Edward," he attributed thirty years later to Dalrymple. And the third, "Sir Patrick Spens"— or "Spence," as Percy spelled it—was taken from "two MS. copies transmitted from Scotland," one of them apparently by Dalrymple and the other by McGowan.[76] Percy's was the first printing of "Sir Patrick Spens" and "Edward, Edward," two of the best known Scottish ballads, and his version of "Sir Patrick Spens" has understandably remained a general favorite. This story of a ship's master ordered to sea in foul weather by a king who

> . . . sits in Dumferling toune,
> Drinking the blude-reid wine

has been celebrated, perhaps more than any other ballad, for its drama, characterization, and imagery:

> O quha is this has don this deid,
>   This ill deid don to me;
> To send me out this time o'the zeir,
>   To sail upon the se?

> Mak haste, mak haste, my mirry men all,
>   Our guid schip sails the morne.
> O say na sae, my master deir,
>   For I feir a deadlie storme.

> Late late yestreen I saw the new moone
>   Wi' the auld moone in hir arme;
> And I feir, I feir, my deir mastèr,
>   That we will cum to harme.

O our Scots nobles wer richt laith
   To weet their cork-heild shoone;
Bot lang owre a' the play wer playd,
   Thair hats they swam aboone.

O lang, lang, may thair ladies sit
   Wi' thair fans into their hand,
Or eir they se Sir Patrick Spence
   Cum sailing to the land.

O lang, lang, may the ladies stand
   Wi' thair gold kems in their hair,
Waiting for thair ain deir lords,
   For they'll se thame na mair.

Have owre, have owre to Aberdour,
   It's fiftie fadom deip:
And thair lies guid Sir Patrick Spence,
   Wi' the Scots lords at his feit.

Grateful though he was to McGowan, Percy continued to look to Dalrymple, a much more reliable correspondent, for new poems and variants of the old, as well as for details to correct and enliven his introductions to individual poems. "Lady Anne Bothwell's Lament" and "Hardyknute," a modern Scottish imitation widely accepted as a genuine early work, both benefited from Dalrymple's knowledge of Scottish balladry; and Percy printed "John Anderson My Jo" more for an anecdote that Dalrymple sent with it than for the poem itself.[77] To Dalrymple he also confided some of his editorial views, though not without giving the impression that he had some uneasiness about them.

His editing of the ballads posed more than one dilemma for Percy. Although an antiquary, he did not wish to be lumped with those antiquaries whom he looked upon as "void of all taste and feeling";[78] he hoped to attract a large readership among people of taste. But his desire to please conflicted time and again with his scholarly instincts, which led him naturally to seek authentic texts, as he was doing for his editions of Surrey and Buckingham. With the ballads, the archaic and often obscure language, the texts garbled by careless scribes, and the missing words and stanzas of otherwise excellent poems all stood in the way of reader acceptance, and he set to work clearing them out like underbrush or patching and filling in the hope of restoring something of a poem's original structure and flavor. Variant texts caused problems also, which he frequently resolved by joining together the best from each. The Scottish "Edom o'Gordon" and English "Adam Carre," for example, were border cousins with a striking family resemblance, and to achieve his final text he took a few stanzas from the seriously disfigured "Adam Carre" of his folio manuscript, gave them a Scottish twist, and grafted them to "Edom o'Gordon."[79]

No doubt such tampering—usually noted only in general terms—troubled his conscience less and less as he became accustomed to it, but he was probably never totally without misgiving. It seems unlikely that he would have remarked upon Sir David Dalrymple's apparently freehanded editing if he had not welcomed it as an endorsement of his own. Alluding to the ballads edited by Dalrymple for the Glasgow publisher Foulis in 1755, Percy wrote in his letter of January 7, 1763: "I suspect that they received some beauties in passing thro' your hands. This was not only an allowable freedom (if they did) but absolutely necessary to render them worth attention. You will hence infer that I take the same liberty myself; I do it when it seems wanting, and in that case I mention it in my introduction, without any scruple."[80]

Percy confronted another dilemma because he could never quite satisfy himself that ballad editing was a suitable employment for a conscientious churchman, and his uneasiness was intensified by the countless hours the ballads exacted from him. The project that began with Johnson's suggestion that he publish the poems in his folio manuscript had reached into every part of the British Isles—and even into the empire beyond the seas! Impelled to go on—"Ancient English Poetry will ever be my favourite subject," he wrote to Warton in 1765—his conscience was nonetheless aroused, and he tried to soothe it, and to disarm criticism, by understating both the importance and the magnitude of his work.[81] "I bestow upon a few old poems," he wrote to Dalrymple on January 25, 1763, "those idle moments, which some of my grave brethren pass away over a sober game at whist."[82] Similarly, in the preface to the *Reliques*, he observed that preparing his "parcel of OLD BALLADS" for the press had been "the amusement of now and then a vacant hour amid the leisure and retirement of rural life, and hath only served as a relaxation from graver studies."[83] For most of his days those statements would have held true, but a clergyman who left his parish for more than two weeks, as Percy did when he visited Cambridge in August 1761, would have had much to answer for if the object of his visit had been not a "parcel of OLD BALLADS" but a continuing party of whist.

Percy was not called to account for his ballad editing; indeed, the only one who seems to have questioned its propriety was Percy himself. His friends offered a support that he needed, and the light provided by such a galaxy as Johnson, Shenstone, Grainger, Farmer, Warton, Evans, Lye, Dalrymple, and Astle was more than enough to guide a wanderer who was reluctant at times to venture forth alone in the dark. Percy kept going, and, hesitant though he was, he frequently asserted his independence, as when he held out for three volumes of of the *Reliques* against Shenstone's insistence upon two. He did look constantly to his friends for advice and was at times almost too ready to accept it. "You find fault with my *Mad-Songs*," he wrote to Farmer on February 28, 1764, about the six poems that formed a sequence in volume 2 of the *Reliques*: "See how Doctors differ! they were particularly selected and recommended to me by poor Shenstone, whose opinions have now acquired a kind of prophetic authority with me.— Yet to tell you true, I long ballanced with myself whether I should admit them or not: and if I had previously had your opinion it would have been decisive with me."[84] These were the poems, as G. E. Bentley noted, that were to be the inspiration for William Blake's "Mad Song."[85]

Reliant as Percy was on his friends, it is not surprising that he tried to bring a number of them to Easton Maudit as his work on the ballads approached its end. Gratitude, his convivial nature, the need for varied intellectual stimulation—these must also have been motivations even if none was so pressing as the desire to draw upon his friends' knowledge and experience. In late December 1762 he sent an invitation to Warton, who declined because he was about to begin a period of required residence at Oxford. With Farmer, Percy was more persistent but no more successful. "My wife reminds me to inquire, when we may expect to see you at Easton," he wrote on June 16, 1763. On October 9 he renewed the invitation: "I have a thousand literary topics to discuss with you, many literary curiosities to shew you, and many literary doubts relative to the progress of some of our publications for you to determine for me."[86] Farmer's responses to these invitations have not survived, but he gave Percy hopes of seeing him at Christmas, by which time the poems for his second volume had been printed and those for the third were being readied for the press. The hopes were not realized, however, much to the disappointment of Percy, who was eager for Farmer's advice on the songs and ballads that illustrate Shakespeare, which he was then editing. A leading authority on Shakespeare, Farmer was at work on his *Essay on the Learning of Shakespeare*.[87]

In the summer Percy tried again with Johnson, who had given him reason two years before to believe that he would one day make the trip to Easton Maudit, even if only for a short stay. In an undated letter possibly written in late August 1763, Percy supported his invitation by reporting that Edward Lye, recovering from a "severe fit of Illness" [the gout], joined him in wishing that Johnson would make his promised visit; it was Lye's hope that he could confer with Johnson about his Anglo-Saxon dictionary and other projects. Mrs. Percy also joined in the invitation, which was extended to both Johnson and Miss Williams.[88]

On September 3 Johnson wrote to assure Percy of his desire to enjoy his company in his own "fields and groves." "I purpose to bring Shakespeare with me and strike a stroke at him with your kind help."[89] With Johnson about as close to completing his edition of Shakespeare as Percy was to completing the *Reliques*, he must have had a fairly early visit in mind, but the year ended with no sign of Percy's long-awaited guest.

The friend whom Percy probably least expected to see was James Grainger, who seemed permanently settled in St. Kitts. Because only one letter from Grainger to Percy and none from Percy to Grainger is extant for the last eight months of 1763, it is impossible to know if Percy received advance notice of Grainger's return to Britain in the fall. Grainger's April 18 letter gave no hint of such a trip, and his next letter was written from London on November 30 after he had spent some weeks settling his family business in Scotland following the death of his brother. Two letters from Percy had been held for him in London, and one, which Grainger said drew tears from his eyes, contained news of the deaths of Shenstone and Binnel in February and April of that year. "What would become of me were you too snatched away?" he wrote on November 30.[90]

"How can I see you?" Grainger asked. "My time is short, and yet I must see you." Percy must have responded promptly, and on the evening of Friday, December 16, Grainger arrived at the vicarage. He brought with him his "Cane Piece," corrected and entitled *The Sugar-Cane*, and on the next day he and Percy began the work of reading and further correction. Their time was not totally given to business, but they made their way steadily through the poem's four books, the first on Saturday and the other three on Monday, Wednesday, and Thursday. On Sunday Percy conducted services at Easton Maudit and Piddington, and on Tuesday he and Grainger accompanied Richard Orlebar to Olney field, drove around Yardley chase, and called on Edward Lye, with whom they dined twice during the following week. On Friday, apparently leaving Grainger at the vicarage, Percy rode to the hunt with John Ward's hounds. In spare moments, Grainger later recalled, they sat by the fireside reading tales of King Arthur and his court.[91]

Grainger left on December 30, taking with him some half a dozen of Percy's letters to post in London. *The Sugar-Cane* had been revised, presumably to his and Percy's satisfaction. But Grainger, without consulting Percy, was shortly to replace a mock-heroic introduction to book 2 with a curious invocation that evoked considerable merriment when it was read aloud to a group at the home of Joshua Reynolds: "Now, Muse, let's sing of rats." Perhaps, as Percy recalled in 1791, the reader on that occasion was Thomas Warton; but one must wonder if it was not Samuel Johnson, an intimate Reynolds friend to whom Grainger had sent the manuscript of book 2 in early or mid-January.[92] Johnson was to remember Grainger's rats.

With his passage already engaged on a ship to St. Kitts, Grainger made a hurried trip to Easton Maudit in mid-February to inoculate young Anne and Barbara against smallpox—"an anxious time with us," as Percy wrote to Farmer on February 12. But the Earl of Sussex's concern that the Percy girls might infect his own daughter compelled a delay while Grainger tried to dispel the Earl's fears. His passage to St. Kitts was lost. On February 24, with the last chance for another ship about to be missed, Percy informed the Earl that Grainger was now "very sure" that the three-year-old Lady Barbara was in no danger, and he asked for leave to have the inoculations the next day.[93] Perhaps the Earl continued to demur, since Grainger seems to have lost his passage on the second ship as well.

For Grainger the visit also had an unfortunate sequel, which he took with his customary good spirit. On his way back to London his coach was held up about three miles below St. Albans. Luckily, Grainger wrote to Percy on March 24, the robber "did not ask for my watch, and went off by telling me he was sorry to be obliged to take our money. So civil are our highwaymen. In France or Spain our death would have preceded the robbery."[94]

Before he left London on April 30 to board the ship at Southampton, Grainger corrected proof of *The Sugar-Cane* and learned from Johnson that he would be reviewing the poem in the *Critical Review*. "He talks handsomely of you," Grainger reported to Percy on April 6.[95] Johnson also expressed a desire to see Percy's "Dissertation on the Drama," which Grainger had called to his attention. This was one of four essays—the actual title was "On the Origin of the English Stage"—that Percy was to prepare for the *Reliques*. Not long before the Grainger meeting with Johnson, he had, in fact, asked Thomas Apperley to convey a request that Johnson, in the table of contents of his edition, classify Shakespeare's plays as comedies, histories, or tragedies, as was done in the first folio of 1623; and in support of his request he had extracted a few historical paragraphs from a draft of his essay.[96] With Johnson's interest made known to him by Grainger, it seems certain that he would have sent the entire essay, which was in proof by the end of March.[97]

No doubt much of the final work for the *Reliques* was tedious for him. In deciding upon the plates he felt keenly the loss of Shenstone, who had "the most happy talent at designing," but by October 1763 seven plates for the first two volumes had been engraved by Charles Grignion from designs by Samuel Wale.[98] For the obscure Scottish words of the glossaries, he was pleased to be able to turn to Dalrymple, who enlisted the aid of his friend John Davidson with the glossary of volume 2.[99] To illustrate the music of the ballads, he asked Farmer to transcribe the notes of "For the Victory of Agincourt" from the Pepysian collection, after Warton had lost Percy's own transcription. "I know nothing of Music myself," he confessed to Farmer.[100] Materials continued to arrive well into 1764, sometimes prompting him to cancel pages in the poems already printed and print them anew. Warton sent a list of ballads in Anthony à Wood's Ashmole collection in mid-March 1764, and Percy responded with a request for one of its Robin Hood poems, which he did not use. In May Warton sent the ballad of the unsaintly "George Barnwell," which Percy inserted in his first volume between "The Birth of St. George" and "St. George and the Dragon."[101]

A decision that Percy acted upon on March 10 was to lead to still further changes in his collection of poems—not yet given the title of *Reliques*. It was, in fact, to change the whole course of Percy's life. For some months he had planned to dedicate the collection to Shenstone's memory, a fitting recognition of the central role that Shenstone had played in its inception and development. But on March 10 Percy wrote to Elizabeth Percy, Countess of Northumberland, to ask her permission to dedicate his collection to her.[102] What happened to effect this change is not apparent. Of his close friends, only Grainger had been with him shortly before he wrote to the Countess, and Grainger may either have proposed the idea or been consulted on it. Perhaps the Earl of Sussex urged the desirability of a noble patron or patroness. Percy, of course, may have needed no prompting. His connection with the earls of Sussex, particularly Augustus, had brought him into close association with English court and upper-class life, which he found very much to his taste.[103] The Countess of Northumberland, matriarch of the Percy family, was an imposing and influential figure in London and court society. Her evening routs at Northumberland House, the palatial home of the Percys at Charing Cross, were a popular feature of fashionable London until she left for Ireland with her husband after his appointment as lord lieutenant in 1763. And the Percy name, sung through the ages, was the most prominent of all in the poems that dominated the third volume of the *Reliques*: "The Ancient Ballad of Chevy-Chase," "The Battle of Otterbourne," John Skelton's "Elegy on Henry Fourth Earl of Northumberland," "The More Modern Ballad of Chevy Chace," "The Rising in the North," and "Northumberland Betrayed by Douglas." Indeed, the Percys were introduced in the very first stanza of volume 3:

> The Persé owt of Northombarlande,
>   And a vowe to God mayd he,
> That he wolde hunte in the montayns
>   Off Chyviat within dayes thre,
> In the mauger of doughtè Dogles,
>   And all that ever with him be.

The Thomas Percy who had changed his name from Piercy would have readily appreciated the value of linking such an influential Percy as the Countess of Northumberland to a "parcel of OLD BALLADS" with which he hoped to please readers of taste.

Percy's letter took four weeks to reach the Countess, who replied from Dublin on April 10 that she was flattered by his compliment and gratefully accepted his offer of the dedication. Her acceptance, which he received on April 29, left him with much to get ready before he set out for London to discuss its implications with Dodsley and the printer, John Hughes. But overlooking the last press runs of his poems was not the sole reason for a trip to London. While awaiting the Countess's reply, he had apparently received a firm invitation from Jacob Tonson to direct a new edition of the *Spectator*, for which he would supply occasional notes and compare the modern editions with the original *Spectator* papers. A formal contract remained to be signed in London, but on April 23 Percy began writing to scholarly friends— first Dalrymple, then Farmer, Birch, and Warton—for help in explaining particular passages and identifying the authors of anonymous letters published in the essays.[104]

A third objective of the trip was to renew the longstanding invitation for Johnson to visit Easton Maudit, and, with the collection of poems approaching its final form, he had to act quickly if he had any thought of calling upon Johnson for further assistance. Edward Lye set the stage for him in April when he was in London on business related to his Anglo-Saxon dictionary. "I have seen Mr. Johnson," he wrote to Percy from London on April 10. "He inquired much after you, and doth not despair of seeing Easton."[105]

Percy thus had much to hope for when, with Anne accompanying him as far as Newport Pagnell, he set out for London on the morning of May 22. Surprisingly, his diary records little more for this eventful trip than that he stayed in Cecil Street with James White, a friend of Grainger's who had written a book called *The English Verb* and translated *The Clouds* of Aristophanes. The contract which Percy signed with Jacob Tonson and his brother Richard on May 25 has survived, however, and reveals that he was to be paid a hundred guineas for editing both the *Spectator* and the *Guardian* and that he was to deliver the first volume of the *Spectator* within a month and the other seven volumes before Christmas. No schedule was set for the *Guardian*.[106]

Percy had been given a head start on the project, but even with a March or April beginning the schedule was an optimistic one. With the *Reliques* close to demanding its last irrevocable changes, the writing of *A Key to the New Testament* only recently begun, and the Mallet translation and the editions of Buckingham and Surrey still bidding for attention, the schedule was hardly short of visionary. "I find you are indefatigable," Evans exclaimed in a letter of April 17 as he contemplated the publications Percy was engaged on.[107] The adjective was one that all of Percy's friends might have agreed upon, as its application to him by Rice Williams and Shenstone as well as by Evans suggests.[108] And it is exemplified continually in his letters and his diary. The diary entry for May 17, 1764, when he was preparing for his trip to London, may not be typical, but it shows what he was capable of: "This day I translated 22 pages in 4ᵗᵒ of Chevʳ Mallet & wrote 10 Letters by yᵉ Post, & took 2 rides. I was up from 4 in the morning till 12 at night."

With Dodsley and his printer, Percy had much to attend to. Because his collection was now to be dedicated to a lady, as he wrote Dalrymple on December 16, he felt "obliged to cancel all the more indelicate pieces and substitute others more inoffensive."[109] Three neighbors in volume two, "Cock Lorel's Treat," "The Moral Uses of Tobacco," and "Old Simon the King," were dispossessed by "The Heir of Linne," hapless victims of an enclosure movement; and in the third volume another seven poems were similarly forced out. Occasional lines in other poems were given a hurried scrubbing: "Jesus God! what a griefe is this?"—the opening line of "The King of Scots and Andrew Browne"—became " 'Out alas!' what a griefe is this?" with Percy calling attention to the change from the original text by the use of single quotation marks, as he frequently did elsewhere.[110] He concluded also, though perhaps somewhat later, that it would now be inappropriate for him to issue the book anonymously; his name would not appear on the title page, but he would sign the dedication.[111] With *Hau Kiou Choaan*, it might be noted, he had remained anonymous throughout, even though he had dedicated the book to the Countess of Sussex; but perhaps his relationship with his patron's wife was close enough for him to ask, and to be granted, permission to preserve the anonymity that he commonly sought.

Percy's most far-reaching decision was also dictated by his change in plan for the dedication. The first volume of his collection opened with the ancient ballad "The Boy and the Mantle," which magically exposes the rampant cuckoldry in King Arthur's court, with a special rebuke for Queen Guenever in a series of uncourtly five-letter words:

> Shee is a bitch and a witch,
> And whore bold:
> King, in thine owne hall,
> Thou art a cuckold.[112]

Whatever the likely general appeal of the ingenious mantle, or of the loathly lady turned beautiful in "The Marriage of Sir Gawaine," which followed "The Boy and the Mantle," Percy could be forgiven if he felt reluctant to place his noble patroness in close proximity to them, particularly when he had an obviously preferable alternative. The Northumberland poems that opened and dominated the third volume were rich in Percy lore and Northumberland history, and with his own bit of magic he simply transformed volume 3 into volume 1 and volume 1 into volume 3. This shift required some canceling of pages and a printed instruction to the binder to make sure that he bound the already marked sheets in their new volumes. It also had the curious effect of moving a very free rendition of "The Boy and the Mantle" by Shenstone to the end of the new third volume, where it closed the entire collection. So Shenstone, though deprived of the dedication, was given the last word.

The interchange of the two volumes took place in June, and all in all it was accomplished with a minimum of inconvenience and distortion.[113] By June Percy had also decided on a title for the collection, the pages for which had gone through the press identified in the running heads only as "Ancient Songs and Ballads." "I think to intitle my Book," he wrote to Dalrymple on June 2, " 'Reliques of Ancient Poetry: Consisting of old heroic ballads, songs, and other compositions of our earlier poets; chiefly of the Lyric Kind.' "[114] Long though the title was, it did not encompass all the poems in the collection, and before publication Percy changed *Reliques of Ancient Poetry* to *Reliques of Ancient English Poetry*, replaced "compositions" with "pieces," and added at the end "Together with some few of later Date." The last of these changes took into account a number of recent poems, including Grainger's ballad "Bryan and Pereene" and Percy's own "The Friar of Orders Gray" and "Valentine and Ursine"; but the insertion of "English" in the main title may have seemed to slight the numerous ballads that northern pride would justly have claimed for ancient *Scottish* poetry. It would have been difficult to adapt the title to include Percy's translations of two Spanish poems, which he appended to the original third volume.[115]

Percy was still in London on Friday, June 15, when he wrote to Thomas Birch, but he probably left for Easton Maudit the next morning to be back in time for his Sunday duties.[116] This was the longest of his London visits, and it permitted him to be on hand for Dodsley's publication of *The Song of Solomon* on June 13. He probably also found time to confer with Lockyer Davis, publisher of his *Key to the New Testament*, and he met with various friends including Johnson and Miss Williams. On June 8 he gave Christopher Smart 5/3 as a first payment on Smart's translation of the Psalms of David.[117] It is not clear whether Johnson, who had almost reached the end of his last volume, still hoped to "strike a stroke" at Shakespeare with Percy's help, or to what extent Percy, with a dedication, preface, essays, and glossary still to complete, was counting on Johnson's last-minute assistance with the *Reliques*. Actually Percy had been given something of a reprieve with the *Reliques*, which Dodsley informed him would not be published until late in the fall. But he thought that the moment to press for Johnson's visit had come, and this time—perhaps with some urging by Miss Williams—Johnson acquiesced. "I expect him down here next week," Percy wrote to Farmer on Tuesday, June 19, three days after his return to Easton Maudit.[118]

NOTES

1. Both Farmer and Blakeway were fellows of their colleges, and Farmer, who was also a tutor, was elected Master of Emmanuel in 1775. He and Percy were brought together by Edward Capell (*The Percy Letters*, 2:106–7). Blakeway, a native of Shrewsbury, appears to have been related to Robert Binnel (Letter Percy to Binnel, 27 July 1762 [Beinecke Library, Ms. Vault File]).

2. *The Percy Letters*, vol. 3, *The Correspondence of Thomas Percy & Thomas Warton*, ed. M. G. Robinson and Leah Dennis (Baton Rouge: Louisiana State Univ. Press, 1951), 1–10.

3. Ibid., 10–22. Warton published the first letter (*Observations*, 1:139–42).

4. Ibid., 7.

5. *The Percy Letters*, 7:98.

6. See pp. 42–43.

7. Nicholas Rowe, *Jane Shore*, act 2, sc. I, lines 148–49; Joseph Cradock, *Literary and Miscellaneous Memoirs* (London, 1828), 1:239.

8. B.L. Add. MS. 32,326, f. 28. The other godmother was Martha, Dowager Lady Drury of Overston, Northamptonshire. The godfather was John Robinson, Esq., of Cransley, Northamptonshire.

9. *The Percy Letters*, vol. 5, *The Correspondence of Thomas Percy & Evan Evans*, ed. Aneirin Lewis (Baton Rouge: Louisiana State Univ. Press, 1957), vi, 156.

10. Ibid., 1–5. Whatever his intention, Percy's attribution of the runic translation to "a friend" served to obscure the fact that the three projects were being conducted by only two people just one and a half miles apart in rural Northamptonshire.

11. Ibid., 5–12.

12. Ibid., 13–14.

13. *The Percy Letters*, 7:105.
14. Ibid., 109–10 (Letter to Shenstone, 19 July 1761).
15. *Lit. Illus.*, 7:281. The misspellings of *Caribbean* and *aught* are Grainger's.
16. *The Percy Letters*, 7:109. The ballads supplied by Dicey are in the Houghton Library. For information on Dicey, see Diane Dugaw, "The Popular Marketing of 'Old Ballads': The Ballad Revival and Eighteenth-Century Antiquarianism Reconsidered," *Eighteenth-Century Studies*, 21(Fall, 1987): 71–90.
17. *Reliques* (1765), 1:xiii.
18. S. H. Harlowe, "Letters from Dr. Percy to T. Astle, Esq.," *Notes & Queries*, 4th ser., 3(1869):25–27.
19. Tonson's first extant letter to Percy, dated 10 Oct. 1761, acknowledges Percy's return of nine volumes of Garrick's plays and a request for more (Folger Shakespeare Library, w.b. 475, opp. p. 96). All told, Percy borrowed thirty-seven of Garrick's volumes (Bodl. MS. Percy c. 9. ff. 94–105).
20. Letter Griffiths to Percy, 23 April 1762 (Hyde Collection).
21. *The Letters of William Shenstone*, ed. Marjorie Williams (Oxford: Blackwell, 1939), 597 (Letter Shenstone to McGowan, 24 Sept. 1761). Percy also looked into the Scottish poems in the Pepysian Library's Maitland MS.
22. *Correspondence of Thomas Gray*, ed. Paget Toynbee and Leonard Whibley (Oxford: Clarendon Press, 1935), 2:746–47. R. W. Ketton-Cremer, *Thomas Gray: A Biography* (Cambridge: Cambridge Univ. Press, 1955), 183. *The Letters of William Shenstone*, 596, 598. Gray had contemplated translating most of the poems that Percy translated for his *Five Pieces of Runic Poetry*.
23. Fuller information on the letter can be found in Bertram H. Davis, "The Anonymous Letter Proposing Johnson's Pension" (Johnson Society: *Transactions 1981*), 35–39. The letter is in the collection of the Marquess of Bute.
24. *The Letters of Samuel Johnson*, 1:135–36.
25. *The Percy Letters*, 5:20.
26. Ibid., 7:100 (Letter Percy to Shenstone, 20 June 1761).
27. *British Magazine* (Dec. 1761), 662; *Critical Review* (Nov. 1761), 373; *Monthly Review* (Dec. 1761), 430. A correspondent who signed himself "V. A." commented similarly to Griffiths in the *London Chronicle* of 2–5 January 1762.
28. *The Percy Letters*, 7:121.
29. Letter Griffiths to Percy, 23 April 1762 (Hyde Collection).
30. In the advertisement Percy identified James Wilkinson as the translator of the first three books but did not reveal his own identity.
31. *The Percy Letters*, 7:119–20; 137 (Letter to Percy, 3 Feb. 1762).

32. For a full discussion of the first draft, see Albert B. Friedman, "The First Draft of Percy's *Reliques*," *PMLA* 69(Dec. 1954):1231–49.

33. *The Percy Letters*, 3:33. About half the original was torn away.

34. Ibid., 7:170 (Letter Percy to Shenstone, [16–18?] Nov. 1762); 3:77 (Letter Warton to Percy, 1 Jan. 1763).

35. Northamptonshire Record Office, Sotheby Ecton Collection, Box x 1079, Folder E(S) 1206, f. 31.

36. *The Percy Letters*, 7:150. *The Letters of William Shenstone*, p. 597.

37. *The Percy Letters*, 3:31 (Letter Percy to Warton, 28 Feb. 1762); 2:16–17 (Letter Percy to Farmer, 18 Oct. 1762).

38. Ibid., 5:30–31.

39. Ibid., vol. 4, *The Correspondence of Thomas Percy & David Dalrymple, Lord Hailes*, ed. A. F. Falconer (Baton Rouge: Louisiana State Univ. Press, 1954), 1.

40. Ibid., 5–6 (Letter 18 Nov. 1762).

41. *Monthly Review* (March 1763), 173; *Critical Review* (Dec. 1762), 445.

42. See p. 48.

43. *The Matrons* (London, 1762), ii.

44. *The Percy Letters*, 2:28–29 (Letter to Farmer, 10 Jan. 1763).

45. *Miscellaneous Pieces Relating to the Chinese* (London, 1762), 1:[vii–xii].

46. B.L. Add. MS. 32,329, f. 4.

47. Ibid., f. 8 (undated letter). Percy's last stanza is as follows: "Yes, generous Friend, / Thy Skill attempts the nobler Part, / The Will deprav'd to mend, / To probe and cleanse the ulcerous Heart, / And, thro' the Saviour's all-restoring Blood, / To raise to endless Life, the Penitent and Good."

48. Ibid., f. 9.

49. *The Percy Letters*, 7:138–39.

50. *Lit. Illus.*, 7:276–80.

51. Northamptonshire Record Office, loc. cit., f. 34 (Letter Farmer to Percy, May 1762); *The Percy Letters*, 2:2 (Letter Percy to Farmer, 5 June 1762); 7:155.

52. Northamptonshire Record Office, loc. cit., ff. 41–42; James L. Clifford, *Dictionary Johnson* (New York: McGraw-Hill, 1979), 267–68. Percy thought that the pension was intended to blunt criticism of a pension given to the Scot John Home (Bodl. MS. Percy d. 11, f. 7).

53. *The Percy Letters*, 7:154 (Letter 16 May 1762).

54. *The Letters of William Shenstone*, 452 (Letter Shenstone to Robert Dodsley, 20 Nov. 1762). *The Percy Letters*, 2:11 (Letter Percy to Farmer, 9 Sept. 1762); 7:160 (Letter Percy to Shenstone, 5 Oct. 1762).

55. B.L. Add. MS. 32,333, f. 31 (Letter to William Cleiveland, 23 Jan. 1763).

56. *The Percy Letters*, 2:33 (Letter to Farmer, 30 Jan. 1763).

57. B.L. Add. MS., 32,326, f. 27. Henry's other godfather was Charles Stuart,

Esq., of Town-Malden in Kent. His godmother was Anne, the wife of Ambrose Isted.

58. *The Percy Letters*, 2:37.

59. *The Works in Verse and Prose of William Shenstone, Esq.* (London, 1764), 2:333–71.

60. *The Percy Letters*, 4:49 (Letter Percy to Dalrymple, 30 Aug. 1763).

61. B.L. Add. MS. 32,326, f. 27.

62. Emmanuel MS. Lib. 2.1, p. 96. In London Percy received, £100/3/10 ½ for the *Reliques* on 25 March and, on 26 March, twenty guineas for his *Miscellaneous Pieces Relating to the Chinese* and ten guineas as a first payment for *Five Pieces of Runic Poetry (Willis's Current Notes*, no. 47 [Nov. 1854], 90).

63. *Lit. Illus.*, 7:567–68 (Letter Percy to Birch, 21 April 1763).

64. Letter Tonson to Percy, 23 April 1763 (Hyde Collection). The contract to edit Surrey's poems was signed on 24 March (*Lit. Illus.*, 6:560).

65. On the day after his return he called on "poor Mr. Lye," who would probably have been the first of his friends to be given a copy of the book.

66. It is difficult to assess Percy's relationships with his Wilby parishioners, whom he generally saw only on Sundays and sometimes irregularly, as when he traveled to London. In a letter to the Rev. Charles Lawrence written in 1780, Samuel Johnson recalled Percy's saying—when he was "a little rector in Northamptonshire"—that one could discern "whether or no there was a Clergyman resident in a parish, by the civil or savage manners of the people" (*The Letters of Samuel Johnson*, 2:401). One might infer from Percy's comment that he looked upon his Easton Maudit parishioners as rather more civil than those in Wilby and that he, as resident clergyman in one parish and non-resident in the other, was responsible for the difference. Whether or not such an inference reflects the reality cannot be determined from Percy's sketchy references to Wilby, which usually consist of nothing more than the terse weekly note, "Duty at Wilby." That a clergyman could influence the manners of his parishioners more by his presence than his absence seems indisputable, but he was not likely to be the sole influence. Addison and Steele, for example, perceived a major community force in their lord of the manor, Sir Roger de Coverley. It would have been natural for Percy to feel more affection for his Easton Maudit parishioners, with whom he lived closely from day to day, than for those in Wilby, whom he saw only in the formal setting of a weekly church service. And it is possible as a consequence that he sensed some hostility at Wilby and that the new agreement of April 7 was forced upon him by parishioners resentful of being served from a distance; but there is no apparent way of confirming those possibilities. For all that is known, his Wilby parishioners' conduct toward

him, and toward each other, was no less civil than that of his Easton Maudit parishioners.

67. *The Percy Letters*, 2:38–41.
68. *The Song of Solomon* (London, 1764), v, xiv, xxi, 102. Percy's translation, parts of which follow the King James version exactly or very closely, was praised by the reviewer for the *Critical Review* (July 1764, 78–79).
69. *Lit. Illus.*, 7:282–83.
70. *The Percy Letters*, 2:42–43.
71. *Shenstone's Miscellany,* xiv–xv (Letter Hylton to Percy, 26 June 1763).
72. Letters Millar to Percy, 12 Dec. 1762; Newbery to Percy, 9 June 1763 (Hyde Collection); *Five Pieces of Runic Poetry* (London, 1763), x.
73. *Lit. Illus.*, 7:569 (Letter Percy to Birch, 2 July 1763). Percy's copy is in the University of Edinburgh Library.
74. *The Percy Letters*, 2:47 (Letter Percy to Farmer, 9 Oct. 1763); Appendix, 193–200.
75. Ibid., 4:48 (Letter Percy to Dalrymple, 30 Aug. 1763).
76. On 16 June 1763 Percy requested what Dalrymple called his "imperfect" copy of "Sir Patrick Spens," and on 30 August 1763, in the same letter that he informed Dalrymple that he had received McGowan's packet, he mentioned receiving "Sir Patrick Spens." A letter from Dalrymple, however, had arrived in the same post and may have contained the copy that Percy requested (*The Percy Letters*, 4:39, 48). "Sir Patrick Spens" was printed at 1:71–73 of the published first volume of the *Reliques*, from which the text quoted below is taken. For the attribution to Dalrymple, see *Reliques* (1794), 1:61.
77. *The Percy Letters*, 4:29 (Letter Percy to Dalrymple, 25 Jan. 1763).
78. Ibid., 56 (Letter Percy to Dalrymple, 8 Sept. 1763).
79. *Reliques* (1765), 1:99.
80. *The Percy Letters*, 4:20.
81. Ibid., 3:114 (Letter 5 May 1765).
82. Ibid., 4:30.
83. *Reliques* (1765), 1:xiv.
84. *The Percy Letters*, 2:66.
85. G. E. Bentley, Jr., "Blake and Percy's *Reliques*," *Notes & Queries*, New ser., 3(1956):352–53.
86. *The Percy Letters*, 3:82 (Letter Warton to Percy, 9 Jan. 1763); 2:44–45; 2:46–47.
87. Ibid., 2:57 (Letter Percy to Farmer, 31 Dec. 1764); 2:50 (Letter Percy to Farmer, 9 Oct. 1763).
88. B.L. Add. MS. 32,325, f. 238. The letter could have been written as late as the early spring of 1764.

89. Mary Hyde, " 'Not in Chapman' " (*Johnson, Boswell and Their Circle*, ed. Mary M. Lascelles et al. [Oxford: Clarendon Press, 1965], 306).

90. *Lit. Illus.*, 7:284.

91. Ibid., 285 (Letter Grainger to Percy, 22 Jan. 1764).

92. Ibid. See also an unsigned note, *TLS*, 16 Feb. 1951, and Boswell's *Life*, 2:453–54 and 533–34. Percy's later recollection was noted in a letter to Boswell of 12 March 1791 (*The Correspondence and Other Papers of James Boswell Relating to the Making of the* Life of Johnson, ed. Marshall Waingrow [New York: McGraw-Hill, 1969], 394).

93. *The Percy Letters*, 2:65. Letter Percy to the Earl of Sussex, 24 Feb. 1764 (Osborn Collection, Yale University).

94. *Lit. Illus.*, 7:286.

95. Ibid., 287.

96. Percy's letter, which lacks a salutation and a date, is in the Osborn Collection. It could have been written at almost any time between Grainger's return to London at the end of November, which is mentioned in the letter, and his meeting with Johnson on 6 April. Johnson observed the divisions in printing the plays, but did not include a general table of contents.

97. Of Percy's four essays, the first to be completed was "On the [Alliterative] Metre of Pierce Plowman's Visions," a proof of which he shared with Farmer on 9 October. It was followed by the essay "On the Origin of the English Stage," which he sent to Farmer and Evans in March and to Dalrymple in April for their reactions. On 20 March 1764, he informed Evans that he was planning "a short essay on the origin and progress of our English Poetry"—later entitled "On the Ancient English Romances"—but it was not in final form until 1 November. On 16 August he began writing his preface, of which the "Essay on the Ancient English Minstrels" was originally a part. The preface and the essay were separated before the *Reliques* was published.

98. *The Percy Letters*, 4:64 (Letter Percy to Dalrymple, 18 Dec. 1763); 2:49 (Letter Percy to Farmer, 9 Oct. 1763).

99. Ibid., 4:71 (Letter Percy to Dalrymple, 28 Feb. 1764).

100. Ibid., 2:68, 70 (Letters 28 Feb. and 5 April 1764).

101. Ibid., 3:98–99, 104 (Letters Percy to Warton, 27 March and 2 June 1764).

102. B.L. Add. MS. 32,334, f. 2 (Letter Countess of Northumberland to Percy, 10 April 1764).

103. H. E. Boyd, Percy's secretary at Dromore, informed the Rev. G. Bellett that the Earl of Sussex introduced Percy to the Earl and Countess of Northumberland (*The Antiquities of Bridgnorth*, 240).

104. *The Percy Letters*, 2:72–73; 3:105; 4:81–82. *Lit Illus.*, 7:573–74.

105. B.L. Add. MS. 32,325, f. 212.

106. B.L. Add. MS. 38,728, f. 168.

107. *The Percy Letters*, 5:82.
108. See pp. 84 and 91.
109. *The Percy Letters*, 4:91–92.
110. L. F. Powell, "Percy's Reliques," *The Library*, 4th ser., 9, no. 2 (Sept. 1928):131–32; Rodney M. Baine, "Percy's Own Copies of the *Reliques*," *Harvard Library Bulletin*, 5(1951):246–51.
111. *The Percy Letters*, 5:102–3 (Letter Percy to Evans, 18 Dec. 1764).
112. *Reliques* (1765), 3:1–11.
113. Powell, "Percy's Reliques," 121.
114. *The Percy Letters*, 4:83–84. The running title on the first proof sheets was "Select Songs and Ballads" (Baine, 247).
115. *Reliques* (1765), 1:317, 324. The poems were "Rio Verde, Rio Verde," which he rendered as "Gentle River, Gentle River," and "Alcanzor and Zayda." He accompanied the first with its Spanish text.
116. *Lit. Illus.*, 7:576–77.
117. Arthur Sherbo, *Christopher Smart: Scholar of the University* (East Lansing: Michigan State Univ. Press, 1967), 191.
118. *The Percy Letters*, 2:75; 4:83 (Letter Percy to Dalrymple, 2 June 1764).

CHAPTER VI

A Year of Celebrations:
1764–1765

J OHNSON'S LETTER announcing that he and the blind Anna Williams
would visit Easton Maudit must have reached Percy only the day
before their arrival on Monday, June 25. "I should not think our
visit an event so important," Johnson wrote on June 23, "as to require
any previous Notification, but that Mrs. Williams tells me, such was
your desire."[1] The visit, to be sure, was not an event that could hold
love-stricken Edward Blakeway, who had fairly flown through Easton
Maudit on June 19, "so hot after his Mistress that there was no de-
taining him a moment."[2] But to tiny Easton Maudit, its history an
ebb and flow of baptisms, marriages, and burials almost as constant
as the tides, the visit was an occasion for celebration, and Johnson,
Mrs. Williams, and Johnson's servant Francis Barber were scarcely
settled in the vicarage when the first celebrant arrived.[3] Edward Lye,
by this time virtually a cohost, came from Yardley Hastings on the
evening of their arrival, the first of numerous visits he was to make
in the course of their stay. On the second day they were greeted by
the London printer Edmund Allen, a Northamptonshire native who
would be Johnson's landlord when Johnson moved into his final residence in London's Bolt Court. Other callers were to follow, but the
chief celebrant was the thirty-five-year-old vicar of Easton Maudit,
for whom Johnson's presence in his vicarage was the fulfillment of a
five-year dream.

No doubt the eminently sociable Johnson welcomed the attention
that even an obscure country village could assure him. I "never found
. . . [Johnson] more cheerful or conversible" than he was in 1764, Percy
recalled many years later.[4] This was not the brooding Johnson who,
scarcely two months before the trip to Easton Maudit, had confessed
in his diary that "A kind of strange oblivion has overspread me."[5] Sir

John Hawkins, an intimate friend, called Johnson's melancholy "habitual."[6] But in June of 1764 everything seems to have combined to remove any apparent signs of stress: the prospect of a quick release from the tedium of editing Shakespeare, the change of scene and company, and perhaps most of all the good spirits of a host and hostess eager to make his stay pleasant and comfortable.

It was not all a social visit, of course. Percy had church and community duties to attend to, and his numerous literary projects to advance; and proof sheets of *Othello* kept arriving for Johnson's inspection.[7] Probably at this time Percy provided the five notes which Johnson inserted at the end of his last volume, along with late notes contributed by other Johnson friends.[8] Johnson supplied information for Percy's recently undertaken edition of the *Spectator*, proofs of which began arriving during the summer.[9] He also read through the glossary of the newly designated first volume of the *Reliques*, though even his vast lexicographical knowledge was not sufficient to penetrate some of the ballads' obscurities.[10]

During Johnson's first week Percy had to devote time to haymaking on June 27 and to a turnpike meeting the next day. Percy's diary does not reveal whether Johnson joined him in either activity, but as one who "well understood . . . the management of a farm," Johnson would probably have enjoyed observing Percy in his glebe lands, if not actually assisting with the haymaking process.[11] Perhaps it would be too much to hope that the young ladies of the village carried out tea for their refreshment as they did for Percy in his bachelor days, but it is tempting to picture Johnson on a haycock—probably no less at ease than in a tavern chair—drawing a coterie of new village friends about him.[12] The villagers, in any event, were well aware of his presence. Even today they think of one of the terraces in the vicarage's back garden as "Johnson's Walk," and the tradition persists among them that Johnson slept in the bedroom on the third floor overlooking the back garden.

On one literary project Percy must have enlisted Johnson's aid fairly promptly. Grainger's *Sugar-Cane* had been published on May 26, and Percy, solicitous of Grainger's fame, undertook to write a review, in which Johnson became a reluctant collaborator. Percy "had a mind to make a great thing of Grainger's rats," Johnson later said to Boswell;[13] and, committed already to review the poem in the *Critical Review*, he understandably drew back from another review in which Percy's partiality for Grainger would inevitably limit his freedom. A likely obstacle for Johnson was Grainger's implicit acceptance in the poem of the detested institution of slavery. By April 1763, in fact, Grainger had invested all his available money in Negroes.[14] In the end, Johnson consented—"in jest"—and, though he told Boswell that he only helped Percy, the review's critical sections are clearly in Johnson's style and survive in a manuscript in Johnson's hand.[15] Perhaps Percy selected the illustrative quotations and prepared a first draft for Johnson's revision. The review, in any event, must have been sent to the *London Chronicle* toward the end of Johnson's first week at Easton Maudit, since the *Chronicle* published the first of the review's three installments in its issue of July 3–5. None of them contains any reference to slavery.[16]

Probably most villagers had their first glimpse of Johnson at church on the Sunday morning after his arrival. Percy selected for the occasion a sermon he had first preached at the little Shropshire church of Tasley in 1752, when he was just starting out as a curate, and its central theme should have had a special appeal for Johnson, who had written similarly in the fourth essay of his *Idler*. "The transcendent Excellence of the Christian Religion," Percy wrote, "[is that it] makes cordial Charity and Love the great distinction & mark of its genuine Votaries."[17]

Percy rode to Wilby to conduct the service that evening, but Johnson apparently did not accompany him. And within a day or two he was called away to Bridgnorth to attend his widower father, who—blind and worn out with troubles and disappointments—was dying of dysentery and dropsy, though still a few weeks short of sixty.[18] Percy made only one diary entry for the two weeks between July 1 and July 15, but it shows him in Bridgnorth with his brother Anthony on July 4. In a July 6 letter from Bridgnorth he asked Anne to inform Johnson that he had inquired about "old M.ʳ Higgs," the clergyman, recently deceased, who had substituted for him occasionally at Astley Abbots and Tasley.[19] On July 8 he preached at Bridgnorth's two churches, St. Leonard's and St. Mary's, and he administered the eucharist to his father before returning to Easton Maudit to resume his parish duties on July 15. On that day he preached the same sermon he had preached at St. Mary's the week before, a funeral oration on the vanity of human wishes obviously reflecting his distress as he saw his father's life slipping from him.[20] No doubt it was delivered also with a consciousness of Johnson's presence in the congregation and of works in which Johnson had addressed the same theme.

Home again with his family and guests, Percy attended to some of the duties as host which his forced absence had kept him from. On July 18 he and Johnson dined at Ecton with Ambrose Isted, Ecton's lord of the manor. On July 21 they visited the Orlebars at Hinwick, and on July 23 Percy and Anne introduced Johnson at the public day at Castle Ashby, the Earl of Northampton's resplendent estate just two miles from Easton Maudit. Mrs. Williams joined the other three for an "airing" by the neighboring village of Bozeat on July 25, and two days later the same group visited Lord Halifax's estate at Horton, where they also had dinner.[21]

On the evening of their return from Horton, Percy received word that his father had died on July 22. Just why Anthony, who had remained in Bridgnorth, did not notify him more promptly is not clear, but the delay precluded Percy's attendance on July 24, when his father was buried next to Percy's mother in St. Leonard's churchyard.[22] Difficult as it would have been to absent himself again from the guest he had waited five years to entertain, it is hard to imagine that Percy would have put his obligation as a host before his obligation as a son. Percy took his family ties seriously, and though he never ceased to deplore his father's imprudence in financial matters, he was grateful to him for sparing no expense in his elder son's education, and he revered him as one "incapable of doing the least action that he thôt mean or dishonorable." He was, in sum, a "most Gentleman-like man."[23]

By July 27 Johnson and Mrs. Williams had spent a little more than a month at Easton Maudit, and Johnson began talking of going away. He would leave Mrs. Williams at the vicarage for two or three weeks and then return for a second visit later in the summer.[24] Perhaps, with the family in mourning, Johnson thought it an appropriate time to visit his "harried" friend the Reverend John Taylor, to whom he had earlier suggested a summer meeting; at Easton Maudit he had already traveled about half the distance from London to Taylor's home in Derbyshire.[25] Whatever his intentions, he stayed on at the vicarage, visiting and being visited, reading and writing, working and talking with Percy, and enjoying Anne's company. Anne recalled that one morning, when her husband announced that he had set out some books for Johnson to look at after breakfast, Johnson replied very courteously, "No, Sir, I shall first attend upon Mrs. Percy to feed her ducks."[26] Perhaps feeding the ducks together had been a daily ritual during Percy's absence in Bridgnorth.

Doubtless there were stresses also. With Johnson and Mrs. Williams probably occupying the vicarage's two "capital" bedrooms,[27] the Percy's had, of course, to withdraw into less than capital quarters, where family privacy must have been as much a burden as a blessing. For by the summer of 1764 the Percy children included Anne Cleiveland, aged four; Barbara, aged three; and Henry, aged one and a half. However comfortable, a cottage with three toddlers underfoot, a blind woman inevitably groping in unfamiliar surroundings, and two scholars bringing major works to completion must have taxed even the "gentleness and joy" for which Joseph Cradock thought Anne Percy so attractive.[28] Even for the indefatigable Percy, the pace of life must have seemed oppressive. "I have for these 3 months past hardly had time to breathe," he wrote to Evan Evans on July 23; and to Richard Farmer he commented on July 29 that "ever since I was in London I have been either hurried extremely, or have had the interruptions of company, or have been absent from home." Yet he could urge Farmer to join them at the vicarage before Johnson left, if he would excuse the "very indifferent accommodations" resulting from his guests' filling the house "so as to leave... never a room entirely vacant for an accidental friend." Whatever the inconveniences, Percy obviously took great pride in his guest.[29]

Farmer did not come. But there were others, usually for dinner or tea, including Anne's brother, William Gutteridge; her sister and brother-in-law, Mary and Samuel Edwards; Percy's brother Anthony; John Orlebar; and Edward Lye and his housekeeper, Mrs. Calvert. August 3 was Barbara Percy's third birthday, but, though Percy noted it in his diary, he gave no indication how it was celebrated. On August 4 he and Johnson visited Richard Backwell in Northampton, and on August 5 Johnson accompanied him to the evening service at Wilby. On August 12, five days after Percy had driven Mrs. Williams to Horton to catch the stagecoach for London, Johnson also accompanied him to an evening service and a burial at Piddington.

In spite of the numerous visits, Percy's literary work—and probably Johnson's—was never interrupted for long. Percy corrected a proof sheet of his *Key to the New Testament* on July 16 and another on August 6, when he also prepared copy of his chapter on St. Matthew for the press. The edition of the *Spectator* seems to have progressed as Percy struggled to meet the deadlines he had agreed to on May 25. On July 24 he began reading to Johnson from his translation of Mallet's *Introduction à l'Histoire de Dannemarc*, presumably unaware how much Johnson disliked being read to.[30] Somehow Johnson bore up well enough to endure a second session on July 26, when, with Mrs. Williams present, Percy read from both Mallet and his version of *The Song of Solomon*. On August 16 Percy read some of Pope— *with* Johnson, not *to* him—and he spent part of the same day preparing his preface to the *Reliques*, which at that time included his "Essay on the Ancient English Minstrels." For his leisure reading Johnson, who was particularly fond of romances, selected Percy's folio of the old Spanish romance *Felixmarte of Hircania*,[31] and he also read Evan Evans's *Some Specimens of the Poetry of the Antient Welsh Bards*, which Dodsley had published on June 5. Percy, with a proprietary interest in Evans's book, read it, too, of course—with "great pleasure," as he informed Evans on July 23, although he conveyed at some length his and Johnson's reasons for concluding that Evans had given too much credit in his preface to the pretensions of James Macpherson and his Erse poems.[32]

In August Johnson gave Percy the assistance for which his visit has been best remembered. Percy's typically terse diary entry for the thirteenth—"Preparing dedication of old Ballads"—affords no hint of Johnson's role in the dedication, which was to remain a secret until the publication of Boswell's *Life of Johnson* in 1791.[33] Understandably Percy wished his dedication to the Countess of Northumberland to be a model of its kind, and in Johnson he had at hand the most accomplished writer of prefaces and dedications of his day. Taking up what Percy had apparently begun, Johnson turned it into the graceful tribute of the published work:

> These poems are presented to your LADYSHIP, not as labours of art, but as effusions of nature, shewing the first efforts of ancient genius, and exhibiting the customs and opinions of remote ages: of ages that had been almost lost to memory, had not the gallant deeds of your illustrious ancestors preserved them from oblivion.
>   . . . [they] now return to your LADYSHIP by a kind of hereditary right.[34]

Johnson stayed only a few days longer, and on August 18 Percy drove him and Francis Barber to Newport Pagnell in his chaise to catch the berlin for London. Before leaving, Johnson presented Percy with his inkhorn, a bulbous, long-necked container very convenient for Johnson, who, as Percy noted, often wrote standing.[35] He also gave Percy the *Nouvel Abregé Chronologique de l'Histoire de France*, which he had brought to read on the June 25 trip from London.[36]

Johnson, of course, left a permanent mark on Percy's little village. Percy himself had celebrated Johnson's presence unpretentiously: letters to his friends, an open door to guests, introductions at nearby places, casual notes in a diary that he scarcely had time to keep up to date. But no pretense was needed to give the vicarage a special aura: "Johnson walked here"; "Johnson slept in that room." An enthusiastic twentieth-century vicar, not content with such vague traditions, rummaged in his imagination for details that he could not find elsewhere. Johnson, wrote Dr. F. T. B. Westlake among Percy's entries in the 1764 parish register, came to Easton Maudit with London club members Goldsmith, Sir J. Reynolds, Garrick, and Shenstone—an entry all the more visionary when one considers that Reynolds was not knighted until 1769, Garrick was not yet a club member, and Shenstone, never a club member, had been dead since February of 1763. Dr. Westlake even illustrated his 1929 book *Fame and Faith* with a photograph of Johnson and Goldsmith being served tea in the vicarage garden—cutout figures, of course, superimposed on an authentic background.[37]

Unbridled though it was, Dr. Westlake's enthusiasm was understandable. In a remote village of a hundred people an event like Johnson's nearly eight-week visit may not occur once in a millennium, and its prominence underscores the touching modesty of Johnson's letter announcing it: an event which he did not think "so important as to require any previous Notification" and which, but for Mrs. Williams's prodding, he would not have mentioned at all. One wonders if Johnson, when he left London, had any idea that he would be staying in Easton Maudit for almost two months. And could he really have enjoyed himself in this rather lonely outpost far from the London attractions that he prized: the excitement of Fleet Street and Charing Cross, the stimulus of club conversation, or the unmatched felicity of a tavern chair?

Perhaps the best answer to this question can be found in the sheer length of Johnson's stay. The hapless Dick Shifter in Johnson's *Idler* No. 71 cut short his country idyll on the fifth day and retreated to his sanctuary in London's Temple, though of course Dick had illusions about the country that Johnson was quite free of. Nor did he have such a host and hostess as Thomas and Anne Percy, who had done much to make Johnson's sojourn varied and comfortable. They had given him the opportunity to hasten his long-awaited edition of Shakespeare to a conclusion. They had provided him with company and modest diversions, including an extended relief from the depression that made his life often such a torment. Percy could talk from a full mind: anecdotes flowed from him "like one of the brooks here," Boswell commented to Johnson approvingly during their 1773 tour in Scotland;[38] and Joseph Cradock described Percy—"when in good mood"—as "one of the most entertaining companions he had known."[39] Johnson plainly admired Anne, who knew well how to manage her household, and presumably he also found time to enjoy the Percy children, as he generally did in the families of his friends. "After 165 years," wrote Dr. Westlake, "the shaft of the swing on which Dr. Percy's children flew high and low on the lawn remains to-day and is embedded deep in the heart of the great tree under which Dr. Johnson often took tea."[40] It is not easy to take issue with a man who can see into the heart of a great tree.

With Johnson and Mrs. Williams returned to London, the Percy household settled back into its normal activity. Work on most of Percy's projects progressed, even the edition of Surrey's poems, which Tonson had put aside temporarily in his eagerness to republish the *Spectator* and *Guardian*: on December 11 Percy sought Warton's help in recovering the versions of the Psalms and Ecclesiastes by Surrey and Thomas Wyatt, whose comparatively few poems he planned to include with Surrey's.[41] On November 1 he returned further proof of the *Key to the New Testament* to the printer. His translation of Mallet— assured of publication by a letter of John Newbery dated June 9, 1763, and probably contracted for shortly thereafter—was advanced through the fall and winter, and by May 4, 1765, Percy could inform Evans that the first of the two volumes was almost printed off.[42]

On September 23, 1764, Robert Dodsley died, and James Dodsley assumed sole responsibility for their publishing business. Much of Percy's work had probably been done with the younger brother, and, though he must have regretted the loss of a friend and sponsor, Robert's death seems not to have affected his own very pressing schedule for the *Reliques*. On November 1 he corrected proofs of his essay on the English romances. He sent Farmer proofs of his preface in early November and asked his advice about detaching from it everything relating to the minstrels and calling it "An Essay on the Ancient English Minstrels." He would make no alteration, he said, until he consulted his "oracle," Johnson.[43] His foremost concerns for the moment were the dedication, which had been reset in larger type, and the impending presentation of the first copy to Lady Northumberland. He was afraid that she might expect the contents of his volumes "to be of a higher nature than she will find them to be," he wrote to Dalrymple on October 23 when he sent him a proof of the dedication. "To prepare her for this was therefore what I had principally in view."[44]

Percy made it clear in his letter to Farmer that his need for advice was urgent: he would be leaving for London on November 12, and he asked Farmer to send his answer under cover to Dodsley, "*to be forwarded on to me with all Speed.*" An opportunity had arisen to present the dedication copy to Lady Northumberland in late November, when she would be back from Ireland, and much remained to be done to prepare a finished copy for her. Percy set out as planned on Monday morning, November 12, and in the evening he reached James White's in London, where he would stay until he moved to other lodgings in Cecil Street on the seventeenth. Wasting no time to consult his oracle, he dined the next day with Johnson at the Mitre Tavern, and what questions remained after that meeting were probably resolved when he met with Johnson again on the fourteenth or when he had supper with James Dodsley on November 13 and 16.

With much depending upon Lady Northumberland's reaction to his book, the London visit was an anxious one for Percy. He spent most of his time with close friends, no doubt for the encouragement and advice they could give him: Thomas Apperley, whom he saw on the thirteenth and dined and had tea with on the fourteenth; Goldsmith, with whom he had tea on the sixteenth and supper on the seventeenth, after calling on Mrs. Williams for tea; and John Orlebar and his family, who had come up to London from Hinwick. The entries for November 19 and 20 have been torn out of his diary, but apparently on one of those days he was notified that Lady Northumberland would receive him at Northumberland House on the morning of the twenty-second. On the twenty-first he wrote to her and then dined at the home of Thomas Davies in Russell Street, Covent Garden, the scene of Boswell's historic first meeting with Johnson on May 16, 1763. The other guests at Davies's dinner—together perhaps to wish Percy well on his next morning's adventure—were Johnson, Goldsmith, and John Hoole, the translator of Tasso, with whom Percy spent the evening.

On Thursday, November 22, he called at Northumberland House

and presented the dedication copy of his book, but he recorded no details of this significant moment in his life. From Northumberland House he walked along the Strand to Johnson's rooms in Inner Temple Lane, a fitting attention to the oracle who had initiated the idea of editing the poems in his folio manuscript. He dined with Goldsmith; and that evening Percy, Johnson, Goldsmith, and others gathered at Edmund Allen's, in all likelihood to celebrate the official launching of the *Reliques* in high places.

The *Reliques* was launched, but, with Dodsley having decided to postpone publication until Parliament convened in January, it was to lie in harbor for nearly three months before setting out on its maiden voyage.[45] Meanwhile the first reaction was heartening. On Saturday, November 24, Percy was delivered a card from the Earl of Northumberland, and, after attending church at court the next day, he dined at Northumberland House, where the other guests were the Irish Earl of Drogheda and the Northumbrian Sir Francis Delaval. On Monday he attended Lord Northumberland's levee. Since that, too, was by invitation, Percy would have been safe in assuming that both he and his book had made favorable first impressions. In addition, a visit to Percy's lodgings on November 29 by a Mr. Church, accompanied by the Duke of Hamilton and the Duke's brother, Lord Douglas Hamilton, suggests that word was beginning to spread of his newly found favor.

Percy returned to Easton Maudit on Saturday, December 1, after two visits to the British Museum and frequent visits with the old friends he had turned to before the presentation.[46] Possibly he was back in London on January 7, as he expected to be when he wrote to Warton on December 11, but no record of such a trip remains.[47] It could not have extended beyond January 12, in any event, because on January 13, he conducted the services at Easton Maudit and Wilby, where he preached on the duties of parents to children.[48]

As the February 11 publication date for the *Reliques* approached, Percy's anxieties erupted once again.[49] "Tell me what the Critics say of it at Cambridge," he wrote to Farmer on February 10. "When I consider what strange old stuff I have raked together, I tremble for its reception with the fastidious public. What rare hacking and hewing will there be for Mess.rs the Reviewers!"[50] A like concern lay behind the apologetic and defensive tone of his preface, epitomized in his slighting reference to his collection as a parcel of old ballads. As most of the poems, he wrote, "are of great simplicity, and seem to have been meerly written for the people, he was long in doubt, whether in the present state of improved literature, they could be deemed worthy the attention of the public. At length the importunity of his friends prevailed, and he could refuse nothing to such judges as the author of the RAMBLER, and the late Mr. SHENSTONE."[51]

With these names, supplemented by those of Farmer, Warton, Dalrymple, Garrick, Birch, Lye, and others, Percy had devised what he called an amulet to guard his book against "every unfavourable censure,"[52] though even that was not considered sufficient protection by the cleric who had likened his ballad activity to a game of whist.[53] He wished it known that preparing "this little work" had been only "the amusement of now and then a vacant hour amid the leisure and retirement of rural life, and . . . a relaxation from graver studies." At the same time he was careful not to disparage his poems to the point where no justification could be found for either publishing or reading them. With "nothing immoral or indecent" admitted, he remarked in closing the preface, "the Editor hopes he need not be ashamed of having bestowed some of his idle hours on the ancient literature of our own country, or in rescuing from oblivion some pieces (tho' but the amusements of our ancestors) which tend to place in a striking light, their taste, genius, sentiments, or manners."

Percy's defenses were virtually impenetrable, at least for the moment. Making no extravagant claims for his collection, he flattered the taste of his contemporaries, appealed to their native pride, and subtly urged them to add their own testimony to that of Johnson, Shenstone, and his other authorities. Whether or not at the call of Percy's preface, they complied. Six hundred of the fifteen hundred sets were sold by March 23, "far better than I could have expected," Percy informed Dalrymple on that date.[54] And the dreaded reviewers, instead of hacking and hewing, joined in the book's praise. The *Monthly Review*'s crusty William Kenrick, the husband of Percy's second cousin Elizabeth Perrins, was uncharacteristically gentle, perhaps out of respect for a family connection as well as for Percy's book. With a limited knowledge of the ballads, he was content by and large to echo Percy's own comments about them and to focus instead on such lyric poems as Thomas Carew's "Unfading Beauty" and Henry Wotton's "You Meaner Beauties," though he did observe that the "pleasing simplicity" and "artless graces" of many of the ballads compensated for their want of "superior beauties."[55] The unidentified reviewer for the *Critical Review*, on the other hand, brought a scholar's knowledge of the Scottish dialect and history to his task and was able to supply about a dozen corrections or additions, most of which Percy later incorporated in his second edition: *hauss bane* in "The Ew-Bughts, Marion," for example, was not the top of the stocking, but the neck bone. Yet whatever his concern for particulars, the reviewer was lavish in his general praise: "This writer possesses the uncommon merit of joining exquisite discernment to indefatigable industry, and we know not in which character to admire him most, that of a critic or an editor."[56]

Of the three reviewers of the *Reliques*, the anonymous reviewer for the *Gentleman's Magazine*—probably John Hawkesworth—best fitted the stereotype to whom Percy had directed the comments in his preface: the *Reliques*, he asserted

> will please, persons that have a taste for genuine poetry, chiefly as an object of curiosity; here and there however will be found some approaches to harmony, and here and there some poetical beauties of a superior kind. There is a class of readers and of writers too, that profess themselves to be admirers of *simplicity*, to delight in the stanza of *Spencer*, and to prefer both our language and our versification in their rudiments to the correct elegance of later times. To these gentlemen this work will afford great pleasure, setting curiosity wholly aside.[57]

The review in this most influential of the century's periodicals suggests that the *Reliques* had still a distance to go before the richness and variety of its poems would be recognized. Aside from the care with which he had brought the poems together, of course, Percy had done little to discourage such a reaction. Even in sending an advance copy to Thomas Birch on February 2 he had described the *Reliques* as a "strange collection of trash," and though such a description hardly represents his considered opinion, it is of a piece with other statements and lends support to the conviction that he was himself unaware of what he had achieved. No doubt his depreciation of his own efforts was a way of courting the indulgence that modesty draws to itself; and he looked about for praise—from his friends, the reviewers, the Cambridge critics, Thomas Birch, and even Horace Walpole, to whom he sent a prepublication copy though they had never met[58]—because he perceived a serious risk in his association with those literary urchins, the ballads, and he wished to be assured that he had run it successfully. Inferior though they were to the *Reliques*, he had made no such disparaging comments about *Hau Kiou Choaan*, *The Matrons*, *Five Pieces of Runic Poetry*, or his other works. They had exacted no investment of time and effort comparable to that of the *Reliques*, but, more important, he had seen no need to satisfy his contemporaries, or himself, that they were acceptable diversions for an aspiring scholar and cleric.

Percy had reason to be pleased with the reactions of Birch and Walpole, both of whom wrote cordial letters of thanks, and he received the gratifying news from Warton in April that the *Reliques* was a favorite work at Oxford.[59] The only apparent harsh notes of this period were struck by Edward Capell, who accused Percy of "forestalling" him by printing the ballad of "Titus Andronicus," and by Johnson, who spoke critically of Percy in a visit to Cambridge in February.[60] Johnson "throws about rather too much of what some *Frenchman* calls the *Essence* of BUT," Farmer wrote on February 25, reporting on Johnson's visit: "in plain *English*, he seems to have something to *except* in every man's Character. *Hurd* for instance comes off badly, and *Shenstone* still worse: he pitys *You* for your opinion of the latter. indeed what he takes from *you*, he gives to your better half—Mrs Percy's judgment is, he assures me (where there has been an equall opportunity of information) much to be prefer'd to her husbands!"[61]

Percy replied graciously, but he must have been stung by Johnson's comments. "I see Johnson often, who speaks of you respectfully and without a *But*," he wrote from London on March 26, adding that he was glad to have Johnson give to his wife what he took from him. As he perceived it, he had suffered in Johnson's opinion because of the respect he had shown for Shenstone: "I know very well he can never forgive me for mentioning him and Shenstone in the same Page."[62]

Percy's March 26 letter was written from Dodsley's during the second of either three or four trips to London between early March and late June.[63] Not since 1756, when he was awaiting word from the Earl of Sussex about the Wilby living, had he visited London more than twice in one year. Now, once again, his fortunes were becoming dependent upon a nobleman. Of the 1765 trips, only the first seems to have had a strong literary motivation: on March 15 he corrected in London the final proofs of his *Key to the New Testament*, and on March 16 he signed contracts with Dodsley for two hundred guineas for an unexplained purpose and with Jacob Tonson for fifty guineas for an edition of Sir Richard Steele's *Tatler*.[64] Even during that trip, however, he was savoring his new success and pressing the advantage that the *Reliques* had given him. His first extant diary entry, written on March 11, shows him attending Lord Northumberland's levee and then calling on Horace Walpole, whom he visited again on the thirteenth.[65]

His activities during these trips, of course, reflected a number of his interests. He finally secured printed copies of his edition of *The Rehearsal* and of his new key for Birch and Lord Hardwicke, and he discussed with Birch, a trustee of the British Museum, the possibility of his filling a vacancy on the Museum staff.[66] He saw Otway's *Venice Preserv'd* on March 14, sat through an evening lecture on portraits on April 19, and on April 26 selected books at Lockyer Davis's shop, apparently the agreed-upon payment for his *Key to the New Testament*. Of his London relatives, he seems to have visited only Anthony Nott and George Haslewood, but his brother Anthony was his guest at breakfast on three occasions, one of them with Mary Perrins's sons-in-law, the writers William Kenrick and Richard Rolt. On the fifteenth he dined at Rolt's with Kenrick, the dramatist Hugh Kelly, and Kelly's wife. He was frequently with Johnson, Goldsmith, Mrs. Williams, Apperley, the Orlebars, or another old friend, George Durant, whose name had long been absent from his diary.[67] On April 26 he spent the last night of his April visit with Johnson and Mrs. Williams at Johnson's new quarters in Johnson's Court, Fleet Street, presumably to be close to the Smithfield stagecoach, which left for Northamptonshire regularly at four in the morning.

However numerous Percy's activities, the focal point of his interests in early 1765 was Northumberland House, which by late April he was visiting almost daily—for breakfast or dinner, the Earl's levee or the Countess's rout, or a conference with the Earl's principal agent, Thomas Butler. Early in their acquaintance the Earl seems to have suggested that he write a history of the House of Percy, and Percy, taken with the idea, shared it with Grainger in a letter probably written in January or February. Grainger was not encouraging; the subject struck him as "limited" and "disagreeable":

> Can you vindicate . . . the conduct of the old Earl of Northumberland in James the First's time, who was so long imprisoned on account of the Gunpowder Treason? How can you cast a veil on the conduct of his son, with regard to his gratitude to King Charles? In short, my friend, . . . if your patrons cannot bear to hear the severity of historical truth, you should handsomely decline writing the history of their ancestors.[68]

Percy had probably begun collecting materials for a Percy history before this letter of March 25 could reach him from St. Kitts, and by May 24 he was outlining the project enthusiastically for Dalrymple and soliciting information from him and his Scottish friends. Exploring the Percy family's connection with Scotland—"from their situation on the borders"—would provide an opportunity to introduce much that was curious concerning the ancient Scottish nobility. "Whatever throws light on the History of Manners," he informed Dalrymple, "I shall seize as my proper prey," and he added that Lord Northumberland was lending him numerous manuscripts, one in particular on the regulation of the domestic economy of the House of Northumberland in the reign of Henry VII.[69] Perhaps his interest in the Scottish nobility helps to account for his spending the morning of April 18 walking with Mr. Church and the Scottish Duke of Hamilton.

By early April Percy had received an invitation to visit Alnwick Castle, where Lord and Lady Northumberland usually spent their summers, but he doubted that he would be able to enjoy that pleasure during the 1765 summer. The Earl himself had not yet determined upon a summer visit to Alnwick, and Percy thought that Anne's fourth pregnancy, which was well advanced, might keep him at home under any circumstances.[70] Events, however, were to take an unexpected and, for Percy, not unwelcome turn.

Percy went to London in mid-April to witness the trial of Lord Byron—William, fifth Baron Byron of Rochdale—for killing William Chaworth in a duel fought on January 26, 1765.[71] On April 15, the day of his arrival, he attended the evening rout at Northumberland House and apparently spoke with Lady Northumberland about the trial, which was scheduled for the House of Lords the next day. In the morning, as he noted in his diary, "Lady North.ᵈ sent for me to go with her Son to Lord Byron's Trial," and accordingly he was driven to the House of Lords with her fifteen-year-old younger son Algernon Percy. Percy was impressed by the trial—a "grand sight"— and, much as he disapproved of dueling, which he thought criminal, he applauded the Lords' decision to discharge Lord Byron under his privilege as a peer even though they had found him guilty of manslaughter. There was "nothing in the Evidence," he wrote Farmer, "that bore hard upon him."[72] What young Algernon thought of the trial is not known, but he and Percy proved sufficiently compatible for his parents to judge Percy a suitable companion for the last months of his private tutelage before he entered the University of Edinburgh. In June Algernon's tutor, Dr. Charles Dodgson, was appointed Bishop of Ossory, Percy offered to replace him, and the offer was accepted.[73]

By late June Lord Northumberland had decided to go to Alnwick, and between July 1 and July 4 Percy wrote to his four chief correspondents of this period—Farmer, Warton, Dalrymple, and Evans—to apprise them of his plans.[74] Anticipating an absence of two or three months, he asked both Farmer and Warton to suggest a clergyman who might make the weekly trip to Northamptonshire to serve his two churches. Had the position been a regular one, it would doubtless have been of interest to Evans, who on May 24 had sought Percy's assistance in finding him a new curacy.[75] "I should be very happy to gain so ingenious a friend for my neighbour," Percy responded on July 1, but he thought it difficult to secure a post that would provide an adequate living: "The Run of our Curacies is about 40^{lb} per annum for which you serve two parishes, once a day each. But then boarding, provisions &c. is dear." If Evans continued to wish to move, he would keep alert to any vacancy that would provide a maintenance; and he had also mentioned Evans's situation to Johnson when he was in London the week before. It was Johnson's view, he reported, that Evans should by no means leave Wales, "as your great acquaintance with British antiquities will make you more useful to the World there, than any where else." Percy suggested that Evans write to Johnson, give him the name of his bishop, and explain how he would have Johnson serve him.

Percy, of course, could not leave his desk for any length of time without some final attention to his literary concerns. He informed Evans that Thomas Apperley was carrying the first volume of his Mallet translation to Chester, to be left there until Evans called for it; he would welcome Evans's reactions to it before he sent the second volume to the press. He mentioned to Dalrymple, whom he hoped to meet while he was in the North, that among the innumerable projects that filled his "waking dreams" was a collection of "the best fugitive old pieces" of both England and Scotland. He looked forward to examining the William Carmichael collection of poems—later known as the Bannatyne Manuscript—as part of that project.[76] To Farmer he renewed a request made on April 20 for any remarks on the *Reliques* that occurred to him and others. Had Hurd seen the *Reliques?* he asked. "Or Mr Gray?—What faults do they find in them? tell me, that I may cor[rec]t them, in case of a second Edition."[77] He also sought Warton's remarks on the *Reliques*, which Dodsley, he stated on July 2, "entertains hopes" of reprinting, and he reminded Warton of his request for help with the *Spectator*, *Guardian*, and *Tatler* and commended him for moving ahead with his *History of English Poetry*. At about the same time he wrote to Edward Blakeway in Shrewsbury to ask if Blakeway could identify the prototypes of George Farquhar's characters in *The Recruiting Officer*, whom Percy believed to have been drawn from "living originals" in Shrewsbury, the scene of the play.[78]

In the letters to Farmer, Dalrymple, and Warton of July 2 and 4, Percy announced that he would be leaving for Alnwick the next week—that is, the week beginning Sunday, July 7. If that was in fact his intention, the opportunity for employment with the Earl of Northumberland's family had clearly overridden his concern to be at home with Anne when their fourth child was born. But perhaps his vagueness about the precise date merely reflects a failure by Lord Northumberland to set a date for the departure, and an expectation by Percy, that, wish it or not, he might soon be required to leave for Alnwick. As it turned out, he was still at Easton Maudit on July 11 when their child was born—the third Percy daughter, whom they named Elizabeth in "compliment" to her godmother Elizabeth, Countess of Northumberland.[79]

Six days later Percy was on his way to Stamford, where he joined the Earl of Northumberland and Algernon for the last three days of the journey to Alnwick Castle.

NOTES

1. *The Letters of Samuel Johnson*, 1:168. Unmarried women were frequently referred to as Mrs., particularly in later life.

2. *The Percy Letters*, 2:75 (Letter Percy to Farmer, 19 June 1764). Blakeway married his second cousin Mercy Brickdale on 3 September 1764.

3. Barber is not mentioned in Johnson's letter or Percy's diary, but Percy informed Boswell in a letter of 29 February 1788 that he had been part of the company (*The Correspondence and Other Papers of James Boswell Relating to the Making of the* Life of Johnson, 268).

4. Robert Anderson, *The Life of Samuel Johnson, LL. D.*, 3d ed., 300n.

5. *The Yale Edition of the Works of Samuel Johnson*, I: *Diaries, Prayers, and Annals*, ed. E. L. McAdam, Jr., with Donald and Mary Hyde (New Haven: Yale Univ. Press, 1958), 77. The date of Johnson's entry is 21 April 1764.

6. Sir John Hawkins, *The Life of Samuel Johnson, LL.D* (London, 1787), 559.

7. *The Percy Letters*, 2:76–77 (Letter Percy to Farmer, 29 July 1764).

8. *The Plays of William Shakespeare* (London, 1765), vol. 8 (Notes to *Henry IV*, pt. 1 [2]; *King Lear; Romeo and Juliet;* and *Othello*).

9. Percy inked over three entries related to the *Spectator*, probably because he wrote them later when he was bringing his diary up to date and was unsure of the exact days. They show him well into the second volume by mid-August.

10. *The Percy Letters*, 4:85 (Letter Percy to Dalrymple, 21 Aug. 1764).

11. Hawkins, 469.

12. See p. 42.

13. *Boswell's Life of Johnson*, ed. George Birkbeck Hill, rev. and enlarged by L. F. Powell (Oxford: Clarendon Press, 1934–50), 6 vols. 2:454, 532–34; 4:556.

14. *Lit. Illus.*, 7:283 (Letter Grainger to Percy, 18 April 1763).

15. The manuscript is in the Hyde Collection.

16. *London Chronicle*, 3–5, 5–7, and 7–10 July 1764. Johnson did not ignore the issue of slavery when he reviewed the poem in the *Critical Review* (October 1764, 270–77).

17. Bodl. MS. Percy d. 3, f. 242.

18. B.L. Add. MS. 32,326, f. 20.

19. D. M. Barratt, "The Diaries, Sermons, and Other Papers of Richard and John Higgs, 1677–1754," *Bodleian Library Record*, 4 (Sept. 1953):273–77.

20. Collection of Kenneth Balfour. The sermon preached at St. Leonard's on 8 July was preached at Wilby on the fifteenth (Bodl. MS. Percy d. 3, ff. 259–72).

21. It seems likely that Percy escorted the group to Horton, but it is not clear from his diary record that he did: "Fri. 27 M.' Johnson, Miss W.'s & Wife &c. went to see L.ᵈ Halifax's at Horton. Dined there: home." John Orlebar, who died in 1765, was succeeded as Hinwick's lord of the manor by his son Richard, Clerk of the Privy Council and a captain in the Bedfordshire militia.

    The absence from Percy's diary of any reference to a visit to the Earl of Sussex, whose manor house was just a three- or four-minute walk from the vicarage, suggests that the Earl was not in residence during Johnson's stay.

22. B.L. Add. MS. 32,327, f. 168.

23. B.L. Add. MS. 32,326, ff. 20, 22.

24. *The Percy Letters*, 2:77 (Letter Percy to Farmer, 29 July 1764).

25. *The Letters of Samuel Johnson*, 1:167–68.

26. Cradock, *Literary and Miscellaneous Memoirs*, 1:240.

27. See p. 68.

28. Cradock, 1:239.

29. *The Percy Letters*, 5:95; 2:76–77.
30. Boswell noted that, when Bennet Langton read Robert Dodsley's *Cleone* aloud to him, Johnson "turned his face to the back of his chair, and put himself into various attitudes, which marked his uneasiness" (*Life*, 4:20).
31. Boswell's *Life*, 1:49.
32. *The Percy Letters*, 5:96–98.
33. Boswell canceled a page in the *Life of Johnson* on which he revealed Johnson's authorship of the dedication, but failed to remove an index reference to it.
34. *Reliques* (1765), 1:v–viii.
35. The inkhorn and a Percy note describing it are in the collection of Kenneth Balfour.
36. *The Library of Thomas Percy* (London: Sotheby's, 23 June 1969), no. 273. The library was purchased by the Queen's University of Belfast.
37. Reverend F. T. B. Westlake, D.D., *Fame and Faith* (London: Skeffington, 1929), opp. 22. Dr. Westlake seems also to have attached the explanatory label, similarly inaccurate, to the front pew at the south side of the church: "D.ʳ S. Johnson / O. Goldsmith / D. Garrick / worshipped here in this pew / with other members of / the Garrick Club, London." The Garrick Club was established in 1831, forty-seven years after Johnson's death.
38. Boswell's *Life*, 5:255.
39. Cradock, 4:292–93.
40. *Fame and Faith*, 22.
41. *The Percy Letters*, 3:110.
42. Ibid., 5:105–6. Newbery's letter is in the Hyde Collection.
43. Ibid., 2:78–80. Percy also asked for Farmer's reaction to the apology he had prepared for the preface to the *Reliques*.
44. Ibid., 4:88–89.
45. Ibid., 3:110 (Letter Percy to Warton, 11 Dec. 1764).
46. He also noted in his diary two meetings (one at breakfast on 24 November) with a Mr. Stuart. This was probably James Stuart, better known as "Athenian" Stuart from the *Antiquities of Athens*, the first volume of which he coauthored with Nicholas Revett in 1762. Percy later gave Andrew Caldwell an account of Stuart's escape from the Turks on which Caldwell, in 1804, based a single-sheet *Account of the Extraordinary Escape of James Stuart* (*Lit. Illus.*, 8:57).
47. *The Percy Letters*, 3:112. No Percy diary entries are extant between 3 December 1764 and 10 March 1765, and I have seen no letters to or from him between 19 December and 28 January.
48. Bodl. MS. Percy d. 4, ff. 208–32. This was Percy's last delivery of the sermon, on which he wrote, "Not fit to be used again."
49. Publication was announced in the *Public Advertiser*, 11 Feb. 1765. The price of the three volumes, bound, was half a guinea.

50. *The Percy Letters*, 2:82.

51. *Reliques* (1765), ix–xiv.

52. Percy stated that he had found many pieces of ancient poetry in the plays lent to him by David Garrick.

53. See p. 104.

54. *The Percy Letters*, 4:94. On 2 July Percy told Warton that eleven hundred copies had been sold (*The Percy Letters*, 3:119).

55. *Monthly Review* (April 1765), 241–53. Kenrick had also reviewed *Five Pieces of Runic Poetry* and *The Song of Solomon*.

56. *Critical Review* (Feb. 1765), 123.

57. *Gentleman's Magazine* (April 1765), 180. John L. Abbott, *John Hawkesworth: Eighteenth-Century Man of Letters* (Madison: Univ. of Wisconsin Press, 1982), 97–98.

58. *The Percy Letters*, 2:82–83 (Letter Percy to Farmer, 10 Feb. 1765); *Lit. Illus.*, 7:577 (Letter to Birch).

59. Letter Birch to Percy, 12 Feb. 1765 (Hyde Collection); *The Yale Edition of Horace Walpole's Correspondence*, vol. 40, *Horace Walpole's Miscellaneous Correspondence*, ed. W. S. Lewis and John Riely (New Haven: Yale Univ. Press, 1980), 1:372–76 (Letter to Percy, 5 Feb. 1765); *The Percy Letters*, 3:113 (Letter Warton to Percy, 29 April 1765). Walpole, "particularly struck . . . [by the] good sense and conciseness" of Percy's dissertations, invited Percy to visit him when he came to London and sent him a ballad of Lord Lovel and Lady Hounsibelle.

60. *The Percy Letters*, 2:87 (Letter Percy to Farmer, 26 March 1765). Percy thought that Capell bore a grudge also because of their differences on the date of "The Nut-brown Maid."

61. Ibid., 84–85.

62. Ibid., 87.

63. Percy's diary shows him in London from 11 to 17 March and 15 to 27 April, but it does not span the entire period of his March trip. He informed Warton on 5 May that, after going to London in early March, he stayed the entire month. But he addressed a 23 March letter to Dalrymple from Easton Maudit. Perhaps he returned home briefly to conduct the services on Sunday, 24 March. In any event, he was in London on 26 March, when he wrote to Farmer and when Dodsley paid him the £4/16/1½ still owed to him for the *Reliques* (*Willis's Current Notes* [Nov. 1854], 90). Although there is no diary record for June, Percy informed Evans on 1 July that he had been in London the week before (*The Percy Letters* 3:116; 4:94; 2:86; 5:111).

64. *Lit. Illus.*, 6:561. It is not apparent what the 16 March contract with Dodsley was for. By that time Percy had completed all his projects for the Dodsleys, and James Dodsley's next publication for Percy, not yet decided upon, was a second edition of the *Reliques*, which Percy told

Farmer on 2 April 1767, he revised without compensation (*The Percy Letters*, 2:134). What seems to me likely is that James Dodsley, whom Percy always thought more generous than his brother, was paying him for the four essays published in the *Reliques* and reserving the right to publish them separately, as he did in 1767 under the title *Four Essays, as Improved and Enlarged in the Second Edition of the Reliques of Ancient English Poetry*.

65. Percy was doubtless attracted to Walpole both for his stature as a man of fashion, rank, and taste and for his literary achievements, which included *Royal and Noble Authors* (1759) and *The Castle of Otranto* (1764), Walpole's authorship of which was revealed in April 1765. Percy visited him again on 23 and 25 April.

66. B.L. Add. MS. 35,230, ff. 24–25 (Letters Birch to Percy, 9 May and 30 July 1765). In conveying the information that no vacancy existed, Birch wrote on 25 July: "You know how ardently I wish you the best place in that Foundation, if it were open, from a Conviction of your Merit; or any other important Addition to your Fortune."

67. See p. 39.

68. *Lit. Illus.*, 7:288 (Letter Grainger to Percy, 25 March 1765).

69. *The Percy Letters*, 4:98–100. Percy was to edit the household book a few years later.

70. Ibid., 98. Percy wrote to Dalrymple that "some particular affairs in my own little family will I fear prevent me from obeying his [the Earl's] kind Invitation this year."

71. Ibid., 2:89 (Letter Percy to Farmer, 20 April 1765).

72. Ibid., 90.

73. Ibid., 4:107 (Letter Percy to Dalrymple, 4 July 1765).

74. Ibid., 2:90–93; 3:119–22; 4:106–9; 5:110–13. Percy also wrote to Edward Blakeway about 1 July.

75. Ibid., 5:107–9.

76. Percy also informed Dalrymple that he had forwarded to Farmer and Warton his request for help with materials in the two university libraries. For part of Dalrymple's request he had to plead the inaccessibility of the Yelverton manuscripts in the Earl of Sussex's manor house at Easton Maudit: "they are kept locked up in great Chests where no man of Letters is suffered to Examine them with any attention. At least I could never obtain that pleasure since they have belonged to the present Possessor." "I write this in *confidence*," he cautioned (*The Percy Letters*, 4:107–8).

77. *The Percy Letters*, 2:89–90 (Letter Percy to Farmer, 20 April 1765).

78. *Lit. Illus.*, 5:643–45 (Letter Blakeway to Percy, 4 July 1765). Percy's letter to Blakeway is not known to have survived.

79. B.L. Add. MS. 32,326, f. 28. Elizabeth's other godmother was Percy's aunt Elizabeth Nott. The godfather was George Durant, who was living at Tong Castle in Shropshire. Young Elizabeth was baptized by Edward Lye on 24 August and received into the church on 14 November.

CHAPTER VII

Northumberland Years: 1765–1769

To PERCY, a stranger to Northumberland except in his "waking dreams," his first sight of Alnwick Castle must have marked indelibly the end of an era and a new beginning. Much had happened since 1756, when, with a stroke of his pen, Thomas Piercy had allied himself in name with the Percys of renown: marriage and a family; friendships with Johnson, Goldsmith, and Shenstone; contracts for a dozen books; a collection of poems that catapulted him into the affections of the latest guardians of the Percy titles and fortunes. Now, escorted by one of England's wealthiest and most influential noblemen, he was making his entrance upon a stage for which his studies and dreams had well prepared him.

After Lord Northumberland's accession to his title in 1750, when he also changed his name legally from Hugh Smithson to Hugh Percy, he and his countess had begun restoring the castle from an abandoned ruin to its former eminence; and they annually planted the country between Alnwick and Newcastle—once "almost a desert"—with a million or more forest trees.[1] Their success was remarkable. By Percy's day the great castle seemed to belie its long history of bloodshed and intrigue. A home rather than a fortress, it stood hospitably by the eastern road from Scotland where the Aln River winds through farm and woodland before giving itself up to the North Sea. The castle had become a showplace, with public days every Sunday and Thursday, and the country around it fairly invited exploration. For Percy, made to feel at home from the start, his new position must have been nothing less than enchantment: the scholar whose favorite subject was ancient English poetry had been magically transported to the very heart of the country where much of the poetry he liked best had its origin.

Percy did not have to wait long to see the local places of interest or to begin his duties as Algernon's tutor. After an apparently quiet first day, July 22, when he wrote letters to Anne and to Edward Lye, he started Algernon's tutorial sessions with Virgil's *Aeneid* and William Robertson's *History of Scotland*, the latter dictated by the plan for Algernon to pursue his studies in Edinburgh during the fall. Lord and Lady Northumberland rode with him on the same day to view the sea and, on the twenty-fourth, to survey the ruins of the thirteenth-century Hulne Abbey in nearby Hulne Park. On the twenty-fifth Algernon rode with him to the seaside village of Alnmouth, and they began the second book of the *Aeneid*.

These were the first of many short jaunts during the summer of 1765, although after the introductory visits Percy was seldom accompanied by Lord and Lady Northumberland, for whom the sights around Alnwick were hardly new. By August 5 he and Algernon had visited Brisley Hill at the crest of Hulne Park, the ruined castle of the Northumberlands at Warkworth, and an ancient hermitage carved into the rock beside the River Coquet, about half a mile from Warkworth Castle. The castle and hermitage were to inspire his *Hermit of Warkworth* a few years later, but in 1765 he was attracted especially to Hulne Park and Hulne Abbey, perhaps because they were the first and closest of the places he visited. Lady Northumberland was so pleased with an account of the ride to Hulne Abbey that he wrote for Edward Lye on August 5 and later revised that she had it printed in the fall, and in subsequent summers it seems to have been given routinely to castle guests.[2] As soon as he was familiar with the castle environs, Percy seems to have assumed responsibility for conducting guests on the various local tours.

How well Algernon's tutorial sessions progressed is not apparent, but Percy was kept busy. He preached at Alnwick Church on July 28 and August 4, and, after Lady Northumberland left for London on August 18, he spent a number of evenings conversing with and writing letters for Lord Northumberland, who was often indisposed with the gout. Even before the trip to Alnwick, Lady Northumberland had apologized for being unable to present him with a living of £350 a year that became vacant with Dr. Dodgson's elevation to a bishopric; it had been promised to someone else before she and her husband became acquainted with Percy, but she assured him that they would make it up to him in some other way.[3] At Alnwick, Percy—characteristically seeking "to conciliate the favour" of those he "conversed with" and "to profit by all opportunities that offered"—was steadily making himself all but indispensable.[4]

He obviously enjoyed discharging the duties that came to be expected of him, and he also took pleasure in the almost continuous company. Christopher Smart came to dinner on July 31, and Thomas Gray stopped by on August 19. Newcastle's scholar-cleric, Dr. John Brown, known as "Estimate" Brown from his book *An Estimate of the Manners and Principles of the Times*, became a close enough friend to accompany Percy and Algernon on part of an extended tour later in the summer. Dignitaries, knights, and peers were numerous, and Percy recorded their names and titles and treasured up information for a new edition of the *Reliques*. He could now conjecture that the name Lovele, celebrated in "The Ancient Ballad of Chevy-Chase," was that of "*the ancient family of* Delaval, *of* Seaton Delaval, *in North-umberland,*" whose descendants—Sir John and Lady Delaval, Sir Francis Delaval, and Mr. Thomas Delaval—he dined with on August 12 and then accompanied to a performance of *Alexander the Great* by a traveling theater group:

> Thear was slayne with the lord Persè
>   Sir John of Agerstone,
> Sir Roger the hinde Hartly,
>   Sir Wyllyam the bolde Hearone.
>
> Sir Jorg the worthè Lovele
>   A knyght of great renowen,
> Sir Raff the ryche Rugbè
>   With dyntes wear beaten dowene.[5]

A visitor of special interest to Percy was Hugh Percy, Lord Wark-worth, who arrived with Lady Warkworth for dinner on August 2. Not yet twenty- three, this older of the two Northumberland sons had already served for two years in Parliament as member for West-minster and had distinguished himself sufficiently in the Seven Years' War to be given command of a regiment. In 1762 he rose from captain to lieutenant-colonel in the Grenadier Guards, and in October 1764 after his marriage to Anne Stuart, third daughter of the Earl and Countess of Bute, he was promoted to the rank of colonel and ap-pointed aide-de-camp to George III. When he met Percy on August 2, 1765, he and his wife were living at Stanwick near Richmond in Yorkshire.

Percy presented Lord Warkworth with a genealogy of the Percy family that he had drawn up in anticipation of his visit, and on August 6 he accompanied him to the assizes at Newcastle, where they dined with the mayor, Sir Walter Blackett, and spent the night before returning to Alnwick. Percy's primary duties, however, were still as tutor to Algernon, whom he was preparing to conduct on a tour through northern England and southern Scotland before delivering him into the charge of Hugh Blair, Regius Professor of Rhetoric and Belles Lettres at the University of Edinburgh. His future with the Northumberland family after the accomplishment of that mission had not yet been settled, but any concern that Percy might have felt was soon to be alleviated. Accompanied by Lord Northumberland, he and Algernon left Alnwick on August 29, with a week's or ten-day visit with Lord and Lady Warkworth at Stanwick as their first major objective; and by September 3, when Lord Northumberland continued on to London from Stanwick, Percy had been invited to join the Earl's household in the fall as domestic chaplain and secretary. "This will cause me to remove my family to town," he wrote to Farmer from Stanwick on September 8, "as soon as I can get a house or convenient Lodgings for them near Northumberland House."[6]

The days at Stanwick must have brought back memories of Percy's visits to Newport Pagnell with the young Earl of Sussex.[7] From the third to the fifth of September Lord and Lady Warkworth, their guests, and numerous military and titled friends devoted themselves to the festivities at Richmond, which began each day with a dinner at the race course, continued through a single race, and closed with an evening ball. On September 9 and 10 Percy attended races of gentlemen riders, and at various times went riding himself with Lord Warkworth's officers, visited Richmond Castle, and played cards at Stanwick with Lord and Lady Warkworth and their guests.

Percy and Algernon left Stanwick on Wednesday, September 11, were met by Dr. Brown at Barnard Castle, and the next evening arrived at Lowther Hall, the country estate of Lady Warkworth's sister Mary and her husband, Sir James Lowther, who was absent on a shooting party. After providing for them overnight, Lady Lowther escorted them on a morning ride through the woods, and they then set out along Ullswater for Keswick, where they spent their first full day exploring the hills and islands of Derwentwater. At Keswick their guide was probably Dr. Brown, who not long before had published a brief *Description of the Lake at Keswick*, a copy of which he had sent to Percy on August 17.[8] On Sunday, after church, they climbed the three thousand feet to the top of Skiddaw. It was a clear day that afforded a delighted Percy his first sight of Scotland, the Irish Sea, and the Isle of Man, along with a view of the country they had just traveled through: "a prodigious tract . . . towards the inland parts of England."[9]

From Keswick they turned north toward Carlisle, which they reached on September 17, once again in time for the races and their attendant activities. They were entertained almost constantly by Sir James and Lady Lowther and their daughter, with whom Percy danced at the balls on September 18 and 21. On the nineteenth, in a nice blend of duty and pleasure, he and Dr. Brown dined with Charles Lyttelton, Bishop of Carlisle, and then joined the evening card assembly.[10] On the twentieth Percy toured the cathedral and walked around the city walls before dining with Sir James and making his regular appearance at the race course and the evening ball. On the twenty-fourth, the day before a departure delayed by continual rain, he visited Carlisle Castle with Sir James and his wife and spent much of the rest of the day in their company. By that time Dr. Brown seems to have returned to Newcastle.

Had the rain not relented, Percy would have canceled a scheduled visit to Glasgow, but with a turn in the weather he and Algernon set out with a guide on the twenty-fifth according to their original plan.[11] They crossed into Scotland north of New Town Bridge, dined at Annan, and reached Dumfries, where the magistrates, discovering Algernon's lineage, could be kept from presenting them with the freedom of the town only by Algernon's promise to inform his parents of the intended honor. The next three days brought them to the Duke of Queensberry's palace at Drumlanrig, the lead-mine country north of it—"a horrid scene of desolate nature"—Douglas Castle, and the Duke's palace at Hamilton, from which they followed the Clyde into Glasgow on September 28. Most impressive to Percy, caught up in the contemporary passion for the picturesque, was the succession of falls in the Clyde above Douglas: "the wild irregular cliffs, thro' the breaks of which the whole river comes foaming down, . . . are all overhung with shaggy Woods, . . . [and] upon one of the cliffs that project over the Cataract, arises an ancient venerable ruin; so that we have here assembled, all in one scene, whatever is most striking in Landscape."[12]

Throughout their trip Percy had been received as the tutor and companion of a great nobleman's son. At Glasgow he was welcomed as the editor of the *Reliques of Ancient English Poetry*. Most attentive among his Glasgow hosts was Robert Foulis, publisher of ballads and printer with his brother Andrew to the University of Glasgow, who introduced Percy and Algernon to members of the university faculty and showed them through his own academy of fine arts. On October 2 the lord provost presented them with the freedom of Glasgow and invited them to a "great dinner," and on the first, second, and third Percy sat for his portrait, perhaps to be hung in Foulis's academy.[13] On the fifth Percy and Algernon visited Loch Lomond and Dumbarton Castle, and on the fourth and the sixth they entertained the Foulises at supper.

They left for Edinburgh on October 7, tracing as they went the remains of the Antonine wall between the Firth of Clyde and the Firth of Forth. At Stirling, where they spent the night, they surveyed a largely wild country from the high vantage of the castle walls, and Percy marveled at the River Forth, which reeled through twenty-four miles on its way to a village only four miles off. On the eighth, with the Stirling piper to guide them, they stopped at Linlithgow Castle and the Earl of Hopetoun's house, and then rode into Edinburgh in time for dinner. By evening they were at Hugh Blair's flat, where Percy was to stay while Algernon boarded with Dr. Gregory Grant in the flat above.[14] They had completed on schedule a tour, by Percy's calculation, of more than three hundred miles.[15]

At Edinburgh Percy must have felt among old friends, even though he had never before seen any of his hosts, and Algernon too was quickly made to feel at home. Blair invited guests for dinner on the ninth and the eleventh, including the historian William Robertson, who was Principal of the University; Adam Ferguson, Professor of Moral Philosophy; John Jardine, an Edinburgh divine; and two of Algernon's fellow students, Charles and Robert Greville. "Dr. Blair has brought the two Mr Grevilles to . . . [Algernon]," Percy wrote to Lady Northumberland on October 11, "and a great friendship seems to have commenced on both sides."[16] The meeting most eagerly anticipated came on October 10, when Percy waited on Sir David Dalrymple, who later joined him and Blair for dinner with John McGowan and John Davidson, Dalrymple's aide in correcting the glossaries for the *Reliques*. Percy was also taken to places of special interest to him: the university, the Advocates' Library, Holyroodhouse, and the castle, the last of these with Davidson as his guide. On October 12 Dr.

Robertson rode with him to the site of the 1666 Battle of the Pentlands and then entertained him at dinner. On Sunday the thirteenth, the day before his departure, he went to hear Blair preach, and in the afternoon he and Blair had tea at Ferguson's.

Among such a group, Scottish literature and history and Percy's own recent publication must have dominated the conversations, but no topic could have been pressed with more fervor than the Erse poems translated by James Macpherson. Blair himself had urged Macpherson to translate the Erse pieces that Macpherson claimed to possess and had written the preface to his 1760 *Fragments of Ancient Poetry*. Although the book found an enthusiastic audience, there were of course skeptics, particularly in England. Skepticism multiplied as Macpherson followed up his triumph with translations of two epics, *Fingal* in 1762 and *Temora* in 1763, both alleged to be the work of the ancient Scottish bard Ossian. To allay suspicion, Blair published in 1763 a *Critical Dissertation on the Poems of Ossian* and, in early 1765, produced a second edition with an appendix containing "undoubted Testimonies" to the poems' authenticity. A persistent and notable skeptic was Samuel Johnson, who, in Blair's presence, denied not just the authenticity of the Ossian translations but their merit as well. Asked by Blair in the spring of 1763 if he thought that anyone in modern times could have written such poems, Johnson replied, "Yes, Sir, many men, many women, and many children."[17]

Percy, reflecting Johnson's influence, had declared the poems an "imposture" when he wrote to Evan Evans on July 23, 1764.[18] In Edinburgh he voiced his doubts again, and his Scottish friends, unlike Evans, took up the challenge. At tea on the thirteenth, Percy later reported, Adam Ferguson introduced a student from the highlands "who recited several passages or verses, in Earse [*sic*] (some of which he afterwards sung to me) as what he had heard in his own country; and I perfectly remember, that when he interpreted the verses to me, some of them appeared to contain part of the description of Fingal's chariot. Dr. Ferguson also gave me, in his own hand-writing, some specimens of Earse poetry in the original."[19] The doubting Percy was won over: I "could not resist the Evidence that poured in upon me," he wrote to Evans on December 24. Now, ironically, it was Evans's turn to set Percy right. He granted that there might be some pieces in Erse that Macpherson translated, but saw nothing in them to point to Ossian's authorship or to support the claim of such antiquity. "The

Scots," he added, "have made it a national affair, and therefore what they say in it's plea ought to weigh the less." Percy did not reply, but he came in time to believe that he had been the victim of a hoax.[20]

Percy left Edinburgh on the fourteenth and reached Easton Maudit on the nineteenth after stops at Berwick and Alnwick, at Newcastle with Dr. Brown, and at York and Grantham. Reunited with his wife and children after a three-month separation, he might have been expected to settle back promptly into the relaxing routine of Northamptonshire life, particularly since a letter from the Earl of Northumberland that arrived on the twentieth offered him a reprieve until the end of November. Lord and Lady Northumberland would be leaving for Bath as soon as his gout would permit, and Percy need not hurry to town.[21] But Percy could not wait to see his new quarters and to confer with his patron and patroness. After attending the service conducted in his own church by a Mr. Rogers—perhaps his summer replacement—he set out, probably on Monday, October 21, and reached London on the twenty-second. He planned to return to Easton Maudit for the month of November, but in the last full week of October, as he wrote Richard Farmer on October 24, he moved into "two very handsome apartments" in Northumberland House overlooking the Strand, where he spent his time "in the most agreeable manner in the World."[22]

Percy's delight was understandable. Always adaptable, he had warmed equally to his two Shropshire curacies and his Northamptonshire vicarage and rectorate. Now, after a summer's probation at Alnwick Castle, he had been elevated to a third-story apartment in one of England's great houses, a landmark familiar to Londoners since the first decade of the seventeenth century, when it had been built by Henry Howard, Earl of Northampton. Welcomed by an earl and countess whom he had come to revere, surrounded by comfort and elegance, and with Charing Cross—"the full tide of human existence"—at his doorstep, Percy had every reason to be pleased with his lot.

Just what he did in his first days beyond savoring the pleasures of Northumberland House is not apparent. Perhaps he began looking out for a suitable house for his family, whom he hoped to remove to London as spring approached. By November, in any event, he was back at Easton Maudit. In December he had young Henry and Elizabeth inoculated against the smallpox and remained anxious until he saw the effect of "that perillous operation." "You will . . . be glad to hear," he wrote to Farmer, "that my little folks went very happily thro' the Small-pox."[23]

He returned to London a day or two before Christmas, probably laden with books for use during an unexpected three- or four-month stay in his new apartments, and was whisked almost immediately off to Bath with Lord Northumberland. In London again on January 20, he spent the morning with George Steevens in the Temple, and during the week that followed he visited, among others, Johnson, Apperley, and the writer Richard Owen Cambridge and saw Garrick in a performance of Aaron Hill's *Zara* attended by the King and Queen. On Sunday the twenty-sixth he attended Whitehall Church and conducted prayers for the family at Northumberland House.

The rest of the year was a busy one, though less eventful than some. He came quickly to admire his new friend Steevens, who was beginning his revision of Johnson's Shakespeare. "He is a Man after your own heart," he wrote to Farmer on February 1, "and I want to bring you two acquainted. . . . He has all the Zeal and diligence of Capel, with the utmost openness and generosity of Heart." Capell, an on-and-off friend, had also shown some generosity: with the help of 1557 and 1585 editions of *Tottel's Miscellany* lent to him by Capell, Percy had been able to complete his text of Surrey's poems and submit it to Tonson's printer. Scarcely two months later, however, he was announcing to Farmer that he and Capell were "never to speak to each other more." The "final rupture" had come when the two met at court on Sunday, March 16, and Capell reported that he had never taken time to look into the three volumes of Percy's *Reliques.* "Was ever so provoking a speech to an Author?—Seriously: was it not very unaccountable that he should never have the curiosity to look into a book so much in his own way."[24]

At Northumberland House Percy's social duties compelled an unwelcome change in his habits. A water drinker, he had taken only two glasses of wine in his life: when he married Anne in 1759 and when he baptized Lady Barbara Yelverton, the first child of the Earl and Countess of Sussex, in 1760. But the fine dinners at Northumberland House, as he wrote in his diary, required that he drink "a little wine for my Stomach's sake"; and at Dodsley's in the spring of 1766 he tried a little Madeira to prepare himself for taking a glass regularly at the Earl's table. Although he never acquired a taste for wine, he was able "by degrees . . . to join with the company."[25]

In May Lockyer Davis published the *Key to the New Testament*, which the *Critical Review* noticed in two sentences and the *Monthly Review*, at much greater length, acknowledged as "this little, useful book."[26] Percy later informed George Paton that he printed the *Key* for the use of his parishioners, and perhaps he made copies available to them; but clearly it was intended for a larger audience.[27] Even the humblest among his parishioners, to be sure, would have had no trouble with occasional sentences, particularly in the introduction: "The holy Scriptures are divided into The OLD and NEW TESTAMENT." Much of the rest, however, derived as it was from the learned and abstruse works of J. D. Michaelis, Nathaniel Lardner, Henry Owen, and others, would have found its readership among university students and Percy's fellow clergymen, many of whom must have welcomed his lucid and concise exposition of what they should know about each of the New Testament books. The *Key*, in fact, proved a popular work. It went into a second edition in 1773 and third and fourth editions in 1779 and 1792, a record of publication that kept pace with that of the *Reliques*. It was reprinted at Cambridge as late as 1823.[28]

With a curate appointed to conduct the services at Easton Maudit and Wilby—the twenty-three-year-old John Liptrott, a recent Emmanuel College graduate probably recommended by Farmer—Percy set out for Alnwick Castle on July 4, 1766. He took time during the four-day trip to have tea at Stamford with Richard Orlebar's sisters, Mary, Elizabeth, and Constantia, and to tour the York Minster. On his first day in Alnwick, as though impatient to be reunited with a favorite, he rode out to Hulne Abbey with Lord and Lady Warkworth. As for the rest of his seven weeks' activity, much of it followed the pattern of his 1765 summer. He attempted nothing so extensive as his three-hundred-mile tour with Algernon, but he managed a three-day jaunt into the Cheviot Hills with Lord Warkworth and one of his captains, as well as two-day trips to Melrose Abbey with Lady Northumberland and Lady Warkworth and to the Farne Islands with Lord and Lady Warkworth and Algernon.[29] Hugh Blair, who arrived from Edinburgh with Algernon on July 20, was the beneficiary of two of Percy's guided tours around Hulne Abbey before he left the castle on July 23. Percy himself stayed on until August 25, making numerous short trips, compiling Percy genealogies, perhaps editing the sixteenth-century Northumberland household book, assisting occasionally at Alnwick Church, and preparing the castle servants for confirmation in anticipation of a visitation by the Bishop of Durham on August 11. On August 29 he rejoined his wife at Stamford, where she was visiting the Orlebar sisters, and, after viewing the paintings at Burleigh House, went on with Anne to Easton Maudit the next day. On Sunday the thirty-first he preached in his own church, "for M.ʳ Liptrott."

In October Percy's patron was named Duke of Northumberland, and Percy, still at Easton Maudit, sent a note of congratulation to the new duchess, who was traveling on the Continent with Algernon and Henry Reveley. He regretted, he wrote, that he was kept from paying his respects to the Duke of Northumberland in person by Anne's lying "dangerously ill," information that brought a message of sympathy when the Duchess replied from Antwerp on November 11: "Mrs. Percy is too aimable [sic] to be seen without being loved, I hope she is well before this Time."[30] Anne's illness lingered at least until October 22, when Percy informed Richard Farmer that she was "very poorly," but he was able to spend part, if not all, of November at Northumberland House.[31] He had still not found a London house for the family to move into.

Earlier that year James Grainger had announced to Percy that he was considering a return to England. His medical practice was not prospering as he wished, and he was lonely. "I am lost, murdered, for want of company," he wrote on February 29, 1766, when he sent congratulations on the success of the *Reliques* and predicted, as he had done before, that Percy would one day be a bishop: "The lawn can add no real dignity to you, but may receive it from you." But by December 4 Grainger had decided to remain in St. Kitts and had moved into a house of his own. If he should send his eldest daughter to England next year, he asked, "Might I presume to recommend her to your and Mrs. Percy's care?"[32]

Percy's reply is not known, nor was Grainger to know it. Twelve days after writing his letter he died very suddenly, leaving a wife and two daughters, the younger of whom was Percy's goddaughter. Perhaps Percy's distress at this loss of a close friend was mitigated by the distance and time that had separated them; he could hardly have learned of Grainger's death for a month or more after it occurred. But he was to retain his affection for Grainger's memory throughout his life, and rose more than once in support of his friend's reputation.

In the fall of 1766 Percy was occupied with family history, both his own and that of the Northumberland Percys. He secured pictures of the first five earls of Northumberland for the Duke and Duchess to hang at Sion House, their country home on the Thames at Brentford. From his cousin William Cleiveland, in the first letter between them in three years, he requested information about all the Percys in the registers of Worcester's St. Martin's parish, including the variant spellings of the Percy name. He asked in addition for an account of the prebendaries of Worcester Cathedral, specifically "their several ages, degrees of health & the Chance any of them offers of a vacant Stall." A prebend at Worcester, he explained, would be the most agreeable of several preferments that the Duke and Duchess had encouraged him to aspire to.[33]

Will called on Percy in London, but not finding him in sent the desired account of Worcester prebendaries by letter, without holding out any hope that Percy might add another appointment to his already considerable list. He announced also that he was engaged to be married and enclosed verses, probably inspired by his bride-to-be, which, Percy informed him on January 19, both he and Anne much admired. Perhaps this evidence of a lyric strain in Will prompted Percy to suggest, when he wrote again on February 16, that the two of them collaborate in completing the translation of Ovid's *Epistles* he had begun some years before: "the Booksellers w.[d] be very glad of such a Publication & have long since made me offers: but I have not time myself."[34]

Although Percy might have been happy to enlist a partner in a project he had probably grown tired of, he could reasonably plead want of time to complete it himself. The demands on him were numerous, particularly during December and January, when the Duke customarily distributed his charities, and some of Percy's own projects were in need of attention. He seems to have been willing to let the editions of the *Spectator, Tatler,* and *Guardian* lie idle following the initial rush to meet the exacting schedule set out in his 1764 agreement with Tonson. But, as his diary reveals, he was revising his translation from Mallet of the Norse prose *Edda* during the first week of September 1766, and he was preparing the second volume of Mallet's history of Denmark for the press on February 7, 1767. Of greater urgency, however, was the second edition of the *Reliques*, in which Percy perceived a challenge that he could not afford to resist.

In July 1766 he had secured from Sir Joseph Ayloffe, one of the governors of the Society of Antiquaries, a copy of a paper written by Samuel Pegge and read to a meeting of the society on May 29.[35] The subject of Pegge's paper was Percy's "Essay on the Ancient English

Minstrels," which, Pegge argued, gave "a false, or at best, an ill-grounded idea" of the minstrels in Saxon times, a defect he considered to have arisen out of Percy's assumption that, because the French and the Danes accorded high places to their minstrels, the Saxons would have done so as well. The customs of these people, Pegge contended, were simply too different to warrant such an assumption. He also questioned, as of doubtful authority, Percy's stories of King Alfred and the Danish King Anlaff disguising themselves as minstrels, Alfred to gain access to the Danish camp and Anlaff to the Saxon.[36]

Although annoyed that Pegge would address his criticisms to a society of which he was not a member without favoring him with a copy, Percy saw the justice of much of Pegge's argument and, as soon as time permitted, he set about establishing the essay on firmer ground.[37] "I shall correct whatever faults I think he has truly hit off," he wrote to Farmer on October 22, 1766; "and shall obviate all the rest of his objections that are worth notice."[38] On January 2, 1767, Percy's amanuensis, James White, was admitted to the reading room of the British Museum for a six-month period, probably to assist in this effort.[39] And on February 11 Percy opened a correspondence with John Bowle of Idmiston, near Salisbury, whose interest in minstrels he had learned of in the shop of a little-known collector of literary curiosities, Andrew Jackson of Clare Court.[40] According to his 1767 diary, Percy spent the whole day of April 29 preparing notes for the essay, and then continued working on them the next day and May 2 until he was finished. On June 17 he offered Farmer a trade: "Send me up Your *first* Edition of the Old Ballads, and I will send you down the *Second* which is now printed off and ready for Publication."[41]

Perhaps some unexpected event occasioned a delay, for not until December 3 did Dodsley issue the newspaper advertisements that normally signaled the appearance of a new work.[42] Percy nonetheless had secured a number of advance copies by mid-June and was distributing them freely. He made Joshua Reynolds the same offer he had made Farmer, and he sent sets of the three volumes to Granville Sharp, John Bowle, William Cole, and probably others who had lent him assistance.[43] Obviously he was pleased to be able to correct the errors of the first edition, but with one exception he made no extensive changes. All the poems of the first edition were retained, although eighteen were given new positions, the texts of a few were modified, and one, "My Mind to Me a Kingdom Is," was divided into two poems. The prefaces to about two dozen of the poems were revised, though most only slightly, and notes were added to about a dozen poems. Only three new poems were included: "Jephthah Judge of Israel," called to Percy's attention by George Steevens and placed among the "Ballads that Illustrate Shakespeare"; Dryden's "Jealousy Tyrant of the Mind"; and, the very last poem of volume 3, a translation into French of John Lyly's "Cupid and Campaspe" written by a Percy friend expressly for the *Reliques*. Percy seems to have been unconcerned by the thought that he was now concluding his collection of "Ancient English" poetry with a poem in modern French.

The one extensive revision was to the "Essay on the Ancient English Minstrels," which Percy lengthened from nine pages to twenty to meet Samuel Pegge's objections.[44] But Percy was not content with a mere revision of the essay. In addition to the footnotes on many pages, indicated by the century's characteristic asterisks, daggers, and crosses, he appended a second series of notes indicated by letters which ran through one alphabet and into a second—A to Z followed by Aa to Af. Starting at the end of the essay, Percy's additional documentation spread like a flood through thirty-eight pages, almost twice as many as the revised essay and more than four times as many as the original essay.[45] Clearly the scholar Percy had risen to the challenge of a fellow scholar, who acknowledged that his doubts had been satisfied.[46] But in gaining his success Percy yielded to the very impulse that Shenstone had warned him against more than once. Interesting in numerous parts—for their description of the roles of the minstrels, for example, and their demonstration that the Anglo-Saxons held music and musicians in high regard—the thirty-eight pages must nonetheless have proved impassable for many readers, some of whom would have been swept away by the torrent of Percy's scholarship, including untranslated passages in Latin, French, and Spanish and a five-page disquisition on the Anglo-Saxon language.

Yet Percy's essays for the *Reliques*, which Dodsley also published separately in 1767 as *Four Essays, as Improved and Enlarged in the Second Edition of the Reliques of Ancient English Poetry*, were a major achievement, the most comprehensive and authoritative literary history that Percy's contemporaries could turn to until Thomas Warton published his *History of English Poetry* about a decade later. Always the pioneer, Percy was the first English scholar, as René Wellek noted in *The Rise of English Literary History*, "to demonstrate that alliteration was the principle of Anglo-Saxon and Germanic verse generally," the first to look closely at English romances, and the first to make any real advance in probing the origins of the English stage.[47] Although long since superseded, the essays remain of interest as the essential foundation stones on which subsequent history could be built.

Percy's preoccupation with his own work never kept him from enjoying the successes of his friends. He received four copies of Farmer's *Essay on the Learning of Shakespeare* from Dodsley before the book's publication in January 1767 and gave the extra copies to Astle, Steevens, and Johnson, the last of whom, he reported to Farmer on January 15, "speaks of it with the most unreserved applause." He had read his own copy over three times "and shall 3 times more before I part with it out of my hands." He had also scribbled innumerable "queries and memorandums" into the book, many of which he sent to Farmer with his letter. "You are so deep read," he commented, "that things that are familiar to you are hardly known in the slightest degree to common Readers.—Even I myself, who have been pretty much conversant with old English Books, am hardly able to follow you in your researches; and you refer to many curious Tracts, with all the ease of familiar acquaintance, which I never so much as heard of."

He expressed a regret that Farmer had included one bit of information in his book: that Percy was the editor of the forthcoming edition of Surrey's poems. He had never intended to affix his name to it, he wrote, "Not from any Coxcomical Reserve: but from a difficulty I should be exposed to, about dedicating it to one of . . . [the present Earl of Surrey's] Family.—I have particular reasons for using some *Management* on this subject."[48]

Jacob Tonson, who was to have published the Surrey and Buckingham editions, as well as the *Tatler, Spectator,* and *Guardian,* died on March 31, 1767, a loss that Percy did not fully appreciate until he discovered some years later that no progress had been made in printing his various projects since Tonson's death. Much of his own work on Surrey had been done, but in 1767 he was still searching for Surrey's version of *Ecclesiastes,* a search that was not successful at least until 1773.[49] Other projects also occupied him from time to time in 1767. In John Bowle, whom he had consulted about the minstrels, he found a scholar who shared his love of *Don Quixote* and was ready to assist him in building what Percy called his "Quixotic Library." "I shall sometime attempt," he wrote to Bowle on April 2, 1768, "if not a new edition, of the Original: yet an improved Translation with large Notes & Illustrations: as well containing Criticisms on the Spanish

Phraseology of the Author, as large Extracts from the old Romances by way of a Key to his Satire."[50] Still another project, the printing of the Northumberland household book, was well advanced by July 1767, when Percy sent printed sheets to Thomas Warton at Oxford.[51] On August 5 he offered to send a copy, if possible, to Samuel Pegge, with whom, in spite of their first differences, he maintained a cordial correspondence. In the same letter he reported that he had an amanuensis transcribing old romances at the British Museum with a view to publishing a collection such as Pegge had recommended.[52]

Percy's association with the Northumberland family brought him numerous new friends and improved his opportunities to meet with the old. His visitors at Northumberland House in the first half of 1767 included Joseph Warton, Tom Woodington (who came to view a portrait of Percy), Thomas Apperley, Chairman John Hawkins of the Middlesex Quarter Sessions, and James Devey and Oliver Goldsmith, who arrived together on June 7 and then walked with Percy in St. James's Park. Evan Evans, urged by Percy in a March 1 letter to help himself in his quest for a curacy by greater "temperance and sobriety," stopped by on May 23 and, unresentful of Percy's advice, proceeded to borrow five guineas.[53] On May 29 Percy took the occasion of the Duke's absence at Sion House to conduct the Notts, Edward Lye, and Thomas Apperley on a tour of Northumberland House.

Himself a frequent visitor, Percy started off the 1767 new year at court with the Duke of Northumberland and then spent the evening at Tom Davies's in the company of Johnson, Joseph Warton, John Hoole, the dramatist Arthur Murphy, and William Rose. On January 21 he dined at the Mitre Tavern with Goldsmith and another Irish dramatist, Isaac Bickerstaff. He called on his cousin Mary Perrins on January 23 and again on May 30, when, accompanied by Goldsmith, he also visited Anthony Nott, and on February 7 he spent the evening with Tom Woodington. He journeyed to Sion House with the Duke on May 28 and with the painter Hamilton (probably Hugh Douglas) on June 15. Although he went to the theaters occasionally, he was most impressed by a private performance of Nicholas Rowe's *Jane Shore* at the Duke of York's house, to which he was invited by Lady Delaval, the wife of Sir John Delaval. The Countess of Mexborough, he reported in a letter to Anne written immediately after the performance on June 20, played the lead role, supported by Lady Stanhope, Sir Francis Delaval, and the Duke of York himself. He thought Lady Stanhope in the role of Alicia "equal to any actress that ever appeared on any stage." The Duke of York as Hastings was on the whole a pleasing figure, but Percy took special note of the "most ungraceful part of him . . . [,] his legs & knees, which bend in."[54]

At Alnwick, where he resided from July 25 to September 9 in 1767, he cultivated his acquaintance with the Bishop of Carlisle and the Bishop of Ossory, his predecessor as Algernon's tutor, with whom he rode to Hulne Abbey on August 31. The Bishop of Carlisle was given a tour to Warkworth Castle and the hermitage on August 26, a natural sequel to an account of Warkworth that Percy had sent him on August 5.[55] Elizabeth Montagu, leader of London's bluestockings, was a guest at the castle in early September, perhaps Percy's first meeting with her. And on September 5, after a trip to Warkworth "with the Ladies & much Company," Percy stayed with a friend to measure the hermitage, no doubt in anticipation of writing his poem *The Hermit of Warkworth*, which he began at Easton Maudit on September 25.

That Percy contributed much to the pleasure of the castle's guests is evident. He seemed never to tire of escorting them to Hulne Park and Warkworth—history and romance to the scholar and poet, places to be studied, venerated, and enjoyed—and it is understandable that he would gain many friends among them. His good nature, moreover, was well suited to the atmosphere generated by a duke and duchess who wished to set their company at ease and spared few efforts to that end. Yet beneath the informality that they aspired to they found it essential, in so complex a community as Alnwick Castle, to impose a regularity which would not at the same time preclude the independence and privacy of their guests. A casual orderliness, strict but not exacting, characterized castle life, and it is nowhere better exemplified than in a set of "Laws" drawn up by the Duchess on July 20, 1767.[56]

The first ten laws related to the events of the day, in sequence, beginning with a servant's morning call at each apartment to ask if the company would breakfast in their rooms or with "the rest of the Family" and if they chose to walk, ride, or go out in carriages. The dining hours followed: breakfast at 9:30, dinner except on public days at 3:30, coffee "to be ready" at 5:00, tea at 7:15, and supper at 10:00 followed by a "Summons to bed" at 11:30. Carriages were to be ordered after breakfast, and prayers were held on Wednesday evenings at 9:00.

The final six provisions dealt rather with conduct than with time.

Guests' servants should attend them in their own rooms and wait upon them at table, where there was to be no ceremony: "No Precedency is to be observed, but whoever is next the Door is to go in first," and all are to be seated where they choose and "help themselves to what they like." Indeed, no one was obliged "to attend at any of the stated hours," but could eat any meal out without giving previous notice. The drawing room and red closet were common rooms to be resorted to "at will and pleasure," and they were to be stocked with "Books, Pens, Ink &c &c," which could be freely used. Those who chose to walk or ride should go "their own way without interruption to each other."

In this world of opulence and high fashion, rural Northamptonshire must sometimes have seemed remote, but in the summer of 1767 two events occurred to remind Percy that it was very close. On August 19, Edward Lye, aged seventy-three, died at Yardley Hastings from what Percy called "a severe fit of the Gout," with which he had long been afflicted.[57] Percy, who valued him both as friend and mentor, had consulted him on most literary matters, including the recent revision of the essay on the minstrels, and his death left a gap which no one in that part of England seemed likely to fill. At the time of his death, Lye had not completed his Anglo-Saxon dictionary, but he left the project to Owen Manning, who carried it through to publication in 1772. Percy, who had secured fourteen subscriptions for the dictionary, assembled what he could of Lye's correspondence and also supplied Manning with biographical information for use in his introduction.[58] Under the terms of Lye's will, most of his estate went to Elizabeth Calvert, his housekeeper of thirty years: his silver plate, £500, and an annuity of £200. Thirty guineas were left also to Frances Reynolds, Joshua's sister, and a guinea to each member of the Percy family for the purchase of mourning.[59]

The second event to occur during Percy's absence at Alnwick was the birth on September 1 of the Percys' fourth daughter. Named Charlotte in honor of George III's queen, she was baptized in Percy's church on October 5, with Hugh, Earl Percy as godfather and Lady Percy and Mary Dickens, the wife of Ambrose Dickens, Esq., of Wollaston in Northamptonshire, as godmothers.[60]

By the time of Charlotte's baptism Percy had secured lodgings for his family in London, and on October 12 they settled into apartments in St. James's Place, close to both Piccadilly and Green Park, where Anne went for a walk just a day after their move. Visitors were numerous during the family's first days in St. James's Place: Henry Reveley, for example, Tom Woodington and his wife, and, on October 18, the Duchess of Northumberland, who called to see Anne and the children. For Anne, however, St. James's Place proved to be only a waystation. On November 2 a prince was born to Queen Charlotte, and on the same day Anne—probably on the recommendation of the Duke and Duchess of Northumberland—was appointed to be his wet nurse. Required by her position, for which she received an annual salary of £200, to reside in the royal household, she was to spend the next year and a half either at Buckingham House or at Kew.[61] The prince was baptized at St. James's Palace on December 30, 1767, and given the name Edward in compliment to his uncle, Edward, Duke of York, who had died on September 9, two and a half months after Percy saw his performance as Hastings in *Jane Shore*. Later named Duke of Kent, Anne's charge is remembered today primarily as the father of Queen Victoria.

It is not clear what arrangements the Percys made for managing the new apartments and—with Henry having started school at Oldbury in Shropshire—caring for the four girls during Anne's absence at court.[62] Probably they had brought a housekeeper and nursemaid with them from Easton Maudit and, with Anne's appointment in mind, engaged a wet nurse in London for the infant Charlotte. With all the family but Henry in London, a chaise became, if not a necessity, a much desired convenience. Percy probably made use of it in his visits to Anne at Buckingham House, and on May 9 and 10, 1768, he called on Johnson and carried him in the chaise for what he recorded in his diary as "a airing."

His opportunities to see Anne during her royal service were limited by the demands of both her position and his, but the few extant diary entries for the months after her appointment show that he dined with her on four occasions between late November and mid-February. Goldsmith dined with them on February 12, on the evening of which Percy, wrapped in a mourning cloak, went to St. Clement Danes for the funeral of Mary Perrins, who had died of a stroke on February 9.

Perhaps at the February 12 dinner the Percys discussed with Goldsmith a suggestion that he occupy the Easton Maudit vicarage during the family's absence in London. In a letter, undated but written early in 1768, Goldsmith submitted to Percy a list of questions about his "Northamptonshire offer": "are there any prying troublesome neighbours?," for example, "Can I have milk, meat, &c tea, in the place?," and "when will you want to be down yourselves?"[63] All were questions that could have been readily answered during the February 12 dinner, but Goldsmith decided in favor of a cottage near Edgware, where he entertained Percy at dinner on May 7.

Percy was himself a frequent dinner guest during this period, and at tables that he must have found unusually attractive. He dined at Mrs. Montagu's on November 25 with the Bishop of Carlisle and others and on January 6, when the company included David Garrick and his wife, Edmund Burke, the writer Elizabeth Carter, the painter Allan Ramsay—son of the poet—and the eminent philosopher and historian David Hume, to whom Percy had sought an introduction through Hugh Blair.[64] Even among such a distinguished group Mrs. Montagu found Percy impressive: "I have got a new blue stocking with whom I am much pleased," she wrote to Elizabeth Vesey on February 2, "a Mr. Percy who publish'd ye Reliques of ye ancient Poetry, he is a very ingenious man, has many anecdotes of ancient days, historical as well as Poetical."[65] On February 11 he was again at Mrs. Montagu's, for dinner with Richard Owen Cambridge and "much Company." On January 4 he dined at Joshua Reynolds's with another select group that included Burke, Thomas and Joseph Warton, and Samuel Dyer, editor of Plutarch; all were joined in the evening by Burke's father-in-law Dr. Christopher Nugent, Thomas Francklin, Giuseppe Baretti, and Goldsmith.

Aside from the pleasure such company gave him, it proved fortunate for Percy in still another way. Reynolds, Burke, Dr. Nugent, Dyer, and Goldsmith constituted more than half the membership of the club established by Reynolds and Johnson in the winter of 1764— "The Club," as its members called it, which met each Monday at seven for supper and conversation at the Turk's Head in Gerard Street, Soho. Percy was already a good friend of both Johnson and Goldsmith, and perhaps he was known to the Club's three other members, Anthony Chamier, Topham Beauclerk, and Bennet Langton, the last two of whom he may have met at Johnson's. With his recent literary success, his broad knowledge of literature and theology, and his acquaintance with at least six of the Club's members, it was probably inevitable that Percy would be considered for membership after the Club, following the withdrawal of John Hawkins, decided in the winter of 1768 to expand its membership from nine to twelve. The balloting, in which one blackball would have been decisive, was held on February 15, and Percy was welcomed to membership that evening along with Robert Chambers, Vinerian Professor of Law at Oxford, and George Colman, the playwright and manager of Covent Garden Theatre.

Percy relished his membership in the Club and seems to have attended its meetings whenever he was free of pressing engagements. He was the only one of the three new members present on the Monday following their election, when Bennet Langton, under the Club's practice of rotating the chairmanship, presided over a group that included all the old members except Topham Beauclerk. Percy's diary breaks off at that point, but resumes briefly on Monday, March 28, when he passed up the Club meeting to spend the evening with his wife—an eventful day during which he saw John Wilkes and the other candidates in the Middlesex election convene at the Green Park Coffee House and then head off for the polls at Brentford pursued by what Percy called a "Dreadful Mob" of Wilkes supporters. No diary entries for April remain, but on Monday, May 9, he attended the Club with Chambers, Colman, Dyer, Dr. Nugent, and Reynolds. The next entry for a Monday, May 23, shows him spending the evening at Vauxhall with Hugh Blair and Algernon Percy, who had arrived at midday from Scotland; but he was back at the Club on May 30, when the only other member present was Chambers.

Club members had been selected from the beginning with the expectation that if only two of them should meet they would find subjects of common interest to discuss, and Percy and Chambers, who became good friends, probably had no difficulty enjoying their evening together. Along with Goldsmith and Johnson, Percy was invited by Chambers to Oxford in February 1769, when Chambers was to deliver the second series of his law lectures: in a letter dated February 10 Chambers expressed his pleasure at the prospect of Percy's visit and informed him that he had reserved a place for him in the February 14 Oxford coach.[66]

Percy's relationship with one literary acquaintance of this period suffered a break which has never been explained. His diary, probably because it is far from complete, records only one meeting with Thomas Gray—at Alnwick Castle on August 19, 1765—in the six years following Percy's visit to Cambridge in August and September 1761. It seems likely, however, that they would have met on other occasions at Alnwick Castle or Northumberland House, particularly since both were favorites of the Duchess.[67] But something happened during that time to turn Percy so vehemently against Gray that by 1767 he could not conceal his hostility. In a letter of March 28 in that year, he asked William Cole to procure from Gray some anecdotes about Jane Shore that Cole had mentioned to him; "but then," he added, "I must beg the favour not to have my name used to him; as I do not chuse to apply to him for any favour of any kind."[68] A year later he expressed the same attitude toward both Gray and Gray's friend William Mason. "What Mr Mason is this?" he asked on March 26, 1768, after Farmer had written him about some Surrey materials that "Mr *Mason* says" are in the British Museum; "pray apply to him for further information—Yet not in my Name if it is Mr Mason the Poet:—I would rather go a hundred miles in search myself, than ask a single Question either of him or his Brother Gray."[69]

Six weeks later Percy was reconciled to Gray and perhaps to Mason as well.[70] On May 7 he and Gray tried without success to gain admission to Westminster Hall during the pleadings on John Wilkes's outlawry, one of the sequels to his conviction in 1762 of a libel against the King. And within a day or two the Percy who would seek no favor and ask no question of Gray was looking to him for assistance. When a newly discovered Percy relation, Mme Faubert de Percy, wrote to him on April 2, 1768, after her return to France from a London visit, Percy submitted a draft of his reply in French for Gray to supply the finishing touches. Gray returned a freshly copied draft with a polite note informing Percy that he had made only a few modifications to accommodate what Percy had written "to the french manner." Percy's letter to "Madame & tres chere Cousine," in which he assured her of his desire to visit her family in France, was ready for posting on May 10.[71] Subsequent diary references to Gray, extending to June 17, 1775, suggest that they remained friends. They spent the evening of May 25, 1768, with Algernon Percy and others at Ranelagh, saw Garrick play Hamlet on May 31, when they were accompanied by Hugh Blair and Henry Reveley, and went with Blair the next night to see Samuel Foote's farce *The Devil on Two Sticks.* At Alnwick, in 1769, they walked into town together on the evening of August 1.

Percy saw much of his Scottish friends in the spring of 1768, particularly Blair, who was a guest at Northumberland House for two or three weeks. On June 7 he dined at the Crown and Anchor Tavern, where Boswell had assembled three Scottish compatriots, Blair, William Robertson, and John Douglas, to meet Johnson, and had also included Percy, Langton, and Thomas Davies in his invitation. The

Scots scarcely spoke through dinner, Boswell noted, except "to say something which they were certain would not expose them to the sword of Goliath." Percy on this occasion would have done well to remain silent also. When Johnson grew "vehement" against Dr. Messenger Monsey of Chelsea College as "a fellow who swore and talked bawdy," Percy interjected that he had "been often in his company, and never heard him swear or talk bawdy." That seemed to conclude the discussion of Monsey. But Davies, who sat next to Percy at the end of the table and conferred with him privately, announced that he had discovered why Percy had never heard Dr. Monsey swear or talk bawdy: "he never saw him but at the Duke of Northumberland's table." "And so, Sir," Johnson said loudly to Percy,

> you would shield this man from the charge of swearing and talking bawdy, because he did not do so at the Duke of Northumberland's table. Sir, you might as well tell us that you had seen him hold up his hand at the Old Bailey, and he neither swore nor talked bawdy; or that you had seen him in the cart at Tyburn, and he neither swore nor talked bawdy. And is it thus, Sir, that you presume to controvert what I have related?

Boswell noted that Percy seemed displeased and soon left the company. Although Johnson took no notice of his departure at the time, he was apparently waiting for an opportunity to put Davies in his place for occasioning his rebuke of Percy. It came during an exchange with Dr. Douglas concerning Swift's *Conduct of the Allies*, which Johnson called "a performance of very little ability. . . . Swift has told what he had to tell distinctly enough, but that is all. He had to count ten, and he has counted it right. Why, Sir, Tom Davies might have written 'the Conduct of the Allies'."[72]

Early in May Percy and his daughters had journeyed to Shropshire, probably to visit Henry at school, and to other Midland counties, but again his major journey of the year was to Alnwick, where he resided from August 2 to September 9.[73] On September 2 he began a four-and-a-half-day tour that took him to Otterburn and Holy Island, with a stop along the way at Norham to dine with the Reverend Robert Lambe, who had sent him a number of old poems on August 17.[74] On September 6, the day of his return, a little white horse arrived as a gift from Algernon to young Henry. The most dramatic events were a show of lions at the castle on September 1 and the celebration of the Prince of Wales's birthday on August 22, when, after the Duke raised his glass and recited the names of all the royal family, a dozen cannon were fired from the castle ramparts. As the volley echoed along the hills and valleys, Percy informed Anne in a letter that night, the whole country roared with applause.[75]

From Alnwick Percy rode almost to Birmingham with the Duke and Duchess and Henry Reveley, along a week's route that included Hadrian's Wall, Prudhoe and Naworth Castles, Carlisle, Ullswater, and Lancaster. He stopped at Newport, his old school town, on September 17, before going on to Oldbury, near Bridgnorth, to visit Henry, with whom he attended morning and evening services on the eighteenth.[76] At Bridgnorth he was given almost a hero's welcome. Bailiffs old and new—the chief magistrates—turned out to greet him on September 21 when Percy, the son of Bailiff Arthur Lowe Percy, was honored with the title of burgess. On October 2 he preached at St. Leonard's.[77] On his way to London from Bridgnorth he stopped at Worcester to visit William Cleiveland and his recent bride and then spent two days with Anne at Kew. Back in London he took a special pleasure in attending the opera on October 11, when he sat below the box occupied by the young Christian VII, King of Denmark.[78]

September brought word of a nephew named for him: Thomas Percy, born on September 13 to Percy's brother Anthony, who had married Mary Mason of London on April 16, 1767, and was now in "a fine way of business" in Southwark.[79] In October Percy had news for Will Cleiveland, who in February of 1767 had responded to a number of Percy's requests with a request of his own: could Percy secure him a chaplaincy?[80] "Dear Cuz," Percy wrote on October 22, 1768,

> I give you Joy of your new Scarf, and wish it may be only a prelude to higher & greater honours: The inclosed Qualification gives you a full power to wear as good a one, as the best right reverend of them all.—I got you this by the greatest chance in the world: walking yesterday in the park, I accidentally met with my Lord Home, whom I had the pleasure of seeing this last Summer at Alnwick, his Lordship renewed his acquaintance with me in so obliging a manner that it occurred to me to ask him the favour, which he in the most polite manner immediately granted: In return for which I desire you will purchase a very fine silk Scarf against next Sunday and pray for his Lordship in the face of all your Congregation.[81]

Because Will's chaplaincy was merely nominal—an opportunity, as Percy suggested, for him to display himself with greater luster before his congregation—Percy continued his search for "a real actual" chaplaincy, and by the end of 1769 he had secured promises of assistance from the aging Lord Sandys's successor and from the Scottish Lord Eglinton.[82] At the same time he was pursuing an honor of his own. As early as February 1766 he had asked Farmer for information about the Cambridge requirements for the doctor's degrees, and in 1769 he set his course in earnest toward the degree of Doctor of Divinity.[83] Meanwhile he remained much in demand as a preacher, his position as chaplain and secretary to the Duke of Northumberland making him both desirable and accessible to the London churches. In 1768 he preached twice at Temple Church and once each at St. George, Bloomsbury, and Kew Chapel. In St. Paul's Cathedral, on May 11, 1769, he preached the "Sermon before the Sons of the Clergy" at an annual charity service for the benefit of clergymen's widows and orphans; and in November, at Johnson's request, he preached at the Ladies Charity School in Snow Hill.[84] The St. Paul's sermon was published in 1770.[85]

Percy's diary contains only a handful of entries for the first months of 1769, but among other activities it shows him presenting the children to the Duchess at Northumberland House on January 16, before he spent the evening at the Club, and then escorting them to court the next day to celebrate the Queen's birthday. That afternoon he and the children dined with Goldsmith and then went to the theater to see Garrick's *The Country Girl* and *Harlequin's Invasion*. In mid-February he spent four days at Oxford with Chambers, Johnson, and Goldsmith, and on April 27 he was at Reynolds's for "a Treat": a celebration of Reynolds's knighthood to which Reynolds had invited five other members of the Club— Johnson, Burke and Dr. Nugent, Chambers, and Langton—plus John Hawkesworth, the linguist William Jones, and the Reverend Dr. Thomas Leland of Dublin.

At Oxford Percy dined with Thomas Warton on February 17 and probably heard then of plans to republish the 1744 Hanmer edition of Shakespeare, the first Oxford edition. Although attractively printed, the edition had contributed little to Shakespeare scholarship, but Percy, as he wrote Warton on March 3, conceived that it might yet have an advantage over all the other Shakespeare editions, "that is in having a good *Glossary* to it.—From the Notes of Theobald's, Warburton's, and especially *Johnson's* Editions might be selected a most excellent

Glossary of the unusual and obsolete Words; sufficient to compensate in a great measure for all the other Defects of the Book."[86] Percy offered, if Warton would provide him with a copy of the present glossary, to add to it from "a sketch of the same kind in MS. in my own possession." Warton seems to have raised no objection and, with some help from John Hawkins, Percy contributed to an expanded glossary which was published with the new edition in 1771.

In May came the good news that Anne Percy, who had expected to spend a full two years in the royal household, had been released under a recent regulation of the Queen and was now "her own Mistress again." Free to travel together, they left for Shropshire during the week of May 21, stopping on their return to visit William Cleiveland and his wife.[87] Percy had suffered from piles in the spring, and he looked for relief in a country excursion and a break in his sedentary regimen of writing and "other literary application." Not surprisingly, the trip did not prove to be all relaxation: Percy preached at St. Mary's in Bridgnorth on June 4 and at All Saints, Will Cleiveland's church, on June 18.[88]

In July 1769 he was off again for a two-month stay at Alnwick, where the major event was another trip to Holy Island. The company at the castle included Thomas Gray, the Primate of Ireland Archbishop Richard Robinson, and John Calder, to whom, in 1773, Percy would relinquish his editorship of the *Tatler, Spectator,* and *Guardian.* On August 4 he conducted Archbishop Robinson, the brother of Elizabeth Montagu, on a tour of Warkworth Castle and the hermitage. Toward the end of his Alnwick stay Anne visited Brighton at the invitation of Johnson's friends Henry and Hester Thrale, when Johnson was also a visitor. "The Thrale's have made him quite a new Man," she wrote to Percy on September 2, "and he looks so smart that you wou'd hardly know him."[89] Probably it was during this visit that Anne showed Johnson and the Thrales her letters from her husband, in one of which, Mrs. Thrale later recalled, Percy mentioned enjoying "the fall of a murmuring stream" and then added, "but to you who reside close to the roaring Ocean, such scenery would be insipid." Johnson, laughing at Percy's comment, called it "ridiculous Affectation."[90]

"God grant us a happy meeting which I hope will not be long now," wrote Anne in concluding her letter, "for I want to see you; it's a great while since I had that happiness, nine weeks this day." Reunited at Easton Maudit later that month, they dined with the Earl of Sussex on September 25 and 27 and two days later set off with their daughters to visit Mrs. Percy's brother at Thurmaston in Leicestershire. Once again Percy was called upon to preach, at Thurmaston on October 1.

Autumn was kind to the Percys. On October 10 Anne, though employed by Queen Charlotte for less than two years, was granted a pension of £100 a year, which was paid to her in quarterly installments for the rest of her life.[91] And on November 24 Percy was appointed one of the King's Chaplains in Ordinary to fill a vacancy left by the promotion of Dr. John Hinchcliffe to the bishopric of Peterborough. No doubt the appointment reflected the Duke of Northumberland's influence, although Percy was hardly without qualifications for such a position. Indeed, at least one well-wisher expressed a hope for more. "I beg leave to wish you joy of being appointed Chaplain to his Majesty," Algernon Percy wrote from Turin in response to one of the numerous letters he received from Percy while on the Grand Tour; "(I wish it was of being made a Bishop)."[92]

Probably the chaplaincy was granted the more readily because Percy was well on his way to the Doctor of Divinity degree at Cambridge—what Farmer called the "*Watch-word* to Preferment."[93] On December 2 he finished writing the required Latin sermon, and on December 8 he rode to Cambridge in the stagecoach, Anne having taken the chaise to visit an uncle at St. Ives some two weeks earlier.[94] After being admitted as a member, first of Emmanuel College and then of the university, he preached an English sermon in St. Mary's Church on Sunday the tenth and then had a free day, which he spent visiting university friends. On the twelfth he was "very busy . . . in going round the university with Farmer petitioning for my Grace"— apparently submitting himself to questioning by university doctors of divinity for the required "Act in Divinity," a "more *serious* thing," according to Farmer, than the defense of a thesis required for the Doctor of Laws.[95] He preached his Latin sermon, on the prophecy concerning Shiloh, at St. Mary's on December 13, and in the afternoon attended a dinner for the vice-chancellor at Emmanuel College. On the fourteenth Farmer drove him to St. Ives to see Anne and returned to Cambridge that evening, with Percy and his wife following the next evening in the chaise. On December 16 Percy was admitted in congregation to the Doctor of Divinity degree; and in the evening he and Anne, in keeping with tradition, gave a treat: a tea and supper for an unrecorded number of guests. The final event in Percy's candidacy had to await the commencement on July 3, 1770, when he preached the commencement sermon and was, as he wrote, "Created" a Doctor of Divinity.[96]

NOTES

1. Arthur Collins, *The Peerage of England*, 5th ed. (London, 1779), 2:486 (Percy revised the article on the Northumberlands for this edition); Alnwick Castle MS. 93A/19.
2. It was given the title *A Letter Describing the Ride to Hulne Abbey from Alnwick in Northumberland*. It has been reprinted in *Lit. Illus.*, 8:152–57.
3. B.L. Add. MS. 32,333, f. 34 (Letter Anthony Percy to Cleiveland, 27 June 1765).
4. See p. 9.
5. *Reliques* (1767), 1:14.
6. *The Percy Letters*, 2:94. On the way to Stanwick, Lord Northumberland, Percy, and Algernon stopped at Newcastle, where Dr. Brown had supper with them on 29 August. Algernon went on to Stanwick the next day while Percy stayed with Lord Northumberland and also paid morning and afternoon visits to Dr. Brown. He and Lord Northumberland completed the journey to Stanwick via Durham on 31 August. Probably it was during this period together that they discussed Percy's future with the Northumberland family.
7. See p. 43.
8. Letter John Brown to Percy, 17 Aug. 1765 (Florida State University, Special Collections). Brown's pamphlet, adapted from a letter to Lord Lyttelton, developed quite similarly to Percy's *Ride to Hulne Abbey*. Brown committed suicide in 1766.
9. B.L. Add. MS. 39,547, f. 1 (Letter Percy to Anne Percy, 15 Sept. 1765). Percy, who kept the Countess of Northumberland informed of their progress, also wrote to her on 15 September (collection of Kenneth Balfour).
10. The Bishop of Carlisle, the brother of Lord Lyttelton, was elected president of the Society of Antiquaries in 1765.
11. *The Percy Letters*, 4:112–15 (Letters Percy to Dalrymple, 22 Sept. and 4 Oct. 1765). The 11 October date given in the published text is an error for 4 October. Percy was already in Edinburgh by 11 October.
12. B.L. Add. MS. 32,334, ff. 3–6 (Letter to the Countess of Northumberland, 29 Sept. 1765). At one of the lead mines they were shown the whole process from digging the ore to melting the lead into pigs.
13. Neither the portrait nor the artist has been traced. Foulis's academy was dissolved in 1770, and his pictures were sent to London in 1776 to be auctioned (*DNB*, "Robert Foulis").

14. National Library of Scotland, MS. 2524, ff. 7–8 (Letter Hugh Blair to Baron Mure, 5 Oct. 1765).

15. B.L. Add. MS. 32,334, f. 9 (Letter to the Countess of Northumberland, 11 Oct. 1765).

16. Ibid., f. 10.

17. Boswell's *Life*, 1:396, 548.

18. See p. 125.

19. *Lit. Illus.*, 6:569.

20. *The Percy Letters*, 5:117, 121–22 (Letters Percy to Evans, 24 Dec. 1765; Evans to Percy, 17 Jan. 1766).

21. Northumberland Miscellaneous Papers, Alnwick G/2/1. The letter is undated, but a partially blotted stamp suggests that it was posted on 16 October.

22. *The Percy Letters*, 2:96–97.

23. Ibid., 100 (Letter to Farmer, 1 Feb. 1766).

24. Ibid., 101–2, 106–7 (Letter to Farmer, 29 March 1766). The Percy-Steevens friendship was to flourish long enough for Percy to contribute sixty-eight new notes to the Johnson-Steevens edition of Shakespeare in 1773, and another fourteen to the 1778 edition. These have been analyzed in considerable detail in Arthur Sherbo's *The Birth of Shakespeare Studies* ([East Lansing: Colleagues Press, 1986], 39–44, 71–73). Inevitably, many of the notes reflect Percy's literary work, particularly for the *Reliques*, which had drawn him deeply into the study of early English drama as well as early poetry.

25. Diary, 17 March 1766. Percy dictated this entry on 22 April 1809.

26. *Critical Review* (June 1766), 460; *Monthly Review* (May 1766), 401–3.

27. *The Percy Letters*, 6:12 (Letter 12 June 1768).

28. *A Key to the New Testament* (London: L. Davis & C. Reymers, 1766), xxxviii. Percy's chief sources were Michaelis's *Introductory Lectures to the Sacred books of the New Testament* (1761), Lardner's *History of the Apostles and Evangelists* (1760), and Owens's *Observations on the Four Gospels* (1764). Percy did not disclose his authorship until the second edition, which he dedicated to Shute Barrington, Bishop of Llandaff.

29. Diary, 14–16, 28–29 July; 4–5 Aug. 1766.

30. Northumberland Letters and Papers 1766–1769, Alnwick 23/1, ff. 11–13 (Letter to Duchess of Northumberland, 5 Oct. 1766) (from L.C. microfilm); B.L. Add. MS. 32,334, ff. 13–14.

31. *The Percy Letters*, 2:114.

32. *Lit. Illus.*, 7:292–94.

33. B.L. Add. MS. 32,334, ff. 15–17 (Letter Percy to Duchess of Northumberland, 15 Nov. 1766); B.L. Add. MS. 32,333, ff. 35–37 (Letter to Cleiveland, 1 Dec. 1766).

34. B.L. Add. MS. 32,333, ff. 38–41.

35. Bodl. MS. Percy c. 11, f. 17 (Letter Sir Joseph Ayloffe to Percy, 5 July 1766).
36. "Observations on Dr. Percy's Account of Minstrels among the Saxons," *Archaeologia* (London, 1773), 2:100–6.
37. Bodl. MS. Eng. Lett. d. 46, ff. 653–56 (Letter Percy to Pegge, 13 July 1767).
38. *The Percy Letters*, 2:112.
39. B.L. Add. MS. 45,867, B. 41.
40. *Thomas Percy & John Bowle Cervantine Correspondence* (Exeter Hispanic Texts), ed. Daniel Eisenberg (Exeter: Univ. of Exeter, 1987), 3. The original letters are in the University of Cape Town Libraries, BC 188, Bowle-Evans Collection. Percy noted the following in his diary after dining with Johnson at a tavern on 21 February 1759: "Recommended by M.' Johnson for any literary Curiosity to apply to M.' Jackson in Clare-Court, Drury Lane."
41. *The Percy Letters*, 2:138.
42. *London Chronicle* and *London Evening-Post*, 1–3 Dec. 1767.
43. Letters Reynolds to Percy, 13 July 1767 (Hyde Collection); Sharp to Percy, 9 June 1767 (B.L. Add. MS. 32,329, f. 36); Percy to Bowle, 25 June 1767 (*Thomas Percy & John Bowle*, 6); Percy to Cole, 25 June 1767 (B.L. Add. MS. 5825, f. 12).
44. *Reliques* (1767), 1:xix–xxxviii.
45. Ibid., 1:xxxix–lxxvi.
46. *Lit. Illus.*, 8:164 (Letter Pegge to Percy, June 1773).
47. René Wellek, *The Rise of English Literary History* (Chapel Hill: Univ. of North Carolina Press, 1941), 144–59.
48. *The Percy Letters*, 2:120–30. Percy's probing questions prompted Farmer to make a number of changes in his second edition (1767).
49. Cleanth Brooks has provided a detailed account of the progress of Percy's Surrey edition in an appendix to *The Percy Letters*, 2:175–200.
50. *Thomas Percy & John Bowle*, 13.
51. *The Percy Letters*, 3:128 (Letter Warton to Percy, 25 July 1767).
52. Bodl. MS. Eng. Lett. d. 46, ff. 650–51.
53. *The Percy Letters*, 5:124; Diary, 23 May 1767. The IOU is pinned into Percy's copy of Evans's *Some Specimens of the Poetry of the Antient Welsh Bards*, now at the Queen's University of Belfast (*The Library of Thomas Percy* [London: Sotheby's, 1969], no. 184). The portrait viewed by Woodington has not been identified.
54. B.L. Add. MS. 39,547, ff. 3–4.
55. Alnwick Castle MS. 93A/29.
56. Ibid., 93A/43.
57. B.L. Add. MS. 32,325, f. 1.
58. Ibid., f. 245.

59. Public Record Office, Prob. 11/932–33/346.

60. B.L. Add. MS. 32,327, f. 175.

61. Information supplied by the Royal Archives, Windsor Castle. See also B.L. Add. MS. 32,326, f. 28.

62. B.L. Add. MS. 32,327, f. 175. At Oldbury Henry, not yet five, seems to have been under the care of his great aunts of the Nott family.

63. B.L. Add. MS. 42,515, f. 42. Goldsmith's letter has been printed in *The Collected Letters of Oliver Goldsmith*, ed. Katharine C. Balderston (Cambridge: Cambridge Univ. Press, 1928), 79–80.

64. *The Letters of David Hume*, ed. J. Y. T. Greig (Oxford: Clarendon Press, 1932), 2:134 (Letter Hume to Blair, 1 April 1767).

65. Huntington Library MS. MO 6393.

66. Houghton Library, Harvard Autograph File.

67. The Duchess wrote them and Reveley a joint letter from Germany in May 1768 (B.L. Add. MS. 32,334, ff. 18–19).

68. B.L. Add. MS. 6401, f. 157.

69. *The Percy Letters*, 2:144–45.

70. By March 1772, Percy was seeking information from Mason on the Percys of Yorkshire, and in 1773, probably at Percy's request, the Duke of Northumberland sent Mason a copy of the *Northumberland Houshold Book* (B.L. Add. MS. 32,329, ff. 44 and 68).

71. Alnwick Castle MS., Northumberland Misc. Papers G/2/44 and 48.

72. Boswell's *Life*, 2:63–65.

73. *The Percy Letters*, 2:146 (Letter Percy to Farmer, 7 May 1768). Percy called on Farmer's mother and probably visited Anne's relations in Leicestershire.

74. Houghton Library, Harvard bMS Eng 893 (128E).

75. Northumberland Letters and Papers 1766–1769, Alnwick 23/1, ff. 108–9 (from L.C. microfilm).

76. Percy was greeted at Newport by Thomas Marshall, who had married Percy's distant cousin Abigail Congreve (B.L. Add. MS. 32,326, f. 25).

77. Bodl. MS. Percy d. 5, f. 60.

78. B.L. Add. MS. 32,333, ff. 42–43 (Letter Percy to Cleiveland, 12 Oct. 1768).

79. B.L. Add. MSS. 32,327, f. 177; 32,333, ff. 44–45 (Letter Percy to Cleiveland, 22 Oct. 1768).

80. Ibid., 32,333 (Letter Percy to Cleiveland, 16 Feb. 1767).

81. Ibid., ff. 44–45.

82. Ibid., ff. 52–53 (Letter Percy to Cleiveland, 25 Nov. 1769; ff. 54–55 (Letter Percy to Cleiveland, 31 Jan. 1770).

83. *The Percy Letters*, 2:104–5 (Letter Farmer to Percy, 12 Feb. 1766).

84. Bodl. MSS. Percy d. 3, f. 242; d. 5, ff. 35 and 60. *The Letters of Samuel Johnson*, 1:231–32.

85. *A Sermon Preached before the Sons of the Clergy, at Their Anniversary Meeting, in the Cathedral Church of St. Paul, on Thursday, May 11, 1769* (London: Rivington [1770]). According to Joseph Cradock, the sermon was published over Percy's objection. Cradock stated (*Literary and Miscellaneous Memoirs*, 1:241–42) that Percy, having forgotten his engagement until the time was nearly at hand, "freely engrafted the greatest Part" of Johnson's *Idler* No. 4 onto his sermon in his haste to meet his deadline. Essentially, however, the two pieces are alike only in their general treatment of the theme of Christian charity, and Percy could hardly have felt the serious embarrassment that Cradock, claiming firsthand knowledge of the incident, attributed to him. It should be noted that G. B. Hill, in refuting Cradock's account, stated that the sermon was preached seven years before Cradock met Johnson (*Johnsonian Miscellanies* [New York: Harper, 1897], 2:65). Whether or not that is so, Cradock *was* acquainted with Percy, whose diary shows that he and his wife had tea with the Cradocks in Leicestershire on 29 September 1769.

86. *The Percy Letters*, 3:131–32. Sherbo, *The Birth of Shakespeare Studies*, 29–31. Percy's manuscript glossary is in the Folger Shakespeare Library.

87. Letter Percy to Cleiveland, 15 May 1769 (collection of Kenneth Balfour).

88. Alnwick Castle MS., Northumberland Misc. Papers G/2/41 (Letter Lewis Dutens to Percy, 3 June 1769); *The Percy Letters*, 4:117 (Letter Percy to David Dalrymple, by then Lord Hailes, 16 July 1769); Bodl. MS. Percy d. 5, f. 80.

89. *Notes & Queries*, New ser. 26 (1979): 38. The original of Anne Percy's letter is in the collection of Kenneth Balfour.

90. *The Letters of Samuel Johnson*, 1:294 n. 3.

91. Information supplied by the Royal Archives, Windsor Castle.

92. Alnwick Castle MS., Northumberland Misc. Papers G/2/32 (Letter 13 March 1770). Algernon was traveling abroad with the Reverend Lewis Dutens, with whom Percy also corresponded.

93. *The Percy Letters*, 2:104 (Letter to Percy, 12 Feb. 1766).

94. B.L. Add. MS. 32,333, f. 49 (Letter Percy to Cleiveland, 23 Nov. 1769).

95. *The Percy Letters*, 2:104–5.

96. B.L. Add. MS. 32,327, f. 172. William Cole spent the day and evening of 17 December with Percy "and was much entertained with his company" (*The Yale Edition of Horace Walpole's Correspondence*, vol. 1, ed. W. S. Lewis and A. Dayle Wallace [New Haven: Yale Univ. Press, 1937], 193 n. 2).

CHAPTER VIII

King's Chaplain:
1769–1773

By DECEMBER 1769 Percy had secured new lodgings for Anne in York Buildings, Villiers Street, only a short walk from Northumberland House, but sometime before April 1 she moved to Bolton Street, just off Piccadilly.[1] At that time at least the older children were in Shropshire visiting their great aunts, and Percy hoped to take them back to Easton Maudit after he traveled with Thomas Apperley to Wynnstay in Wales for the coming-of-age feast of Sir Watkin Williams Wynn in mid–April. Perhaps, as Percy feared might happen, the Duke's gout forced a postponement since there is a record of a May but not an April trip to Shropshire. On May 13 he preached at Oldbury, where Henry was completing his first schooling before being enrolled at Oakham in Rutland during the summer, and Percy probably drove Henry and the girls to Easton Maudit very shortly thereafter. He arrived there, in any event, in time to conduct the service on May 27.[2]

Perhaps the trip to Wynnstay attracted him in part because it would take him close to Brynypys, which he seems not to have visited for some years. On November 3, 1769, Mrs. Price had died after a series of strokes, and it would have been natural for him to extend condolences personally, if possible, to her son, daughter-in-law, and grandson.[3] But he must particularly have welcomed the opportunity to enjoy the company of Apperley, the confidant and most devoted correspondent of his early years in the church.

Percy's most frequent correspondent of the late 1760s and early 1770s was George Paton, a clerk in the Edinburgh custom house whose literary interests had been called to his attention by Robert Lambe. Paton proved a tireless supplier of books, manuscripts, and information intended to assist Percy with his ballad work. In his very first letter, dated May 9, 1768, he listed four books and some old ballads and songs in manuscript that he planned to ask Hugh Blair to deliver to Percy in London. Assuming these to be loans, Percy sent a number of them back when Blair returned to Edinburgh in June. But in time, after he requested books that he expected Paton to purchase for him, he found them arriving with no indication of their cost and not so much as a hint that Paton wished to be reimbursed. By August 18, 1769, Percy, embarrassed by his mounting indebtedness, pleaded for relief. He asked Paton to send him two copies of David Herd's second volume to *Ancient and Modern Scottish Poems* whenever it should be published, "but not unless you let me repay you for this and your former disbursements." When he replied on December 9, informing Percy that Herd's second volume would go to the press in the spring, Paton not only ignored Percy's insistence upon repaying, but also announced that he would be sending William Adlington's translation of Apuleius, which he had purchased for Percy at auction. On December 20 Percy tried again: he could not think of receiving the Apuleius without paying for it, and he asked to be informed how much he was indebted for that book and the others that Paton had been "so good" as to send him; otherwise it would be impossible for him to trouble Paton again. "I can by no means trespass upon your good nature in the manner in which your benevolence would invite me," he added. But if Paton would point out any "Services of the same literary kind" by which he might return his favors, he would then be encouraged to apply to him again.

Paton proved incorrigible. He informed Percy in a letter of December 26 that the Apuleius was on its way and that he was still looking for another book, and he suggested no services of any literary kind that might interest him. "It gives me great Concern," he wrote, "to be in Danger of procuring your Displeasure, and denied the Opportunity of the Pleasure of serving you, which I beg you will alter your Intention of, as the few things sent are Trifles, so hope to enjoy future Occasions of serving you." After an almost identical exchange in September 1773, Percy concluded that he could pay for books obtained by Paton only by asking that he have the Scottish booksellers bill him through a London bookseller. Money and Paton simply did not mix.[4]

Paton's assistance, useful though it was to become, had no impact upon Percy's major 1770 publication, which had been at the press since 1767. Dedicated to the Duke of Northumberland and given the title *Northern Antiquities*, Percy's two-volume translation of Paul Henri Mallet's *Introduction à l'Histoire de Dannemarc* was published on June 8, 1770, two and a half years after Percy, confident of quick publication, had referred to it in the 1767 edition of the *Reliques* as though it was already available to the public.[5] The delay has not been explained, but at least one benefit can be attributed to it. Percy's title for the book in 1767 was *A Description of the Manners, Customs, &c. of the Ancient Danes and Other Nations*. The title *Northern Antiquities*, if not a master stroke, was clearly worth waiting for.

One needs to turn to only a few sentences in Percy's translation to understand his fascination with Mallet's book. Drawn to literature as one of the few surviving records of ancient times, Mallet asks whether it is not history just as much as a "recital of battles, sieges, intrigues and negotiations." The most credulous writer, he asserts,

> he that has the greatest passion for the marvelous, while he falsifies the history of his contemporaries, paints their manners of life and modes of thinking, without perceiving it. His simplicity, his ig-norance, are at once pledges of the artless truth of his drawing, and a warning to distrust that of his relations. This is doubtless the best, if not the only use, we can make of those old reliques of poetry, which have escaped the shipwreck of time.[6]

This was the voice, not just of Mallet but of the Percy who sought to recover the ancient poetry of different nations and who selected for the *Reliques*, as he wrote in its preface, "such specimens . . . as either shew the gradation of our language, exhibit the progress of popular opinions, display the peculiar manners and customs of former ages, or throw light on our earlier classical poets."[7] Holding so much in common with Mallet, Percy was happy to track him through his examination of the ancient Danish culture: the religion of Odin, the forms of government, the passion for war, and the relentless explo-ration and conquest of Britain and northern Europe. His admiration did not blind him, however, to a significant shortcoming, Mallet's failure to distinguish the Celtic people from the Gothic, and adjusting this distortion in Mallet's picture became a primary objective of his preface to the two volumes. Assisted by his correspondence with Evan Evans on this very subject, he was able to cite distinctions between the two peoples in their manners and customs, institutions and laws, religion and language, and even their physical appearances.[8]

The publication of *Northern Antiquities* marked the high point of Percy's literary activities for the year, but there were other gratifications. He was elected a member of the Society of Antiquaries in February, and at Alnwick he cataloged the Duke's library and wrote the second part of *The Hermit of Warkworth*, which seems to have remained untouched since September 1767.[9] He wrote the final part at Tunbridge Wells in late September.

His summer stay at Alnwick was cut short by the need for him to return to London for his first period of "waiting" as a King's Chaplain. He had hoped for a winter month, but—after a call to preach before the King on March 28—he was assigned initially to a shorter period in late August.[10] On the way south from Alnwick he stopped at Oakham to see Henry, who rode part of the way with him to Easton Maudit, where he arrived on August 20, and on the twenty-fourth he and Anne traveled to London together. His only record of this first waiting, in his diary, shows him preaching the early and midday sermons at St. James's Chapel on August 26 and entertaining James White and one or two others at the chaplain's table in the palace on August 25 and 26. Since he appears to have been in Bridgnorth by September 6, he probably concluded his duties on August 31.[11] Thereafter, beginning that year, December was to be his regular month.

Although illness had from time to time disturbed the generally even tenor of the Percys' lives, it had left no permanent scars. In early June of 1770, for example, Anne suffered what Percy called a "dangerous Illness," but by June 19 she was "much restored," and he was able to leave Easton Maudit to attend to his Northumberland House duties. But their fortunes were soon to change. On the night of October 27, Barbara and Henry, the latter just returned to Easton Maudit from school, were stricken with the ulcerated sore throat, a disease not yet given the name diphtheria and frequently confused with the scarlet fever, with which it had much in common.[12] Percy himself fell ill with it the next day. With the disease known to be highly contagious, Anne sent Elizabeth and Charlotte to stay with her sister, who had moved to Wellingborough after the death of Samuel Edwards in 1766; but, hardly knowing how she could spare their oldest daughter in such an emergency, she kept young Anne, "a very sensible womanly little Girl" of ten and a half, to help out at the vicarage. To avoid infection both Annes took the same bark administered to the three patients and observed other "proper precautions."[13]

"Bab," as she was known, soon grew better, and Percy was also much improved by the end of the week. Henry, on the other hand, grew much worse and, "after every application that the art of Medicine could offer, was pronounced to be at the point of Death." But by "a happy Providence," Percy wrote, the house had been stocked with a large quantity of Dr. James's Fever Powder, and on November 4 he administered seven grains with the intention of repeating the dosage every six hours. From that moment Henry "hourly mended" so that by November 8, after having taken over ninety grains, he was able to resume the bark, which completed the cure. For some time, however, he was so weakened by the disease that he was as "helpless as an infant."

About the time that Henry was beginning to recover, young Anne, in spite of all precautions, contracted the disease. She too was given the fever powder and, though still "very indiff[eren]t," there seemed no reason to despair of her life as there had been with Henry. On November 12, however, her fever rose sharply and she grew delirious. Again the fever powder "removed her Fever, and mitigated many of the Symptoms," but its relief was only temporary. A violent intestinal disorder ensued, which terminated only with her death on Sunday morning, November 18.

She was buried on November 20 in a small vault beneath the middle aisle of the church, between the Earl of Sussex's pew and Percy's.[14] The effect of her death on her parents was more easily conceived than described, Percy wrote to William Cleiveland on November 22, in a flood of words reflecting his troubled state:

> This sweet child was so engaging and pretty a companion to her Mother in my absence and under the ill health she [Mrs. Percy] has for some time past suffered was really so useful and already took so much trouble off her hands, by carrying Messages to the Servants, by being intrusted with her Mother's Keys, had so much judgement & penetration, and had so much solid Piety for so young a Child, that the Loss of her has almost broke both our hearts (tho it is happiest for the dear Child) indeed her poor Mother has been quite ill ever since.

The letters of condolence included one from Johnson on behalf of Mrs. Williams and himself, and one from Edmund Allen, who reported that he had printed about one hundred eighty copies of the sixteenth-century household book— *The Regulations and Establishment of the Houshold of Henry Algernon Percy.*[15]

Percy spent the last week of November writing the preface to the household book, perhaps to clear his desk before being called to London for his December waiting at court. Fortunately when the call came it was for Sunday, December 9, credit apparently having been allowed him for his waiting during the last week of August. Some of the effects of his illness had lingered, so that he did not attempt even the duties of his own church until December 2.

His record of the December waiting consists largely of the names of his guests at the chaplain's table in St. James's Palace, a privilege of which he regularly took advantage. On December 21, for example, his guests were Johnson, Goldsmith, Dyer, Reynolds, Sir John Delaval, and John Oldershaw, and, on December 24, Thomas Francklin, Edmund Allen, Percy's brother Anthony, Mr. Wright from his Bridgnorth days, and Ralph Griffiths. He even preserved a number of menus. On December 31, when Richard Penneck of the British Museum was his sole guest, the dinner included lamb boiled and fried, spinach, paté of goose and giblets, and venison, with a dessert of creamed tart and cheesecakes.[16] For evening diversion he saw three plays, one of which was the annual Latin play—Terence's *Andria*—performed by the boys of Westminster School, and he attended the Club on December 17 and 31.

His duties as chaplain included preaching the noon service at the Chapel Royal on December 23 and the early service on Christmas morning, after which he assisted the Bishop of Winchester in administering the sacrament to the King and Queen at Buckingham House. On December 30 he preached at the Chapel Royal in the presence of the King and then attended court in St. James's Palace.

As he was making his way to Buckingham House on Christmas Day, he was delivered a letter from his wife informing him that Charlotte had been taken ill with the ulcerated sore throat. There was nothing he could do for the moment. But as soon as his Christmas duties permitted, he hurried off a note to Dr. Henry Owen, rector of St. Olave's Hart Street, asking if he could assume his responsibilities for the remainder of the waiting. Unfortunately Owen, who replied on December 26, had been afflicted for a month with "a violent hoarseness," and his wife, too, had just fallen ill.[17] It is not evident whether Percy sought assistance from other friends, but he apparently found no alternative to completing his assignment. He left London at the turn of the year and reached Easton Maudit, probably on January 2, to find Charlotte as critically ill as Henry and Anne had been almost two months before. She clung to life for another week, but even her "uncommon health and vigour" were inadequate to protect her against the ulcerated sore throat. She died about three in the morning of January 9 and was buried with Anne beneath the church floor on January 10.[18]

Inevitably Mrs. Percy's illness, brought on by the loss of young Anne, was exacerbated by still another such loss. She "has never been well since this fatal Shock," Percy informed William Cleiveland on March 25; "and is at times very much afflicted with a bilious Complaint, which often fills me with Apprehensions." The family's removal to London was put off until late winter, although Percy was himself at Northumberland House on January 30, when he wrote to John Bowle.[19]

In town, while five-year-old Elizabeth remained in the country with her aunt Mary Edwards, Percy supervised Barbara's and Henry's studies until Henry returned to school at Oakham. Under his guidance they read Roman and Grecian history, the first of these in his friend Goldsmith's recently published *Roman History*, and they looked in a book of ancient maps for all the new places mentioned. They "come on as well as I could wish," Percy told Will. Later he introduced Henry to two books from his own boyhood library, Basil Kennett's *Antiquities of Rome* and John Potter's *Antiquities of Greece*, with illustrations Henry was "so fond of, that his common play with his Sisters was to act a Roman Triumph, Sacrifice or Funeral."[20]

On May 21 *The Hermit of Warkworth* was published, its dedication to the Duchess of Northumberland set in one of the eighteenth century's few Spenserian sonnets:

> O Lady, may so slight a gift prevail,
> And at your gracious hands acceptance find?
> Say, may an ancient legendary tale
> Amuse, delight, or move the polish'd mind?

In addition to the dedication copy for the Duchess, Percy gave sixty of the edition's five hundred copies to friends and relations, including the eleven other members of the Club. One of the copies went to George Paton, to whom he had also sent the two volumes of *Northern*

Antiquities—his attempt to strike the balance for which money had proved unequal.[21]

The hermitage of Percy's poem had drawn him time and again to Warkworth during his Alnwick summers and teased him with its questions. Who had hewn this solitary outpost out of the rock and carved its chapel with such devotion that it was vaulted like a miniature cathedral? Who was its first inhabitant? And who were the stone figures in the window niche scarcely a whisper from the River Coquet, a woman lying as though dead and a man standing over her at her feet? The questions defied response. But Percy's imagination could not rest until it had fitted a romantic tale to this romantic retreat: of lovers separated, a tireless search, a pilgrim, a maidenly voice heard lamenting in a tower, a night rescue down a rope ladder, a tragic mistake of identity, a withdrawal into penance and solitude. Almost "all the fictions of the last age will vanish," Johnson wrote in *Rambler* No. 4, "if you deprive them of a hermit and a wood, a battle and a shipwreck." Percy, writing twenty years after the *Rambler*, managed without the shipwreck. And in substituting some two hundred ballad stanzas for the prose of the earlier romantic fictions, he was expressing his faith not just in the quality of his verse, but in the ability of the ballad stanza to sustain a poem much longer than any of those in the *Reliques*. Like most of Percy's work, *The Hermit of Warkworth* was a pioneer effort that helped to point the way for poets who were to follow. Though his faith in his poetic powers may have been misplaced, his faith in the ballad stanza was not, as Coleridge's success with "The Ancient Mariner" less than thirty years later was to make clear.

Percy's poem, it must be said, enjoyed a considerable success itself. A second edition of five hundred copies was called for within two months, and numerous other editions and reprintings were to follow.[22] Although John Langhorne, writing in the *Monthly Review*, concluded that Percy had not made a virtue of simplicity, the reviewer for the *Critical Review* singled out the poem's "beautiful simplicity" for special praise. The poem, he wrote, "pleases by the genuine graces of nature, undebased with the ornaments of art; and whether we consider it in regard to imagery, sentiment, or diction, we may fairly admit it to rival the most celebrated model of the English ballad."[23] The "most celebrated model" was the ballad of "Chevy-Chase."

"Simplicity" was the cant word for *The Hermit of Warkworth*, as it was for the ballads generally. Shenstone's first reaction, when he heard from Percy about the folio manuscript in 1757, had been to praise the "simplicity of style and sentiment" of the old ballads.[24] And at an Oxford coffee house in 1771, when Johnson was present, many of the assembled scholars praised *The Hermit of Warkworth* particularly for "the great *Classical Simplicity of the Poetry*." "Poetry!" Johnson is said to have cried out, "I could speak such Poetry extempore for seven Years together, If I could find Hearers dull enough to attend to me." To support so extravagant a claim, he immediately recited a quatrain that he improvised for the occasion:

> I put my hat upon my head
>   And walked into the Strand,
> And there I met another man
>   Whose hat was in his hand.[25]

Earlier that year, after Percy had shown his poem to Club members at a meeting on March 19, Johnson described it in a letter to Bennet Langton as "a long Ballad in many *Fits*," an amused reference to the antiquated word by which Percy chose to designate the poem's three sections. It is "pretty enough," Johnson added. No doubt he would have been content to leave his friend Percy's poem with that bit of bland praise, had he not seen the turn that reaction to the poem was taking. What Percy's admirers looked upon as the virtue of simplicity in the ballad imitations, Johnson recognized—to use John Hawkins's word—as "inanity," a kind of verse that required almost no imagination and merited little praise for its "imagery, sentiment, or diction."[26]

For modern readers, Johnson's parody has won the argument. *The Hermit of Warkworth* simply lacks the fire and color of the ballads in the *Reliques*. It is interesting historically, and the hermit Bertram's recounting the story of his tragic pursuit of Isabel to the young lovers, Hotspur's son Henry and Henry IV's half-sister Eleanor, permits a second level of narrative without distracting from the first. Percy's Northumberland setting, buttressed by an introductory "Advertisement" and a "Postscript" containing a history of the castle and hermitage, lends some reality to the contrivance of his tale. At dramatic points, however, the poem lapses into commonplaces, and elsewhere its language seldom rises above the pedestrian into a cogency of phrase or vividness of imagery that strikes one as compelling and inevitable. In the climactic scene Percy seems almost at a loss for the right words.

With Bertram's younger brother traveling north to aid in the search for Isabel, Bertram went west and found the castle in which she was imprisoned. On his third night of watching, he spied a rope ladder hanging from the castle wall:

> And soon he saw his love descend
> > Wrapt in a tartan plaid;
> Assisted by a sturdy youth
> > In highland garb y-clad.

Assuming the youth to be her abductor, Bertram rushed upon him with his sword drawn "And laid the stranger low."

> Die, traitor, die!—A deadly thrust
> > Attends each furious word.
> Ah! then fair Isabel knew his voice,
> > And rush'd beneath his sword.

> O stop, she cried, O stop thy arm!
> > Thou dost thy brother slay![27]

In his earlier years Percy had written occasional pieces that deserved to be called poetry, but altogether too many of *The Hermit of Warkworth's* eight hundred lines were merely rhymed verse for which Johnson's "pretty enough" was ample recognition.[28]

On his way to Alnwick in early August Percy visited old castles and monasteries in Yorkshire formerly belonging to the Percy family, including the site of the abandoned Lekinfield Castle near Beverley and probably Wresill Castle a few miles away, which had been largely destroyed by parliamentary forces in 1648.[29] It was for these two castles that the fifth Earl of Northumberland had prepared his household book in 1512. From Beverley Percy went on to Scarborough and to Whitby Abbey, and on August 7 he reached Alnwick Castle, where he found Algernon, Thomas Gray, and Lewis Dutens already in residence. During the next few weeks he rode out from the castle frequently with Algernon (*Lord* Algernon, as he had been known since coming of age)—to watch the duck hunting on August 9, for example, and to visit Dunstanburgh Castle on the twenty-first.

It was a reunion summer for the Northumberland family, with the Duchess and Lord Algernon returned from their continental travels and Lord Percy arriving from military duty in Ireland on August 11.

But the most memorable event was the visit of the twenty-five-year-old Prince Henry Frederick, Duke of Cumberland, the brother of King George III. From the moment of his arrival on the evening of August 22 the days were filled with grand dinners and suppers, balls and card assemblies, processions, bonfires, and twenty-one-gun salutes. At the dinner on Sunday, August 25, 177 dishes were served—"exclusive of the Desert," the Duchess emphasized in her diary—and two days later, after the Alnwick group had moved in procession to Berwick and enjoyed a dinner and ball sponsored by the town corporation, the Duke of Northumberland provided a supper with 240 dishes.[30] Percy, understandably, made no attempt to record them.

But he recorded much else, both in his diary and in letters to his wife and William Cleiveland, and it shows him playing an important role in the festivities.[31] Even before the feasting began he conducted the Duke of Cumberland on a tour of the castle. And during the first two full days, when all the party attended their royal guest on the customary tours of Hulne Park and Warkworth, it may be assumed that the Duke turned to the best informed person among them to point out what was of interest and answer his questions. Sometime on that second day he read to Percy "The Ballad of the Hermit"—probably Goldsmith's "Edwin and Angelina"—a nice link in the unavoidably tenuous connection between the King's brother and the King's chaplain. He is "one of the best Readers I ever heard," Percy noted in his diary, "tho' he speaks fast & thick." Later during the visit the Duke read to Percy from Pope's "Epistle from Eloise to Abelard," with remarks on the poem that Percy found "always just."

On August 25 Percy preached at Alnwick Church, adapting his sermon to the Duke of Cumberland's "situation," including a well-deserved reputation as a libertine. Just the year before, Lord Grosvenor had been awarded £10,000 in damages because of the Duke's adulterous relationship with his wife.[32] Percy hinted—"as gently as I could"—the necessity for people of the first rank to remain circumspect in their conduct, since everyone's eyes were upon them and there was a "Malignity" in the world that would exaggerate their failings until it was disarmed "by the exercise of every virtue and amiable quality." The Duchess of Northumberland thought it an excellent sermon.[33] The Prince himself, who listened intently, spoke kindly to Percy afterwards, commended him to others, and invited him to call on him often in London. He is not a "Libertine from Principle," Percy wrote in his diary; and to William Cleiveland he described him as "a good-humoured indiscreet young Man, with a strong appetite for pleasure which has made him fall a Victim to Temptations . . . purposely thrown in his way."

At the grand dinner that night Percy headed one of the three tables, and as the tables broke up the Duke of Cumberland drew him into an adjoining room where Lord Algernon was plying the Berwick aldermen with claret. When the Duke began a round of corporation toasts—"highly alarming," as Percy wrote Anne, "to so puny a drinker as myself"—he perceived Percy's uneasiness and, giving him leave to withdraw, had the rector of Alnwick take his place.

On Monday Percy received a note from James Boswell, who had just arrived at Alnwick with his wife during a short trip in northern England, and he took time out from his castle duties to spend an hour with them at their inn.[34] The next day the festivities moved to Berwick, where, during the dinner at the Red Lion Inn, Percy sat near the middle of the table at which the Duke of Cumberland presided. Close to Percy, and tottering each time the table was moved, was a "monstrous high pyramid of Jellies," which the Duke, winking at Percy to protect himself, did his best to topple without being seen. Luckily, Percy noted, he was too far off to succeed, or "many a pompous Periwig" would have suffered in the crash.

The festivities continued through the week, with the Alnwick group returning to the castle on Wednesday and the Duke of Cumberland proceeding to Newcastle for another corporation dinner on the thirtieth, in which the Alnwick group joined. Percy remained in Newcastle until Sunday morning and then, having declined an invitation to dine with the Duke of Cumberland at Seaton Delaval, returned to Alnwick.

With the close of festivities, the Duke of Northumberland and Lord Algernon set off for the southern part of Northumberland to pay some visits, the Duchess went north for a short tour in Scotland with Lord Percy and Thomas Gray, and Percy headed off into the Cheviot Hills. The Duke of Cumberland returned to London, leaving Percy a pair of his white leather gloves and presumably taking with him copies of the *Reliques* and *The Hermit of Warkworth* that Percy had presented to him. In October he married the widowed Anne Horton of Derbyshire secretly, an event he did not inform the King of until November 1.[35] Percy, unaware of the marriage but remembering the Duke's invitation, called on him in London on October 30 and spent the morning with him. What he thought of the marriage when he learned of it on November 7 is not known, but his counsel to the Duke on August 25 leaves no doubt that he would at the least have been dismayed by the Duke's lack of circumspection on this occasion. The King made no attempt to conceal his displeasure. He virtually forced a Royal Marriage Act through Parliament in 1772, forbidding members of the royal family to marry without the Crown's consent, and he announced that he and Queen Charlotte would receive no one who paid court to the Duke and Duchess of Cumberland.[36] For Percy, King's chaplain, the threat of the King's disfavor would have precluded any further response to the Duke's invitation.

Percy left Alnwick in late September and, after being met by his wife on the road, spent two weeks with her relations in Leicestershire.[37] Henry joined them briefly from his school in Oakham, to which he had returned only in August, his parents having thought it best to keep him at home following his nearly fatal experience with the ulcerated sore throat. Percy was much pleased with this "very orderly good Boy" now that he was not being spoiled by "the foolish indulgence of his old Aunts," who had looked after him at Oldbury. He was pleased with the progress of his studies also. Henry's fondness for classical literature had given him an incentive to learn Latin and, though in a class with six boys two to five years older than himself, he had outstripped nearly all of them.[38]

Percy's October 13 letter to William Cleiveland reveals that he had at last secured the "real actual" chaplaincy that Will desired. Asked by Will if, in bidding prayers, he should pray for both his patrons, Percy answered with a categorical "No": Will is "legally and properly" the chaplain of Lord Sandys and needs to name only him; it is sufficient if he remembers Lord Home in his private devotions.

Percy and Anne were back in Easton Maudit on October 10, and on October 28 he left for London, where his most frequent companions during the first two weeks of his stay were Lord Algernon and Clayton Mordaunt Cracherode, a wealthy collector of books, prints, and curios. The bond between Percy and Lord Algernon had grown steadily, a consequence in part of Percy's concern to keep his former protégé abreast of news at home when he was abroad, as well as to convey the interest of the Duke and Duchess in their son's activities and his sometimes precarious health. Lord Algernon repaid his attention by writing freely to him of his health and his love for Lady Betty Windham, of which he was pleased to have both Percy and Anne approve.[39]

In January 1772 Percy accompanied him to Dover, where Lord Algernon took passage for Calais on the start of another continental tour. By that time the Percy family had probably moved into its new lodgings in Half Moon Street, once again close to Piccadilly.[40] Percy took Anne for occasional drives in the chaise, and on March 21 they dined at Sir Joshua Reynolds's with Johnson, Burke, Cambridge, Dyer, and others. During the spring he assisted the Duke of Northumberland in distributing copies of the *Northumberland Houshold Book*, with most of them going to the Duke's friends among the peerage, but some to such Percy friends as Johnson, Hawkins, Tyrwhitt, Astle, and Blakeway. A second distribution followed in early 1773, when James Boswell and William Mason asked Percy to convey their thanks to the Duke for his gift.[41] As word spread of this first publication of its kind, Percy received requests for it from other friends, but did not find it easy to secure additional copies from the Duke, who had the sheets bound in lots of about thirty copies as he needed them.[42]

Percy was drawn inexorably to the fifth Earl of Northumberland's household book as an authentic record of the life and manners of a time reflected, more colorfully but in less detail, in the popular poetry that had set him on his way to the *Reliques of Ancient English Poetry*. At once a budget, a calendar, and a census, the book laid out precisely and comprehensively the economy of the Yorkshire castles of Wresill and Lekinfield: the number and cost of larks and swans for the Earl's table as meticulously as the wages for 166 household positions. But Percy, himself enthralled with castle life, looked beyond the household minutiae to the "state and splendour," much like the Royal Court's, that had sprung from the soil of this vast inventory:

As the King had his Privy Council and . . . Parliament, to assist him in enacting statutes and regulations for the public weal; so the Earl of Northumberland had his Council, composed of his principal officers, by whose advice and assistance he established this Code of Oeconomic Laws. As the King had his Lords and Grooms of the bed-chamber, who waited in their respective turns; so the Earl of Northumberland was attended by the Constables and Bailiffs of his several castles, &c. who entered into waiting in regular succession. . . . Among other instances of magnificence, we cannot but remark the number of PRIESTS that were kept in houshold, not fewer than ELEVEN, at the head of whom presided a Doctor or Batchelor of divinity, as dean of the chapel.[43]

Books about other households were to follow, and the *Northum-berland Houshold Book* itself enjoyed a continuing popularity, at least in scholarly circles.[44] It was reprinted in *The Antiquarian Repertory* in 1809 and in separate editions in 1827 and 1905. Percy, doubly sensitive because of the Duke's interest in the book as well as his own, reacted quickly when he was shown a rather harsh assessment of the fifth earl's economy that David Hume had prepared for a new edition of his *History of England* on the verge of publication. Writing to Hume on January 5, 1773, he took exception particularly to a note in which Hume branded the earl's management of his expenses as "very rigid, and . . . even somewhat niggardly." Hume replied graciously and made an effort to have the passage changed, but apparently by then the book was out of the printer's hands. He did remove the word *niggardly* from the 1778 edition, but permitted other unflattering comments to stand.[45]

With Hume's fellow Scot, Boswell, Percy's friendship continued to progress, though it never achieved the warmth of his friendships with Apperley, Grainger, Shenstone, Farmer, and Goldsmith. On March 26, 1772, Boswell called on him at Northumberland House and was pleased to find him in a large room looking into the Strand, and at the same time crowded with books and papers in apparent disarray—"as much a library . . . as any room in a college." Percy brought out some of his more curious volumes and displayed his collection of Spanish romances, praising as he did so the Spanish learning of John Bowle, who was helping him build the collection. When Boswell repeated a story told by his barber of the poet Edward Young's keeping a mistress, Percy dismissed it as "mere scandal," comparable to saying that Johnson kept Mrs. Williams. He added that he had just begun to make Young's acquaintance: they had not met, but Young had written him a letter. Later he accompanied Boswell to General Paoli's, where Boswell confessed that a story printed in the *London Chronicle* some months earlier—of Dr. John Brown's leaving a memorial of the Corsicans to be published in Petersburg—was a fiction of Boswell's invention. The fiction had sent Percy rummaging fruitlessly through Brown's papers for General Paoli, after Paoli's visit to Alnwick Castle in the summer of 1771.[46]

In 1772, with both the Duke and Duchess traveling on the Continent, Percy was free to spend his first summer at Easton Maudit since 1764, and he was thus at hand for the birth on July 4 of another daughter and for the initial weeks of her life.[47] Named Hester after her godmother Hester, Countess of Sussex, she was baptized privately by Percy on September 17 and received into the church on October 21, in the presence of the Countess and her daughter Lady Barbara, together with young Hester's other godmother, Mrs. Robinson of Cransley.[48] Her godfather, the Duke of Northumberland, did not attend. One of the well-wishers was Anna Williams, who wrote on August 5 of her pleasure in Mrs. Percy's safe delivery and informed her that Johnson asked how she did whenever he came to town from the Thrales' home at Streatham. She hoped that her "dearest Favourite Miss Bab," who had just turned eleven, would write her a full letter so she might answer Johnson's question.[49]

The Duke's absence from England also freed Percy for scholarly activity, some of it long overdue. He finished revising the *Key to the New Testament* for the second edition, to be published in 1773, and he put his correspondence with Shenstone in order and arranged and selected his own letters to his wife. From Joseph Warton, Bishop Warburton, and the Reverend John Hoadly he sought information about the *Tatler* and *Spectator*, probably his last burst of activity, at least for the *Tatler*, before relinquishing the editing to John Calder and turning his notes over to the publisher.[50] His transcription of Scottish ballads from Cambridge's Maitland MS. stimulated thoughts of a new collection, as he wrote David Dalrymple—Lord Hailes since his appointment to the Court of Session in 1766—on August 23. It would be similar to the *Reliques* but not a continuation of it: "Ancient English and Scottish Poems, chiefly of the more popular cast, accompanied with some few modern pieces, 3 Vol[s] 12 mo." Boswell, to whom Percy broached the plan on August 24, gave it his endorsement after discussing it with Bennet Langton and offered to contribute a few pieces.[51]

Percy's letter to Boswell was in part a response to a request for permission to give Garrick a list of Johnson's writings that Percy had compiled. Percy granted the permission, but he must have been disturbed to have Boswell inform him that the list contained several errors that Johnson had allowed his housemate Dr. Robert Levett to dictate to him. Apparently Boswell was right. On July 18, 1773, when Mrs. Thrale asked Johnson who could supply information about his early years, he replied, "Boswell and Baretti; and myself from Time to Time have a trick of writing down Anecdotes Bon Mots &c. [Mrs. Thrale:] & Doctor Percy will be busy at this work I warrant him: He would replied M[r] Johnson, but I have purposely suffered him to be misled, and he has accordingly gleaned up many Things that are not true."[52]

In December Percy was back at St. James's, preaching before the King and Queen on December 13 and entertaining such guests at the chaplain's table as Astle, Chambers, Colman, Goldsmith, and the recently knighted Sir John Hawkins, plus friends of fellow chaplain-in-ordinary Dr. Nicholas Boscawen. On December 7 and 11 he was at the Club for its final Monday and first Friday meetings, and on December 9 he accompanied Goldsmith and Chambers to the "Italian Show of Birds" in Cockspur Street.

In 1772 a petition and an action of the House of Commons cast Percy briefly in an unfamiliar role. "This day," he wrote in his diary for February 6, "the Petition for abolishing the 39 Articles was presented to the House of Commons & rejected by a great Majority." The House of Commons's rejection did not conclude the doctrinal controversy, which provoked discussion in the press, Parliament, and private circles for another year or two. In March Percy himself had three meetings with Dr. Beilby Porteus, who, as rector of Lambeth, was closely associated with the Archbishop of Canterbury and thus took a vital interest in any attempt to modify church doctrine. Neither his nor Percy's interest, as it turned out, was entirely defensive. Although they had no intention of supporting an effort as radical as that of the petitioners, they perceived, to use Percy's words, that "several obscure Points of Doctrine" that church leaders at the Reformation had felt obliged to insist upon were "now almost universally allowed to be of no great Importance"; and they believed that, if these could be removed or altered, many "moderate and well disposed" Dissenters could be brought into the Church of England.[53] The problem was of special concern to the universities, whose students, in order to matriculate, had to subscribe to the whole of the Thirty-nine Articles.

There is no evidence to show that Percy and Porteus met again during the summer or much of the fall. But early in December Francis Wollaston, rector of Chislehurst in Kent, published *An Address to the Clergy of England in Particular, and to All Christians in General* outlining positions on the controversy in accord with their own and an approach to it that they could approve. On December 10 Percy and Porteus spent the evening together, and on December 15 they participated in a meeting held in the library of St. Martin's in the Fields with Dr. John Yorke, dean of Lincoln; Dr. Henry Owen; Samuel Salter, Master of the Charterhouse; Thomas Hollingbury, Archdeacon of Chichester;

and Wollaston. Dr. Yorke presided, and Wollaston became their self-appointed spokesman, to the annoyance of Porteus, who sensed the need to avoid publicity if they were to have any success. "I wish he would be quiet," he wrote to Percy at one point.

The group concluded that a statement should be prepared requesting the bishops to consider reviewing the Thirty-nine Articles, the requirements for subscription, and the liturgy, but that two of the group should first consult the Archbishop about the propriety of their proposal. On December 18 Percy and Owen dined at Porteus's to prepare the statement, a draft of which in Percy's hand Porteus showed to the Archbishop, who "seemed to like it much." When the two members of the group—probably Yorke and Porteus—met formally with the Archbishop, he agreed to present the proposal to the bishops after the Christmas holidays and indicated that he saw no need for a written statement, at least for the moment. On February 11, 1773, he informed Yorke and Porteus that the bishops, as Porteus wrote Percy on February 12, were of the opinion that nothing could be done in the matter with "prudence & safety."

Percy's role in the controversy seems to have ended at that point, as perhaps did that of the other participants. In all likelihood he was not seriously disappointed by the failure of their effort. On December 15, after the meeting in the St. Martin's library, he had written to ask Farmer what he and his "most judicious friends" thought of the Wollaston tract—the kind of sounding that Percy commonly took when he was less than sure of himself. Farmer's reply, delayed until February 18, came in a postscript to a long letter that he called a "*Folio* of Repentance":

> I have totally forgotten the *Reformation* of the *Church*! Seriously, Mr *Woolaston's* Pamphlet is a very sensible one; and could what he talks of, be done without noise, it might be well. But suppose the Remedy should prove worse than the Disease—it would at least make one *Schism* more—We should have the *old Liturgists*, and they join'd by the *Methodists*, would make a formidable figure. Those, who are able to find Difficulties in the old Form, are able likewise to explain them: and these bear a very small proportion to the Bulk of Mankind.[54]

Though hardly a stimulus to further action, the letter may have given Percy some comfort, whether or not he shared Farmer's reservations. Perhaps, if he needed it, he found further comfort in the hope of eventual success. But that hope was not to be realized in his lifetime. Not until 1865 were entering clergymen of the Church of England permitted to make only an affirmation of general assent to the Thirty-nine Articles rather than a subscription to the whole. And not until 1871 was the requirement of subscription lifted for entering students of the two universities. Percy's pioneering spirit was not confined to literature.

NOTES

1. B.L. Add. MS. 32,333, f. 58 (Letter Percy to Cleiveland, 1 April 1770).
2. Bodl. MS. Percy d. 4, f. 70. Beginning in late 1769, Percy seems to have left much of the work at Wilby to a curate: William Procter until 1773 and William Underwood until 1781 (Wilby parish register, Northamptonshire Record Office).

    Apperley had been young Wynn's governor until he reached his majority.
3. B.L. Add. MS. 32,333, ff. 48–55 (Letters Percy to Cleiveland, 23 and 25 Nov. 1769; 31 Jan. 1770). Mrs. Price left Cleiveland an estate in Birkenhead in reversion (i.e., when she had no further direct heirs) with £5000 to be paid to Percy out of that estate.
4. *The Percy Letters*, vol. 6, *The Correspondence of Thomas Percy & George Paton*, ed. A. F. Falconer (New Haven: Yale Univ. Press, 1961), 1–5, 26–30, 68–73, 95, 167–68. Percy opened the correspondence on 30 April 1768.
5. The first advertisement was in the *Public Advertiser*, 8 June 1770; *Reliques* (1767), 1:xx.
6. *Northern Antiquities* (London: T. Carnan & J. Newbery, 1770), 1:55–56.
7. *Reliques* (1765), 1:ix.
8. *Northern Antiquities*, 1:ii ff.; *The Percy Letters*, 5:88–94. *Northern Antiquities* was reprinted in the Bohn Library in 1847. For its influence on William Blake, see Northrop Frye, *Fearful Symmetry: A Study of William Blake* (Princeton: Princeton Univ. Press, 1947), pp. 172–73.
9. Osborn Collection, Yale University (Receipt for admission, 22 Feb. 1770); B.L. Add. MS. 32,327, f. 172; Alnwick Castle MS. 93A/16.
10. Percy's 28 March call was from Dr. Frederick Cornwallis, Archbishop of Canterbury (Letter 15 Jan. 1770, Hyde Collection).
11. During his tenure as a King's chaplain (1769–78), Percy wrote to Thomas Stedman from Bridgnorth on "Thursday Morn^g" and, some days later, "Thurs Morn^g 13th Sept." In those years September 13 fell on a Thursday only in 1770. The Percy-Stedman letters are in the Osborn Collection, Yale University.

12. *The Percy Letters*, 2:155 (Letter Percy to Farmer, 19 June 1770).
    Dr. John Wall of Worcester, writing in the *Gentleman's Magazine* for Nov. 1751 (497–501) stated that the disease had first appeared in England in 1748 and at the beginning was called "the scarlet fever."

13. This account of the illness in Percy's family is based on the information in Percy's diary and in his letter of 22 November 1770 to William Cleiveland (B.L. Add. MS. 32,333, ff. 60–61).

14. B.L. Add. MS. 32,327, f. 174. Dr. James's Fever Powder, a compound largely of phosphate of lime and oxide of antimony, tended to reduce fever by inducing sweating.

15. *The Letters of Samuel Johnson*, 1:247 (Letter to Percy, 27 Nov. 1770); Letter Allen to Percy, 28 Nov. 1770 (Hyde Collection).

16. "When Dr. Percy presided at the King's Chaplain's table," wrote Cradock (IV, 296), "perhaps no literary dinner was superior." Percy recorded his guests' names in his diary. The menu is in the collection of Kenneth Balfour.

17. Bodl. MSS. Percy d. 5, f. 115; Add. A. 266, f. 2.

18. The account that Percy sent to William Cleiveland on 25 March 1771 differs from that in the diary by conveying the impression that he returned to Easton Maudit as soon as he learned of Charlotte's illness: "I was attending my Waiting at S.ᵗ James's in the Christmas, when I was fetched into the Country with the alarming Account that my youngest Daughter *Charlotte*, was seized with the same dreadful Disorder, which . . . [carried off] Sister Ann: I hastened into the Country, but it was only to be witness to her Death!" (B.L. Add. MS. 32,333, f. 62). Percy seems to have hastened home after the completion of his waiting, but his letter obscured the fact that a week elapsed between the receipt of his wife's letter and his departure for Easton Maudit.
    The inscription on the floor over the graves of Percy's daughters gives the date of Charlotte's death as 10 January. The parish register, Percy's diary, and his note in B.L. Add. MS. 32,327 (f. 175) give the date as 9 January.

19. B.L. Add. MS. 32,333, f. 62. *Thomas Percy & John Bowle*, 13.

20. B.L. Add. MS. 32,333, ff. 62, 67 (Letters to Cleiveland, 25 March and 13 Oct. 1771).

21. Bodl. Libr. (John Johnson Collection); MS. Percy c. 4, f. 1. *The Percy Letters*, 6:40–41 (Letters Paton to Percy, 3 Jan. 1771 and 17 Oct. 1772).

22. Bodl. Libr. (John Johnson Collection). Edmund Allen's bill dated the printing of the first edition in May and the second in July.

23. *Monthly Review* (Aug. 1771), 96–103; *Critical Review* (May 1771), 390–95.

24. *The Percy Letters*, 7:5 (Letter to Percy, 4 Jan. 1758).

25. *Baldwin's London Weekly Journal*, 21 Sept. 1771. The account of the meet-

ing was sent from Oxford by someone who used the initials "T. R." The text of Johnson's parody is from *Boswell for the Defence 1769–1774*, ed. William K. Wimsatt and Frederick A. Pottle (New York: McGraw-Hill, 1959), 177–78.

26. *The Letters of Samuel Johnson*, 1:249–50 (Letter 20 March 1771); Sir John Hawkins, *The Life of Samuel Johnson, LL.D.*, 389.

27. *The Hermit of Warkworth. A Northumberland Ballad. In Three Fits or Cantos* (London: T. Davies and S. Leacroft, 1771), 37–38.

28. Shortly after the poem came out, the Percys visited John Hawkins and his wife at Twickenham (Bertram H. Davis, *A Proof of Eminence: The Life of Sir John Hawkins* [Bloomington: Indiana Univ. Press, 1973], 107.

29. B.L. Add. MS. 32,333, ff. 64–65 (Letter Percy to Cleiveland, 13 Oct. 1771).

30. *The Diaries of a Duchess*, ed. James Greig (London: Hodder and Stoughton, 1926), 141, where the year is mistakenly given as 1770.

31. B.L. Add. MSS. 32,333, f. 64; 39,547, ff. 9–14 (Letters Percy to his wife, 30 Aug. and 3 Sept. 1771).

32. John Brooke, *King George III* (New York: McGraw-Hill, 1972), 272.

33. *The Diaries of a Duchess*, 141.

34. *The Correspondence of James Boswell and John Johnston of Grange*, ed. Ralph S. Walker (New York: McGraw-Hill, 1966), 271 (Letter Boswell to Johnston, 27 Aug. 1771); *Boswell for the Defence*, 21. Percy's statement in his diary that he saw Boswell at the Swan Inn may be an error resulting from his making the entry at a later date. Boswell's note invited him to a meeting at the White Hart Inn.

35. Brooke, 273. The gloves are in the collection of Kenneth Balfour.

36. Ibid., 275.

37. A late season guest at Alnwick Castle was General Pasquale Paoli, hero of the Corsican revolution, who impressed Percy as "a fine steady manly Character, fully equal to the high conception entertained of him by the English Nation" (B.L. Add. MS. 32,333, f. 64).

38. B.L. Add. MS. 32,333, f. 66 (Letter to Cleiveland, 13 Oct. 1771). Henry's master at Oakham was the Reverend Baptist Noel Turner (B.L. Add. MS. 32,327, f. 175).

39. Alnwick Castle MS., Northumberland Misc. Papers G/2/30–32 (Letters Lord Algernon Percy to Percy, 13 Nov. 1768; 4 Jan. 1769; 13 March 1770).

40. Ibid., 33 (Letter Lord Algernon Percy to Percy, Jan. 1772). Percy noted in his diary that he spent the morning of 17 March in Half Moon Street, and Richard Cumberland wrote to him at that address in a letter in the Hyde Collection dated Monday, 16 March—probably 1772, when 16 March fell on a Monday.

41. *Letters of James Boswell*, ed. Chauncey Brewster Tinker (Oxford: Clarendon Press, 1924), 1:192 (Letter 1 March 1773); B.L. Add. MS. 32,329, f. 68 (Letter 8 April 1773). Johnson's copy is at Yale University.

42. Bodl. MS. Percy c. 6, ff. 46–50. There seem to have been various delays in completing the book, the text of which was first printed in July 1767, when Percy sent sheets to Thomas Warton (*The Percy Letters* 3:128). In July and August 1768 he sent bound copies of the text to Samuel Pegge and Richard Farmer (Bodl. MS. Eng. Lett. d. 46, f. 667; *The Percy Letters* 2:147), both of them probably with title pages dated 1768, as in one of the British Library copies. The initial delay was apparently caused by Percy, who did not complete the preface until the end of November 1770. It is not clear when he completed the notes, which were appended to the printed volume. On 20 June 1770 Percy sent Edmund Allen a downpayment of £20 on the printing, and Allen submitted his bill of £90/7/6 sometime in 1771 after completing the printing, including a title page updated to 1770. The Duke of Northumberland paid the balance of £70/7/6 to Allen on 23 July 1771. The subsequent delay probably resulted from either the binder's slowness or the Duke's indisposition with the gout. Three persons to request copies were Samuel Salter, George Paton, and Thomas Davies (Letters Davies to Percy, 16 Sept. 1772 [Hyde Collection]; Paton to Percy, 17 Oct. 1772 [*The Percy Letters*, 6:43]; Salter to Percy, 27 Sept. 1773 [*Lit. Illus.*, 8:161–62]).

43. *The Regulations and Establishment of the Houshold of Henry Algernon Percy, at His Castles of Wresill and Lekinfield in Yorkshire. Begun Anno Domini M.D.XII* (London: privately printed, 1770), vi–vii.

44. John Pickford listed ten such manuscripts published between 1787 and 1844 (*Bishop Percy's Folio Manuscript*, 1:xl).

45. *Letters of Eminent Persons Addressed to David Hume* (London and Edinburgh, 1849), 317–24 (Letters Percy to Hume, 5 and 22 Jan. 1773); the date of Percy's opening letter is mistakenly printed as 5 Jan. 1772. *New Letters of David Hume*, ed. Raymond Klibansky and Ernest C. Mossner (Oxford: Clarendon Press, 1954), 197–99 (Letter Hume to Percy, 16 Jan. 1773). David Hume, *The History of England from the Invasion of Julius Caesar to the Revolution in 1688* (London, 1773; 1778), 3:461.

46. *Boswell for the Defence*, 65–66.

47. BC 188, Bowle-Evans Collection, University of Cape Town Libraries (Letter Percy to Bowle, 2 June 1772). B.L. Add. MS. 32,334, ff. 28–29 (Letter Duchess of Northumberland to Percy, 12 Aug. 1772).

48. B.L. Add. MS. 32,327, f. 175.

49. Mrs. Williams's letter is in the Hyde Collection.

50. B.L. Add. MS. 32,329, ff. 52–61 (Letters Warton to Percy, 30 March 1772; Warburton to Percy, 9 May 1772; Hoadly to Percy, 5 July and 17 Nov. 1772). Calder was secretary to the Duke of Northumberland.

51. *The Percy Letters,* 4:122. Yale Boswell Papers (Letter Percy to Boswell, 24 Aug. 1772). *Letters of James Boswell,* ed. Chauncey Brewster Tinker (Oxford: Clarendon Press, 1924), 1:191. Percy also revised Elijah Fenton's edition of Edmund Waller's poems for Thomas Davies, who indicated that he would publish the revision in two elegant volumes, but seems to have done nothing with it (Letter Davies to Percy, 16 Sept. 1772 [Hyde Collection]).

52. Letter Boswell to Percy, n.d. (Hyde Collection). *Thraliana: The Diary of Mrs. Hester Lynch Thrale (Later Mrs. Piozzi) 1776–1809,* 2d ed., ed. Katharine C. Balderston (Oxford: Clarendon Press, 1951), 1:173. Boswell, *Life of Johnson,* 3:321.

53. Bodl. MS. Add. A. 266, ff. 1–19. The manuscript contains statements by Percy and Owen, plus letters from Porteus to Percy dated 26 December 1772, 2 January 1773, and 12 February 1773. Porteus was appointed Bishop of Chester in 1777 and Bishop of London in 1787. In 1772 he was one of Percy's fellow Chaplains in Ordinary to George III. On 15 March 1772, at Owen's request, Percy preached a charity sermon at St. Olave's Hart Street (*Gazetteer,* 14 March 1772; diary, 15 March 1772).

54. *The Percy Letters,* 2:159–60; 170–71.

CHAPTER IX

Years of Waiting:
1773–1778

IN FEBRUARY 1773 Percy fulfilled a long-cherished dream by entering Henry—Harry, as he called him—at Westminster School. They arrived at Northumberland House from Easton Maudit on the evening of February 13, and on the next day, after introducing him to the Duchess, Lord Percy, and Lord Algernon, Percy escorted his son to Dean's Yard to present him to the headmaster, Dr. William Smith. On the fifteenth Harry was formally enrolled and presented to the undermaster, William Vincent, and probably on the same day he moved into the Dean's Yard house of John Jones, with whom he was to board.[1] No doubt the problem of adapting to a new school with numerous boys older than himself—he had celebrated his tenth birthday on February 7—was lessened by both his father's closeness and the presence among his schoolmates of Frank Price, grandson of the late Alice Cleiveland Price of Brynypys. The two boys, who were bedfellows and formfellows, quickly became close friends.[2]

Outside of school hours Harry and Frank seem to have been free to leave the school grounds in Percy's custody very much as he wished. He treated them to a performance of Dryden's *Double Gallant* on the evening of Thursday, February 18 and walked with them in the Mall on Sunday, March 14. On February 21 he took Harry to see Johnson, Mrs. Williams, and John Hoole, and on March 9 and 11 Harry joined him at Northumberland House to do his school exercises. On the twenty-fifth father and son walked together in Kensington Gardens and then dined at Northumberland House. Two days later, when Harry became feverish, Percy nursed him with Dr. James's Fever Powder and kept him at Northumberland House overnight.

Harry was recovered sufficiently the next day to accompany his father and Thomas Butler to Henry Reveley's for dinner, although afterwards he grew so ill that Percy took him to the doctor, who diagnosed his illness as measles and ordered him to stay in his room. During his week's confinement Percy visited him several times a day, and then, as Harry recovered, gave him a daily airing in the chaise. By April 13 Harry was ready to resume his school work.

It was a season of illnesses. On February 17 Percy saw Lord Algernon off on another continental tour by accompanying him as far as Dartford, and after Lord Algernon wrote home of vomiting blood Percy urged him to relieve his parents' anxiety by writing to them frequently of his progress, and he offered himself to go to his assistance. In late February or early March he returned to Easton Maudit because Barbara, in Percy's usual term, had been taken "dangerously ill," but she had recovered when he wrote to Lord Algernon on March 10.[3] At Northumberland House the gout was taking its toll. Lord Percy was stricken with it during the second week of March, and on April 5 the Duke was crippled by a serious attack that was still troubling him when Percy read to him on April 12.

In January Percy renewed his activity on the edition of Surrey's poems. With Surrey the first English poet to write in blank verse, he thought it appropriate to fill out his second volume with a history of blank verse and a list of nondramatic blank verse poems before *Paradise Lost*. John Bowle provided him with an account of blank verse in Italy and Spain. And, on February 18, Farmer sent him Thomas Wyatt's translation of the Psalms, which Percy, eager to add it to his Surrey edition, promptly transcribed and edited for the press.[4]

With the Club in the process of expanding its membership to twenty, he attended meetings on March 12, when David Garrick and Lord Charlemont were admitted, and on April 2 when the orientalist William Jones was admitted. He was also present on March 26 when Goldsmith arrived with a bloody face from a fight with Thomas Evans and William Kenrick over a personal attack upon him in Evans's *London Packet* of March 24. On three or four of its twenty-four days he attended the auction of James West's books and pictures and came away with his most coveted prize, the Isaac Fuller portrait of the poet John Cleiveland, for which he paid six guineas.[5] His diary contains the names of seventeen persons that he called upon on April 12, the day after Easter, including Mrs. Montagu, Lord Charlemont, and Sir Joshua Reynolds. On April 3 he went to Milton's house in Westminster's Petty France and, on April 17, with Goldsmith and William Jones to the house where the seventeen-year-old Thomas Chatterton committed suicide in 1770. On April 21 he took Harry and Frank to a performance of *Alexander the Great* at Covent Garden.

Another aspiring member of the Club that spring was James Boswell, whom Percy, walking with Sir John Hawkins, met by chance on April 7 as Boswell was leaving Topham Beauclerk's house. It was the first meeting of Boswell and Hawkins, the two men who in little more than a decade would be the chief rivals in writing Johnson's biography; and after introducing them Percy invited them to North-umberland House to view his portrait of Cleiveland. Over a dish of chocolate, Boswell recorded in his journal, he "listened with pleasure to Percy's active schemes of curious and amusing literature."[6] On April 16 he asked Percy to remember him at the meeting of the Club that evening; Johnson, Goldsmith, and Reynolds, he was pleased to say, had engaged to support him for membership.[7] Percy seems to have had no objection to Boswell's candidacy. But, while he attended that meeting and the next, he was apparently absent on April 30, when the balloting took place.

In April, with George Paton acting as intermediary, Percy ar-ranged to borrow the Bannatyne manuscript of early poems from Edinburgh's Advocates' Library, with the understanding that he could retain the manuscript for six months. It did not reach him until June, however, and on October 23 he requested an extension of the loan, his attendance on the Duke of Northumberland, he observed, having kept him from home much longer than usual that year. A two- to three-month extension was granted on November 15.[8]

On May 26 and 29 he sat for his portrait by Sir Joshua Reynolds, but its completion was delayed until the next year, perhaps by the death of Anne's mother and the need for Percy himself to leave for Alnwick shortly after the funeral.[9] His 1773 residence at Alnwick, the longest of his nine years' summer service for the Duke, extended from early or mid-July until late October. He had the pleasure once again of seeing Christopher Smart, who arrived for dinner on July 25 and spent the night. But for Percy the high point was a trip to Scotland, even though it meant missing the opportunity to show the castle to Johnson, who passed through Alnwick on August 13 on his way to join Boswell for their tour of Scotland and the Hebrides.[10] By contrast Percy's own tour was modest, a week's jaunt undertaken on an im-promptu invitation from his old friend George Durant, who stopped at the castle on August 7 on his way north with his fiancée, Maria Beaufoy, her brother Henry, and Mrs. Sarah Biddle. With the

Duke and Duchess away, Percy was free to accept the invitation, and the five of them left together that evening.[11]

It proved to be no ordinary tour. At Edinburgh, the next evening, they gathered in the chief Episcopal chapel, where Percy joined Durant and Miss Beaufoy in marriage. In the morning the five members of the wedding party were tourists again, making the rounds of Edinburgh Castle, Holyroodhouse, and the new town, although Percy disengaged himself long enough to pay his first visit to George Paton and to call on John Davidson and Boswell. Boswell also entertained him at breakfast on the morning of the tenth and took him to the Court of Session.

Leaving Henry Beaufoy behind, the others set out that afternoon for Inverary, with a first night's stop at Glasgow. They drove north the next day along Loch Lomond, which Percy, viewing it with the mountains behind it, thought "astonishing & fine beyond all description," and they reached Tarbet as night was approaching only to find the inn already filled. For fourteen miles they pushed on toward Cairndow, enjoying the view of Loch Long in the waning light; then, as the darkness intensified, they had to alight frequently and grope their way behind the coach. It was midnight when they reached the inn at Cairndow and roused the host and hostess from their bed.

What followed was not without elements of a medieval fabliau. Admitted reluctantly, they were nonetheless fed well in "the best Chamber," where room was made for them by the removal of an old man and woman from the bed. In the midst of supper they were surprised by the sound of snoring, which Percy traced to a large clothes press. "Unbuttoning" its door, he disclosed a bed and "the naked hairy arm of a Highlander, who lay there snoring & sleeping beside us." After supper a private room was found for the newlyweds, and Mrs. Biddle was offered the supper room, but "could not think of passing the night in . . . the Best Chamber with a naked Highlander." So, while she was shown to a room below stairs, Percy lay down between "very sweet clean Sheets" and fell sound asleep.

Below stairs Mrs. Biddle, preparing to lie down "(as she protests) *in her Cloaths*," was alarmed by the sound of snoring issuing from another press, but was quickly assured by the hostess that it was only her "*Papa* and *Mamma*."

> Upon wch supposing she m^t safely venture herself along with two decripid old People, she lay down with great composure. But in

the morn.ᵍ she heard one of the bare-footed Damsels of the House, come & open two or three Presses, & whisper to the Persons within to make no Noise, for "*Missy* lay there": and presently she saw come forth, buttoning up their Cloaths, 3 Soldiers and 2 Highlanders; who, to her great astonishment, she found had slept all night with her in the same chamber!

On the next morning, August 12, they proceeded around the head of Loch Fyne to Inverary Castle, which all agreed was much inferior to Alnwick, though its "great and noble" situation seemed to Percy all the more wonderful in a remote part of the country where "all the arts of life" fell far short of the perfection he considered to have been attained in England. The common people, he remarked to Anne, lived in rude stone huts covered with turf, usually without chimney or window, so that the smoke from the peat fires made its way out the same door that the light came in.[12]

The four travelers returned to Cairndow in the afternoon, and while dinner was being prepared at the inn, Percy slipped out to the little highland kirk on the edge of the loch. Inside, a group of barefooted boys and girls were reading to an elderly man with spectacles and a blue bonnet, while others pored over their lessons among the pews. To impress his visitor the schoolmaster called up two of his boys and placed a book in their hands, from which they began to read aloud. But they spoke in such a "Yelping Tone, so unnatural in accent & such a gutteral roughness," that after five minutes Percy, unable to detect the sounds of any language familiar to him, concluded that they were speaking their native Erse. To his astonishment, he discovered that they were reading Dryden's *Ode on St. Cecilia's Day*.

After dinner he and his companions set out for Tarbet along the military road constructed after the Jacobite rebellion of 1745. As they passed through Glen Croe, they came upon what Percy described to Anne as "the most extraordinary Scene in the World":

> We were got up a great height amid the hills, & yet in this elevation a clear level narrow Lake ran for two miles beside the road: beyond the lake rose a huge rocky mountain of great height; having its summit all the way ingulphed in a Cloud, that spread along it's brow like a Curtain; and here we saw a Couple of Eagles on the Wing soaring over our heads, and every now & then alighting on a huge craggy rock that projected out of the Cloud, but at such a tremendous height that we should not have known they were birds

of that size, if we had not compared them with the sheep that were grazing at nearly the same distance.

They spent the night of the twelfth at Tarbet and the next day drove eighty-one miles through Dumbarton and Glasgow to Edinburgh, where Percy took leave of his friends. On the fourteenth he returned to Alnwick and was drawn almost immediately into the controversy over the poems that Thomas Chatterton had asserted to be the work of a fifteenth-century monk, Thomas Rowley. Percy had expressed doubts more than once about the poems' authenticity, most recently during meetings with Lords Dacre, Camden, and Charlemont, but had withheld final judgment pending an opportunity to examine the manuscripts. On April 28, 1773, Lord Dacre had sent him a transcription of a Rowley manuscript made by William Barrett of Bristol, hoping that it would help to resolve his doubts, but it gave him no clues to the quality of the original manuscript. By midsummer, however, Lord Dacre had secured two of the Rowley parchments from Barrett, and he forwarded them to Percy on August 15 with a request that he make no copies and that he return the originals to Barrett when he finished with them. One of the parchments, known as the "Yellow Roll," contained two prose works. The other contained the "Song of Aella," "To John Lydgate," and "Lydgate's Answer."[13]

Percy's response to Lord Dacre was detailed and unequivocal: the works attributed to Rowley, he wrote on September 6, were undoubtedly "spurious and modern." By good fortune, he noted, he had with him the Duke of Northumberland's principal agent, Thomas Butler, whose long custody of the family's records and charters had qualified him as one of the best judges of old writings in England, and Butler without hesitation had pronounced Chatterton's work one of the "most bungling" forgery attempts he had ever seen. Handwriting, spelling, idiom—all were uncharacteristic of the fifteenth century; and even the discoloration, suggestive of age, had been superinduced by yellow ochre, which could be readily rubbed off. Yet, compelled though Percy was to dismiss the parchments as forgeries, he could not withhold his admiration for Chatterton's poetry. A collection of his pieces in one volume, he stated, would prove him, considering his youth and limited education, "one of the greatest Geniuses that ever existed in the World." He himself would subscribe to such a volume with pleasure.[14]

Unwilling to trust the parchments to the post, Percy informed

Lord Dacre that he was sending them to him in the care of his "faithful friend" Robert Chambers, who had accompanied Johnson as far north as Newcastle and was visiting at Alnwick. Chambers, who had been appointed a judge of the Supreme Court of Bengal, seems to have left Alnwick about the time of Percy's letter. But on October 8 Lord Dacre informed Percy by letter that the parchments had not yet been delivered, and Percy, understandably anxious, sent off a letter on October 15 urging Chambers to leave them at Lord Dacre's house as soon as possible but without fail before his departure for India. On October 28, after returning to Easton Maudit, he sent another reminder, and on November 7 he assured Lord Dacre that he had asked Chambers to deliver the parchments promptly. But by November 22 Lord Dacre had still not heard from Chambers and was pleading with Percy to secure the parchments before they were carried off to India.[15]

Percy's efforts were unavailing. Chambers had lost or misplaced the parchments, and Percy suffered the acute distress of one who knows that, whatever the circumstances, he will probably himself be held responsible. Lord Dacre, at least, was sympathetic. Do not blame yourself, he wrote on February 8, 1774: "Certainly whatever has happened wrong by perverse accident; was occasioned by your acting right. . . . The only person to blame is M.ͬ Chambers who if the things are lost has been guilty of a carelessness hardly to be excused." All they could do was to make the best of it and let Barrett know the truth. As a further gesture of good will, he invited Percy to have dinner with him on February 10.[16]

How conscientiously Chambers searched for the parchments is not apparent. Nor is it known whether he replied to Percy's two October letters, although Lord Dacre's February letter leaves no doubt that there had been some communication between them. But Chambers's preoccupation with both his removal to India and his impending marriage seems to have drawn him away from more than one of his friends. He is "so hurried, or so negligent, or so proud," Johnson wrote to Boswell on February 7, "that I rarely see him."[17] On March 8 Chambers married the sixteen-year-old Fanny Wilton, daughter of the sculptor Joseph Wilton, and in April he and his bride sailed for India, where he was to reside for the next thirty years. The parchments remained undelivered, the castoffs of an incredible negligence.

Four years later Percy made one more attempt in the hope that Chambers might have chanced upon the parchments while dipping into some of his books. Rowley's "pretended poems," he wrote on March 9, 1778, had gone through two editions and were received as genuine by numerous critics, "who make a great clamour about the disappearance of these two parchments." It would thus be most fortunate "if they could at last be produced, with all the evidence they carry of fraud and imposture." Entrusted to one of Percy's Woodington relations on his way to Bombay, the letter did not reach Chambers in Calcutta until 1785, by which time some of the more ardent Rowleians had accused Percy of willfully destroying the evidence of Rowley's authorship. Chambers replied in 1789, still unable to account for the parchments. They were to remain unaccounted for until his death in 1803, when his widow, going through his papers, discovered them among his letters.[18]

Among the Rowley believers in 1773 was Oliver Goldsmith, whose strongly held views probably helped to enliven the Club's discussions on March 26—the day that Goldsmith arrived with a bloody face—when Lord Charlemont read from the Rowley poems, and on April 16, when Garrick brought some of Chatterton's letters to the meeting. Joseph Cradock, sighing, "How frail, alas! are all human friendships!," asserted that their differences over Rowley drove Goldsmith and Percy to "an entire separation."[19] But if there was any break in their friendship it was certainly brief. Neither their letters nor Percy's diary suggests any coldness between them, and, however vehement their disputes about the authorship of the poems, they shared an unqualified admiration for the author's genius.

The evidence of the last twelve months of Goldsmith's life points, in fact, to a relationship as close as it had ever been. On March 13, 1773, Percy and Beauclerk enjoyed the privilege of special friends to attend a rehearsal of *She Stoops to Conquer* at Covent Garden, and on March 15 Percy went to the theater for the opening performance only to be turned away by a full house. He settled for watching the fourth performance from the Duchess of Northumberland's box on March 18.[20] On March 22 he spent the evening with Goldsmith, and on April 11 Goldsmith and Cradock called on him at Northumberland House. On April 21, four days after their visit to the house where Chatterton died, he and Goldsmith had breakfast together. Perhaps on that occasion, as Ralph Wardle suggested, Goldsmith asked Percy to be his biographer, for at their next meeting, on April 28, he dictated a memorandum about his early life and left Percy a small bundle of letters and other biographical materials.[21] On May 23 Goldsmith was the Duke of Northumberland's dinner guest at Sion House, in a company that included Percy, Walpole, Burke, Beauclerk, Joseph Banks, and Richard Owen Cambridge.

Later that year, rather than return to town from a pleasant sojourn at Windsor, Goldsmith asked Percy and Cradock to stop by his room in the Temple to correct a proof of his *History of the Earth, and Animated Nature*. Supplied with a note for Goldsmith's servant—"Honest John Give Doctor Percy, My History of Animals. Which you will find among my books"—they met by appointment and found a proof of a section concerning birds, with numerous reference works lying open near it. "Do you know anything about birds?" Percy asked. "Not an atom," Cradock replied; "do you?" "I scarcely know a goose from a swan," said Percy. But, Cradock reported, they set to work and found the task not very difficult.[22]

On March 10, 1774, Goldsmith called on Percy and they dined together at the Turk's Head, "tête-à-tête." But when Percy returned the visit on March 28 he found Goldsmith ill with a fever; and on Sunday, April 3, Percy wrote, Goldsmith was so "dangerously ill" that he "just knew me." That night he suffered a series of convulsions, and he died the next day. Percy, absent for a week in Sussex, returned on April 9 in time to view "poor Goldsmith's coffin" before he was buried privately in the Temple Church.[23]

The early weeks of the year brought illness and tragedy to the Percy family also, interspersed with some brighter moments. Harry, home at Easton Maudit, was busy at a very long school task when Percy wrote to William Cleiveland on January 17: twenty nonsense and ten sense verses to write in Latin and a hundred lines of Ovid to learn by heart. He had also played an important role in *The Siege of Tamor*, performed at Castle Ashby by the Earl of Northampton's children, and was presented with a guinea by Lord and Lady Sussex as he left the stage after the performance. Most of the players, his father observed, were twelve to fifteen, but Harry, though tall for his age, would not be eleven for another month. After the play, when the Earl of Northampton treated the company to a supper and ball, Percy and a neighboring clergyman danced by agreement with each other's wife, with Anne catching a terrible cold as a result, even though she rode home in Lord Sussex's coach. Twelve-year-old Barbara danced at the ball, too, but without any ill effect.[24]

Percy for a time was "very much indisposed" with an unidentified ailment and was forbidden by the doctor to do any writing. But the most serious illness to attack the family was the chincough—whooping cough—which, Percy informed Paton, threatened the lives of most of the children.[25] The older ones recovered, but Hester, not yet twenty months, was unable to fight it off and died on February 19. She had "just begun to prattle and be very engaging," Harry wrote to William Cleiveland on August 30, and her death "very much affected my Mamma's health." She was buried on February 23 in a small vault near her sisters beneath the aisle of the church.[26]

Percy's indisposition did not prevent him from responding to a scurrilous memoir of Grainger printed in the December *Westminster Magazine* and reprinted in the *Whitehall Evening-Post* of January 4–6. According to the anonymous memoirist, Grainger, having a daughter who "he had but too many reasons to be convinced was not his own," left St. Kitts for England "full of chagrin and despair," his peace of mind destroyed by the suspicion of his wife's infidelity.[27] Perhaps without the interposition of Edmund Allen, who was on the scene in London, the newspaper would have ignored Percy's dismissal of the allegation as "utterly false." But Allen threatened the proprietors with a prosecution for libel, and they inserted the response in the issue of January 11–13—without a fee, he informed Percy on January 15.[28] During his whole time in England, Percy wrote, "the Doctor appeared to correspond in the most affectionate manner with his wife and family; whose absence from him he mentioned, upon all occasions, as the subject of his most tender regret."[29]

Perhaps at this period, when he was away from London for six weeks, Percy occupied himself also with putting together a forty-five-page manuscript dated 1774 and entitled "A Dictionary of the Peculiar Words and Phrases used in or near the Town of Bridgnorth in Shropshire."[30] The entries were written in a copy book used by young Henry in April and May 1771, when he was kept at home following his nearly fatal bout with the ulcerated sore throat, and they reflect not only Percy's intimate knowledge of his home town but his considerable artistic talent as well. Under "Bylet," defined as "any island in the river Severn," he noted that "The *Bannut-tree Bylet* [is] an island below Bridgn.: Bridge, formerly remarkable for a large Bannut or Walnut Tree." For "Caff," a small pickaxe for cutting roots, "Drag," a horse-drawn sledge or cart "Not unlike an Irish Car," and "Hod," a wooden scuttle, he even inserted small pen-and-ink drawings in the manner of modern dictionaries. In introducing the letter "H" he reported that the "Bridgnorth Dialect is distinguished by an universal misap[p]lication of the Aspirate H.—applying where it sh.ᵈ not be and omitting it where it should." No doubt as Percy wrote this he recalled the inscription over the hearth of his Bridgnorth "owse," a word that he included in the dictionary under "O."³¹

On October 19, 1769, Johnson had advised Boswell to complete a dictionary of words peculiar to Scotland, of which Boswell had shown him a specimen: "Ray has made a collection of north-country words," said Johnson. "By collecting those of your country, you will do a useful thing towards the history of the language."³² Perhaps a similar suggestion by Johnson had started Percy on his own modest compilation, which, though it probably went further than Boswell's, seems never to have been made ready for a publisher.

On May 30, 1774, Percy resumed sitting for the portrait that Reynolds had begun a year before, and he returned for a final sitting on June 1.³³ Reynolds himself pronounced the portrait "a well finished piece," Percy informed the Duchess of Northumberland on May 31, and perhaps one reason for the Percys' entertaining Johnson, Mrs. Williams, and the Hoole family at dinner and supper on June 4 was to show them the new portrait, which Percy later hung in his apartment in Northumberland House.³⁴ These days, one can judge it only from the engraving in mezzotint made of it by William Dickinson in 1775: the original has been destroyed, and a copy of it made sometime before March 1780 has disappeared from public view.³⁵ The half-length Dickinson engraving—a fine one—shows Percy in velvet cap and gown and clerical bands, with the folio manuscript clutched in his left hand: handsome, alert, and dignified, and proud to a degree perhaps not unbecoming a King's chaplain who had edited the *Reliques of Ancient English Poetry*.

Percy crowded other activities into the late spring of 1774. He had supper with Garrick in late May and, having garnered the latest theatrical gossip, sent it on to the Duchess of Northumberland in his letter of May 31. On the thirty-first he and Anne also drove to Harrow for dinner and tea, and on the next day he was visited at Northumberland House by Goldsmith's brother Maurice and by one of the Rivingtons of the bookseller family. On the morning after the June 4 dinner for Johnson, Mrs. Williams, and the Hooles, he preached at Spring Garden Chapel in Charing Cross, and then, after a drive with Frank Price, he and Anne entertained Michael Lort at home in the evening. Toward mid-June he was engaged by Frances Reynolds, Sir Joshua's sister, to meet Hannah More and her sisters, who, as Miss

More wrote, were surprised to find him "quite a sprightly modern, instead of a rusty antique."[36]

Percy had probably met Miss Reynolds through either her brother or Edward Lye, and both he and Anne found her a good friend. His diary shows her spending the evening with Anne on two of his Club nights: on March 23, 1772, when they went to Drury Lane to see Garrick, and on May 13, 1774, when they had supper together. But her best-known connection with Percy was through another Johnson parody of *The Hermit of Warkworth*, which, according to George Steevens, was composed impromptu at Miss Reynolds's tea table in Percy's presence. Responding to the customary praise of the poem for its artful simplicity, Johnson announced that he could rhyme just as well in "common narrative and conversation." And he started in:

> I therefore pray thee, Renny dear,
>   That thou wilt give to me,
> With cream and sugar soften'd well,
>   Another dish of tea.
>
> Nor fear that I, my gentle maid,
>   Shall long detain the cup,
> When once unto the bottom I
>   Have drank the liquor up.
>
> Yet hear, alas! this mournful truth,
>   Nor hear it with a frown;—
> Thou canst not make the tea so fast
>   As I can gulp it down.

"And thus," wrote Steevens, "he proceeded through several more stanzas, till the Reverend Critic cried out for quarter."[37]

On July 6, 1774, Percy left for Alnwick, where he was drawn inescapably into an activity for which he had little taste. Lord Algernon, by then twenty-four, and Sir John Delaval, an experienced politician, were seeking election to Parliament as Northumberland's two knights of the shire, and in a summer that fell almost midway between the Boston Tea Party and the Battle of Lexington, the campaign was heated and intense. Although Percy managed a tour along the border during the September audit week, there was little other relief. The canvassing for votes began at Alnwick on July 27 and within a week took him to Belford, Bambrugh, and (perhaps as a diversion) the

Farne Islands, but probably his most effective persuasion came through his pen, for which, even before the Northumberland campaign was concluded, an urgent call came from the south: "After fighting in the Papers for three Months . . . without intermission, Parliam! was unexpectedly dissolved, & we were suddenly obliged to hasten up to Westm! where came on, one of the most busy contests ever known in the Kingdom."[38]

In Westminster Lord Thomas Pelham Clinton and Lord Percy, absent with his troops in America, were running mates for the city's two seats in the House of Commons. Inevitably Lord Percy was attacked as an absentee candidate, but in 1774 his position of leadership in America could be turned to his advantage. A notice printed in the October 18 *Public Advertiser*, perhaps one of many written by Percy, commended him for his loyalty and devotion to England's interests and quoted from one of his letters to demonstrate his compassion for the Americans. When the final count was taken on October 26, he had drawn 4994 votes, 250 more than his successful running mate and almost 2500 more than his closest opponent, Lord Mountmorres.

In Northumberland, where the polls were closed on October 21, Lord Algernon outdrew even Sir John Delaval, who defeated his closest opponent by a mere handful of votes. The contests north and south, Percy commented to William Cleiveland, "ended so much to the Honour of the Family I reside with as to make one amends for all the fatigue."[39]

By July of 1774 Percy had secured a further extension of his loan from the Advocates' Library and had taken the Bannatyne manuscript to Alnwick, fully intending to complete his work on it and return it before the summer's end. It was not impossible, he had written Paton on March 24, that he would personally carry it to Edinburgh in a post-chaise. But politics was no respecter of scholarly intentions. With no progress to show for weeks of his Alnwick residence, he had to plead for more time, which—with or without the intervention offered by Boswell in mid-August— was readily granted. As late as December 1, Alexander Brown, the librarian of the Advocates' Library, conveyed to him through Paton that he need not hurry to return the manuscript. By then, of course, it was in London or Easton Maudit once again.[40]

Percy's problem in finding time for the manuscript was compounded by other developments. About August 20 he received the manuscript he had requested of the second volume of David Herd's *Ancient and Modern Scottish Songs*, and his quick review of it persuaded him that some changes were desirable. With so many mutilated or fragmentary poems, he wrote Paton on August 22, it would be improved if most of them were repaired like some of those in the *Reliques*, or if they were replaced by more perfect copies that might be found elsewhere. A search of that kind would take time, however, and to avoid a long delay he suggested that Herd "collect all that are tolerably perfect, in this or any other Collection," and supplement them with Scottish poems that Percy would supply from Cambridge's Maitland manuscript. Others, he added, might be transcribed by the editor from the Bannatyne manuscript "when I return it." As for some of the more fragmentary poems, with Herd's permission he would make up their deficiencies and insert them in the collection that he himself planned to publish in three or four years. Herd could then reprint as many as he wished in a third volume of his own collection.[41]

Paton replied on August 29 that Percy's proposal was acceptable to both Herd and his printer. Thus Percy, unable to complete his examination of one manuscript, had set himself a formidable task with another. Perhaps, if little had distracted him, he might have been able to live up to at least part of his intentions. But Percy's life was never that simple. In London he suffered a fall and returned to Easton Maudit in early November, confined to his room while he nursed a "very disagreeable" swelling in one of his legs. At almost the same time Anne became "extremely ill" with an abdominal inflammation that lasted till the end of the year. Percy himself remained a cripple throughout the month of December and missed his regular tour of waiting at St. James's. It was sometime in January before he was able to resume his duties at Northumberland House.[42]

There were further complications. In the spring of 1775 the Duchess of Northumberland lay "for many days at the point of death," keeping Percy, as he wrote William Cleiveland, "in a close & unremitted attendance upon her" at Sion House. The Duchess had scarcely recovered when Percy himself became ill. In June Algernon returned from abroad to marry, not Lady Betty Windham, his love of a few years before, but Isabella Susanna Burrell, daughter of Peter Burrell, Esq., of Beckenham in Kent. Percy officiated at the wedding, held on June 8 in the drawing room of Sion House in the presence of the Duke and Duchess, the bride's mother, and a few other relatives and friends. At the end of June Anne was afflicted once again with her severe illness "of the bilious kind."[43]

Somehow, in spite of illnesses and the necessary attendance on his own and his patron's families, Percy managed to complete some scholarly work. On June 15, at Sion House, he prepared copy of the *Reliques*'s third edition for the printer, and on June 24, in London, he wrote an account of Prudhoe Castle for Captain Francis Grose's *Antiquarian Repertory*. He finished his examination of the Bannatyne manuscript, but he never undertook the major revision of Herd's manuscript that he had proposed on August 22, 1774. With Paton having reminded him on March 25 and July 21 that Herd and his printer were waiting to send it to the press, Percy packed up the Herd manuscript together with the Bannatyne manuscript and a small parcel for Lord Hailes, and on July 28 sent them off to Paton in the Edinburgh wagon.[44]

He had held the Bannatyne manuscript for twenty-five months and the Herd for eleven, long by almost anyone's standards, though perhaps not Percy's. William Cole noted that he lent Percy the manuscripts of John Crew's poems in 1767 and got them back fourteen years later![45] Generous with his own books and manuscripts, Percy assumed that others would be equally generous, and by and large he was proved correct.[46] He could hardly count on such liberality from a library, however, as he had discovered in 1762 when he asked Farmer for some of Cambridge's manuscript treasures. What is surprising with the Bannatyne manuscript is not that Percy kept it as long as he did, but that the library permitted it to circulate at all. Gracious as well as generous, the librarian, after the manuscript's return, commended Percy for improving it by inserting additional references in the index.[47]

With the Herd manuscript Percy had more to answer for. He promised much and gave nothing but a year's delay. Perhaps the best that can be said is that, as often happened, he was dreaming in good spirit even though beyond his means. It would nonetheless have been appropriate for him to offer Herd a more attractive compensation than he outlined to Paton in his July 28 letter: "I hope now in the Course of next Winter to prepare a 4th Volume of Reliques for the Press, and when I have selected some of Maitland's Poems for my own Work, I shall see what I can spare for your friend's Publication." The dreamer was dreaming still, but the dream contained only a few leftovers for David Herd.

In the late winter and early spring, before the succession of illnesses that preempted his attention, Percy continued his social activities much as in previous years. His curiosity about China led him on March 11 to seek out a visitor from Canton with the unlikely name of Whang-a-tong; and on March 24 Dr. Daniel Solander called at Northumberland House with Omai, the attractive young Tahitian who had captured Londoners' hearts. That evening he attended the Club, where, as Boswell reported, Johnson was in high spirits and attacked Swift. Boswell wondered, as perhaps Percy did also, to hear him say of *Gulliver's Travels*, "When once you have thought of big men and little men, it is very easy to do the rest." On March 27 Percy was among the group that Reynolds gathered for Frances Abington's benefit performance at Drury Lane Theatre, but, arriving late, was unable to sit with his friends. Boswell spent several hours with him the next day, reading a collection of letters from Voltaire to Richard Rolt and listening to the anecdotes that Percy had recorded during his interview with Goldsmith on April 28, 1773. Percy also showed him a bunch of the papers that Goldsmith had given him, a mere handful, as Boswell observed, of the letters, notes, newspaper clippings, and scraps that Percy had assembled for his projected life of Goldsmith. On April 2, when they walked together in the Mall, they were joined by John Hoole, who invited them to dine with him. Although Percy at first agreed, he recalled later that the Duchess was at home alone and might want him—an excuse to get a better dinner, Beauclerk surmised when Boswell told him of it.[48]

In early August, while the Duke stayed behind nursing his gout, Percy attended Lord Algernon and his bride into Northumberland to meet the gentlemen of the country. The Duchess, whom he found much improved in health, was already in residence at the castle, as was Thomas Gray, who had also been at Sion House with Percy in mid-June. Lord Percy, by then a major general, was still in America, encamped near Boston. On August 12 he wrote to Percy from "Mt. Whoredom"—an odd place, as he noted, to be writing to a clergyman—to thank him for about twenty letters, all apparently received since his previous letter to Percy on November 25, 1774.[49]

Particularly welcome to Percy was an October letter from Thomas Apperley, who had married Anne Wynn and was living in Wales. The letter, Percy replied on October 14, "recalled a thousand pleasing ideas, & gave me the most sincere delight. I had heard so high a character of Mrs. Apperley & always had so good an opinion of your taste and judgment, that I knew you must be very happy in your choice." Much less welcome was the news a few weeks later of fifteen-year-old Lady Barbara Yelverton's elopement to Gretna Green with Colonel Edward Gould. Percy wrote a consoling letter to the Earl of Sussex, who seems never to have been reconciled to the marriage.[50]

Percy's chief scholarly accomplishment in 1775 was the publication of the third edition of the *Reliques*, for which Dodsley had paid him twenty guineas on June 21, 1774.[51] Although the text was ready by June 1775, publication seems to have been delayed until December, when Dodsley advertised the new edition in a list of books bearing his imprint.[52] Surprisingly, considering how many new poems Percy had acquired since 1767, the third edition was not appreciably different from the second, but, of course, he was setting poems aside for his projected *Ancient English and Scottish Poems* or a fourth volume of the *Reliques*.[53] Most notable among the changes were the substitution of an entirely new text for "The Battle of Otterbourne" called to his attention by Thomas Tyrwhitt, and the replacement of "The Wanton Wife of Bath" with the saintly "Bride's Burial."[54] No doubt the King's chaplain was reluctant to continue his public association with an unrepentant sinner like the Wife of Bath, who at heaven's gate asserts her moral superiority to such biblical worthies as Adam, Jacob, David, Solomon, Paul, and Peter.

Another project, probably of late 1775, was carried to the verge of publication and then abandoned. Attracted to Spanish poetry almost as early as to *Don Quixote*, Percy, to show the similarity between early English and Spanish poetry, had published his translations of two Spanish poems at the end of the *Reliques*'s first volume, one of them with its Spanish text. By 1775 he had translated five additional poems, one from *Don Quixote* and four from the *Historia de las Guerras Civiles de Granada*, the source of both poems in the *Reliques*. He had also engaged Samuel Leacroft, publisher of *The Hermit of Warkworth*, to publish them in a sumptuous quarto edition entitled *Ancient Songs Chiefly on Moorish Subjects* and illustrated with engravings and woodcuts. Before giving up the project he had annotated the texts, read proof, and secured illustrations for both the title page and a frontispiece. On March 2, 1776, he paid Leacroft £25 out of his account at Drummond's Bank and on June 10 another £10, an indemnification perhaps for Leacroft's investment in the publication.[55]

Why Percy stopped short of publication is not apparent, but if, as D. Nichol Smith suggested, he was dissatisfied with his translations, his dissatisfaction may have been compounded by the fear of what a critic like Johnson would do with them.[56] Johnson, in fact, had already found fault with one of his translations in the *Reliques*, which Percy opened with the following stanza:

> Gentle river, gentle river,
>   Lo, thy streams are stain'd with gore,
> Many a brave and noble captain
>   Floats along thy willow'd shore.

When Mrs. Thrale praised the translation to Johnson, he replied that "he could do it better himself—as thus":

> Glassy water, glassy water,
>   Down whose current clear and strong,
> Chiefs confus'd in mutual slaughter,
>   Moor and Christian, roll along.[57]

Perhaps Percy was unaware of Johnson's verses, which were uttered privately to Mrs. Thrale and not published until 1786. He had had enough experience with *The Hermit of Warkworth* to know what Johnson was capable of, however, and he was too proud and sensitive to expose himself unnecessarily to further ridicule. Yet whatever his motives, his attention to Spanish poetry deserves to be remembered as one more manifestation of his pioneering spirit, for no one else in England was translating Spanish poetry for publication as early as the 1765 *Reliques* or even the proposed *Ancient Songs* of 1775.[58] When John Pinkerton published translations of six Spanish poems in his *Select Scotish Ballads* of 1781, he acknowledged that Percy's translations had excited his curiosity.[59]

In the autumn of 1775 Percy enjoyed what he called a "comfortable respite" with his family in Easton Maudit. Back in London by the third week in November, he called on his brother, Reynolds, John Calder, and others, took a walk into the City with Michael Lort, and attended the November 24 Club meeting, when Adam Smith was elected to membership. On December 4 Harry was his father's guest at the chaplain's table along with Reynolds, Cambridge, Thomas Barnard, dean of Derry, and Richard Hind, vicar of St. Anne's, Soho, who had been Percy's tutor at Christ Church. On the tenth Percy preached at the Chapel Royal before the King and Queen, and, his period of waiting shorter than usual, he returned to Easton Maudit in time to conduct the Christmas services at his own churches. The high point of his post-Christmas activities was a dinner at Reynolds's on January 11 with Johnson, Burke, Adam Smith, Gibbon, Henry Thrale, Charles Burney, and four or five others from the Johnson circle. After the dinner Percy went to tea with Miss Reynolds.[60]

Early in 1776, when the family was again residing on Bolton Street, he gave some attention to a project that one would hardly have expected of a literary scholar. "I have been lately amusing myself," he wrote to Lord Hailes on February 29, "by tracing the existence of the *Wolf* and ascertaining the time of its extinction in different parts of this Island. I can prove by records," he went on, "that it existed in the Northumberland Wastes since the Conquest.—In the Marches of Wales as late as the reign of K. Edwd I. . . . And I have been told, that it is hardly a century ago, since the last of them was killed . . . [in the Highlands] by Sr Huon Cameron of Lochiel."[61] He concluded by asking for any information on the subject that Lord Hailes and his friends could provide.

Lord Hailes's reply has not survived, but Boswell learned from Percy on March 17 that he was writing a history of the wolf in Great Britain, and he passed the information on to Johnson while they were traveling from Stratford to Henley in Warwickshire on their way to Lichfield. Why the wolf? snorted Johnson. "Why does he not write of the bear, which we had formerly? Nay, it is said we had the beaver; or why does he not write of the grey rat?—the Hanover rat as it is called, because it is said to have come into this country about the time that the family of Hanover came? I should like to see *The History of the Grey Rat, by Thomas Percy, D.D. Chaplain in Ordinary to His Majesty.*" "I'm afraid," said Boswell, "a court chaplain could not decently write of the grey rat." "He need not give it the name of the Hanover rat," replied Johnson.[62]

Percy probably did not carry the project far, but, Johnson's laughter notwithstanding, it had at least one literary application, as Percy had shown at a meeting of the Club on April 7, 1775—perhaps the occasion when the idea of writing such a history occurred to him. During a discussion of Ossian, he remarked that it was an "objection to the antiquity of the poetry said to be Ossian's, that we do not find the wolf in it, which must have been the case had it been of that age."[63] Whether or not he found other applications, Britain's extinct wolf was an unlikely candidate for Percy's prolonged contemplation, and it is not heard of again in his letters or other papers.

During the spring or summer of 1776, Percy turned his Goldsmith materials over to Johnson, whom he considered best qualified to write Goldsmith's biography. He was not present at a dinner at Reynolds's in May and thus was unable to join in the unsuccessful round robin, signed by Reynolds and his eleven guests, asking Johnson to revise the epitaph that he had prepared for Goldsmith's monument in Westminster Abbey's Poets' Corner and to change it from Latin into English. Percy had a small part in the epitaph nonetheless: he was to supply the date of Goldsmith's birth. Relying largely on Goldsmith's "uncertain recollection," he settled on November 29, 1731, which was duly graved in the epitaph. As it turned out, at least the day was incorrect. Goldsmith was born on November 10, probably in 1730.[64]

The war in America, particularly after the Declaration of Independence, became the daily focus of newspaper report and public discussion. For the Northumberland family, with the elder son a key figure in the effort to suppress the rebellion, it was a source equally of pride and concern. Percy, assuming the only role available to him, continued to correspond with Lord Percy—promoted by 1776 to the rank of lieutenant general—and he kept the Duke and Duchess abreast of the news when they were out of reach of the London newspapers. From the country he submitted occasional short pieces to the newspapers, eager tributes to a young leader whose rise, by age thirty-four, if not unprecedented, was certainly extraordinary. Both the Duke and the Duchess expressed their appreciation in letters, he on October 19 and she on the thirty-first. The Duchess was pleased to have Percy confirm her suspicion that he had written the unsigned pieces, especially one in which a returning soldier lavished praise on Lord Percy for his humanity and generosity to his troops and to the widows of those who had fallen at Bunker Hill. "I . . . am very glad I was not mistaken," she wrote, "as I look upon it as a Mark of your Friendship to me & mine wch I assure you I value very much."[65]

The Duke announced in his letter that he and the Duchess would not be leaving for Bath until close to Christmas, and that Percy meanwhile should feel free to remain in the country pursuing the researches he was "so obligingly engaged in." No doubt he had in mind Percy's inquiries into the history of the House of Percy, a project the Duke had commended to him almost from their first acquaintance. Although Percy had responded enthusiastically, his work on the project had been largely sporadic and indirect. But its usefulness could hardly have been questioned. His editing of the border ballads for the *Reliques*; the background studies for *The Hermit of Warkworth* and the Northumberland household book; the compilation of Percy genealogies; the tour of the Percys' Yorkshire estates; even the summer excursions out of Alnwick—these and other activities had steeped him in the Percy lore and mystique and qualified him at least to attempt the ambitious history which, in his first rush of excitement, he had laid out for himself: "following the thread of this family, . . . to trace out the various changes in taste, customs, fashions and opinions, and all the revolutions which the Human Mind has undergone from it's earliest state of savage ignorance and rudeness, to its present state of politeness and refinement."[66]

A mass of detail remained to be uncovered and assimilated, but by 1776 Percy seems to have found the time and inclination to probe more deeply and comprehensively. Perhaps his efforts were stimulated by the knowledge that a new edition of Collins's *Peerage of England* would soon be in preparation and he could thus put his information and experience to use in revising its lusterless article on the Percys. A further impetus must have come from his correspondence with Lionel Charlton, who was writing a history of Whitby and Whitby Abbey, other ancient Percy centers, and, having received much help from Percy, shared with him the results of his own investigations.[67]

The Northumberland branch of the family was not the only one to draw Percy's attention in 1776. He had long hoped to find conclusive evidence of a link between the Worcester and Northumberland Percys that he had heard his father talk of; and, in changing the spelling of his name from Piercy to Percy in 1756, he was, in fact, asserting a connection between the two families. On September 2, 1775, he was startled, even angered, by a brief notice in the *Newcastle Journal* touching on this very subject: "It is said that the————chaplain to a certain great man not far from Alnwick Castle, owes his present situation and success in life to the happy thought of changing his name from Pierce or Pierson, to that he bears at present." Percy did not reply to this bit of malice. But on the day of the notice he wrote out, apparently for the Duke and Duchess, an explanation of the change in spelling, noting at the end that he had made the change many years before he had the honor to know them.[68]

Replied to or not, the notice was to have a lasting effect. "I judged it necessary," Percy wrote on April 24, 1776, "to collect, and leave with my Family such plain Proofs, and to make an Assemblage of such attested Papers, as should vindicate my Memory from this, or any other similar Charge. . . . I could not be indifferent to the removal of a calumny, which seemed to affect my Character as an honest Man, and to represent me as a base unprincipled Impostor."

No doubt he had reason to believe that questions about his change of name would persist. "The late Bishop Lyttleton," he added as a footnote to his April 24 statement, "once told me he had heard my Name was Pershouse: Mr. [James] Bindley tells me, he has been informed that it was Pearsall."

The fruit of Percy's determination was not just one collection but two. Although by no means identical, the two volumes duplicate each other at numerous points and contain between them a variety of anecdotes, memoirs, letters, certificates, records, and illustrations. The first, in which Percy pasted the newspaper clipping and entered his April 24 statement, was "Original Papers relating to the Percys of Worcester, first begun to be collected in 1776 and afterwards continued occasionally."[69] The second—"Collections relating to the Percy Family, &c. but Chiefly to the Percys of Worcester"—was begun in 1778.[70] It became the more substantial of the two, and Percy continued to add to it through much of the rest of his life.

He probably began the first at Northumberland House early in 1776 and added to it during a shorter than usual summer residence at Alnwick. He may also have done some further work at Bridgnorth, where he preached at St. Mary's on September 8 and St. Leonard's on September 15 before settling down at Easton Maudit to await his call to St. James's.[71] His interests, of course, were numerous: recording, for example, the births, baptisms, marriages, and burials of his parents, children, and other relations. But his overriding concern was his Percy ancestry. He could trace it back through six generations without difficulty: through his grandfather Arthur Percy, the first Percy to leave Worcester for Bridgnorth; Arthur Percy's grandfather Thomas Percy, mayor of Worcester, who died in 1663; and Thomas's grandfather James Percy, who died at Worcester in 1574. At that point certainty had to yield to conjecture and oral tradition. James Percy *appeared* to be the grandson of the first Percy to settle in Worcester, a "Gentleman," Percy had heard his father say, "descended from a younger Branch of the Earl of Northumberland's Family." "The first PERCY . . . retired to Worcester for Concealment; And brought with him one Son, then very young. As also what he could save out of the Wrecks of his Fortune in Money & Jewels. . . . My Father had understood that He had been obliged to withdraw from his native County in consequence of his having had the misfortune to kill his adversary in some Duel or Fray."[72] Percy's examination of evidences at Alnwick Castle and Sion House led him to believe that the first Worcester Percy was John Percy, Esq. "sometime of Newton by the Sea in Northumberland, who was son and heir of Sir Henry Percy knight, who was eldest son and heir of Sir Ralph Percy knight the Third Son that left Issue of Henry Percy Second Earl of Northumberland."[73]

As Percy discovered, the tradition concerning the first Percy had also come down in the Worcester families of Mary Perrins, daughter of Anthony Percy, and Anne Davis, daughter of Captain Thomas Percy. Mrs. Davis died before Percy began his serious inquiries, but because her husband had been a tenant of Sir Hugh Smithson before he became Earl of Northumberland, she had become known to the future Duchess of Northumberland, who attested on January 21, 1769, to having been informed by Mrs. Davis that she had seen the Percy arms "on the groin'd arches of her father's cellar at Worcester." A letter of inquiry by Percy later that year brought the disappointing news that the house had been rebuilt as an inn and no evidence of the arms was to be found.[74]

The Duchess apparently accepted Percy's proofs of lineage. And James Boswell, describing himself as "a Lawyer accustomed to the consideration of evidence, and as a Genealogist versed in the study of pedigrees," was "fully satisfied." Modern genealogists have been less receptive to them. One of the editors of *The Complete Peerage* informed L. F. Powell that Percy's "claim will not bear examination. The ancestor from whom Percy professed to derive his descent, namely Sir Ralph Percy, . . . died unmarried."[75] There are good reasons to question Percy's claim: John Percy and his son remain shadowy figures in his account, their migration to Worcester not demonstrated beyond a doubt and their marriages totally unaccounted for. But, when he came to revise the article on the Percys for *The Peerage of England*, Percy explicitly refuted the view that Sir Ralph Percy died unmarried by citing evidences at Alnwick Castle and Sion House to show that he married Eleanor, the daughter of Laurence Acton, Esq. [76]

As he was about to begin his December waiting in 1776, Percy invited Johnson and Langton to dine with him at the chaplain's table on December 3, but, though Johnson accepted for both, he developed a cold on December 2 which he feared might hinder his attendance. And something much more serious than a cold may have held Percy at Northumberland House. "A return of all her former symptoms,"

Percy wrote the Countess of Aylesford, "... for some days filled us with all the most alarming apprehensions for the Duchess of Northumberland." She died late in the evening of December 5, the day that she would have been celebrating her sixtieth birthday.[77]

The Duke, who was only just recovering from the gout, was inconsolable, and he was persuaded to move into Lord Algernon's house in Harley Street as preparations for the funeral began. Percy probably wrote the obituary printed in all the London newspapers; and on the eighth he excused himself from conducting prayers for the princes in order to sit with the Duke. The scattered remnants of his diary for this period show that he sat with him again on December 15 after preaching the noon service at the Chapel Royal and visited him on the sixteenth and seventeenth. On the eighteenth, the day of the funeral, he was able to carry him news of Lord Percy, and that evening he and Theophilus Lindsey, the Duke's other chaplain, rode in the lead coach to Westminster Abbey, where the Duchess was interred in the small Chapel of St. Nicholas. According to newspaper report, a crowd of three thousand had gathered to view the funeral, and in the confusion some people were injured and some of the monuments damaged.[78]

In the Duchess—"Ever distinguished for the most tender Affection for her Family & Friends," as he wrote for the inscription on her monument— Percy had indeed lost a good friend.[79] She had encouraged his writing, been grateful for his attention to all her family, and welcomed his correspondence. Her letters to him from the Continent are filled with her impressions of towns and palaces, art treasures and people: a varied stream of amusement, admiration, and ridicule flowing out of her knowledge that in Percy she could count on an appreciative audience. Her death, of course, raised questions about his future, but, as he had done before, the Duke sought to allay his fears. Being "the only patron I could look up to for active Services," Percy wrote to William Cleiveland on January 9, 1777, a day before setting out for Easton Maudit, "[the Duke] has twice since her death renewed the kindest promises to me & apologized for its not having been in his power to serve me hitherto."[80]

Within a week Will, married to Mary Jones of Stadhampton since 1767, had a happiness of his own to share. "Good news, rare news!" he wrote to Percy on January 14: his wife had given birth to a daughter just the day before, "on my dear Father's Birth-Day." On the eighteenth Percy wrote to express his pleasure in Will's news; but three days later word came from Will that his "poor dear little Girl" had died on the fifteenth of injuries received in her difficult birth. Will's "melancholy news," Percy replied on the twenty-first, came "so close on the heels of your former joiful account" that it was all "the more affecting." But Will's wife having been spared, he went on, "has been a most happy providence, & will tend to console you for your disappointment."

Once again their letters crossed in the mail. On the very next day Percy responded to Will's "short but afflicting" letter of January 19 containing the news that his wife—"my dear Invaluable Partner"— had died that morning. The letter, Percy wrote, "was read by my Wife with many tears, & the shock of such unexpected News, has made her quite ill.— How shall we be able to give you comfort under a Distress, which no Misfortune in this Life can equal? When I reflect what my own feelings would be under such a Calamity, I cannot even attempt to console you."[81]

In the hope that a change of scene would benefit him, Percy urged Will to join his family for the month at Percy's disposal before the Duke returned to London from Bath. "Books," he argued, "rural Solitude & the soothing quiet converse of a Family attached to you by every tye of Blood & Friendship, must suit best the present drooping State of your mind." But Will was not easily moved from his lifelong home in Worcester, where he continued to reside with his sister, although he managed to visit the Percys briefly in London four months later. Percy hoped meanwhile to take Will's mind from his misfortunes by asking him to secure some information for an article on the Lowe family that Percy was preparing for Treadway Nash's history of Worcestershire.[82]

Just before leaving London for Easton Maudit Percy had received from John Bowle a copy of his *Letter to the Reverend Dr. Percy, concerning a New and Classical Edition of . . . Don Quixote de la Mancha*, a sixty-seven-page pamphlet in which Bowle outlined his plan for an edition of *Don Quixote* in Spanish and appended some samples of his work. Percy, of course, was flattered by such attention, though Bowle's tribute to him was perhaps a natural consequence of his encouragement and his generous sharing of both information and his "Quixotic Library." About Cervantes—"our favourite author," as Percy frequently called him—he and Bowle were of one mind, particularly in their recognition that appreciating Cervantes's satire and erudition required a knowledge of the romances that were the heart of Percy's Quixotic Library. When Percy wrote to Bowle on February 3, he had first to apologize for his delay in writing, occasioned in good part by the death of the Countess of Sussex on January 11 and the need for him to help prepare for the funeral and conduct the service. He went on to express the hope that Bowle's work might "meet with the general attention it deserves," but was afraid that it would be "Caviare to the Million": that Bowle must be content to please a few readers like himself who try to enjoy Cervantes in his own language.[83]

In the spring Lord Percy, heir to a peerage on the death of his mother, was back in London, having been recalled at his demand following a dispute with General Howe. Before leaving for Alnwick in July, Percy sought his assistance in securing a government post for Anthony, who had labored without much success as a brandy and hop merchant in Southwark. Although Lord Percy was ready to try to help, as he informed Percy, he could do nothing until Parliament convened in October, and he was not in such favor that he could approach Lord North in person. He would have to work through an old schoolfellow, Lord Suffolk, who was secretary of state for the Northern Department. Writing to Anthony on September 18, shortly after his return to Easton Maudit, Percy thus urged him not to press at the moment, but simply to provide the salient information about the position he was seeking.[84]

In his letter Percy also stated that he "would have" Anthony defer removing his only son, Tom, who was attending the Merchant Taylors School, to Westminster until Anthony could see where he might be stationed. A change of that kind, Percy commented, "always throws a young Scholar a Year back at least." Percy was to take an active interest in his nephew, who, at age nine, had already written a poem that another precocious child, Charles Wesley's son Samuel, was to set to music.[85] The tone of Percy's letter suggests either that Anthony expected to be guided by his literary brother in Tom's education, or that Percy assumed that he did. In any event, Tom remained at the Merchant Taylors School, and, with Lord Percy's efforts coming to nothing, his father kept to his trade in Southwark. Lord Percy's failure in no way diminished Percy's regard for him: when he met Boswell near Whitehall on March 21, 1778, Percy boasted that Lord Percy was maintaining the family's high reputation.[86]

On March 25 Percy replied to his first letter from the twenty-year-old Scot, John Pinkerton, who had sent him manuscript copies of several poems, including a second part of "Hardyknute," without reporting that he had written the continuation himself. His silence on that point was rewarded with Percy's blunt opinion that the second part was "hardly equal to the first," though he added that he would be pleased to include all the pieces whenever he published an "additional volume." Presumably he had in mind the fourth volume of the *Reliques* that he had mentioned to George Paton on July 28, 1775. When he replied on July 20 to a second Pinkerton letter, he stated his intention of availing himself of the poems whenever he gave the world his "additional volumes," an obvious reference to the proposed *Ancient English and Scottish Poems.*

The truth is, Percy continued, he no longer had the time or taste for "amusements of this kind" that he had when he was younger:

> I only considered these things as pardonable, at best, among the levities (I had almost said follies) of my youth. However, as I must confess that I have always had a relish for the poetic effusions (even the most sportive and unelaborate) of our ancestors, I have commonly taken up these trifles, as other grave men have done cards, to unbend and amuse the mind when fatigued with graver duties, till they have insensibly grown into a regular series ready for the press.

His real purpose in keeping the poems by him, Percy wrote, was to give his son, "a tall youth of fifteen," the merit of editing them after he leaves Westminster for the university.[87]

On April 12, 1778, Johnson, Boswell, and Mrs. Williams were the Percys' dinner guests at their house off Piccadilly, an occasion that gave rise to one of the more dramatic episodes in Boswell's *Life of Johnson.*[88] In addition to the three special guests, the company included the Reverend Robert Boucher Nichols, a British army chaplain recently returned from America; an unidentified young woman; Percy's nephew; and the Percy children: sixteen-year-old Barbara, whom Boswell called "a pretty, genteel girl"; Harry, "a fine Westminster lad"; and twelve-year-old Elizabeth.

The engagement began inauspiciously. Johnson, having felt faint on the ride to Piccadilly, asked for brandy or wine immediately upon his arrival and withdrew to an open window, where he quickly emptied the bottle that was brought to him. Before long he was talking spiritedly of Goldsmith: "He had so much envy, that he could not conceal it." A "good neat dinner" followed, during which Percy read aloud a fifty-line pastoral of his nephew's about to be published in the *Gentleman's Magazine,* and the company then retired to "the cheerful front room" for a dessert of oranges and raisins.[89] After dessert, while the others talked, Johnson fell asleep; and Percy, catching a glimpse of the Duke returning from Sion House across Green Park, dashed out to meet him. When he came back, Johnson was awake, perhaps aroused as much by Percy's absence as by the serving of coffee and tea.

When the discussion turned to books of travels, Johnson put Percy on the defensive by praising Thomas Pennant, whose disparaging comments on Alnwick Castle in his 1771 *Tour in Scotland* ("You look in vain for any marks of the grandeur of the feudal age") had offended the Northumberland family.[90] Percy responded with a sharp attack upon Pennant and drew an equally sharp retort. "Pennant," said Johnson, "has done what he intended. He has made you very angry. The stigma of such a man will stick."[91]

"He has said the garden is *trim*," replied Percy, "which is representing it like a citizen's parterre, when the truth is, there is a very large extent of fine turf and gravel walks."

"According to your own account, Sir," continued Johnson, "Pennant is right. It *is* trim. Here is grass cut close, and gravel rolled smooth. Is not that trim? The extent is nothing against that; a mile may be as trim as a square yard. Your extent puts me in mind of the citizen's enlarged dinner, two pieces of roast-beef, and two puddings. There is no variety, no mind exerted in laying out the ground, no trees."

For Percy, proud of the Duke's extensive planting at Alnwick and elsewhere in Northumberland, the presumption of "no trees" was a signal for still another line of attack: "He pretends to give the natural history of Northumberland, and yet takes no notice of the immense number of trees planted there of late." But Johnson was arguing for victory, and he parried with an amusing bit of sophistry that threw Percy off stride and effectively put an end to rational debate: "That, Sir," said Johnson,

> "has nothing to do with the *natural* history; that is *civil* history. A man who gives the natural history of the oak, is not to tell how many oaks have been planted in this place or that. A man who gives the natural history of the cow, is not to tell how many cows are milked at Islington. The animal is the same, whether milked in the Park or at Islington."

PERCY. "Pennant does not describe well; a carrier who goes along the side of Loch-lomond would describe it better."
JOHNSON. "I think he describes very well." PERCY. "I travelled after him." JOHNSON. "And *I* travelled after him."
PERCY. "But, my good friend, you are short-sighted, and do not see so well as I do."

Johnson, sensitive about his physical defects, was momentarily stunned by this unexpected blow. But, as Boswell wrote, "inflammable particles were collecting for a cloud to burst," and, when Percy renewed his attack against Pennant, Johnson could no longer hold them back:

> "This is the resentment of a narrow mind, because he did not find every thing in Northumberland." PERCY. (feeling the stroke) "Sir, you may be as rude as you please." JOHNSON. "Hold, Sir! Don't talk of rudeness; remember, Sir, you told me (puffing hard with passion struggling for a vent) I was short-sighted. We have done with civility. We are to be as rude as we please." PERCY. "Upon my honour, Sir, I did not mean to be uncivil." JOHNSON. "I cannot say so, Sir; for I *did* mean to be uncivil, thinking *you* had been uncivil."

Percy got up, took Johnson by the hand, and assured him that his meaning had been misunderstood. They were reconciled immediately: "Sir, I am willing you shall hang Pennant," said Johnson. "Pennant complains," Percy went on, "that the helmet is not hung out to invite to the hall of hospitality. Now I never heard that it was a custom to hang out a *helmet*."

"Hang him up," said Johnson.

They had "a calm after the storm," Boswell wrote, and they stayed through supper and were pleasant and gay; but Johnson's thunderclaps reverberated in Percy's mind. Eight days later, when Boswell called at Northumberland House, he found him still uneasy about Johnson's treatment. Percy had hoped to make a favorable impression on Nichols, who, he said, wished to supplant him in his chaplaincy, and he had brought Nichols and Johnson together with that purpose in mind. "This comes of *stratagem*," Johnson commented when Boswell informed him of Percy's concern; "had he told me that he wished to appear to advantage before that gentleman, he should have been at the top of the house, all the time." He also spoke of Percy "in the handsomest terms" so that Boswell might repeat them to Lord Percy. Thus encouraged, Boswell proposed that he write Johnson a letter on "the unlucky contest" of April 12 and that Johnson reply with the praise of Percy that he had just given. Boswell would then find an opportunity to read the correspondence in Lord Percy's presence during a dinner that he was to attend at General Paoli's. Johnson agreed, and, in response to Boswell's letter, wrote to him on April 23:

> The debate between Dr. Percy and me is one of those foolish controversies, which begin upon a question of which neither party cares how it is decided, and which is, nevertheless, continued to acrimony, by the vanity with which every man resists confutation. Dr. Percy's warmth proceeded from a cause which, perhaps, does him more honour than he could have derived from juster criticism. His abhorrence of Pennant proceeded from his opinion that Pennant had wantonly and indecently censured his patron. His anger made him resolve, that, for having been once wrong, he never should be right. Pennant has much in his notions that I do not like; but still I think him a very intelligent traveller. If Percy is really offended, I am sorry; for he is a man whom I never knew to offend any one. He is a man very willing to learn, and very able to teach; a man, out of whose company I never go without having learned something. It is sure that he vexes me sometimes, but I am afraid it is by making me feel my own ignorance. So much extension of mind, and so much minute accuracy of enquiry, if you survey your whole circle of acquaintance, you will find so scarce, if you find it at all, that you will value Percy by comparison. Lord Hailes is somewhat like him: but Lord Hailes does not, perhaps, go beyond him in research; and I do not know that he equals him in elegance. Percy's attention to poetry has given grace and splendour to his studies of antiquity. A mere antiquarian is a rugged being.
>
> Upon the whole, you see that what I might say in sport or petulance to him, is very consistent with full conviction of his merit.[92]

Exulting in his diplomatic triumph, Boswell showed the letter to William Robertson when he met him on April 24, and that evening at General Paoli's he read it aloud in the presence of Lord Percy, General James Oglethorpe, and two or three others. On the twenty-fifth, after writing Percy a note, he joined him at breakfast and read him the exchange of letters with Johnson. "I would rather have this than degrees from all the Universities in Europe," said Percy. "It will be for me, and my children and grand-children." A bungling surgeon, he added, would go round and round, but Johnson "probed the human heart, where the sore was." After breakfast they walked in the Mall and then went to Northumberland House, where Boswell made copies of the letters to leave with Percy.[93]

On April 27, when Boswell called at Bolt Court, Johnson remained busy at his desk for some time and then began to ask about his letter. "He bid me not show it about," Boswell wrote. And he became very angry when Boswell acknowledged that he had already given Percy a copy. Percy would "run about with it," said Johnson. "I said it would lie in Percy's drawer. 'That,' said he, 'is worse. For it will be published in a collection of letters. That is the mischief of writing a letter,' said he. 'I did this to help Percy. But I would not degrade myself. I have no high opinion of Percy.' " In short, concluded Boswell, it was "a very disagreeable business." He promised nonetheless to get the copy back, uneasy though he felt about Johnson's writing something that he did not wish to have permanently shown. "This must be explained [by] himself," he wrote in his journal.

Boswell was unable to reach Percy on the twenty-seventh, though he stopped at Northumberland House both on his way home from Johnson's and later in the day, when he also called at the Bolton Street house. On the twenty-eighth he hurried to Northumberland House from another visit, found Percy in, and told him that he must have the copy back; Johnson, he said, was very angry that he had given it to Percy. Percy resisted at first, saying that Boswell would have to tell Johnson that he was unwilling to part with it, but he readily gave it up when he saw how concerned Boswell was. Then, wrote Boswell, "he took up a tone of displeasure and said he did not care about it and threw out a rhapsody of affected indifference which I tried to check." Later that day Boswell informed Johnson that he had secured the copy of the letter, but that Percy was vexed. "I don't care about Percy's being vexed," said Johnson.[94]

In his *Life of Johnson* Boswell reported the "Pennantian Controversy" for the purpose of displaying "the truely tender and benevolent heart of Johnson, who, as soon as he found a friend was at all hurt by any thing which he had 'said in his wrath,' was not only prompt and desirous to be reconciled, but exerted himself to make ample reparation."[95] But it took some careful editing to convey such a happy view. When the Duke of Northumberland crossed Green Park on his way back from Sion House, he cast a long shadow upon a cheerful front room off Piccadilly, and touched off a sequence in which none of the three participants was to find much cheer. Percy's desertion of his company to greet his patron, Johnson's goading comments, and Percy's uncivil allusion to Johnson's eyesight were all difficult to excuse in the polite setting of Percy's front room. There was "a violence in . . . [Percy's] temper," wrote Cradock, "which could not always be controlled," though one might have expected him to control it in the presence of his guests.[96] As Johnson suggested in his letter, Percy was practicing to a fault the virtue of loyalty to his patron.

The events subsequent to April 12, blurred by Boswell in his *Life*, raised the most troublesome questions. Why should Percy have brooded for more than a week about the effect of the controversy on the comparatively insignificant Mr. Nichols? How could Johnson, who held the truth almost sacred, reconcile his letter of April 23 and the shattering comment, mercifully not repeated by Boswell, "I have no high opinion of Percy"? And why would he subject Boswell to the embarrassment and Percy to the humiliation of the letter's withdrawal?

No doubt Percy was overly concerned about the competition from Nichols, but, despite the Duke's assurances, he could probably not avoid some uneasiness about his future. Continually at the mercy of the gout, the Duke was not so robust as to go on indefinitely; and, in any event, however much Percy revered his patron, it was not his ambition to dedicate his entire career to a nobleman's clerical needs. The King's chaplaincy, which had brought prestige but no emolument, was commonly a stepping stone to a deanship or bishopric, and at age forty-nine, after eight and a half years at St. James's, he was approaching the point when his chances of preferment were likely to diminish with each passing year. It was thus important for him to retain the good opinion of both the Duke and Lord Percy, without whose influence he knew that he could expect nothing further.

As for Johnson's letter and statement, they can be reconciled on the ground that they were intended to serve different purposes. "I did this to help Percy," Johnson said of the letter—that is, to dispel any false impressions conveyed to Lord Percy as a result of the April 12 dispute. It was, in short, a letter of commendation written for the occasion of the dinner at General Paoli's, when Boswell and Lord Percy were to be together. But when Boswell admitted that he had given a copy to Percy, Johnson became aware that he had been drawn into an encomium of Percy for a purpose which had not been made clear to him and to which he would not have consented. With a copy available to Percy to show about or to print, the context of the letter would in time be lost sight of, and Johnson's praise would be seen as an apology and as a rounded assessment of Percy's character and qualifications, neither of which he had intended. His angry "I have no high opinion of Percy," even if not a fair reflection of his view, must have seemed an essential first corrective of the false impression he perceived had been conveyed. Retrieving the copy of his letter was the second.

The month of May brought Percy better news. Harry, trying for the second time, was elected a King's scholar at Westminster, and Percy, proud of his son's achievement, went with him on May 17 to purchase the gown and square hat that distinguished his new honor. "He is grown nearly as tall as myself," Percy wrote to William Cleiveland on the same day, "& is I flatter myself a very promising & manly Youth perfectly sober & virtuous."[97]

Throughout much of the year Percy busied himself collecting material for the articles on his own and related families for Treadway Nash's history of Worcestershire, and his letters to Cleiveland are filled with requests for family details. At Alnwick and Easton Maudit, between August and late October, he concentrated on revising the Collins article on the Northumberland Percys and writing the history of the Percys undertaken at his patron's suggestion. He was impatient with the Collins work because of its innumerable errors, and also because it kept him from the more attractive companion volume that he was free to develop as he pleased. But he welcomed the opportunity to insert a digression on the Northumberland ancestry of the Worcester Percys and a brief note—doubtless with Johnson and Pennant in mind—on the Duke's improvements at Alnwick: he found the castle "almost a desert" and has already "clothed it with woods." To please the Duke, who read each sheet avidly as it came from the press, he pushed ahead with his *Genealogical History of the Percy Family*, of which, by November 1778, three sheets were in print.[98]

He remained alert to the possibilities for preferment. On August 29 he wrote to John Bowle to inquire about the health of the dean of Salisbury, on behalf of a "friend of mine." By November 12, when Bowle, joining in Percy's game, informed him that his friend would have to wait a little longer, Percy's fortunes had already drawn him in a different direction.[99] On October 24, after the death of Dr. Thomas Wilson, dean of Carlisle, the Duke met with Lord North to follow up a written request that Percy be offered the deanery, along with a vacant living that he and Percy understood to accompany it. Lord North made it clear that they were misinformed about the living, but he readily agreed to recommend Percy to the King for the deanery. "I thought it advisable not to decline," the Duke wrote to Percy later that day, "as it is a situation of credit which I hope may lead to something more advantageous."[100]

The next few days were filled with activity. At the Duke's request, Percy hurried to town, where he arrived on the morning of the twenty-sixth. He met with the Duke and then called on Reynolds and John Singleton Copley, whom he also visited on the twenty-seventh. Perhaps he was seeking advice concerning the copy made, or to be made, of his Reynolds portrait or the mezzotint by William Dickinson, which was reissued after his appointment as dean of Carlisle.[101] On the twenty-sixth Lewis Dutens dined with him at Northumberland House, where no doubt they discussed Percy's collection of romances, which Dutens was to purchase in 1779.[102] On the twenty-seventh Percy and Harry dined with Percy's old friend, Mr. Wright, went to a play, and returned to Northumberland House, where they both spent the night.

In the morning Percy attended the King's levee and kissed the King's hand on his appointment, a ceremony that the Duke, who had left for Bath on the twenty-seventh, expressed regret at having to miss. "I shall always be desirous of giving you every proof of my Regard," he wrote on November 2, "and I assure you it affords me particular satisfaction to have been instrumental in procuring you an appointment of such Dignity in the Church, it is the first favour I have applied for, having never asked any thing even for my own Sons."[103] After the ceremony Percy took Harry with him to visit Anthony in Southwark and Johnson in Bolt Court.

On the morning of the twenty-ninth he was at court to kiss the Queen's hand, and later—perhaps a private celebration in his honor— he had dinner and tea at Reynolds's with Johnson, Charles Burney, Allan Ramsay, Richard Brinsley Sheridan, and Giuseppe Baretti. On the thirtieth he met with Lord Sussex and also with Lockyer Davis, who would be bringing out a third edition of the Key to the New Testament in 1779, and he dined with Dr. Boscawen and perhaps other associates among the King's chaplains.

Impatient to leave for Carlisle, Percy chafed at the bureaucratic machinery that held up the final seals of his appointment. The King and Queen, he wrote to William Cleiveland on November 9, "allowed me to kiss their hands on my Promotion near a fortnight ago: so much more attendance do Ministers & even the Under-Clerks of Office require of us their humble Dependants, than their & our great Master."[104] On the tenth he borrowed £150 from Johnson, perhaps to assist with the expenses attendant upon his appointment; and on the sixteenth, his patent as dean at last delivered to him, he set out with Harry for Carlisle. After spending the night at Royston in Hertfordshire, they called on Richard Farmer in time for breakfast at Emmanuel College, and that day Percy was instituted in his office by Dr. Edmund Law, Bishop of Carlisle, who was in residence at Cambridge.[105] They left Cambridge immediately after the ceremony and reached Carlisle on the evening of November 20.

NOTES

1. Vincent became headmaster in 1788 and dean of Westminster in 1802. Jones's first name is conjectural, based on payments to John Jones out of Percy's account at Drummond's Bank.
2. B.L. Add. MS. 32,333, f. 72 (Letter Percy to Cleiveland, 22 June 1773). Frank Price had been admitted in September 1771 (*The Westminster School Register from 1764 to 1883*, ed. G. F. Russell and Alan H. Stenning [London: 1892], 188).
3. Alnwick Castle MS., Northumberland Add. Papers, F/13/1–3 (Letters Percy to Lord Algernon, 10 March 1773, 2 and 13 April 1773 [from L.C. microfilm]).
4. *The Percy Letters*, 2:164–67 (Letters Percy to Farmer, 25 Jan. 1773; Farmer to Percy, 18 Feb. 1773). BC 188, Bowle-Evans Collection, University of Cape Town Libraries (Letter Bowle to Percy, 23 Feb. 1773).
5. B.L. Add. MSS. 32,333, f. 72 (Letter Percy to Cleiveland, 22 June 1773); 42,516, ff. 68–69.
6. *Boswell for the Defence*, 174.
7. Ibid., 192.
8. *The Percy Letters*, 6:56, 61, 75–76, 173–74 (Letters Percy to Paton, 3 June and 23 Oct. 1773; Earl of Hyndford to Percy, 6 Jan. 1773).
9. B.L. Add. MS. 32,333, f. 71 (Letter Percy to Cleiveland, 22 June 1773). Percy noted that Mrs. Gutteridge, who died in Anne's arms on a visit to Easton Maudit, had left "a very handsome Legacy to my Children: what will be more than £1000 before it is paid in." Her will is in the Public Record Office, Prob. 11, 998 (351).
10. Johnson wrote to Mrs. Thrale from Newcastle on 12 August: "I shall set out again to morrow, but I shall not, I am afraid see Alnwick, for Dr.

Percy is not there" (*The Letters of Samuel Johnson*, 1:318). On 25 August, amusing themselves with the thought of setting up a college at St. Andrews taught by members of the Club, Johnson and Boswell agreed that Percy should teach practical divinity and British antiquities (*Boswell's Journal of a Tour to the Hebrides with Samuel Johnson*, ed. Frederick A. Pottle and Charles H. Bennett [New York: McGraw-Hill, 1961], 78–79).

11. The account of Percy's trip is taken from his diary and, more particularly, his letters to his wife of [12] and 17 Aug. 1773 (B.L. Add. MS. 39,547, ff. 17–31). In 1773 Durant was member of Parliament for Evesham.

12. A year later, after a tour through the border country, Percy noted for Anne a striking contrast between the common people he observed on the two sides of the border: though separated by only a few miles, the English look "clean, wholesome, healthy & comely," the Scots "dirty unwholesome [and] disgusting" (B.L. Add. MS. 39,547, f. 36 (Letter 21 Sept. 1774).

13. *Lit. Illus.*, 8:163 (Letter Percy to Andrew Ducarel, 13 Jan. 1772). Beinecke Library, Ms. Vault File (Letters 28 April and 15 Aug. 1773).

14. B.L. Add. MS. 32,329, ff. 74–77. The letter is printed in A. Watkin-Jones, "Bishop Percy, Thomas Warton, and Chatterton's Rowley Poems (1773–1790)," *PMLA* 50(1935):79–84.

15. Historical Manuscripts Commission, Thirteenth Report, Appendix, pt. 4 (*The Manuscripts of Rye and Hereford Corporations* [London, 1892], 372) (Letter Percy to Lord Dacre, 7 Nov. 1773). Percy's 15 and 28 Oct. letters to Chambers are in the Houghton Library, fMS Eng. 1279 (3–4). Lord Dacre's letters of 8 Oct. and 22 Nov. are in the Beinecke Library, Ms. Vault File.

16. Beinecke Library, MS. Vault File.

17. *The Letters of Samuel Johnson*, 1:395.

18. A. Watkin-Jones, "Bishop Percy, Thomas Warton, and Chatterton's Rowley Poems," 771–72. E. H. W. Meyerstein, *A Life of Thomas Chatterton* (New York: Scribner's, 1930), 456–57.

19. Cradock, 1:206.

20. Gaussen, 161, 163.

21. Ralph M. Wardle, *Oliver Goldsmith* (Hamden, Conn.: Archon Books, 1969), 251–52.

22. B.L. Add. MS. 42,515, f. 51. Cradock, 4:285–86.

23. Gaussen, 168–69. Some diary entries cited by Gaussen are not among the diaries that the British Library bound together as Add. MS. 32,336. I have not found them elsewhere.

24. B.L. Add. MS. 32,333, ff. 77–78.

25. *The Percy Letters*, 6:82, 85 (Letters Percy to Paton, 6 Feb. and 24 March 1774).

26. B.L. Add. MSS. 32,327, f. 175; 32,333, f. 79.

27. *Westminster Magazine* (Dec. 1773), 685–87.

28. *Lit. Illus.*, 7:295.

29. Boswell's *Life*, 2:534–35. In the January issue of the *Westminster Magazine* the memoirist acknowledged that he had not known Grainger personally and apologized for any injury to his widow or her daughters (32).

30. Salop Record Office, 1175/2.

31. See p. 4.

32. Boswell's *Life*, 2:91–92. Percy projected a similar work for Northamptonshire but did little with it (Beinecke Library, Ms. Vault File).

33. There are many unanswered questions about the portraits of Percy painted before the Reynolds portrait. Glasgow authorities have found no record of the 1765 portrait. It is not known what portrait Tom Woodington viewed at Northumberland House in 1767, and it is not known what two portraits Percy paid G. D. Hamilton for on 18 October 1770 (Bodl. MS: Percy d. 8, f. 77), or who G. D. Hamilton was. Of the two Hamiltons known to be actively painting in London after mid-century, Gavin Hamilton had settled in Rome in 1769 or earlier, and the other was Hugh Douglas Hamilton. The latter does seem to have done a portrait of Percy (probably in crayon, which was his preferred medium at the time) since Walpole identified as Percy the subject of one of his portraits exhibited in Spring Gardens on 26 April 1771 (Lewis Walpole Library, 49.3885.2.2–1). In 1783 the Percys took four Hamilton "Pictures" to Ireland, including one of Henry dated 10 July 1771 (collection of Kenneth Balfour).

34. Perhaps it was at this dinner that Johnson, as reported by J. W. Croker, sat one of the Percy daughters on his knee and asked her what she thought of *The Pilgrim's Progress*. When she said that she had not read it, Johnson replied, "No! then I would not give one farthing for you" and took no further notice of her (Boswell's *Life*, 2:238 n. 5). In June 1774 Elizabeth was not quite nine. Percy's 31 May letter is in Northumberland Letters and Papers 1766–69, Alnwick 23/1, ff. 11–12.

35. The copy was bought by the Hammer Galleries in 1948.

36. *Johnsonian Miscellanies*, 2:179–80.

37. *The Yale Edition of the Works of Samuel Johnson*, 6, *Poems*, ed. E. L. McAdam, Jr., with George Milne (New Haven: Yale Univ. Press, 1964): 269–70. The parody was first published in the *St. James's Chronicle*, 13 Jan. 1785. In her *Anecdotes* Mrs. Piozzi included still another Johnson parody without associating it with Percy, but in *Thraliana* (2d ed., 1:398–99) she stated that it "made Percy angry—but he soon came to himself": "The tender infant meek and mild / Fell down upon a stone; / The nurse took up the squealing child / But yet the child squeal'd on" (*Yale Johnson*, 6:269).

38. B.L. MS., 32,333, f. 81 (Letter Percy to Cleiveland, 7 Nov. 1774).

39. Boston Public Library (Letter Thomas Taylor to Percy, 21 Oct. 1774). B.L. Add. MS. 32,333, f. 81.

40. *The Percy Letters*, 6:86, 97, 108, 113. Boswell's offer was reported by Paton on 11 Aug. 1774 (97).

41. Ibid., 101–2.

42. Ibid., 103, 117. B.L. Add. MS.32,333, f. 82. Percy wrote to Cleiveland from Easton Maudit on 4 January, but Anne forwarded a 13 January letter from Paton to him in London (B.L. Add. MS. 32,333, f. 83; *The Percy Letters*, 6:118).

43. B.L. Add. MS. 32,333, ff. 87–90 (Letters 12 May and 7 Nov. 1775). *The Percy Letters*, 6:121–22 (Letter Percy to Paton, 28 July 1775).

44. *The Percy Letters*, 6:119, 120, 122.

45. B.L. Add. MS. 6401, f. 6.

46. Percy would not have lent the folio manuscript.

47. *The Percy Letters*, 6:126.

48. Boswell, *Life of Johnson*, 2:318–19; *Boswell: the Ominous Years 1774–1776*, ed. Charles Ryskamp and Frederick A. Pottle (New York: McGraw-Hill, 1963), 102, 104, 115.

49. B.L. Add. MS. 32,333, f. 89. Lord Percy's letters to Percy are in the Boston Public Library (Ms. G. 31.39).

50. National Library of Wales, MS. 4955D. Gaussen, 11. In his diary Percy mistakenly entered the date of Lady Barbara's marriage as 27 November rather than 27 October.

51. L. F. Powell, "Percy's Reliques," 136. The edition was to consist of a thousand copies, and Percy was not to publish a new edition till the third edition was sold.

52. *Public Advertiser*, 15, 23, 26, 29, and 30 Dec. 1775.

53. For an account of the three-volume collection, see Vincent H. Ogburn, "Thomas Percy's Unfinished Collection, Ancient English and Scottish Poems," *ELH* 3(1936):183–89.

54. Tyrwhitt's text, from the Cotton MS., contained 58 lines not found in the Harleian MS. used for the first two editions.

55. Percy ledger, Drummond's Bank.

56. *Ancient Songs Chiefly on Moorish Subjects Translated from the Spanish by Thomas Percy with a Preface by David Nichol Smith*, vi.

57. *Yale Johnson*, 6:292.

58. For a comprehensive study of the early translations, see Shasta M. Bryant, *The Spanish Ballad in English* (Lexington: Univ. Press of Kentucky, 1973).

59. John Pinkerton, *Select Scotish Ballads*, 2d ed. (London: 1783), xlv (cited in Bryant, 25).

60. B.L. Add. MS. 32,333, ff. 89–90 (Letter Percy to Cleiveland, 7 Nov. 1775). Bodl. MS. Percy d. 4, f. 177. Cradock stated in his *Literary and Miscellaneous Memoirs* (1:243) that Percy introduced David Hume at the

chaplain's table, but gave no precise date. I have been unable to find any time when a Hume visit to London coincided with Percy's period of waiting.

61. *The Percy Letters*, 4:137. Bodl. MS. Add. A. 64, f. 252.

62. *Boswell: the Ominous Years*, 285–86; *Boswell's Life*, 2:455.

63. *Boswell's Life*, 2:347; *Boswell: the Ominous Years*, 134.

64. *Boswell's Life*, 3:81–85; *TLS*, 7 March 1929.

65. Alnwick Castle MS., Northumberland Misc. Papers, G/2/4. B.L. Add. MS. 32,334, f. 34. *Public Advertiser*, 9 Sept. 1776.

66. *The Percy Letters*, 4:98 (Letter Percy to Dalrymple, 24 May 1765).

67. Alnwick Castle MS. 93A/19.

68. *Boswell's Life* 3:521.

69. Collection of Kenneth Balfour.

70. B.L. Add. MS. 32,327. The "Account of the Private Family of Percy, formerly of Worcester, afterwards of Bridgnorth, Shropshire" (B.L. Add. MS. 32,326), cited particularly in the opening chapters, differs from the other two principally through its narrative account of Percy's Worcestershire lineage and his own life until his marriage.

71. Bodl. MSS. Percy d. 3, f. 240; d. 5, f. 115. Percy's notations on the sermons show that he also preached at Alnwick Church on 10 August and Easton Maudit on 1 September.

72. "Original Papers," ff. 1–2.

73. B.L. Add. MS. 32,327, f. 77.

74. Ibid., f. 67.

75. *Boswell's Life*, 3:271 n. 5; 520. The Earl of Leicester informed Percy in 1793, during his presidency of the Society of Antiquaries, that he too was convinced (B.L. Add. MS. 32,327, f. 7).

76. Arthur Collins, *The Peerage of England*, 5th ed. (London, 1779), 2:361.

77. *The Letters of Samuel Johnson*, 2:154 (Letters Johnson to Percy, 1 and 2 Dec. 1776). B.L. Add. MS. 32,334, f. 38 (Letter 6 Dec. 1776). *The Complete Peerage* gives the Duchess's birthdate as 26 November O.S.: i.e., 7 December N.S. The Duchess was the daughter of the seventh Duke of Somerset; the younger countess was the daughter of the sixth Duke by his second wife.

78. Letter Henry Percy to Anne Percy, 19 Dec. 1776 (collection of Kenneth Balfour). *Public Advertiser*, 20 Dec. 1776.

79. Percy had some slight assistance from Horace Walpole when he prepared the inscription in 1780 (*The Yale Edition of Horace Walpole's Correspondence*, vol. 41: *Horace Walpole's Miscellaneous Correspondence*, vol. 2, ed. Wilmarth S. Lewis et al., [New Haven: Yale Univ. Press, 1980], ff. 411–13).

80. B.L. Add. MS. 32,333, f. 106.

81. Ibid., ff. 108–13. Bodl. MS. Percy c. 1, ff. 38–42.

82. B.L. Add. MS. 32,333, ff. 112–19 (Letters Percy to Cleiveland, 22 Jan., 28 Feb., 8 March, and 3 June 1777).

83. *Thomas Percy & John Bowle*, 37–38.

84. Collection of Kenneth Balfour. For Anthony's trade, see *Kent's Directory for the Year 1771* (London, 1771).

85. Daines Barrington, *Miscellanies* (London, 1781), 308.

86. *Boswell in Extremes 1776–1778*, ed. Charles McC. Weis and Frederick A. Pottle (New York: McGraw-Hill, 1970), 227.

87. *The Percy Letters*, vol. 8, *The Correspondence of Thomas Percy & John Pinkerton*, ed. Harriet Harvey Wood (New Haven: Yale Univ. Press, 1985), 1–11.

88. The Percys kept their Bolton Street house (No. 7, just off Piccadilly) until they went to Carlisle in 1780. In the account that follows I have relied upon both Boswell's journal (*Boswell in Extremes*, 272–75 *et seq.*) and his *Life of Johnson* (3:271–78), for which Boswell edited the journal "to display the truely tender and benevolent heart of Johnson."

89. *Gentleman's Magazine* (April 1778), 183.

90. Thomas Pennant, *A Tour in Scotland. MDCCLXIX* (Chester, 1771), 31–32. Bodl. MS. Montagu d. 9, f. 119 (Letter Pennant to Thomas Evans, n.d.).

91. This sentence is quoted from *Boswell in Extremes*, 274. It does not appear in the *Life of Johnson*, from which, except for two or three statements at the end, the argument between Johnson and Percy is taken.

92. Boswell's *Life*, 3:277–78.

93. *Boswell in Extremes*, 309, 310–11. Boswell's *Life*, 3:276.

94. *Boswell in Extremes*, 317–19.

95. Boswell's *Life*, 3:271.

96. Cradock, 1:238–39.

97. B.L. Add. MS. 32,333, f. 130. According to Cradock, Percy ("so bright himself") was never satisfied with Henry's progress at Westminster, with the result that they often quarreled (4:293).

98. *The Peerage of England*, 5th ed., 2:360–68, 456. B.L. Add. MS. 32,329, ff. 101–2 (Letter Percy to Treadway Nash, 7 Nov. 1778). Four sheets of the *Genealogical History*, totaling thirty-two pages, were printed before Percy abandoned the project (Alnwick Castle MS. 93A/11).

99. *Thomas Percy & John Bowle*, 56. According to William Cole, Walpole dropped Percy's acquaintance chiefly because Percy pressed him to get him preferment (Sir Egerton Brydges, *Restituta* [London: 1814–16], 4:243).

100. Alnwick Castle MS., Northumberland Misc. Papers, G/2/5.

101. Percy's diary entry for 27 October is tantalizing: "Shew.^d the Cornaro Family to Copley & Green ye Mezzotinto Scrape." Another possibility

is that Percy was arranging to have the Reynolds portrait copied by someone in Copley's studio. Green was the engraver Valentine Green.

102. A. Watkin-Jones, "A Spanish Hispanist," *Bulletin of Spanish Studies* 14(1937): 9; *Lit. Illus.*, 8:187–88 (Letter Dutens to Percy, n.d. [1779?]).
103. Alnwick Castle MS., Northumberland Misc. Papers, G/2/6.
104. B.L. Add. MS. 32,333, f. 133.
105. Johnson Birthplace Museum MS. 16/38 ("A State of the Account between the Bp. of Dromore & the Exors of the Late D.ʳ Sam.ˡ Johnson," to 10 Nov. 1785). Chapter records, Carlisle Cathedral, XI (1759–92), f. 242. Percy was installed as dean on 21 November (f. 243).

CHAPTER X

Dean of Carlisle:
1778–1782

THOUGH HE CAME to it by the chance death of Thomas Wilson, Percy seemed ideally suited for the deanery of Carlisle. His eight-day visit to Carlisle in 1765 had been a high point of his first Alnwick summer, when he was caught up in the city's relentless social activity and was welcomed at the best tables, including those of Sir James Lowther and Bishop Lyttelton. The Bishop, who died in 1768, had been a frequent companion of his Alnwick tours, an enthusiastic antiquary to whom Percy addressed his first detailed description of Warkworth Castle and the hermitage. Perhaps best of all, Carlisle, a stronghold of England's border, was the scene of poems close to Percy's heart. In the *Reliques's* ballad of three outlaws, "Adam Bell, Clym of the Clough, and William Cloudesley," the bells of Carlisle ring the townspeople to arms, and the mayor, poleax in hand, strides forth to repulse the attack of the three invaders.

> There was many an out horne in Carliel blowen,
>   And the belles bacwàrd dyd ryng,
> Many a woman sayde, Alas!
>   And many theyr handes dyd wryng.
>
> The mayre of Carleile forth was com,
>   Wyth hym a ful great route:
> These yemem dred hym full sore,
>   Of theyr lyves they stode in doute.[1]

By 1778, of course, the bells had long since held their warrior tongues, and the mayor had set aside the poleax for the politer instruments of a less troubled community. Only a week after his arrival in Carlisle, Percy was the mayor's guest at dinner, and the hospitality shown on that occasion typified his reception everywhere. Following his installation on November 21, he dined with the family of the late dean, and, on the next day, with the archdeacon, John Law, the son of Bishop Law. Both of the cathedral's canons invited him to dinner or tea. On November 28 he was a dinner guest of the "Miss Waughs," the five spinster daughters of the late Dr. John Waugh, Dean of Worcester, and on December 1 he and Harry rode with Archdeacon Law to Netherby, about ten miles north of town, to dine with the wealthy clergyman and landowner, Dr. Robert Graham. Though not yet in possession of the deanery house, he was able to reciprocate by using the facilities of the cathedral's fratry to entertain all the clergy at dinner on the twenty-third, the members of the city corporation on the twenty-fourth, and a few unidentified persons on the twenty-fifth.[2]

The Carlisle clergy were a tightly knit group. The chapter consisted of Percy, Archdeacon Law, and prebendaries James Lushington, Roger Baldwin, and Joseph Amphlett, who governed the cathedral subject only to the Bishop's intervention in cases of serious abuse. For the public services the chapter had the assistance of the two canons, six minor canons, and a choir of four men and six boys; and because the cathedral estates lay "all round," as Percy wrote William Cleiveland on December 22, the city and most of the outlying clergymen came under the chapter's protection and were "naturally disposed to be very obliging." In return the chapter endeavored to make their situations as comfortable as possible. As Percy saw it, the whole society lived together in "great amity."

On November 23 he presided over his first chapter meeting, during which the chapter expressed its approval of bills in Parliament to enclose Hutton and Morland Commons, ordered a pump installed in the abbey yard, and authorized an allowance of five shillings a year to William Wales for cleaning the walk under the trees in Castle Street. Perhaps discussions of more serious matters were conducted informally, since a decision to rebuild the library and provide money annually to purchase "the best books on the most useful Subjects" is not mentioned in the chapter records at all. Behind the decision lay a desire to attract scholars to join the "ingenious Scholarlike Men" whom Percy found among his colleagues, an objective to be furthered admirably in 1780 when William Paley accepted appointment as a prebendary.[3] Paley's *Principles of Moral and Political Philosophy* (1785) and *View of the Evidences of Christianity* (1794) were to make him one of the most influential clergymen of his time.

For Percy, money—inevitably one of his reasons for desiring the Carlisle appointment—became a worry almost immediately. He retained his livings at Easton Maudit and Wilby, but because the income from the deanery depended upon rents and fines (renewal fees) that came due at different intervals, it fell short in some years of the more than £550 that he expected. Unfortunately, both 1778 and 1779 were to be short years, so that he could count on making little more than the expenses of his "necessary attendance." As a consequence he and Anne decided to defer the removal of their family and furniture to Carlisle until 1780, the "expected year of plenty."[4]

Percy left Carlisle with Harry on December 2 and headed back to Easton Maudit by way of Oakham. Not yet sixteen, Harry had virtually completed his course at Westminster, but judging him too young to enter the university, Percy left him with Thomas Orme for further private study, which was to be resumed after Harry's final term at Westminster.

Percy reached Easton Maudit on the evening of Saturday, December 5 and the next evening preached the sermon for his young curate, Thomas Bromwich. By December 22 he was again in London, where he was permitted to keep his Northumberland House apartment even though he had given up his post as the Duke's domestic chaplain.[5] He finished out the year playing chess at Mr. Wright's on the evening of the twenty-ninth, dining at Mrs. Montagu's on the thirtieth with Thomas Warton, William Jones, and Mrs. Vesey, and visiting Charles Wesley on the thirty-first to hear a performance of his nephew's "Song of Autumn" set to music by young Samuel Wesley. Later that day he went to see the three-and-a-half-year-old William Crotch, dressed in a white frock, play voluntaries on the organ.[6]

Early in 1779 Percy was at work on the Collins article, which he finished on June 16, and on the sections he had committed himself to write for Treadway Nash's history of Worcestershire. For these he was seeking to expand and correct his genealogies of Percy-related families, primarily Cleiveland, Lowe, Meysey, and Pembruge. Information from John Charles Brooke of the London Herald's Office on a marriage between the Meysey and Pembruge families, the latter of which Brooke called of great antiquity in Herefordshire, probably accounts for the Percy family's journey into Herefordshire in late

September, between a two-week stay with William Cleiveland in Worcester and a week with Elizabeth Nott in Bridgnorth.[7]

On March 16, 1779, Parliament granted Lord Percy a divorce on the ground that his wife had been guilty of "criminal conversation" with William Bird, Esq., of the University of Cambridge. Lord Percy, who had commenced action for the divorce a year or so earlier, confided to Percy in July 1778, that he would not rush into another marriage unless he was so fortunate as to find a second Lady Algernon. By the time Parliament acted good fortune had probably already struck, for on May 8, 1779, he wrote Percy to announce his intention of marrying Miss Burrell about the seventeenth or eighteenth of that month, with Percy's assistance. In short, he had found his bride exactly where Algernon found his. On May 25, at the Berkeley Square home of the Burrell family, Percy united him in marriage with Frances Julia Burrell, third daughter of the late Peter Burrell and the youngest sister of Lady Algernon. Perhaps the week's delay was occasioned by an unidentified illness which, Percy wrote Pinkerton on July 2, had brought him to "the point of Death."[8]

On June 14, the day before leaving for Easton Maudit, Percy took Harry and Tom to see the paintings, literary treasures, and curiosities in Sir Ashton Lever's Museum, which Tom later commemorated in verse.[9] The stay at Easton Maudit was brief, for the midyear audit at Carlisle, when rents came due, was almost at hand. This time Percy made the trip with Anne and Barbara, both of them doubtless eager to see their new home, although, with the Wilsons still occupying the house, the Percys at best could only contemplate what they might do to adapt it to their own taste.

They reached Carlisle on June 21 and stayed for five and a half weeks, during which Percy conducted chapter meetings, inventoried the cathedral plate, collated the chapter's leases, and preached in the cathedral on three successive Sundays beginning on June 27. In his leisure moments he walked with Anne and Barbara in town, round the city walls, on the castle grounds, and by the riverside, and on the morning of July 2 climbed with them to the top of the cathedral steeple. Much visited in their first few days, after the June 23–25 audit they entertained guests at dinner and were in turn frequent guests of Percy's fellow clergy, the five Miss Waughs, and others. On July 3 they dined with Dr. Graham at Netherby. And on July 5, with Carlisle at its most festive, they yielded to the six-day excitement of balls, card assemblies, public breakfasts, and horse races, one of which they watched from the steeple. On the fifteenth they traveled twenty miles south for a five-day visit with the Earl of Surrey at Greystoke, whose entertainment included a morning ride to Lowther and a boating party on Ullswater, with a picnic on one of its rocky islands. Unfortunately Anne caught cold during the visit and was so ill when they returned to Carlisle on the twentieth that Percy sat up with her all night and nursed her with Dr. James's Fever Powder. They were forced to postpone a scheduled three-day visit to Netherby until late in the day on July 25, after Percy had preached at the cathedral service.

They left Carlisle for Easton Maudit on July 30, taking a leisurely route that permitted a three-day stop with Lord Percy and his bride at Stanwick in Yorkshire, a tour of Chatsworth House in Derbyshire, and three days at nearby Matlock, where, though Percy sprained a foot on the first day, they joined in the rambles and other pursuits of relaxed summer vacationers. Percy as they went could have looked back upon the weeks in Carlisle with overall satisfaction. The deanery house was still occupied by Mrs. Wilson and her children, and with Anne's help he could now see that "some alterations and repairs" would be needed, necessitating a delay in the family's plans to give up their London home.[10] But preaching in the cathedral almost every Sunday of his attendance had helped to establish his place in the community more firmly than had been possible during his hurried visit in 1778; the audit had brought him £332—an encouraging half-year's return—and a balance of £30 was still owed to him from it; and the "very hospitable Reception & very great Civilities" shown to him and Anne by such men as the Earl of Surrey and Dr. Graham had made their time pass so pleasantly that they scarcely knew how to leave.[11] Dean Percy is "very *populous*," James Boswell was informed at his inn when he stopped at Carlisle on November 6, 1779.[12]

Percy was back in Carlisle for the November 23 chapter meeting and the audit, but his only surviving record is of a sermon preached at the recently consecrated St. Cuthbert's Church on November 28.[13] During the rest of the year after his June–July visit, as in the first part of 1780, he was free to turn to literary pursuits, most of which he undertook to assist his friends. Nursing the branches of the Percy tree into full leaf for Nash's history remained a major preoccupation, a labor of love for all its exacting detail. On July 27 Lionel Charlton enlisted his aid in distributing copies of his *History of Whitby* to thirteen subscribers secured by Percy, including Johnson, Reynolds, Langton,

Steevens, Astle, Lort, and Bowle.[14] Samuel Pegge, detecting Percy's hand in articles signed "D. C." in the *Antiquarian Repertory*, requested further information about the King's fool in Henry V's time, the subject of one of Percy's contributions.[15] On November 13, in the first of many letters that he was to write to Edmond Malone over a period of thirty-one years, Percy enclosed notes for Malone's *Supplement* to the 1778 Johnson-Steevens Shakespeare, eighty-four of which Malone printed in his second volume.[16] In January 1780 he supplied John Stafford Smith with copies of "long lost madrigals & hymns" and a Purcell song that Smith, an avid collector of Purcell, was particularly pleased to acquire.[17]

On July 21, 1779, responding to a request from John Pinkerton, Percy agreed to recommend to Dodsley the collection of poems sent to him by Pinkerton early in 1778. The collection, however, was locked away in his escritoire at Northumberland House, and with no immediate plans to return to London he felt compelled to inform Pinkerton that his recommendation would have to be delayed until winter. He did not doubt, he added, that any London bookseller would be pleased to print the collection, provided that Pinkerton would permit the bookseller to defray his expenses with the first returns from the book and divide the rest between them. Pinkerton saw no objection to this arrangement.[18]

But Percy did not travel to London in either the last six months of 1779 or the first two and a half months of 1780, and on March 16, 1780, he received a letter from Pinkerton inquiring about the fate of his manuscript. He replied from Easton Maudit on the seventeenth that, without access to the poems, he had not known how to proceed, but he and his family had now settled upon the middle of April for removing to London, and he would then fulfill his commitment with pleasure. He suggested that Pinkerton write to Dodsley in advance to outline the proposed terms and to explain that Percy, prevented by his "Avocations" from providing any additions to the three volumes of the *Reliques*, approved entirely of issuing the Pinkerton poems in a separate publication. With Pinkerton in Edinburgh, he offered to correct the proofs of his volume and, if Dodsley should decline publication, to put him in touch with another bookseller.[19]

Percy was to be called to London much sooner than he anticipated. At five o'clock the next morning a fire broke out in a third-story room of Northumberland House where servants kept their liveries and other clothes, and it spread quickly to the adjacent rooms. Among them was Percy's apartment. With the wind apparently high, the fire was said to have raged until after eight o'clock when it was extinguished by firemen from the Westminster Fire Office.[20] Newspapers during the week that followed estimated the damage variously from £7000 to £10,000.[21]

News of the fire probably reached Percy on the evening of Sunday, March 19, and he spent the next morning hurriedly preparing to leave for London. He had good reason to worry. The Northumberland House apartment had served him as office and residence for more than fourteen years, the repository of a steady accumulation of books, papers, and manuscripts, including one that a young Scottish poet and editor would be counting on him to turn over to a London bookseller in just a month's time. On one of its walls hung Percy's portrait by Sir Joshua Reynolds.

He set out after dinner on the twentieth with his one-horse chair and his two chaise horses and, after stopping overnight at Barnet, drove into town before breakfast the next morning. At Northumberland House, where he was met by the Duke, he was shown what must have been a heartrending sight: his apartment gutted, the Reynolds portrait consumed by the fire, and numerous books, manuscripts, and letters either burned or soaked with water. But he had expected even worse. The alert firemen had literally snatched most of his prized books and papers from the flames, along with the escritoire containing the Pinkerton manuscript and probably other papers. "I shall have the pleasure to save almost every thing that I much cared for," he wrote to William Cleiveland after he had spent more than a week raking through the embers and drying out his water-soaked volumes.[22]

Sometime after the fire he compiled a list of his losses, perhaps to assist the Duke, who filed a claim for indemnification with the Westminster Fire Office on March 23. Furnishings destroyed included three glass book cases, a small table, and "a cedar box for writings." Among some fifty charred books, probably two first editions of *Paradise Lost* were the most valuable, though perhaps no more regretted than his late friend Edward Lye's edition of Junius's *Etymologicum Anglicanum*, four editions of *Don Quixote*, a few Spanish romances, and an early copy of the *Select Collection of Poems* that John Nichols, a distant relation through marriage, had published a few weeks before with a dedication to Percy.[23] The loss of Edward Lye's manuscript translation of Caedmon's poems later drew from him a heartfelt "irreparable!"[24] Among losses not entered on his list were the bulk of his letters from Lord Hailes and "a great part" of his collection of black-letter poems.[25]

To what extent he was indemnified is not apparent. After assessing all damages, the Westminster Fire Office offered the Duke £1280, which he at first rejected, but changed his mind when the Fire Office's directors gave him the alternative of having them arrange for the repairs themselves.[26] The Duke, who had employed the eminent designer and architect Robert Adam at all three of his great estates, could hardly have welcomed the thought of subjecting Northumberland House to the uncertain artistry of the Westminster Fire Office.

Percy returned to Easton Maudit on April 1, and on April 24 left again with his family to move into the Bolton Street house. Having heard nothing from Pinkerton, whom he had written on April 10, he asked on May 20 whether Pinkerton had written to Dodsley and assured him that he was ready to carry out his instructions. The progress of Pinkerton's manuscript from that point is not clear; but, having survived the fire, it apparently failed to survive James Dodsley's scrutiny, and early in January 1781, Percy turned it over to John Nichols.[27] Nichols published it later that year under the title *Scottish Tragic Ballads*.

On May 22 Harry's years at Westminster School concluded with a "Valediction Supper," and the next day his father took him to Lord Percy's and Lord Algernon's, probably to savor their congratulations and good wishes. Percy spent part of the twenty-third with an old Bridgnorth friend, Bryan Bromwich, who paid him sixteen guineas of the £50 still owed on a £100 loan.[28] He dined that night at the Club, when only four members were present, and on the twenty-seventh he called at Bolt Court to finish paying the first year's interest on his own £150 loan from Johnson.

On Friday, June 2, a mob assembled in St. George's Fields under the leadership of Lord George Gordon and marched across Westminster Bridge to protest to Parliament against the relaxation of penalties against the Catholics. "Saw the 50,000 Mob of Protestant Association," Percy wrote in his diary—"Was at M.[r] Nicholls & Dr. Johnson's." And though the mob—the nucleus of the Gordon Riots—roamed through town that night attacking Catholic chapels, he spent the evening in Chelsea and returned to Bolton Street without incident. During a comparatively quiet weekend he dined on Saturday with the Archbishop of Canterbury at Lambeth Palace and walked in the park with the Archbishop and his other four guests; and on Sunday, after attending church at Whitehall, he walked with Clayton Cracherode and William Jones, dined at Lord Sussex's, and spent the evening with a distant relation, Mrs. Meysey.

The rioting intensified on Monday, when the mob set fire to the Langdale distillery in Holborn and liquor literally flowed in the streets. At court, Percy noted, the celebration of the King's birthday was more sparsely attended than usual, but he himself ventured out to dine at the Bishop of London's, Robert Lowth, with the Archibishops of York and Canterbury and many bishops, and spent the evening with a large group at Miss Reynolds's. On Tuesday, June 6, he dined at the Club with Reynolds, Colman, William Scott, and William Jones. During the course of that night the rioters tore down the house of Lord Mansfield, chief justice of the Court of King's Bench; set fire, among others, to the houses of Westminster justices Sir John Fielding and William Hyde; and broke into Newgate, New Prison, and Clerkenwell Bridewell, from which they released many prisoners. On the seventh, Percy wrote, they set fire to "King's Bench: Fleet Prison, &c. &c. &c. &c." until the King authorized the troops to fire and put an end to the week's madness. Percy dined at home that day while the Duke "gave a great Dinner to ye ambassadors."

With calm restored, Percy's interest centered on the troops that had sprung up like poppies in London's parks. On June 8 he walked to Hyde Park to view the encampment before dining at Northumberland House with the Duke and a number of officers. Another encampment drew him to St. James's Park on June 9, and on the fourteenth he called at Lincoln's Inn, where Lord Algernon was quartered with the Northumberland militia. On the fifteenth Edward Blakeway dined at Bolton Street and was taken by the whole family to admire the new splendor of Hyde Park.

When he could shake the military fever, Percy kept busy packing up the books and papers that had survived the Northumberland House fire and preparing to vacate the Bolton Street house. With his chaplaincies for the King and the Duke relinquished and Harry's course at Westminster completed, a London house had become a mere luxury, and the Easton Maudit vicarage would be the Percy's sole residence until the now vacated deanery house, under repair since March, was once again ready for occupancy.

Percy left for Easton Maudit with Harry on June 16, with Anne and the two girls apparently to follow in a day or two; and on the nineteenth father and son set out for the north, Harry to Thomas

Orme at Oakham and Percy to Carlisle. He reached Carlisle on the twenty-second, the day before the start of a four-day audit that was to yield him a half-year's income of £304/10/10.

While work on the deanery house was in progress, he seems to have resided with Archdeacon Law, but joined nonetheless in activities similar to those of the year before, even to ascending the steeple to watch the horse race on July 6. A chapter meeting on June 23, followed by a dinner for numerous guests, gave him opportunities to become acquainted with William Paley, who, along with prebendaries Roger Baldwin and James Lushington, contributed £8 for a gift of plate to Law, while Percy was to contribute £16. Harry's Westminster school-mate Frank Price stopped by on the evening of June 26, and Percy took the next morning off to show him about Carlisle. The deanery house repairs occupied much of his time on July 5 and 7, and perhaps the dust raised by the workmen accounted for the sore throat that afflicted him on the seventh and kept him from the next day's public breakfast, race, and ball. Sore throat notwithstanding, he preached at the cathedral on Sunday, July 9, the second of his three appearances during his 1780 summer residence. On July 14 he put his artistic talents at the service of Dr. Graham, for whom he drew a plan for a tower at Netherby.

In July he paid £25/9/6 to his builder, Daniel Pattinson of Carlisle, for three months' work and materials that included seven and three-fourths days of replacing ceiling joists and sixteen and one-fourth days of plastering, plus the installation of a double chest of drawers in mahogany and an oak bedstead with two carved mahogany posts— the most expensive items at £6/16/6 and £3/18/0.[29] The work, which extended into every room as well as the garden and stable, continued into the fall of 1781, by which time decaying floors and wainscoting had been replaced, windows and doors added, and the whole interior painted or whitewashed. The work also seems to have made good friends of Percy and his builder, who, on Percy's invitation, was later to visit him at Alnwick Castle.[30]

On July 17 Percy was busy all day giving orders about further repairs and alterations prior to setting out for Easton Maudit the next afternoon. The month following his arrival at the vicarage on July 22 was a leisurely one. He sent still further instructions to Pattinson, purchased a new horse for Mrs. Percy, exchanged visits with the Orlebars and others, and went for walks with his family on the Castle Ashby grounds, in Grendon field, and in Horne Wood. On August

6 he preached the same sermon at Wilby that he had preached at the cathedral on July 16, and on August 13 Anne and the girls accompanied him to Wilby for the evening service.[31] Except for preaching the sermon on July 30 and reading prayers on August 20, he seems to have left the Easton Maudit duties to Thomas Bromwich.

On August 21 he set out for Alnwick in his chair, stopping at Kettering to meet with Edmund Allen and at Oakham to spend a couple of days with Harry, whom he drove for an overnight visit with the Gutteridges at Thurmaston and Leicester. Perhaps his stay at Alnwick was intended merely as a relaxing summer interlude for the Duke's former chaplain and secretary, who had been accepted by the Northumberland family almost as one of its own. Percy's services to the family, however, had not terminated with his service, and it seems likely that his 1780 visit was occasioned by the expected completion of one of the Duke's projects in which he had both an interest and a minor part.

In addition to the Duchess of Northumberland's Westminster Abbey memorial, the Duke by 1778 had set his heart on erecting an even more imposing memorial to her at Alnwick. For its architect he probably turned instinctively to Robert Adam. In selecting its site, however, he may have sought Percy's advice, since Percy was as familiar with the environs of Alnwick Castle as the Duke was himself. Percy had visited Hulne Park frequently in the summer of 1778; but on August 26 and 28 of that year he took castle guests not to Hulne Abbey, as in previous visits, but to Brisley Hill, where, by September 24, the Duke was to mark out the ground for a memorial tower. Perhaps Percy was also of some assistance to Robert Adam, if only to reacquaint him with the country.[32] It would have been natural for the architect to be consulted on the site of the proposed tower, and, according to Percy's diary, a "M.r Adams" arrived at Alnwick on August 16, 1778, and was accompanied by Percy to Hulne Abbey on that day and to Warkworth on the next. There is a gap in the diary from August 30 to September 20, but on September 27 Percy was "with M.r Adams about Percy's Cross," as he might have written were he seeking the advice of an expert about the preservation of an ancient monument.[33]

Hulne Abbey and the castles at Alnwick and Warkworth were, of course, Gothic structures, and the Brisley Hill memorial was to be ornamented in the Gothic style also, as though to assure its feeling at home, like the Duchess herself among her ancient family treasures.

The tower continued to rise through the summers of 1779 and 1780, and by the time of Percy's arrival at Alnwick on August 26, 1780, it was probably near completion. Percy noted the presence of "M! Adams" once again on September 21, and on September 30 he was busy preparing a glass vase for the tower into which he placed copies of *The Hermit of Warkworth* and other works, along with a description of Alnwick Castle that he had written for this occasion. No doubt, among other things, it was a satisfaction to him to commend the improvements at Alnwick that Thomas Pennant and Johnson had dismissed with some contempt:

> As soon as this great inheritance devolved to . . . [Elizabeth Percy] and her illustrious Consort, they applied their Attention to restore, repair, and beautify Alnwick Castle, & to improve and cultivate this long neglected Country, which now in 1780, may vie with any Part of England for the extent & number of its young thriving Woods, for the excellence of its agriculture producing all sorts of grain in the greatest abundance, for its well-formed Roads, & beautiful Bridges. And that Posterity may know the extent of the Plantations made by this most noble Pair in this heretofore desolate & naked Country, it appears from the annual Accounts of their Cheif Gardiner [sic], that for near thirty years past, the Duke has caused to be planted out every year, more than a Million Forest Trees, raised from Seeds procured by his Grace from all parts of the World.

On October 3, with the vase hermetically sealed, Percy went with the Duke to deposit it beneath the new tower.[34]

Percy's six weeks at Alnwick seem otherwise to have passed uneventfully, with even the Northumberland election not demanding an effort like that of 1774. On September 11 he rode to Hulne Abbey with a view to revising his 1765 account, which had become outdated with the erection of Brisley Tower. At Alnwick Church, on September 3, he preached the sermon that had already served him that year at Carlisle and Wilby, and he preached there again on September 27 in the presence of Lord and Lady Percy. On September 12 he lost fifteen shillings playing backgammon.

The rest of Percy's autumn was largely uneventful also, but it involved travels that spun him in dizzying succession from Alnwick to Carlisle, London, Easton Maudit, London, Cambridge, London, Easton Maudit, Carlisle, and Easton Maudit. Planting the deanery garden and improving the house held him at Carlisle for only the four days from October 5–9, but he was back again on November 22 for the audit, which brought his year's income as dean to the gratifying total of £738/12/0. Although a guest of Archdeacon Law while the deanery house remained torn up by the workmen, he again had no difficulty carrying on his former activities. He entertained the chapter at dinner on November 23 and the mayor and corporation on the twenty-fourth, stayed overnight at Netherby, joined the card assembly on two evenings, drank tea with the Waugh sisters, and showed off the deanery house improvements to them and others. On November 26 and December 3 he preached in the cathedral.

On all three of his London visits he was a guest of the Duke at Northumberland House. Although the second and third visits were brief, the first extended from October 12, when he spent the evening at Bolt Court with Johnson and Edmund Allen, until October 30, when he caught the early morning Northampton coach after staying overnight at The Ram in Smithfield. Between those dates he had four meetings with his brother, whose worsening finances were a particular worry to Percy, who had pledged himself as surety for Anthony's debts.[35] He also corrected the Percy and Cleiveland pedigrees for Nash's history, probably the reason for his visit to the British Museum on October 24, where he met Steevens and John Stafford Smith. On the next day he was at court to celebrate the anniversary of George III's accession. A "pretty good shew of Company," he wrote in his diary, "for the Town so empty as it is."

After his return to Easton Maudit on October 30, he devoted much of his time to writing an account of Lindridge Parish for Nash's history. On November 3, a day when he and Barbara walked to Grendon to view some new land assigned to him, he sent a servant to Oakham to bring home Harry, who was to enter Emmanuel College in a few days to begin his university studies under Richard Farmer.[36] On Sunday, November 5, Percy gave that year's sermon of choice its fourth delivery, this time at Easton Maudit, and noted in his diary that "the Duke has been ill—I and Harry shall set out for London."

They left the next morning in the one-horse chair, probably carrying some cuttings of white elder that Percy had secured for the Duke, whom they saw that evening. The Duke was better by Wednesday, when Percy, Lord and Lady Algernon, and one or two others dined with him; and though he was very ill that night, Percy and Harry could put off their departure for Cambridge no longer. They reported to Farmer on Thursday evening, and the next day Percy helped with the furnishing of Harry's rooms. He also called on his other Cambridge friends and dined with the Bishop of Carlisle, whose residence at Carlisle from 1778–80 seems never to have coincided with his own.

The Duke was still very ill when Percy returned to Northumberland House on Saturday, November 11. He was better on Sunday, however, and after a visit to Anthony and two days' work on Nash's history, Percy drove back to Easton Maudit on November 15, just three days before he was to set out on the year's final trip to Carlisle. On December 20, on his way to Easton Maudit from Carlisle, he was joined at Stamford by Harry, released for the Christmas holidays after his six-week initiation into university life.

Percy suffered from an old complaint in the spring of 1781. An "Inflammation and Weakness in my eye," he wrote to Lord Hailes on April 14, "has almost deprived me of the power of using a Pen," and he apologized for the numerous blots on his letter.[37] In spite of his eye trouble, April seems to have been a happy month at Easton Maudit. On April 3 young Samuel Isted called at the vicarage, attracted perhaps by nineteen-year-old Barbara, though it was Percy who accompanied him to Whiston after his visit. Harry, home from Cambridge for the Easter holidays, rode with his father around Yardley chase on the tenth, to Wollaston on the eleventh, and to Hinwick and Piddington on the fourteenth. On the thirteenth, Good Friday, Percy conducted the service at Wilby, and on Easter Sunday he administered the sacrament at Easton Maudit to all of his family but fifteen-year-old Elizabeth. With reading and writing all but proscribed, he also turned to a pastime that produced an unprecedented series of diary entries. "Saw the 2^d Swallow at our house," he wrote on Easter Day. "Heard 1st Cuckow in my Lord's Park." Swallows, unnumbered in the diary, continued to arrive each day; but the first nightingale was given a place of honor on the sixteenth, as was the first redstart in the middle of the week.

He spent the last part of April preparing to testify in support of Lord Percy's claim to be designated Great Chamberlain of England, an office made vacant by the death of Robert, Duke of Ancaster, in 1779. The office was hereditary, and Percy's intimate knowledge of the Northumberland pedigrees had made him a vital witness in Lord Percy's cause. More particularly, on June 21, 1780, while on his way to Carlisle, he had copied inscriptions at Well Church in Boroughbridge in Yorkshire that tended to establish Lord Percy's direct descent from John de Vere, fourteenth Earl of Oxford, who had been Great Chamberlain until his death in 1526. As Percy wrote Lord Hailes on April 14, 1781, "if it depends upon the clearest lineal Descent, Lord Percy will undoubtedly carry it." But with another family long in possession of the office, he was not confident that the House of Lords would take its inquiry as far back as the reign of Henry VIII.[38]

He reached Northumberland House on the morning of April 24, two weeks before the case was to be heard in the House of Lords. With time to enjoy London again, he spent the evenings of the twenty-sixth and the twenty-ninth with Farmer, and on the twenty-sixth also attended a dinner at the Middlesex Hospital with Lord Algernon and the Duke, who was the hospital's president.[39] On the twenty-eighth he took physic—one of Grainger's remedies for eyestrain—and on the next day called on Sir John Eliot, who ordered him to go riding for his health. He obeyed promptly by crossing the river to visit his brother. Anne arrived in town on May 5 with Barbara and Elizabeth, a day after the Percy maids, and presumably moved into a house rented for the expected six weeks of their visit.

The pleadings began on May 9 and continued through the eleventh, when they were adjourned until May 18. In the interval Percy dined at the Archbishop of Canterbury's on May 12 and Sir Joshua Reynolds's on the thirteenth, and on the fourteenth he attended the Duke of Cumberland's levee, apparently his first visit since the Duke's rejection by the King in 1771. He spent that evening at Ranelagh with Anne and the girls and the evening of the seventeenth at Miss Reynolds's, where Johnson, probably out of the spirit of contradiction, maintained against him that Chatterton's Rowley poems were written by neither Rowley nor Chatterton but by some "middle man." Percy had been very busy on the seventeenth preparing for the next day's hearing on Lord Percy's claim. But for all his preparation and his faith in the genealogical evidence, the House of Lords decided the case in favor of the Duke of Ancaster's two sisters.[40]

The family was back in the country by Sunday, June 17, when Percy preached at Easton Maudit, and on June 19 he set out for Carlisle to be at hand for the audit. Although some work was still needed, the deanery house was at last in condition to receive the family, and he spent part of his time putting the house in order for the expected arrival of Anne and the girls on June 28. On the thirtieth, with their parcels safely delivered, all four family members were occupied with unpacking and arranging their possessions. Percy himself took charge of trying out the pictures in the "Great Room," among them, no doubt, the Fuller portrait of Cleiveland and some of the engraved "heads" that he took much pleasure in collecting.[41]

Visitors now were numerous, both to greet the new arrivals and to view the house in its nearly finished state. Of special interest was the redecorated prior's room on the second floor, its ceiling paneled in intricate and colorful symbolic designs painted in the year 1500; but no doubt the entire remodeled house was something of a show-piece. The first visits were casual, but on July 3 the two daughters of Roger Baldwin were dinner and theater guests of the Percys, perhaps an effort by Percy and Anne to help Barbara and Elizabeth make new friends. The Baldwin girls were guests at dinner again on July 5 with a group that included William Paley, the eldest Waugh sister, Judith, and Joseph Nicolson, registrar of the diocese and co-author with Richard Burn of the 1777 *History and Antiquities of the Counties of Westmorland and Cumberland*.[42]

Anne and the girls had arrived in time for Carlisle's traditional early July festivities, and scarcely a day went by without their attendance at a horse race, a card assembly, or a ball. Both girls were ill at church on Sunday, July 8—perhaps from sheer exhaustion—but were well enough in the evening to be taken out for a drive. On the next day the Percys were visited by the two youngest Waugh sisters and by "all the Carlisle Family," and on the eleventh Percy seems to have had his first opportunity to dine with Bishop Law at his palace, Rose Castle, where Paley and his son also were guests. On July 12 Harry arrived from Cambridge for the summer.

Ironically, just as Percy and his family were settling in for a long residence at Carlisle, the seeds of another move that he had planted in the spring were beginning to show signs of life. On April 5, 1781, Michael Lort, responding to what he called Percy's "Commission," had called his attention to Dr. Jeffery Ekins, who, as secretary to the Earl of Carlisle, Lord Lieutenant of Ireland, was in line for an Irish bishopric, but seemed eager to exchange it for a deanery. "Possibly," Lort commented to Percy, Ekins "may have no objection to make such an exchange with an English dean."[43]

Such a possibility was not to be overlooked. Taking the kind of circuitous approach typical on such occasions, Percy wrote to Dr. Thomas Barnard, Bishop of Killaloe and a fellow member of the Club, who passed on to Ekins, in confidence, "particulars relating to the deanery of Carlisle"; and through another channel Percy let it be known that he was "desirous of entering *now* into some conditional agreement . . . for an exchange of preferment," if Ekins could procure him a recommendation to a vacant Irish bishopric. Ekins responded on June 21 by assuring Percy that Lord Carlisle would find him "very acceptable" and asserting a willingness to take Percy's deanery in exchange if one of the bishoprics of Down, Waterford, Clonfert, Ferns, Dromore, Killaloe, Killala, or Ossory should fall to his lot.[44] Percy wrote directly to Ekins on July 31 and August 4 after he had had an opportunity to discuss the proposed arrangement with the Duke at Alnwick Castle, and though both letters are known only through Percy's diary record of them, he plainly expressed a desire to continue negotiations.

He himself had arrived at Alnwick Castle on July 18, bringing his family with him on its first Northumberland visit. For three weeks he shared with Anne and the children the attractions that had been a part of his life since 1765, particularly Hulne Abbey, Warkworth Castle and the hermitage, Alnwick Abbey, and the castle itself. They mingled with the Duke's neighbors and guests, welcomed Lord and Lady Algernon on August 5, walked along the seashore, and entered into the fun of the Alnwick fair, with three days of horse races and a performance by a troupe of traveling players.

The family's visit ended on August 10, but Percy, after accompanying the others more than a third of the way to Carlisle, returned to Alnwick, where Dr. Richard Robinson, the Primate of Ireland, arrived on August 14. Whether or not prompted by Percy's negotiations with Dr. Ekins, Dr. Robinson's presence at the castle for two weeks provided more than one occasion for Percy to consult with him about the Irish bishoprics. On August 15, 16, and 17 Percy went riding with him and the Duke, and on the eighteenth, when Dr. Robinson was taken ill, Percy stayed at the castle with him throughout the day.

Percy himself remained at the castle until September 16, when he left for Newcastle with the Duke and then went on to Carlisle on the eighteenth. Eager to continue his quest for preferment, he wrote to Dr. Robinson on October 1 and to Dr. Ekins on October 6 and 18. It was, of course, natural for him to aspire to higher office. Singled out for honors by one of the first noblemen of his day and by the King himself, he was now only one step away from the dignity, respect, authority, and service to church, state, and society that were the ultimate fulfillment of his calling. But Percy had still another motive, perhaps no less common to deans and bishops than to impecunious curates and vicars. By the end of 1781 he was deeply in debt, a condition that one who had lamented the improvidence of his father must have found sorely trying. Outstanding bills on the deanery house amounted to £138/18/3½, including £46/8/3¾ from the upholsterer and £49/14/0 from Daniel Pattinson. He had borrowed extensively: £56 from a Mr. Edward Bishop and £130 from Lord Algernon without interest; and, at interest of five percent, £150 from Johnson, £60 from Paley, £50 each from Henry Selby and a Desborough friend of William Gutteridge, and £40 from a Mr. Lechmere. Owed "On Henry's Account," as he recorded it in his diary, were £100 to Richard Farmer and more than £43 to other creditors. Anthony's finances remained a worry, a drain without a stopper, and Percy was paying the widowed Mary Edwards an annuity of £20 and providing occasional other sums to assist her daughter, Elizabeth Bartin Edwards.[45]

It is thus not surprising to find him consulting Arthur Young's 1780 *Tour in Ireland* and copying out its information on the yearly value of Irish bishoprics: Clonfert, £2400; Down and Connor, £2300; Dromore, £2000; Killala, £2900; Waterford and Lismore, £2500; and so through the twenty-two bishoprics and four archbishoprics.[46] Even discounting 8 percent for the Irish pound, every one of the bishoprics had a higher value than Lincoln, Chichester, Exeter, Hereford, and half a dozen others, for all of which the range was from £1400 to £450.[47] No wonder Percy looked across the Irish Sea for at least temporal salvation. In Carlisle he would be years shedding the burden of debt; in Ireland, with Ekin's help, there was a prospect of prompt relief.

It was fortunate that, in the midst of these worries, he was unaware how close his son had come to terminating his university career. On Thursday, November 8, Farmer sent John Nichols an urgent plea for assistance. Harry, he wrote,

> instead of proceeding to college according to his father's expectations, has suddenly (as I am informed) left the Cambridge road for a scheme to London. Now, Sir, if we cannot get him hither on Monday next, at furthest, he will lose his Term, and probably every expectation in his present line of life.
> I know he has formerly been found at one of the hotels in the

Adelphi, and it may not be amiss to enquire at Northumberland House. I hope he has not much money with him. You know the town better than I do, and I doubt not will make every proper enquiry. I will leave it to his father to express his gratitude.

Luckily, as Farmer wrote Nichols on November 14, Harry met his deadline, giving as the reason for his delay that he had traveled to London to consult his father's physician, Sir John Eliot. Farmer added that "as the Dean knows nothing of the case or the scheme, I believe (if he behaves properly in future) we had better say no more about it. He, however, acknowledges himself under great obligations for your kind attention to him, and I thank you very sincerely."[48]

Whether or not Harry bypassed Cambridge through some questionable scheme, as Farmer seems to have believed, his father—contrary to another Farmer belief—was informed of the London trip and apparently approved it. He noted in his diary that Harry wrote to Mr. Osborne at the Adelphi Hotel on October 20, probably (it seems reasonable to assume) to reserve a room for himself; and he later entered, among the miscellaneous expenses "On Harry's Account," £22 for "Mr. Osborne (Hotel)." Perhaps Harry, caught up in London's attractions, thoughtlessly attempted to stretch his freedom to the limit, since his acknowledgment of an obligation to John Nichols suggests that he may have failed to appreciate the risk he was running until Nichols impressed it upon him.

On November 10, while Harry was probably making his way to Cambridge, his father was busy writing a letter for the newspapers on the Ossian controversy, which he had been drawn into by a passage in William Shaw's *Enquiry into the Authenticity of the Poems Ascribed to Ossian*, published in London during the preceding spring. Shaw had cited the occasion at Adam Ferguson's in 1765 when a highland student had recited and then interpreted verses in the Erse language that Percy recognized as part of the description of Fingal's chariot.[49] The passage was reprinted in the June issue of the *Gentleman's Magazine* and promptly elicited a denial from Ferguson: "I never was present at the repetition of verses to Dr. Percy by a young student from the Highlands," he wrote on July 21 in a letter printed in at least three London newspapers.[50] Shaw, who had included the passage to suggest that Percy was deceived, replied in a public letter of August 31 acknowledging that he had had his information secondhand. "I desire to acquit Mr. Ferguson," he wrote, "whose presence or absence makes no difference in the question [of an attempt to convince Percy]. . . . The attempt was really made, and Dr. Percy was for a while credulous, with which I do not mean to reproach him, for I have confessed that I once was credulous myself."[51]

Percy himself was not prepared to grant such an acquittal. He wrote to Hugh Blair shortly after the publication of Ferguson's denial, no doubt to ask that he confirm his own recollection of the incident, but neither his letter nor Blair's reply seems to have survived.[52] Blair later informed Dr. Joseph Carlyle that he had written to Percy a number of times, and perhaps an exchange of letters now apparently lost accounts for the delay of some three and a half months before Percy decided to enter the public lists with Ferguson.[53] Whatever else he may have written, Blair maintained consistently that he had no recollection of Ferguson's presence during the incident, and Percy was thus compelled to proceed unseconded.

He might have been well advised to hold his pen, but he could not dismiss the incident as insignificant, and Ferguson's denial offended him deeply. His diary entry of the occasion was characteristically terse: "Sun. 13 [October 1765]: . . . Tea at M[r] Ferguson's Professor of Moral Philosophy." But he had found the incident unforgettable; it had marked indelibly at least a partial turn in his assessment of James Macpherson's translations, the authenticity of which he had persisted in questioning until that time. At Blair's request, in fact, he cited the incident two years later when he revised the *Reliques* for the second edition:

> No pieces of their [the Irish bards'] poetry have been translated, unless their claim may be allowed to those beautiful pieces of ERSE POESY, which were lately given to the world in an English dress by Mr. MAC-PHERSON: Several fragments of which the editor of this book has heard sung in the original language, and translated *vivâ voce*, by a native of the Highlands, who had, at the time, no opportunity of consulting Mr. Macpherson's book.[54]

Some years later, as Percy wrote in his November 10 letter to the newspapers, a "very judicious" Scottish friend persuaded him that there might have been "some deception in the case," and he accordingly suppressed the passage in 1775 when he revised the *Reliques* for the third edition. "But," he commented at the conclusion of the letter, "as I never believed Dr. Blair to have been conscious of any deception in what passed between the student and me, so the same may have been the case with Dr. Ferguson also, as he now appears so entirely to have forgot the whole transaction."[55]

Percy kept the November 10 letter by him until November 24, when he sent it to John Nichols with copies of Ferguson's July 21 and Shaw's August 31 letters and requested that Nichols print all three in the *Gentleman's Magazine.* He requested also that Nichols send printed copies of his November 10 letter to seven newspapers, particularly the *Morning Chronicle,* the *St. James's Chronicle,* and the *Public Advertiser,* in which Ferguson's letter had appeared. "I would pay any sum to have my narrative inserted in [these three]," he wrote.[56] With a December 1 publication imminent, Nichols was apparently unable to fit the series of letters into the magazine's November issue, as Percy had hoped, but, good friend that he was, he printed them in the December issue and sent copies of the November 10 letter to the three newspapers that were Percy's first choice.[57]

It was now Ferguson's turn to take offense. Percy had come close to accusing him of deception, and he sent off a spirited reply in which he incorporated a letter he had sent to Blair on August 18 after reading Percy's comments to Blair on his July 21 letter.[58] He acknowledged that he had shown Percy some scraps of Erse poetry in Macpherson's handwriting, but he stoutly denied that a highland student had recited Erse poetry on the occasion in question or had even recited verses in his presence aside from a mere song or catch. He also suggested a basis for Percy's misunderstanding: "I am entirely persuaded Dr. Percy, in recollecting the Passages of his few Days stay at Edinburgh, must have jumbled together Circumstances that, in Point of Time, were actually separate; the Repetition of Verses by a young Student, with the Communication of Verses in Writing by me." As Percy allows, he concluded, "that I may not have been conscious of any Deception, in what passed between the Student and him, I must in Return, allow, that he may not be conscious of any Misrepresentation of Fact. But I cannot allow that he has made the best Use of his Understanding, in thinking it credible, that any Person, possessed of a decent Character, could be concerned in such a Cheat as he supposes to have been practised upon him."[59]

The public debate ended at that point, but Percy was unable to conceal his dissatisfaction from his friends. After his return to London in March 1782 he showed Horace Walpole and others, including Dr. Carlyle, two letters that Blair had written him in 1766 and 1767 identifying the highland student as John Macpherson and alluding to young Macpherson's recitation and translation of some of the Erse poems. Walpole was persuaded that Percy had been deceived, as was Carlyle until Blair pointed out to him that nowhere in his letters had he mentioned Ferguson's presence during the recitation.[60] Blair did not state, when he wrote to Carlyle, that Ferguson was *not* present, nor did he attempt to account for Ferguson's absence while his two guests were entertained by one of his students, but perhaps this information simply eluded his memory after fifteen years. Boswell, to whom Percy later showed his diary and the correspondence, confessed to his journal that his "Countrymen made but a shabby figure," although he thought also that Percy placed too much emphasis on the diary entry, which fixed the date of the tea at Ferguson's but was silent about the recitation. Percy, he noted, "was very keen and violent upon the subject."[61]

On Sunday, March 17, 1782, only a day after returning alone to Easton Maudit, Percy was delivered the letter from Dr. Ekins that was the culmination of their correspondence. He had hoped to be offered the bishopric of Killala, which was valued at £2900 a year. Instead, Ekins reported that he was authorized to offer the bishopric of Dromore, and at his request—a "Summons to Town," as Percy called it—Percy hurried off to London on Monday morning. The see of Dromore, he wrote Anne from Northumberland House that night, "lies very near Carlisle, in a very chearful well-inhabited Part of Ireland. So that your Situation will be much more agreeable than at the other place, and it also is in the Neighbourhood of our good friend the Primate." But then, he added, "the Profits are not so great and I also fear there is a heavy expence to be incurred by a new Palace, wch is just now building & wch I must pay for.—But I shall know more tomorrow, when I can get sight of Dr Ekins."[62]

He had knocked at Ekins's door as he came into town, but finding him away for the evening proceeded directly to Northumberland House. Before scribbling his note to Anne at 11:00 P.M., he wrote letters to Ireland and elsewhere, perhaps in the hope of learning as much as he could about Dromore before he was compelled to give Ekins a definitive answer. He had most of the basic information, of course, but he felt handicapped by not being able to consult the Duke of Northumberland, who was at Newmarket and was not expected back until the twenty-seventh.

No record has survived of the meeting with Ekins, which probably took place the next morning, but Percy's subsequent letter to Ekins reveals that, in exchange for the Carlisle deanery, he was offered the Lord Lieutenant of Ireland's recommendation that he be appointed Bishop of Dromore. With no substantial encumbrance, the offer would probably have taken him little time to consider. His fear that he would have to pay the full cost of the see house under construction proved to be well founded, however, and he returned to Northumberland House to await the arrival of the Duke. Unfortunately the Duke did not return on schedule, and on the twenty-eighth—perhaps pressed by Ekins for an answer—Percy called on Samuel Johnson, his "Oracle" of earlier days.[63]

Percy gave Ekins his decision the next day. He had considered the offer as best he could in the absence of his patron, he explained, and believed that the Duke would concur in thinking him ill-advised, after spending so much on the Carlisle house, to relinquish his present preferments and expectations for a bishopric that required him to pay the whole cost of the new see house immediately. He would be interested, however, in any of the other bishoprics that were not liable to the same objection.[64]

The answer seemed conclusive, but it was not. Within a few days something happened to change his mind. Perhaps a letter from Farmer arrived urging the exchange of positions.[65] Perhaps the Duke returned from Newmarket and advised his acceptance. Or perhaps Ekins persuaded him that the see house would be less burdensome than he had feared: by the end of the year he would have to pay only £1200 of the full £3200, and he or his family would in time be repaid three-fourths of the amount by his successor.[66] However the change occurred, news of the appointment had spread before April 12, when Percy thanked William Cleiveland for his "friendly Congratulations"—a little premature, he noted, since he had not yet resigned his deanery, though all the arrangements were settled.[67] These had their own encumbrance: £219/7/9½ in fees, according to Percy's itemized record,[68] although they were doubtless overshadowed by the excitement of the moment. His appointment was signed by the King on April 17 and was stamped with the privy seal and transmitted to Ireland on the twentieth, when he resigned all his English preferments. He kissed the King's hand on the nineteenth and the Queen's on the twenty-first. The Queen, as he wrote Anne on April 22, "spoke to me very graciously: asked me how you & my family liked removing from England: and when I answered that you were disposed to comply with any thing, that was for the benefit of your family, She gave a Smile of Approbation, and said She had no Doubt, but you would."[69]

The ceremony with the Queen, he wrote, finished all his business on that side of the water.

NOTES

1. *Reliques* (1765), 1:146.
2. The Waugh sisters were named Judith, Isabella, Elizabeth, Mary, and Margaret. Boswell, who dined with them on 23 August 1778, noted that each of the five had inherited an income of more than £500 a year after their brother, a prebendary of Carlisle, was killed by a fall from a horse (*Boswell Laird of Auchinleck 1778–1782*, ed. Joseph W. Reed and Frederick A. Pottle [New York: McGraw-Hill, 1977], 10). In 1775 they had also inherited £1400 from their mother to be divided equally among them (information supplied by the Cumbria County Council).
3. B.L. Add. MS., 32,333, ff. 135–36. Chapter Records, 246–50.
4. Ibid., f. 137.
5. Alnwick Castle MS., Northumberland Misc. Papers G/2/10.
6. Crotch became Professor of Music at Oxford in 1797. The entry concerning his childhood performance is the last in B.L. Add. MS. 32,336. The rest of Percy's diary entries are in Add. MS. 32,337.
7. Alnwick Castle MS. 93A/27 (Letter to Percy, 5 March 1779). B.L. Add. MS. 32, 333, f. 146 (Letter Percy to Cleveland, 4 Oct. 1779).
8. Ibid., Northumberland Misc. Papers G/2/9–10. *The Percy Letters*, 8:22. Percy was apologizing for not replying promptly to a Pinkerton letter apparently received in May.
9. Letter Percy to his nephew, 29 Oct. 1781 (collection of Kenneth Balfour).
10. *The Percy Letters*, 4:142 (Letter Percy to Lord Hailes, 2 Oct. 1779).
11. B.L. Add. MS. 32,333, f. 143 (Letter Percy to Cleiveland, 22 July 1779).
12. Boswell's *Life*, 3:415–16. Replying to Boswell's information on 13 November, Johnson wrote, "If Dean Percy can be popular at Carlisle, he may be very happy. He has in his disposal two livings, each equal, or almost equal in value to the deanery; he may take one himself, and give the other to his son" (*Life*, 3:417). "Where did J. pick up this mistake?" Percy asked when he read Boswell's *Life* in 1791 (Bodl. MS. Percy d. 11, f. 13).
13. Chapter Records, 255; Bodl. MS. Percy d. 5, f. 80.
14. B.L. Add. MS. 32,329, ff. 110–11.
15. Ibid., ff. 112–13. The 1779 issues of the *Antiquarian Repertory*, collected in 1780 and published as volume 3, contain a number of short pieces by Percy: "The Allowance of Cloth, &c. to the King's Fool," translated from

the Latin in Rymer's *Foedera* on p. 29; letter on instances of "uncommon old age" in Northumberland on pp. 41–43, and dated 6 March 1779, the day that, according to Percy's diary, he was visited in London by the magazine's engraver; a sequel, on four vicars who served a total of 199 years at Worfield in Shropshire, on pp. 129–30 and dated 29 May 1779; "An Account of Percy's Cross," with an engraving, on pp. 130–32. According to Percy's article, Percy's Cross, which he first visited on 24 August 1765, was erected in memory of Sir Ralph Percy, one of the younger sons of Henry Percy, second Earl of Northumberland. A brief piece on Warkworth Castle with a full-page print (171–72) and another on Henry Percy, first Earl of Northumberland, with a portrait "engraved from a Drawing in the possession of the Dean of Carlisle" (237–40) were presumably also submitted by Percy.

16. *The Percy Letters*, vol. 1, *The Correspondence of Thomas Percy & Edmond Malone*, ed. Arthur Tillotson (Baton Rouge: Louisiana State Univ. Press, 1944), 1–2. *Supplement to the Edition of Shakspeare's Plays Published in 1778 by Samuel Johnson and George Steevens* (London, 1780). For a discussion of these and later Percy notes, largely on the apocryphal plays, see Sherbo, *The Birth of Shakespeare Studies*, 85–92.

17. B.L. Add. MS. 32, 329, f. 115 (Letter Smith to Percy, 30 Jan. 1780).

18. *The Percy Letters*, 8:24–27 (Letters Pinkerton to Percy, 7 and 27 July 1779; Percy to Pinkerton, 21 July 1779).

19. Ibid., 27–29.

20. *St. James's Chronicle*, 16–18 March 1780.

21. *Whitehall Evening-Post*, 16–18 March; *Morning Post*, 22 March. For a detailed account of the fire, see Bertram H. Davis, "Thomas Percy, the Reynolds Portrait, and the Northumberland House Fire," *Review of English Studies* (Feb. 1982), 23–33.

22. B.L. Add. MS. 32,333, ff. 150–51 (Letter to Cleiveland, 31 March 1780). *The Percy Letters*, 8:29–30 (Letter to Pinkerton, 10 April 1780).

23. Bodl. MS. Percy c. 9, ff. 44–45.

24. Ibid., d. 11, f. 13.

25. *Lit. Illus.*, 8:375. *The Letters of Sir Walter Scott*, ed. Sir Herbert Grierson (London: Constable, 1932), 1:108n. (Letter Percy to Scott, 10 Dec. 1800).

26. Westminster City Library MS. w.f.o. 343/16 (Minute Book 1780, Westminster Fire Office, 13 and 27 April).

27. *The Percy Letters*, 8:31–33 (Letters to Pinkerton 20 May 1780 and 7 Jan. 1781).

28. Bromwich, the father of Percy's curate Thomas Bromwich, had purchased some of Percy's books when Percy moved to Easton Maudit in 1756.

29. Collection of Kenneth Balfour ("Papers relating to Improvements at the Carlisle Deanery").

30. Letters Pattinson to Percy, 14 Sept. and 1 Oct. 1780; 5 March 1781 (collection of Kenneth Balfour); diary, 3 Sept. 1781.
31. Bodl. MS. Percy d. 4, f. 39.
32. Adam had redesigned much of the interior of the castle in the 1760s, primarily to suit Lady Northumberland's taste for the Gothic.
33. Mr. Adams may have been someone other than the architect, but Percy did on occasion enter names imprecisely in his diary, and Mr. Adams's appearances coincide with the selection of the site and the completion of the tower.
34. Alnwick Castle MS. 93A/19. Percy had also arranged to print five hundred copies of a description of Alnwick Castle, probably the same as this one. I have not, however, seen a copy of the printed description. On 22 August 1781 Percy gave a hundred copies to the castle porter and fifty to the housekeeper, apparently for them to distribute to guests.
35. *Lit. Illus.* 6:578 (Letter Percy to Edmund Allen, 28 Dec. 1783).
36. In March 1780 Percy had been hopeful that Harry would be awarded two scholarships at Sidney College, Cambridge, but apparently nothing came of them (B.L. Add. MS., 32,333 f. 151 [Letter to Cleiveland, 31 March 1780]).
37. *The Percy Letters,* 4:146.
38. Ibid., 145–46. Boswell (*Life,* 4:98) says that Percy attended a party at Mrs. Garrick's on April 20; his diary shows him at Easton Maudit.
39. Percy would seem to have been the author of a sixteen-line poem signed "T.P." in the *St. James's Chronicle* for 24–26 April 1766: "On a Concert and Ball, for the Benefit and Building of the Middlesex Hospital, and a Ball for the Lying-in Hospital."
40. A printed copy of Earl Percy's case is in Alnwick Castle MS. 93A/19. Though signed by Earl Percy's four lawyers, much of it was probably Percy's work. For the evening at Miss Reynolds's see *Boswell Laird of Auchinleck 1778–1782,* ed. Joseph W. Reed and Frederick A. Pottle (New York: McGraw-Hill, 1977), 359.
41. Percy's engraved portraits are in the collection of Kenneth Balfour.
42. Burn was chancellor of the diocese. Perhaps it was during this period that Percy succeeded in getting a local bookseller to remove the "libidinous prints books & adulterous trials" from his shop and catalogue (*Lit. Illus.,* 7:491 [Letter Percy to Michael Lort, 2 March 1788]).
43. *Lit. Illus.,* 7:439. At this time Lort was chaplain to the Archbishop of Canterbury.
44. Ibid., 8:191–92.
45. Percy sent Elizabeth Edwards £10 on 12 Feb. and 10 March 1780, and 22 Jan. 1781 (Ledger, Goslings Bank).
46. Collection of Kenneth Balfour. Percy also secured the names and ages of all the Irish bishops, plus information on the see houses and the predom-

inant religion among the people in each diocese. In all it proved to be either Catholic or Presbyterian.

47. Donald Harman Akenson, *The Church of Ireland: Ecclesiastical Reform and Revolution 1800–1885* (New Haven: Yale Univ. Press, 1971), 37.

48. Cradock, *Literary and Miscellaneous Memoirs*, 4:96–97.

49. Shaw, 45.

50. *Morning Chronicle* and *Public Advertiser*, 4 Aug. 1781; *St. James's Chronicle*, 4–7 Aug. 1781.

51. *Lit. Illus.*, 6:568.

52. In a letter to Blair dated 18 August, Ferguson mentioned seeing a letter that Blair had received from Percy (*Morning Chronicle*, 10 Jan. 1782, and other newspapers; see Note 59 this chapter).

53. University of Edinburgh MS. La II 243 (3) (Letter 18 April 1782).

54. *Reliques* (1767), 1:xlv.

55. *Lit. Illus.*, 6:569.

56. Ibid., 567–68.

57. *Gentleman's Magazine* (Dec. 1781), 567–68. *Morning Chronicle*, 14 Dec.; *St. James's Chronicle*, 13–15 Dec.; *Public Advertiser*, 17 Dec.

58. Ferguson asked Blair to share his letter with Percy.

59. *Whitehall Evening-Post*, 8–10 Jan. 1782; *St. James's Chronicle*, 12–15 Jan. 1782; *Morning Chronicle*, 10 Jan. 1782.

60. *The Yale Edition of Horace Walpole's Correspondence*, vol. 29, *Horace Walpole's Correspondence with William Mason*, vol. 2, ed. W.S. Lewis, Grover Cronin, Jr., and Charles H. Bennett (New Haven: Yale Univ. Press, 1955), 239–40 (Letter Walpole to Mason, 22 April 1782). University of Edinburgh MS. La II 243 (4) (Letter Blair to Carlyle, 22 April 1782). In the letter Blair quoted relevant passages from his letters to Percy dated 10 February 1766 and 10 January 1777. The two letters are not otherwise known.

61. *Boswell: The Applause of the Jury 1782–1785*, ed. Irma S. Lustig and Frederick A. Pottle (New York: McGraw-Hill, 1981), 70–73.

62. B.L. Add. MS. 39,547, ff. 40–41.

63. *Yale Johnson*, I, 318.

64. From a photocopy, supplied by Arthur Freeman, of a draft or copy of the letter in Percy's hand.

65. Sir Egerton Brydges, *Restituta* (London, 1814–16), 4:243–44. William Cole was the authority cited for Farmer's urging Percy to make the exchange.

66. *Lit. Illus.*, 6:578 (Letter Percy to Edmund Allen, 28 Dec. 1783).

67. B.L. Add. MS. 32,333, f. 157.

67. Collection of Kenneth Balfour.

69. B.L. Add. MS. 39,547, f. 42.

CHAPTER XI

Bishop of Dromore:
1782–1798

Percy probably left England with few romantic notions about his new homeland. As early as 1758 James Grainger had described the Irish common people to him as "the most indolent and most dirty" that he had ever seen:

> They live in the meanest huts, and feed on the coarsest fare I ever beheld. This shocked me more than I can well describe to you, for I had always given them the preference to the Scots; but in all these particulars they are as far outdone by my countrymen as the English surpass us . . . ; I am now less surprised that Dean Swift gave such a humbling picture of human nature, in his account of the Yahoos, considering the country he lived in.

And in 1780 one of Percy's more recent authorities, Arthur Young, had passed through Dromore with no inclination to linger among what he called this "miserable nest of dirty mud cabbins."[1] Such comments, of course, had not kept Percy from pursuing an Irish bishopric, and, adaptable as he was, it seems likely that when he embarked from Holyhead about the first of May 1782 he had every intention of being pleased with his new situation.

Perhaps it was fortunate, nonetheless, that his first destination was Dublin, where he was consecrated in the chapel of Dublin Castle on May 26 and seated in the House of Lords the next day. Officiating at the consecration was his good friend Dr. Robinson, Archbishop of Armagh and Primate of Ireland, who was assisted by the Bishops of Clogher and Clonfert.[2] His first day in the House of Lords, as he wrote Anne on May 30, brought "one of the most pleasing Events, that this Country ever saw": the Lord Lieutenant, in great state and before a full house, delivered a message from the King and the English Parliament "granting all the desires of this people, w:ch they have been struggling for so long."[3] On May 29, with the streets lined with regiments of Volunteers, the members of both houses were driven in procession to the castle to present the Lord Lieutenant with an address of thanks to the King.[4]

Day by day Percy was making new friends. "This is certainly the most hospitable K[in]gdom that ever was," he informed Anne; "I have been here now near 3 weeks, & in all this time have never dined at home but twice: and now am engaged for many days to come." Understandably exuberant, he ordered a hogshead of claret to be sent from Dublin to his fellow Club members in London "as a small tribute of respect to the society, among whom . . . [he] had spent so many agreeable hours."[5]

Although Percy's assessment of England's largesse was optimistic, Dublin had good reason for its high spirits. The English Parliament had repealed the Declaratory Act of 1719, which had reinforced and clarified the right of the Privy Council under the 1494 Poynings' Law to approve or disapprove all acts of the Irish Parliament in advance; and in the Irish Parliament the Catholic Relief Act of 1778 had been followed on May 2, 1782, by a Second Relief Act admitting Catholics to the same rights of property and leasehold as Protestants. Agitation for an explicit renunciation of Poynings' Law and for other reforms was to continue, but 1782 was Ireland's year of hope, and Percy had the good fortune to join his new countrymen at the very height of their exhilaration.

After Dublin, which he left following the adjournment of Parliament on June 15, Dromore must have been a sobering reality, but Percy gave not so much as a hint of disappointment. With a name that had gone before him, he was accorded a scholar's as well as a bishop's welcome. The Countess of Moira, daughter of the Earl of Huntingdon and an irrepressible antiquary, had inundated him with genealogical minutiae while he was still in Dublin: long letters on English kings and noblemen from a Yorkist to a Lancastrian, as she chose to designate herself and Percy. "When the Bishop of Dromore is so obliging to favour them with his company in the North," she wrote on June 9, "Lady Moira will show his Lordship several memorandums she has taken out relative to genealogical inquiries."[6]

Percy did not slight a neighbor so influential and congenial, but he had to devote most of his brief time in Dromore to his diocesan duties. He was enthroned in the church of Dromore on June 20, when he preached his first sermon. It was not, he insisted, a charge to the clergy of the diocese; but it was an unmistakable call for the clergy to perform their duties faithfully and a pledge, at least implied, that he himself would do no less:

> Neither deep erudition, nor polite learning, nor elegant address, nor convivial Talents, nor a sociable turn, nor any other of the usual recommendations among men of the world can reconcile us to the character of an unfaithful Minister of Christ, to a false or deceitful or careless Steward of the Mysteries of God.
>
> And if ever Fidelity in the Christian Minister . . . were requisite, it is surely in a more especial manner at present, when the Christian Religion is so often either obliquely or fundamentally attacked, and its mysteries ridiculed or explained away by the fashionable writers of the age.[7]

He set to work promptly visiting as many of his twenty-six parishes as time would allow: the vicarages of Aghadery, Donaghmore, Kilbroney, and Seapatrick, for example, and the rectorates of Clonallan, Lurgan, Magheralin, and Moira. At Donaghmore he found the church in excellent repair, "well pewed and painted," with the vicar planning to build a glebe house (vicarage) near the church. But with only thirty communicants among them, the Protestants of the Church of Ireland were outnumbered ten to one by the Dissenters and twenty to one by the Papists. The church at Kilbroney, though delightfully situated on Carlingford Bay, was out of repair, and the forty-five Protestant families were a tiny minority among some two thousand Papists. "Col. Ross, who leases ye great Tythes," Percy noted, "sh^d keep up the Ch[urch] or at least promote its Reparation." At Moira the rector resided in the parish, the church was in excellent condition, and—Percy was perhaps surprised to discover—Lord Moira and Lord Hillsborough had seats in the church with canopies.[8]

At his home parish of Dromore, he thought the church in good repair and the churchyard well walled, but was disturbed that the rector had neither glebe nor glebe house and consequently rented a house two miles from the church. The Protestants in Dromore outnumbered the Papists two to one, but were in turn outnumbered three to one by the Dissenters. Perhaps as he contemplated the cathedral— one of Ireland's smallest and least pretentious[9]—Percy's thoughts turned to the cathedral he had left behind him in Carlisle, a striking eminence of Gothic arches, tracery, and stained glass, small itself by English standards, but expansive enough to embrace half a dozen cathedrals the size of Dromore. Dromore provided no matching splendor. Its history could be traced as far back as St. Colman in the early sixth century, however, and its stubborn determination to survive had twice saved it from extinction, its most recent resurgence the work of Percy's seventeenth-century predecessor, the renowned Bishop Jeremy Taylor.

Close by, the shallow water of the River Lagan slipped unobtrusively past the churchyard; and between the cathedral and the moldering remnants of Dromore Castle a twin-arched bridge directed travelers entering town from the northeast. Further on lay the square, dominated by a market house with stone arches, where the neighborhood gathered on Saturday market days and during the town's two annual fairs. The dirty mud cabins that had repelled Arthur Young were huddled with the rest of the town on the side of a hill, the name "Dromore" signifying "the great Back of a Hill."[10]

On a rise near the Lurgan road almost a mile from town, with a lower access about two hundred yards from the cathedral, Dromore's only attempt at magnificence was still far from ready for occupancy. The bishop's palace projected by Percy's immediate predecessor, William Beresford, who had been translated to the bishopric of Ossory, was a substantial rectangular building of four stories, its lowest floor below ground level with windows opening on a dry moat, and its plainness broken by a small porch at the entrance. A four-hundred-acre demesne, with some parts occupied by tenant houses, spread temptingly around it, an invitation that the gardener in Percy would respond to once he and his family had moved into the palace.[11]

That time was still a year away, for even after the palace was completed months were required for the plaster to dry. When Percy returned to England in early July, he thus rejoined his family in the Carlisle deanery house, where Dr. Ekins let them continue until the Dromore palace was ready to receive them.[12] In addition to Percy's resignation, Carlisle had witnessed other changes since his departure for London in March. John Law had given up the archdeaconry to serve as chaplain to the Duke of Portland, who succeeded the Earl of Carlisle as Lord Lieutenant of Ireland, and William Paley had replaced Law as archdeacon. Within a few months Law was appointed Bishop of Clonfert.

Percy himself, with no further duties at Carlisle and comparatively few demands from Dromore at such a distance, might have been expected to turn his attention to some of his unfinished literary projects. They were not numerous. Before leaving for Dromore he had arranged for John Nichols to print the edition of the *Spectator* that he had turned over to John Calder in 1773. About the same time he had presented to the Lambeth Palace Library his collection of translations of the Psalms, a total of forty-one books and two manuscripts.[13] He seems also by then to have completed his work for Treadway Nash's *Collections for the History of Worcestershire*, the second volume of which Nichols published in 1782. And with the publication of John Bowle's Spanish language edition of *Don Quixote* in June 1781, Bowle no longer had any need for his assistance.[14]

The remaining projects were the history of the house of Percy, a brief biography of John Cleiveland that he had promised for the *Biographia Britannica*, and the long dormant editions of Buckingham and Surrey. Although he apparently did further research for the Percy history at Alnwick in 1781, and possibly 1782, he never got beyond four printed sheets.[15] In 1783 he completed the article on Cleiveland and had the printed sheets of the Buckingham and Surrey editions turned over to Nichols, in whose warehouse they began another long period of neglect.[16]

Pleased though Percy was with his new position, the year 1782 proved to be an anxious one. During the winter at Cambridge Harry had caught a severe cold, which hung on and was exacerbated in the spring by his lying in a damp bed. By July, when he rejoined the family for the summer, he had developed an alarming consumptive cough.[17] Perhaps his illness accounts for a trip that Percy made to London between mid-August and early September, though all that is known of the trip is that Percy dined with Johnson on August 19 and wrote to William Cleiveland from Northumberland House on September 4. But, with Harry's condition growing steadily more critical, it would have been natural for his father to consult Sir John Eliot in London as well as his admired Carlisle physician, Dr. John Heysham.[18]

By the fall Harry's physicians concluded that his life could be preserved only if he was removed to a warmer climate, and Percy booked passage for him and Thomas Bromwich on the *Prince Ferdinand*, a Tuscan brig sailing to Leghorn from Liverpool. With the two of them, Percy settled in at Liverpool in mid-October to await the ship's departure but was called back to Carlisle on business about two weeks before the ship sailed on November 7. One of his last acts before leaving for Carlisle was to present Harry with a 1754 Bible that he had purchased on September 4.[19]

Two months elapsed before the Percys received word that the *Prince Ferdinand* had reached Leghorn safely, after being attacked by a Spanish gunboat as it passed Gibraltar and then outrunning twenty-eight ships of the "Algerines," who would presumably have made slaves of everyone aboard. But, for all its hazards, the voyage of forty-one days proved so beneficial, as Percy wrote William Cleiveland on January 12, 1783, that he was able to "entertain hopes" of Harry's full recovery.[20]

Percy's anxiety over his son's health had already turned his thoughts to the editorial projects that he had hoped some day to see Harry assume. On January 3, when he sent John Pinkerton a transcript of "Peblis to the Play," he reminded Pinkerton that he had held the poem for his son in case he should choose to edit some supplemental volumes of the *Reliques*, "or, if he should decline it, for a very poetical nephew of mine"—his first reference to young Tom in this context. Percy's determination against resuming his own ballad editing had gained strength from his elevation to the see of Dromore. If, as he wrote, Pinkerton should find it necessary to acknowledge in print who had provided him with "Peblis to the Play," he requested that the citation be "by the name of Dr. Percy, or rather the 'Editor of the Reliques of Ancient Poetry,' in 3 vols.; omitting Rev., much more all mention of my present title, &c." Pinkerton might also "speak of my slight poetical pursuits, as what had been the amusement of my younger years and hours of relaxation from severer studies, which, in truth, they were." In the nineteen years since the *Reliques* was printed, he added, he had been so completely preoccupied with "other unavoidable and necessary avocations" that he believed Dodsley to be reprinting the *Reliques* without his having seen so much as a page of it.[21]

Nothing else survives to suggest that Dodsley was contemplating a fourth edition in early 1783, although in 1784 and 1785 he was to inquire about Percy's interest in that possibility.[22] But already Percy was hearing a distant rumble that would in time become so deafening that he could not ignore it. Michael Lort, one of Percy's best sources for church, literary, and social gossip, informed him on January 15 that Joseph Ritson, an explosive young lawyer of Gray's Inn, "has a pamphlet ready to be published against Steevens and Malone's Shakspeare, and also a Collection of Old Ballads, in which I presume a former Editor is to be handled as roughly." On May 19 Lort reported that Ritson had just published a pamphlet "against all the former editors of Shakspeare, and their assistant note-writers."[23]

Doubtless Percy had too much on his mind to give serious attention to someone whom he probably looked upon as a brash and indiscriminate young scholar. Henry's welfare remained the family's overriding concern, but money was a formidable if not a very close second. Dromore had brought in only £900 in 1782, £300 shy of the sum needed for the first payment on the bishop's palace.[24] On January 2, 1782, Percy had repaid the £50 that he owed to Henry Selby, but other loans, like those from Johnson and Paley, were still outstanding, and he was not to finish paying for the improvements to the deanery house until July.[25] It is not surprising, therefore, that he conducted inquiries into other bishoprics. Dr. Shute Barrington, recently translated to the bishopric of Salisbury, informed him on January 29, 1783, that his average income during his first ten years as Bishop of Llandaff had been £734. And Robert Lowth, Bishop of London, who had held the bishopric of St. Davids briefly in 1766, informed him on April 9 that, according to the most recent bishop's secretary, the average income at St. Davids was about £1000.[26] Neither letter could have given him much to hope for.

One bright interval was a visit from James Boswell, who arrived at Carlisle's Bush Inn at four in the morning on Sunday, March 16, slept with his clothes on, and in mid-morning called on Percy in response to an invitation to visit at the deanery house. Percy made arrangements to have Boswell's baggage delivered to the house, and they went to the cathedral together to hear William Paley preach— "uncommonly well," Boswell noted—and then drove for an airing in the coach with Anne, Barbara, and Elizabeth. "It pleased me," Boswell wrote in his journal, "to see him enjoying such a respectable situation, in which he seemed to be easier than I could have imagined, considering how humble his original state was." Boswell was pleased also that, in repairing the deanery house, Percy had "preserved the old gothick stile with modern elegance."[27]

Avoiding what Boswell called the "melancholy subject" of twenty-year-old Henry Percy's illness, they talked about Johnson, Shenstone, and Pennant, and after evening prayers, when Paley and another friend came to dinner, the conversation, "enlivened . . . [by Percy] with literary Anecdote," turned to "the strange state of politicks." At bedtime Percy assembled the family and read prayers, with

Boswell finding it very agreeable to be included in "this decent family Devotion." He retired to "a very excellent apartment" and the next day visited friends in town, read Percy's papers on his dispute with Ferguson, and, after a walk with Percy, dined with the family and left on the five o'clock coach for London.

No doubt Henry was the first object of the family's prayers that Sunday evening, although the hope that had raised Percy's spirits in January had been supplanted by despair and resignation. By the time of Boswell's visit Henry had been removed to Marseilles where, it was thought, the air might prove more beneficial than at Leghorn and Pisa; but, as Percy wrote John Nichols on April 12, the disease had already "taken root too deep to be eradicated." News of Henry's death was expected any moment, a prospect that had almost reduced his mother and sisters to the same state.[28] It came little more than a week later. The last post, Percy informed William Cleiveland on April 21, "brought us the fatal News . . . of the Death of my poor Son, who dec.[d] at Marseilles . . . on the 2[d] of this Month. The proper Sentiments of Devotion, w[ch] the Clergyman, who was with him, tells us he expressed in his last illness, afford us the only Consolation, we can receive under this bitter Stroke."[29] On April 26 Percy asked Edmund Allen to mention the family's loss to his Bolt Court neighbors, Johnson and Mrs. Williams: "I know they will kindly sympathise with us." Johnson, however, seems to have learned of Henry's death about the same time as Percy: "Dr. Percy is now Bishop of Dromore," he wrote Robert Chambers on April 19, "but has I believe lost his only son. Such are the deductions from human happiness."[30]

In June the Percys were ready to move to Dromore. George Rogers, chancellor of the diocese, reported on June 13 that the see house should soon be dry enough to receive them; it should be a comfortable residence once the kitchen garden and enclosures were completed, he assured them. By that time they had probably almost finished packing the dozens of chests and parcels that were to be sent ahead to meet a boat at Maryport on June 23. And by July 26 they were able to move into the new house.[31] It was large and handsome, Percy wrote William Cleiveland on that day, "in a fine country, extremely pleasant & well peopled with genteel & agreeable Families who have shown every mark of respectful attention."[32]

He quickly resumed his visits to the Dromore parishes and found considerable variety among them. At Magheradroll, near Ballynahinch, the church had been fitted up by the Earl of Moira and was "in very good order and repair." At Drumgooland the service was "most carefully performed" by the vicar, Thomas Tighe, and was well attended by "a very decent congregation" of Protestants. Unfortunately the parishioners from Drumballyroney, which had been united with Drumgooland, refused to contribute to the support of the church; but Percy took heart from the ruins of the Drumballyroney church, which he thought might be made the basis of a new church. At Rathfriland in the parish of Drumgath, where he preached on September 28, the church was neglected and in bad repair because the well-meaning but hot-headed vicar, John Stewart, had turned the parishioners against him. At Anaghelone conditions were still worse. In total disorder, the church was without hassocks, the books were torn to pieces, and the service was "shockingly neglected" by the rector, Mr. Mills, who, Percy discovered, often omitted it altogether. "I must have it all amended," Percy resolved.[33]

Doubtless his parish visits were on his mind when he delivered his charge to the clergy during the visitation at Dromore on October 7. Without citing specific instances of neglect, he counseled the clergy to take special care of the souls in their parishes; to visit the sick, help keep the peace, and set good examples by their conduct. Long experienced in the need for precise records, he urged them to comply with the requirement that every parish maintain a register of baptisms, marriages, and burials. "The want of this," he observed, "is a great defect & often attended with much Inconvenience."[34]

Although it had its compensations, 1783 was by no means one of the Percys' happier years. Henry's death had been preceded by that of Anne's brother, William Gutteridge, who left no will; and, though his estate was finally divided between Anne and her sister Mary, Percy was forced to assume much of the burden of managing his deceased brother-in-law's affairs. On September 22 Johnson's companion, Anna Williams, died, leaving Percy distressed by his failure to carry out his intention of supplementing her income with an annuity of £10. He had been able to advance her only five guineas, but had hoped to make it up to her by "greater kindness" in the future. "I wish you would mention this to Dr. Johnson," he wrote Edmund Allen on December 28, "lest I should have suffered in his opinion from what may have appeared a wanton breach of my engagement."[35]

Money was a constant vexation. Richard Rolt's widow, the former Mary Perrins, wrote to request his help with the arrears in her rent, and, though already in debt to Allen, Percy asked him to call on her to see what was needed, offering to advance or repay it if it did not exceed five guineas. The news that bankruptcy proceedings against his brother had been initiated on December 4 was much more disturbing, and Percy, in addition to incurring losses as his brother's surety, had virtually to support him and his family.[36]

He found relief from his worries in work, the see house (which he named Dromore House), his garden, and his correspondence with English friends. Michael Lort and Edmond Malone wrote long letters that kept him as up to date on the literary, religious, and political news as the unpredictable mails between England and Ireland would allow. He responded gratefully and often at length. The discovery at nearby Quilly of fossil bones and what he believed to be the largest fossil horns of a deer ever to be found in Ireland—fourteen feet four inches from the tip of one horn to the tip of the other—prompted letters to Lort and Sir Joseph Banks, president of the Royal Society and a fellow member of the Club. Lort had his account read at a meeting of the Society of Antiquaries on December 4, 1783, and Banks sent an engraving of a horse skeleton to assist Percy in naming and placing the bones. If he ever parted with them, Percy assured Sir Joseph, the fossil remains would go to the British Museum.[37]

At Dromore House he began to improve the house and lay out a garden almost immediately after his arrival: fences and drains at first, followed by trees in the fall; then, bit by bit, like Shenstone with the Leasowes, he planted shrubs and trees, set out a walled garden, and extended the fences around the entire demesne and through various parts of it. By the end of 1784 he had nearly completed a dam of the "great pond," frequented in later years by swans that he delighted in feeding. In 1785 he finished erecting a barn and some smaller out-buildings, and in 1786 he converted an upstairs room of the see house into a library and added what he called "the little private Stairs."[38]

His primary duties as bishop were to ordain clergy, visit the clergy in his twenty-six parishes, and confirm new members of the church.[39] The first of these duties he had few opportunities to exercise, but in 1786 he confirmed over a thousand "young Catechismens," and he continued each year to visit a number of his parishes. In 1783 he corrected the conditions that had shocked him at Anaghelone, and in 1784 he reformed the church at Rathfriland. At Dromore, where the rector of the cathedral church was a chronic absentee, he arranged for the six members of the chapter to preach in turn on the first Sunday of each month, and, though he brought Bryan Bromwich from England to be curate, he himself performed many of the functions of the rector.[40] In 1786 he took special pride in securing a grant sufficient to build a church at Drumballyroney, the only one of his parishes without a church of its own, and in starting a Sunday School at Dromore for the children of his poor tenants.

In a small town and a small diocese, the work of a conscientious prelate inevitably proliferated. Percy, in fact, was a town father as well as a church father. He established the linen market on a monthly, then a fortnightly, and finally in 1786, a weekly schedule, each time "with increasing advantage." The Countess of Moira, eager to assist her daughter's music master, informed Percy of his desire to teach dancing in the Dromore market house, "if your Lordship has no objection to his exercising his talents in that way in your Lordship's town."[41]

Percy did not have to concern himself with parish funds, except insofar as he thought them misused, as at Anaghelone. These were derived from tithes—a tax upon agricultural production usually collected by a local tithe proctor, who paid the clergyman out of the amount that he collected and was perhaps expected to contribute some part to help keep the church in good order and repair. The six cathedral clergy had separate benefices in the parishes—Chancellor George Rogers, for example, was rector of Clonallan, Archdeacon Stewart Blacker was rector of Donaghclone, and Vicar General Osborne Shiel was vicar of Aghadery—but they were paid additionally from cathedral funds representing rents from church lands and fines paid at the renewal of leases, the term of which was usually twenty-one years. Percy's own income and the maintenance of the cathedral were dependent upon the same funds, and making certain that they were collected was his responsibility.[42]

The leases were in some disorder when he undertook their supervision in 1783, perhaps largely through carelessness; one whole townland, he discovered, had been omitted in five successive renewals from 1774–79, and there were other irregularities.[43] Whatever the cause, he perceived the need for both additional revenues and tenants who could be depended upon to meet their obligations. He was aware, of course, that he could not arbitrarily increase rents and fines without incurring the displeasure of the tenants, many of whom were influential members of the diocese.

His record of "Improvements" at Dromore suggests that he proceeded methodically and discreetly. At the death of the previous bishops' agent in 1783, he took the registry of leases into his own hands, classified the papers, and indexed them. By the end of the year he began to increase the rents and fines, starting with his chief tenant, Alexander Knox. He was prepared to negotiate and often did. And he made his task easier by ensuring that civic improvements, like the revised linen market schedule, accompanied the increases. In 1784, with a view to raising the rents of the demesne and securing some more reliable tenants, he opened a new road from the town through the demesne and laid out sixty to eighty acres in town parks. He added several more roads in 1785 and 1786.

Most negotiations seem to have concluded amicably, though one—over the lease of George Tandy—ended up in the Courts of King's Bench and Chancery, which granted Percy both back rent and costs.[44] But by and large in this period Dromore seems to have prospered under Percy's leadership. William Sturrock, whom Percy appointed vicar of Seapatrick in 1787, may not have written with quite the impartiality he professes, but his assessment of Percy was probably shared by many:

> No Bishop in this kingdom exercises the various functions of his office with more ability, diligence, and universal approbation. This is not the partial voice of a person obliged, but it is the sense of the great body of the people, whom he has reconciled, in this neighbourhood, to the otherwise invidious order of Bishops, by the regularity he has introduced into every part of a much deranged diocese, the employment of a numerous poor, encouragement of manufactories, and various improvements in the country around him; but, especially, he has bestowed a more particular attention on the education of the children of the poorer sort, and on the establishment of schools of every sort in all parts of his diocese.[45]

Inevitably Percy's primary associations were with the Anglo-Irish community, particularly the Protestants of the Church of Ireland. That the Dissenters and Catholics would react to him with the enthusiasm of a William Sturrock was hardly to be expected. Both groups resented their inferior political status. They also resented having to pay tithes for the support of a church to which they did not subscribe, though they tended to vent their animosity on the tithe proctors and the lower clergy, with whom they had to deal at first hand. No doubt the size of the Dromore diocese, which had fewer parishes than any of the other Irish dioceses, helped Percy to maintain fairly close ties with his own clergy and their congregations, and perhaps his civic and literary interests brought him closer to other groups as well. In Dromore he is said to have made friends with the Catholic priest and given him a plot of ground for a Catholic chapel as well.[46] He seems also to have avoided, at least publicly, the more divisive controversies, like that precipitated in 1787 by Richard Woodward, Bishop of Cloyne, who contended in his *Present State of the Church of Ireland* that the established church was an essential element of the political constitution and that only its members could be staunch constitutional supporters.[47] In 1786, in an effort that, in his view, helped to prevent the "greatest confusion" to the church, Percy wrote anonymously to the dioceses in his home province of Armagh to dissuade the bishops from assembling the clergy and sending deputies to a Dublin congress, "as some foolish Hotheads had required."[48]

Whatever the demands of his episcopal office, Percy found numerous opportunities to indulge his literary interests. Lort and Boswell kept him apprised of Johnson's health until his death on December 13, 1784.[49] And when Percy's nephew, not yet seventeen, sent him some lines in tribute to Johnson, Percy urged him to extend them and make them public. In 1785 young Tom's *Verses on the Death of Dr. Samuel Johnson* appeared anonymously in a thin quarto volume, with a preliminary "Advertisement" acknowledging the advice and encouragement of "a Friend, whose reputation is great in the literary world, and who had a much better knowlege [*sic*] of the Subject of these lines than the Writer can pretend to." For Boswell's vast tribute to Johnson Percy provided, at Boswell's request, what he could recollect of Johnson's early life. On June 1, 1786, he was elected a Fellow of the Society of Antiquaries.[50]

In Ireland the indigence of Goldsmith's brother Maurice disturbed him deeply, a thorn in his conscience he was determined to remove. Unable to secure him a post in the customs office, he collected thirty to forty guineas in 1785 to supply Maurice with at least some temporary relief.[51] A more promising opportunity arose in early 1785 when Sir William Scott, one of Johnson's executors, turned over to Malone the Goldsmith materials that Percy had given to Johnson shortly after Goldsmith's death in 1774. Malone sent them on to Percy in December 1786, but meanwhile—on June 1, 1785—Percy had issued proposals to print by subscription "The Poetical Works of Dr. Oliver Goldsmith; For the Benefit of his only surviving Brother," with a new life of Goldsmith based on original letters and the account of his life dictated to Percy by Goldsmith on April 28, 1773. Unfortunately the edition, augmented by many of Goldsmith's prose works, was still some years from providing Maurice with assistance; but, after an appeal from Percy in February 1787 Maurice was given a place in the license office by Thomas Orde, the first secretary for Ireland.[52]

On April 2, 1785, Lord Moira invited Percy to join in establishing an Irish society modeled after England's Royal Society but to include antiquarians.[53] Always an eager club member, he accepted promptly and entered into the organizational work by writing to Boswell, Lort, and the historian Robert Henry for copies of the charters and statutes of the English and Scottish societies.[54] The Royal Irish Academy was duly chartered in 1785 under the patronage of George III; Lord Charlemont was elected its first president; and on February 1, 1786, with papers already read, Percy sought the advice of Sir Joseph Banks on the procedures for selecting those to be published. Ten days later he was commended by Dr. Thomas Campbell for his efforts to assure that only the well qualified would be accepted: "You have redeemed . . . [the academy] from a new degree of contempt, into which it must have sunk, if its corporation of literati were to be responsible for those crude effusions which some of its members write with much more facility than I can read them."[55] Perhaps Campbell had in mind one or more contributions of the volatile and quixotic Colonel Charles Vallancey, who, as Percy informed John Pinkerton, "downright quarrelled with me, one evening, at the Society, for presuming to question some of his wild Reveries."[56] Though he must have welcomed Campbell's praise, he was probably at least as pleased with a decision of the academy to make Maurice Goldsmith its mace bearer.[57]

Although he had disclaimed any interest in a new edition of the *Reliques*, he was as unsettled as a weathervane, unable to point a steady course in the midst of conflicting winds. On April 6, 1784, with Dodsley having written that a new edition was called for, he thanked the Reverend William Jessop of Lismore for information that

> would deserve my best thanks, if you were not tempting me to review with too much complacency the Sins & Follies of my Youth. . . . I believe I sh.[d] have let the last Impression have been meerly copied, without taking any farther Interest in this juvenile Work: if you had not excited a wish that it might undergo some revisal . . . : With this View, I cannot but wish to avail myself of your agreeable Correspondence and to beg to be favoured with any other Cor-

rections or Illustrations, &c. which have at any time occurred to you.

A year and a half later he informed Dodsley, who had inquired again, that it was a matter of "perfect Indifference" to him whether or not the *Reliques* was ever republished.[58]

But Percy could not long remain indifferent. On October 17, 1786, he asked Malone to secure from the British Museum copies of the last stanzas of "Richard of Almaigne" and "The Turnament of Totenham," which the "merciless" Ritson had rebuked him for omitting. Ritson, he thought, had not printed the first of these quite correctly in his *Observations on the Three First Volumes of the History of English Poetry*, "and if I could get it perfectly exact I would insert it in the next Edition of the Reliques."[59] On May 10, 1787, Sir John Hawkins, responding to a Percy request, wrote that he had compared the "Remarks" in Ritson's *Select Collection of English Songs* with the *Reliques*, but thinks "so ill of them and the author, that I cannot suggest a wish that your Lordship would alter anything in the next edition. All that can be supposed he has done is, that he has made use of copies of old ballads, different from, and, probably, less authentic than yours; therefore, to follow his corrections, would, in my opinion, be a very futile labour." He knew something of Ritson, Hawkins continued: "a conceited and very impudent fellow, totally ignorant of good manners, regardless of decorum, . . . and of no account among men of literature."[60]

Probably most of Percy's scholarly friends, a number of whom had felt Ritson's lash, would have concurred in Hawkins's assessment, and they took pleasure in passing on bits of information that seemed to confirm it. Steevens wrote on January 11, 1788, that Ritson had assaulted "an inoffensive barber" and been forced to pay dearly in court, and Lort reported on June 14, 1789, that Ritson had been rejected for membership in the Society of Antiquaries, something he could not remember happening before.[61]

No doubt Percy welcomed Hawkins's assessment of Ritson's work, for nothing in his correspondence suggests that he was prepared to undertake any appreciable revision of the *Reliques*. That he might have been ready to settle for a number of textual changes was understandable: Ritson's questioning of his editorial practice was disturbing. Of more concern for the moment, however, was his assault on Percy's essay on the ancient English minstrels: Percy, he charged, had assumed that, because the French had honored the minstrels, the English would have done so as well. There was no proof, he contended in the *Select Collection of English Songs*, that the English minstrels were "a respectable society" or that they could be called a society at all: "That there were men in those times, as there are in the present, who gained a livelihood by going about from place to place, singing and playing to the illiterate vulgar, is doubtless true; but that they were received into the castles of the nobility, sung at their tables, and were rewarded like the French minstrels, does not any where appear, nor is it at all credible."

Percy's essay, Ritson concluded, should really have been entitled an "Essay on the Ancient FRENCH Minstrels," for nothing more was known of the English than that, by a law of Queen Elizabeth's time, they were branded as "rogues, vagabonds, and sturdy beggars" whose business was to sing and play but not to write. Thus their songs perished with them, and the only ballads that could reasonably be ascribed to them were "The Ancient Ballad of Chevy-Chase" and "The Battle of Otterbourne."[62]

Ritson's argument struck at the very heart of Percy's ballad theory: the romantic poet and singer of his essay—the inspiration in 1770 for James Beattie's popular poem "The Minstrel"—had in one stroke been ignominiously reduced to rogue, vagabond, or beggar.[63] Confronted by such a challenge, Percy might have been expected to respond, if not to buttress his essay to meet Ritson's objections, as he had done with Samuel Pegge's in 1767. Perhaps he had absorbed too much of his London friends' contempt for Ritson to consider him worthy of response; perhaps he recoiled in distaste at the thought of resuming a task that had been the major preoccupation of his 1767 edition; or perhaps he simply found the provocation insufficient to distract a busy prelate from his work—to lure him back, as he would have it, to the sins and follies of his youth.

Yet it was not so much a concern for his youthful sins and follies that deterred him as it was the fear of having the Bishop of Dromore associated with them. He had taken an even more restrictive view of propriety than Johnson, who, as Boswell noted, expected from bishops "the highest degree of decorum": "A bishop . . . has nothing to do at a tippling-house. It is not indeed immoral in him to go to a tavern; neither would it be immoral in him to whip a top in Grosvenor-square. But, if he did, I hope the boys would fall upon him and apply the whip to *him*. There are gradations in conduct; there is morality,—

decency,—propriety. None of these should be violated by a bishop."[64]
Editing "a parcel of OLD BALLADS" was a long way from entering a
tippling house or whipping a top in Grosvenor Square, but for Percy,
even as a young vicar, it had raised troublesome questions of propriety;
for the Bishop of Dromore, allowing himself to be identified publicly
with such a work was unthinkable. Clearly Percy had no objection
to seeking the missing final stanzas of "Richard of Almaigne" and
"The Turnament of Totenham," which could be slipped into their
texts unobtrusively, but he had no intention of undertaking a major
revision that the public would know to be his own work.

Johnson might not have disapproved, although perhaps he would
have questioned one or two other decisions taken by Percy in the
name of propriety. After supplying Boswell with what he called "petty
anecdotes" for the *Life of Johnson*, Percy wrote to him three years
later—on March 19, 1790—to ask that he not identify their source,
and he offered to pay the cost of canceling the already printed pages:
"mention if at all necessary that they were communicated by a Person,
who had heard them in Conversation from Dr. Johnson himself, or
from Mrs. Williams, when he was present and admitted the Particulars
to be true." Not at all receptive to Percy's proposal, Boswell replied
that he would do anything to be obliging but that. Nothing that Percy
had contributed, he assured him, even bordered on impropriety, and
Percy was not the only bishop who would be gracing his pages. Percy
tried again on April 24, concerned, he said, that the trifling information
he had provided would subject him to ridicule. But Boswell remained
adamant.[65]

Thomas Campbell, whom Percy had engaged to write the life of
Goldsmith that would preface the edition of Goldsmith's works, had
even more reason to cite Percy by name, Percy having supplied most
of his data, letters, and anecdotes. "Your name," he wrote Percy on
April 6, 1790, "must be introduced, where you took the hints from
his own mouth; and the world must know,—I mean it will find out,—
whence the materials come. . . . It will procure the work a more fa-
vourable reading, and will give me more credit." Unsuccessful in that
attempt, he asked on June 30 that the veil of anonymity be lifted from
the account of Percy's visit to Goldsmith at Green Arbour Court:
"could there be any harm in letting the world know who the visitant
was?"[66] This time Percy had control of the materials, and he too
remained adamant.

In time Ritson would give Percy more than sufficient provocation, and Percy would find a way to revise the *Reliques* that would satisfy his concern for appearances. Meanwhile—between 1784 and 1790—his primary concerns were to discharge his episcopal duties faithfully and manage his personal affairs efficiently. To both these ends his careful administration of the church properties contributed. For him personally it assured the growing income that permitted him to complete his payments on Dromore House in 1785 and 1786 and gradually thereafter to lift the burden of debt that had oppressed him at Carlisle.[67] In 1788, at Francis Barber's request, he sent £50 and a year's interest on his £150 loan from Johnson, Barber, as Johnson's residuary legatee, having inherited all rights in the loan.[68] He also reimbursed John Calder for money lent to Henry and, in 1789, sent Nichols £74/6/0 to cover interest on a £50 loan and Nichols's charges for storing the printed sheets of the Surrey and Buckingham editions.[69]

He was able to continue assisting his relations, sometimes in ways that promised long-term assistance for himself or his family. He paid Mary Rolt an annuity of £10 until her death in 1792, bought out Mary Edwards's share in "the little Estate" at Stoke Albany, a few miles north of Desborough, and provided occasional sums for her son, William Gutteridge Edwards. In 1785 he also bought out Anthony's share in houses that they owned jointly in Bridgnorth, and, following Tom's matriculation at St. John's College, Oxford, in June 1786, "made up" to him and Anthony an allowance of £100 a year.[70] In 1789 he pledged his vote on the Pension Bill in exchange for an agreement by the Marquis of Buckingham, the Lord Lieutenant, to recommend to the prime minister that Anthony be appointed inspector of the window duties, but like other efforts of his in Anthony's behalf, this too came to nothing.[71] A year earlier he had tried unsuccessfully to draw William Cleiveland to Ireland by offering him an attractive living in his diocese that had fallen vacant.[72]

Unlike many of his fellow bishops, he remained constantly in residence in his diocese throughout the 1780s, his only absences of any length occasioned by his attendance at annual sessions of the House of Lords in Dublin. "Few of our profession . . . who have been translated to Ireland," John Douglas, Bishop of Carlisle, wrote to him in 1788, "seem to have been so fortunate as your Lordship, if we may judge from the frequency of their visits to this island."[73] Percy would not have denied his good fortune. He was in the midst of family and friends and, in addition to a new and commodious house, had a vast estate to please his eye and excite his imagination. His diocese, though not immune to troubles, seemed peaceful compared with others. Its Dissenters were less active in politics than those in Belfast and other parts of Ulster, and its Catholics were quieter than those in the predominantly Catholic south. The English Parliament had renounced Poynings' Law in 1783, but Catholics continued to agitate to secure voting rights and the right to serve in Parliament and the Dissenters to reform Parliament, while both sought to rid themselves of the tithes they were forced to pay to the minority Church of Ireland. In Dromore, however, at least during this period, the agitation seems to have been minimal.

Through the Royal Irish Academy and in other ways Percy was able to indulge his literary interests, without impropriety. When John Calder, in a note to the 1786 *Tatler* edition, repeated a charge that Jonathan Swift had been guilty of a rape while he was a curate at Kilroot, Percy conducted an inquiry and submitted a refutation that Nichols, without naming him, published in the *Gentleman's Magazine* for March 1790.[74] In 1790, at the request of Treadway Nash, he prepared a series of notes on Samuel Butler's *Hudibras*.[75] And on April 18 of that year he preached a charity sermon at Christ Church, Dublin, for the Incorporated Society for Promoting English Protestant Schools in Ireland. It was published at the request of the society.[76]

As he noted in the sermon, Percy saw the work of the schools as an antidote to the implacable resentment against law and the landed proprietors built up in the native Irish—untutored but generous and good-natured—through the forfeiture of their lands by earlier generations. "Train up a child in the way he should go, and when he is old he will not depart from it." So went Percy's text, and so went the hopes of the thirty-eight Protestant charity schools that admitted children between the ages of six and ten from the poorest Catholic families. The schools provided educations that mixed labor and instruction, apprenticed the children to Protestant families, and, upon certification of good behavior, gave forty shillings to each boy and a dowry of five pounds to each girl who married a Protestant. Over the years the schools had placed 6647 children in agriculture, trade, or manufacture and given portions to 685 girls.

By the time of the Christ Church sermon Percy had determined to interrupt his long residence in Ireland and visit England with his family.[77] He settled upon the summer of 1790 at first, but a recurrence of Anne's bilious complaint forced a postponement until she was ready to travel. It had attacked her so severely in 1788 that Percy had given up his plans to attend the session of Parliament; after it struck in 1790 it hung on so long that the 1791 summer was almost half over before she was in condition to leave.[78] They sailed about August 1, leaving the management of the church properties to Crane Brush, whom Percy had appointed his attorney on December 24, 1789.[79] Once in England, they drove directly to Bath, where they hoped that Anne would find relief in the waters.

They remained at Bath for more than eight months, with Anne's health apparently improving steadily. Young Tom, who had joined Percy in Dublin on February 9, joined the family at Bath on September 27 while he awaited the opening of Michaelmas term at Oxford, and William Cleiveland was expected shortly after Percy wrote to him on October 10. Meanwhile Percy had traveled to Cheltenham, Oxford, London, and Windsor; and later in the fall he was to go to Northamptonshire and Leicestershire to receive the rents from his wife's properties.[80] Business took him to the Court of Chancery also: he had found reason, as executor of the estate of one of Anne's uncles, to believe that the widow of Anne's cousin Joseph Hill had remarried and thus violated a condition of an annuity provided for her in the will.[81]

In late April 1792 Percy moved with his family to London, no doubt pleased to be back even though membership in the Club had changed appreciably during the ten years of his absence and a number of the persons that he cared about most had died: Johnson and Edmund Allen in 1784, the Duke of Northumberland in 1786, Michael Lort in November 1790, and Reynolds as recently as February 23, 1792. He did find Malone, Steevens, and Cracherode in town; and on June 1 he and Isaac Reed dined at Richard Farmer's.[82] Boswell called one day when Percy was out, intent on explaining the index entry in his *Life of Johnson* that had revealed Johnson's authorship of the dedication to the Countess of Northumberland in the *Reliques*. It was the result of oversight, Malone assured him in a letter of June 5, not artifice, as Percy had surmised; but probably Percy would have an opportunity to talk with Boswell later that day at the Club.[83] On July 5 the Percy family was escorted around Strawberry Hill by Horace Walpole, Earl of Orford since the death of his nephew in 1791.[84]

In London Percy seems to have been more often with John Nichols than with any of his other friends. A "kinsman" with whom he shared numerous interests, Nichols had offered to print the edition of Goldsmith and to guarantee Percy's anonymity.[85] In spite of this inducement, Percy held back, perhaps because, with the Surrey and Buckingham editions already languishing in Nichols's warehouse, he felt some compunction about burdening him with still another. By that time he may also have been aware that Nichols would be printing the fourth edition of the *Reliques* for Charles Rivington, who became the publisher after James Dodsley's retirement. In any event, he was to turn to the publisher John Murray for the Goldsmith edition. He called upon Nichols in 1792, however, for an unusual service that only such a trusted friend could be asked to provide.

Percy had carried his folio manuscript to England, probably with the intention of subjecting the *Reliques* to a careful revision rather than a simple reprinting. His scruples had not been overcome, but he had found a way of accomplishing his purpose without exposing the Bishop of Dromore to the charge of acting with impropriety. The editor—at least the *nominal* editor—would be his nephew, graduate of St. John's College, Oxford and, for a decade, heir to Percy's dreams for his lost son Henry.

Behind Percy's desire to revise the *Reliques*, of course, lay Ritson's criticism, particularly in his *Select Collection of English Songs*. And Ritson kept on with his attacks. Although in his 1791 *Pieces of Ancient Popular Poetry* he treated Percy with uncharacteristic civility, in his *Ancient Songs, from the Time of Henry the Third, to the Revolution*, published in 1792 though dated 1790, he compensated by striking with renewed force at Percy's editorial practices and his essay on the minstrels. He also questioned the very existence of the folio manuscript, as he had done once before.

Since the minstrels, he wrote, never committed their verses to writing, it was extraordinary that this "multifarious collection" could have been compiled as late as 1650. And, to increase the manuscript's singularity, "no other writer has ever pretended to have seen [it]. The late Mr. Tyrwhitt... never saw it.... And it is remarkable, that scarcely any thing is published from it, not being to be found elsewhere, without our being told of the defects and mutilation of the MS." Ritson then cited seven poems printed by Percy from the folio manuscript—"Sir Cauline," "Sir Aldingar," "Gentle Heardsman," "The Heir of Linne," "The Beggar's Daughter of Bednall-Green," "The Marriage of Sir Gawaine," and "King Arthur's Death"—in which Percy noted his emendations and interpolations only in general terms; and he asserted that many "other instances might be noticed, where the learned collector has preferred his ingenuity to his fidelity, without the least intimation to the reader." Thus, he concluded, one can have no confidence in any of the *Reliques*'s "old Minstrel ballads" that are not to be found elsewhere.[86]

In July 1792, when Pinkerton suggested that Percy respond to Ritson by making the folio manuscript available for public inspection, Percy reacted with some heat: "I am now convinced, that This was the very end to which Mr R. has been driving, (Whom wanton Outrage and unprovoked Insult cost nothing)," so that by examining and collating the manuscript he might find pretenses "to justify his antecedent injurious Charges and Insinuations." The manuscript, Percy vowed, would never be shown to Ritson in his lifetime. Two years later, after Pinkerton sided with Ritson in concluding that the word "minstrel" implied a musician and not a poet or bard—and then referred Percy to Ritson's *Ancient Songs* for evidence—Percy abruptly broke off their correspondence.[87]

Before then he had taken a step in the direction of public display by asking Nichols to keep the manuscript in his house and show it to interested friends, who, of course, did not include Joseph Ritson. The obliging Nichols agreed, and the manuscript was left in his custody for much of a year: probably from October 1792 to July 1793.[88] Percy had never before trusted it out of his possession.

The arrangement for publishing the fourth edition of the *Reliques* called for Rivington, after recovering his expenses, to divide the profits equally between Percy's nephew and Nichols. Nichols later gave his share to Percy's nephew, who sold it to Rivington for £60 and might have sold his own for the same amount if Percy, thinking it undervalued, had not purchased it for £100.[89] Probably most of the work for the new edition was done by Percy during his residences in London in 1792 and 1793, without any assistance from his nephew. Tom's contribution, despite the impression that Percy wished to convey, was simply to lend his name as editor.[90] Even the fourth edition's "Advertisement," though signed by his nephew, is unmistakably Percy's, most notably in its dismissal of the ballads as "the amusements of his youth."[91] Young Tom would never have ventured such a comment.

In mid-August, before setting off with his family for a two-month stay in Tunbridge Wells, Percy turned over responsibility for the Surrey and Buckingham editions to his nephew, who had expressed a willingness to complete them.[92] And after his return to London he reached an agreement with John Murray to publish the Goldsmith edition, though he must have been distressed some months later to learn of the death of Maurice Goldsmith, whom he hoped to benefit by the edition.[93]

In 1793 he was honored by his own university during the five-day celebration of the Duke of Portland's installation as chancellor of the university: he was invited to preach the charity sermon for the Radcliffe Infirmary on July 2, the first of the five days. On that morning the proctors, heads of houses, and governors and subscribers to the infirmary marched in procession into the center-aisle seats of St. Mary's Church, its galleries already filled with ladies and its side pews with men. Oxford's Dr. Philip Hayes had composed a Te Deum for the occasion, and the service itself was chanted by choristers from Christ Church and the Magdalen and New College chapels.[94]

For his sermon, adapted in part from his 1769 sermon at St. Paul's, Percy chose his text from John 13:34: "A new commandment I give unto you, That ye love one another." "His Lordship," reported the *Gentleman's Magazine*, "followed the virtue of benevolence through the different periods of society . . . , and adverted to the alarming diminution of the principle in France at this time. He then more particularly, and with greater effect, enjoined the practice of it in this kingdom, and more especially towards institutions [as] useful and comprehensive as that of the Radcliffe Infirmary."[95]

The events that followed included three convocations, orations in Latin and English, poetry readings, concerts, and a ball attended by nearly six hundred people. For Percy the most important was the first convocation, held on July 3. Having already taken the degree of Doctor of Divinity at Cambridge, he was, by university precedence, the first person presented to the new chancellor, who conferred Oxford's same degree upon him.[96] Then came the noblemen and gentlemen selected for the honorary degree of Doctor of Laws, twenty-one in all. On July 4 another twenty-one were awarded the degree of Doctor of Civil Law and six the Master of Arts. On July 5, eighteen, including Edmond Malone, were awarded the D.C.L. and eight the M.A. Even one pickpocket, quipped the *Gentleman's Magazine*, was said to have been seen in a Master of Arts gown.[97]

With Anne's health restored, a publisher secured for Goldsmith's works, progress on the Surrey and Buckingham editions at least promised, and revisions for the *Reliques* submitted to Charles Rivington, Percy had little to hold him further in England, and about the end of July he and his family drove west for the boat to Ireland from Parkgate. They stopped off at Worcester with William Cleiveland and then went on through Ludlow and Shrewsbury to Wrexham, where they dined on August 5 with Thomas Apperley, his wife, and their nine children.[98]

They returned to Dromore in time for the Primate's Triennial Visitation on August 15, when Percy learned from his clergy that every part of his diocese was in "the most perfect Quiet & Tranquillity . . . & all appearance of faction or discontent seems banished from this Country."[99] Whatever Dromore's situation, the Percys themselves suffered a number of setbacks in the year and a half that followed. Anne's illness started up again in the fall of 1794. The death of John Murray forced a search for a new publisher for the Goldsmith edition. Though Rivington had optimistically looked for a spring 1794 publication, the fourth edition of the *Reliques* seems to have been held up by Nichols's extensive commitments and perhaps by Percy's late submissions of corrections and additions.[100] And in October 1794 the family was saddened by the news of William Cleiveland's death on September 28.[101]

By the end of 1794 even Dromore was less than perfectly quiet and tranquil. Fearing trouble between Catholics and Dissenters, Percy had arranged for a party of thirty soldiers to be at hand on December 27, and he asked a justice of the peace to stay overnight at Dromore House to give them the sanction of a magistrate if there should be a riot.[102] The peace seems to have been kept. Despite such fears, Percy could probably still draw comfort from the relative quiet of his own diocese. Thomas Campbell reported, for example, that in a neighboring parish, about fifty miles from Dromore, the Catholics and Protestants had joined forces at the only point where they could agree—in refusing to pay tithes—and were threatening to burn the houses of any jurors at the next manor court who would adjudge a tithe to be due.[103]

Just as Percy was girding for a clash of Catholics and Dissenters on December 27, a chance discovery drew him to a kind of antiquarian activity that he found especially satisfying. On December 21 a Mrs. Byrns of Ballintaggart, making her way through Drumsallagh in Percy's manor of Dromore, had found "a bright substance" among some clay and rubbish tossed up by workmen building an addition to a house. On her return home, she gave it to her husband, who sold it for six guineas to James Neilson, a repairer of clocks and watches in Banbridge. To Vicar General Osborne Shiel, writing to Percy on December 24, the bright substance appeared to be a chain of pure gold terminating in a small flat piece, a relic perhaps from a Franciscan abbey that had once stood nearby. By law, he noted, treasure trove in that area belonged to Percy as lord of the manor, and anyone concealing it could be punished by fine and imprisonment.[104]

Quick to assert his right and to make sure that future discoveries would not be melted down or smuggled to Dublin, Percy dispatched Crane Brush to Banbridge with a commission to pay Neilson twice the amount he had given Byrns and to spread the word that he was ready to pay generously for additional discoveries. It was a useful precaution, probably accounting for a smaller piece, later identified as a gold slug fibula used for fastening sleeves or dresses, that joined his collection of curios. Unfamiliar with such rarities, Percy likened Mrs. Byrns's find to a candlestick branch of "thick gold wires or twin plates twisted into a kind of tripple gold cord," and he too linked it to the ancient abbey, the last stones of which had been carried off some forty years earlier by a builder erecting houses and offices.[105] One can only imagine Percy's excitement if he had known what the Drumsallagh rubbish had in fact yielded to the prying Mrs. Byrns: part of a necklace—a bar torque—fashioned not only before the advent of Christianity in Ireland, but a thousand to twelve hundred years before the birth of Christ. As it was, he was sufficiently stimulated to make a colored drawing of the five-ounce gold piece and to exhibit the discovery at the Royal Irish Academy on May 16, 1795.[106]

William Cleiveland, who had lived alone since the death of an only sister in 1786, died intestate, and his estate descended to Percy as his closest living relation.[107] Probably the need to settle the estate prompted the Percys to return to England in May 1795, for in early June, having taken out letters of administration, Percy was in Worcester trying to resolve the confusion of his cousin's affairs and to find money in the estate to pay off its numerous debts.[108] By July the family had moved to London, where the fourth edition, further delayed by Nichols's problems with his workmen, was at last making its appearance, and where Percy, sustaining the fiction of young Tom's editorship, busied himself in sending copies to friends on his nephew's behalf.[109]

Considerably revised, the fourth edition owes its revisions, if not its very existence, to the acid, arrogant, and often perceptive criticism of Joseph Ritson. Having rejected at the outset the intolerable suggestion that the folio manuscript was a mere fabrication, Percy concentrated on meeting Ritson's objections to his editorial practice and

to his "Essay on the Ancient English Minstrels." The essay, fortified
for the second edition, was almost doubled in size again, and its
supplemental notes, an almost insurmountable barrier for the reader,
swelled from thirty-eight pages to fifty-two. Although he conceded
Ritson's point that, in the centuries immediately following the Norman conquest, only songs in French would have enjoyed the patronage
of the nobility, he assembled a variety of evidence to support the view
that the Anglo-Saxon gentry, subjugated but not "extirpated," would
readily have admitted their own gleemen or minstrels into their households. In his final supplemental note he turned to Ritson's depiction
of the minstrels as mere players "miserably twanging and scraping"
their harps and fiddles "in the booths of Chester fair":

> Merry it is in halle to here the harpe,
> The Minstrelles synge, the Jogelours carpe.

Thus, for example, wrote Adam Davie in the early fourteenth century.
Moreover, Percy went on, by "proving that Minstrels were Singers
of the old Romantic Songs and Gestes, &c. we have in effect proved
them to have been the Makers at least of some of them. For the Names
of their Authors being not preserved, to whom can we so probably
ascribe the composition of many of these old popular rhimes, as to
the men, who devoted all their time and talents to the recitation of
them." But Percy did not rest his case on probability. In old poems—
"Horn-Child," "Emaré," and "Guy and Colbronde"—minstrels were
represented as composers; and even in a royal pronouncement singer
and composer were united, as Henry V decreed that no "ditties [were]
to be made and sung by Minstrels on his glorious Victory [at
Agincourt]."[10]

Editorially, though he made a number of changes, he could con-
cede almost nothing to Ritson's position. He had made some slips, of
course, such as omitting the final stanzas of "Richard of Almaigne"
and "The Turnament of Totenham," both of which he now inserted.
But Ritson, while allowing for the correction of nonsense or obviously
faulty transcriptions, insisted on an otherwise faithful adherence to an
original text, with any interpolations distinguished from the original
by different type.[11] For Percy that was not sufficient. Confronted
with poems often in multiple versions, couched in archaic language,
and—in his folio manuscript—ravaged by Humphrey Pitt's maids, he
had occasionally removed the archaisms, smoothed the meter, modified texts by conjecture or by a blend of different versions, and filled

in gaps of varying length from his own invention. Himself a scholar, he was well aware of the virtues of Ritson's position, which was essentially his own in the edition of Surrey's poems and other projects; but he had long since concluded, with Shenstone, that a collection of ballads without the touch of a careful editorial hand would have little appeal for readers of taste.

In October 1760, when Shenstone gave his sanction to Percy's altering the ballads, he likened the substitution of a line or more to a toe or finger "*allowably* added to the best old Statues."[12] Percy, however, did not always stop with a toe or finger. He fixed whole limbs in place, for even a new foot would not have permitted some of the crippled poems of the folio manuscript to stand erect. Indeed, with two or three he attempted to implant heart and soul. "The Child of Elle," a fragment of thirty-nine lines, emerged from the manuscript with a full two hundred lines and was embraced in the 1765 *Critical Review* as "a most beautiful ballad."[13] "The Marriage of Sir Gawaine," half of each leaf sacrificed for Humphrey Pitt's comfort, was reconstituted from Percy's imagination. "Sir Cauline," which he thought to have been copied from "the faulty recitation of some illiterate minstrell," grew in his hands from 201 to 392 lines.[14]

Percy's fault was not in seeking to make these poems presentable, along with the other four specifically cited by Ritson: "Sir Aldingar," "Gentle Heardsman," "The Beggar's Daughter of Bednall-Green," and "King Arthur's Death." He would hardly have wished to inflict his mutilated pieces upon readers whom he was eager to please. The only alternative would have been to omit the poems altogether. But he sensed that, *un*mutilated, all of them would have ranked among the best in his collection, and the poet in him was stirred to restore them to something close to their original states. His fault was that he provided only general rather than precise guideposts to most of his emendations: "This old fabulous legend," he says of "Sir Aldingar," for example, "is given from the Editor's folio MS. with conjectural emendations, and the insertion of some additional stanzas to supply and compleat the story."[15] And even in the fourth edition he merely added three asterisks at the end of the forty-eight poems in which he had taken "any considerable liberties" with the texts.[16]

Ultimately Percy's defense of his practice was that it accomplished its purpose. The public, he wrote in the fourth edition "Advertisement" signed by his nephew, "may judge how much they are indebted to the composer of this collection; who, at an early period of life, with such materials and such subjects, formed a work which hath been admitted into the most elegant libraries; and with which the judicious Antiquary hath just reason to be satisfied, while refined entertainment hath been provided for every Reader of taste and genius."[117]

His claim was not overdrawn. The four editions of "a parcel of OLD BALLADS" testified to the book's popularity. Indeed, by 1795 its influence had become measurable. It had been followed, between 1769 and 1792, by David Herd's *Ancient and Modern Scots Songs*; Thomas Evans's *Old Ballads, Historical and Narrative*; Pinkerton's *Scottish Tragic Ballads* and *Select Scotish Ballads*; Ritson's *Select Collection of English Songs, Pieces of Ancient Popular Poetry*, and *Ancient Songs*; and Charlotte Brooke's *Reliques of Ancient Irish Poetry*. This was Percy's lay diocese, unruly at times, but taking its lead from him as surely as his clerical diocese of Dromore.

No longer street urchins, the ballads by 1795 were often honored guests at the most polite tables. And poets had been finding their inspiration in the *Reliques*: Chatterton for his Rowley poems, James Beattie for *The Minstrel*, and William Blake for his "Mad Song," described by one critic as a composite of the six mad songs in Percy's second volume.[118] In Germany, where it was read in both English and a 1767 translation, the *Reliques* breathed new life into Gottfried Bürger's poetry and Johann Herder's collection of German folksongs.[119] In turn-of-the-century England, a new race of poets, nurtured on the rich fare of the *Reliques*, was soon to come into its own.

Meanwhile Percy, proud of an achievement not yet at its height, had much else to occupy him before he returned to Dromore. In the fall he officiated at two weddings, the first, at Ham House on September 25, of the Reverend Herbert Croft and Miss Elizabeth Lewis. On October 20, at St. George's Hanover Square, he married his daughter Barbara to Samuel Isted, son of Percy's old Northamptonshire friends Ambrose and Anne Isted of Ecton, where the newly married couple took up residence.[120] In Ecton's card-playing society, which he joined on November 6, Percy ran up losses of three guineas in a ten-day period. He also participated with Northampton freeholders in an address to the King expressing abhorrence at the "daring Outrages" committed against His Majesty as he was driven between Buckingham House and the House of Lords for the opening of Parliament on October 29.[121]

The Percys' pleasure in their new family connection was interrupted by another family development. Anthony, whose wife had died on January 21, was taken ill in early November at the home of William Taylor near Grosvenor Square. A low fever persisting, he suffered a series of spasms and died at Taylor's house on November 7, just after Percy had reached Ecton from London. Perhaps because of the distance, Percy did not return for the funeral, which was held at Gray's Thurrock in Essex, where Anthony and his wife had retired after Tom became vicar of Gray's following his ordination as a priest in 1793.[122] A hapless figure almost constantly in debt, Anthony had never emerged from the shadow of his more talented brother, to whom he had turned for assistance repeatedly. Even two years after his death Percy was called upon to untangle his affairs to prevent a lawsuit.[123]

In London again, beginning December 5, Percy missed few opportunities to attend Club meetings; and on January 1 he joined in the New Year celebration at court, where the King spoke kindly to him and the Queen inquired about his family. On January 4, 1796, he submitted a proposal for the edition of Goldsmith's works to the publishers Cadell and Davies.[124] Sometime during the year, dressed in his bishop's robes, he sat for his portrait by Francis Lemuel Abbott— an excellent likeness, according to George Steevens.[125] By that time Steevens, with some help from Henry Meen, had assumed young Tom's work of seeking examples of pre-Miltonic blank verse for the Surrey edition, and he took pleasure in teasing Percy by carrying the role of nephew still further. "My very good Lord, and most esteemed Uncle," he wrote on October 24, 1796, "notwithstanding you persist in refusing to acknowledge me in the character of your legitimate Nephew, I have not so far forgotten my duty as to neglect your interests on the slightest occasion."[126]

The Percys returned to Ireland in August 1796, as Irish fortunes were taking a sharp turn. A French fleet attempting to land at Bantry Bay in December 1796 was dispersed by hostile winds, which the Lord Lieutenant, Lord Camden, cited in the Irish House of Lords on January 16 as a signal instance of "divine Interposition." Unfortunately for the English, divine interposition provided no continuing guarantee against the combined forces of the "unprincipled, perfidious and detestable" French government, as one speaker in the House of Lords described it, and those leaders of the increasingly militant Society of United Irishmen who looked to the French to help free them from the dominance of the English and Irish Parliaments.[127]

Much of the agitation was in the north, where the leader of the

United Irishmen Wolfe Tone, aboard one of the French ships at Bantry Bay in the southwest, had hoped that the French would land. In the Irish House of Lords on March 18, 1797, Lord Camden enumerated some of the "daring Outrages" committed in many parts of Ulster: murder, robbery, threats against informers, the amassing of arms in secret places, and the forcible prevention of subjects from joining the loyalist yeoman corps. Although Lord Camden had in mind the insurgents of the United Irishmen, its membership largely Presbyterian and Catholic, the violence was by no means all in one direction. In May 1796, for example, the Protestant Peep o' Day Boys were alleged to have burned a mill near Dromore because its owner would not discharge his Catholic employees. Percy's own agent, Crane Brush, was said to have cut down the local Catholic priest, Father Mornan, just as a Protestant mob was stringing him from a tree.[128] Despite the proximity of some of the action, Dromore itself probably remained comparatively quiet. But Percy took no chances. He appointed Brush captain of the local yeomanry, a kind of submilitia authorized and supported in part by the government, which considered the militia dangerously infiltrated by the United Irishmen. Percy himself had recommended a subscription for raising a corps of local yeomen, and he contributed £100 to that end and prevailed upon most of the clergy to subscribe £20. To his nephew, whom he installed on December 3, 1796, as rector of Magheralin and precentor of the cathedral, a sinecure paying £500 a year, he left no choice. He also permitted Brush to advance out of his rentals any sums needed to make up deficiencies in the yeomanry's equipment, a total of about £800, of which he had been repaid only £200 by December 1, 1797.[129]

By April 1797 the Percys were back with the Isteds at Ecton, where Percy remained throughout his visit despite the temptations of London, Bath, and other places of "pleasurable Resort." He was held in part by his delight in his grandson—and godson—Ambrose, who had been born to Samuel and Barbara Isted on February 15, 1797.[130] Withdrawn though he was in rural England, Percy's life was not entirely idyllic. He kept in communication with his diocese. And the Archbishop of Armagh touched a sensitive nerve when he sent him a memorandum on the need for the clergy to reside in their parishes. As one who had counseled his own clergy on the duty of residence, Percy responded with a defense of his absences, the first of which, he pointed out, had followed nine years of continuous residence in Dromore. His reason for returning to England in 1797, he asserted, was that, with many tenants in Ireland's unsettled situation hanging back from renewing leases or paying rents, he was unable to live in Dromore or Dublin as he had been accustomed, and he thus availed himself of the asylum offered to him and his family at Ecton.[131] Whether or not the Primate found this explanation satisfactory is not apparent.

While at Ecton he was deeply affected by news of the death of Richard Farmer—"a friend so beloved."[132] But he was outraged by Steevens, who, as one of Farmer's executors, had gone through the letters that Percy had written to Farmer, and still more by the way in which Steevens called to his attention an unpaid debt of £100 said by Steevens to have been borrowed from Farmer at the time of Percy's Cambridge doctorate. If, wrote Steevens on November 10, 1797, "I may be permitted to advise you (which I do according to my best judgment, and I am sure with the utmost sincerity) the £100 should be immediately re-paid, that no further inquiry may be urged about it. The sum is trifling compared with inconveniences that may suggest themselves to your own consideration."[133]

Percy replied on November 12 that, rather than conceal any indebtedness to Farmer, he would have it mentioned to Farmer's relations, and anyone else Steevens might wish, "because if I do not satisfy every impartial person that the money has been paid, far from taking advantage of the lapse of time, I will still repay it, notwithstanding my own conviction that it has been paid already." He was thankful, he added, that the charge had not been brought after his death, "when it could not have been cleared up by my family, and must have left imputations on my memory."[134]

Steevens, he wrote to his nephew on February 20, 1798, has played me "a most shocking piece of Treachery," so that "we are alienated for ever. It was therefore most unfortunate that he got out of you, that you were only an Umbra in ye Publications."[135]

That was perhaps the least of Percy's troubles with his nephew. At Gray's, Tom's former parishioners, angered by his neglect of the church's "dilapidation," seemed on the verge of bringing a suit against him. With Tom safe from prosecution in Ireland, Percy advised him on January 19, 1798, to return to England only when St. John's College, of which Tom was a fellow, called him back on urgent business; and then he should let only Crane Brush know that he might be gone for some time. When absent he could find excuses to prolong his stay, Percy wrote, conscience-stricken by the advice he was giving one of his own clergymen. "It is really a shocking consideration that I must connive at non-residence in my own family: how can I ever urge it to any other person?"[136]

More troubles were to come. Within a month William Taylor was clamoring for £143 still owed by Tom for his father's funeral and was threatening to bring suit in the Court of King's Bench. Stepping in to defend his nephew, Percy accused Taylor of condoning the "horrible excesses" of his "swindling Upholsterer" but offered to pay part himself, with his nephew paying the rest when he had discharged his other debts. By March 9 Taylor, having rejected this and another compromise, had announced his intention to sue forthwith. "I laugh at his threats," Percy wrote; nonetheless he advised Tom to consult with Crane Brush on the extent to which he might be pursued at law in Ireland. By May 26, however, Percy had brought Taylor to terms. He himself would pay off the debt in three installments of £50, one immediately and the others on May 1, 1799 and 1800. "I then leave you out of the present Agreem." he informed Tom, but he expressed the hope that Tom might someday be able to repay the last two amounts.[137]

Perhaps it was his vexation with these matters that prompted Percy to reply with unprecedented rudeness when Joseph Cooper Walker sent him a variety of information on blank verse to assist his nephew with the editing of the Surrey edition. Dismissing Walker's information as mere "banter and badinage," Percy advised him bluntly not again to presume so much on his ignorance. Walker, who had wished only to be helpful, was stunned. The more he perused Percy's letter, he replied, the more he felt hurt, and he promised not to meddle again in any of Percy's literary concerns.[138]

Perhaps as much as anything else Percy was held at Ecton by the manuscript for the life of Goldsmith, which he had brought with him to revise for publication. Thomas Campbell's draft, unfinished at the time of his death in 1795, had been taken over by Henry Boyd, who had nearly finished revising it when Percy sailed for England on April 9. Percy paid Boyd thirty guineas for the revision, which he thought elegant; but, persuaded that he could improve it out of his own personal knowledge of Goldsmith, he undertook to rewrite the entire manuscript during his stay at Ecton. Under the agreement reached with Cadell and Davies on October 26, 1797, after lengthy and at times abrasive negotiations, Percy was to be given two hundred fifty copies in sheets for the benefit of Goldsmith's relations, with half of the copies to be disposed of in Ireland. He was also to be reimbursed for the thirty guineas paid to Boyd as soon as he delivered the manuscript of the life of Goldsmith to the publishers. He sent the completed manuscript on April 8, 1798, and Cadell and Davies transferred thirty guineas to his account at Goslings Bank on April 10. On the next day, leaving Anne and Elizabeth at Ecton, he left for Worcester on the first part of his journey back to Ireland.[139]

He spent a week in Worcester looking after his properties and then made his way toward the ferry at Holyhead through Ludlow, Shrewsbury, Oswestry, and Llangollen. At Llangollen he was introduced to Lady Eleanor Butler and Miss Sarah Ponsonby, who showed him the hermitage they had formed for themselves, "one of the most delightful . . . that ever was," Percy wrote Anne on April 26:

> they are more acquainted with all that is going on . . . than any Ladies I have seen in the *Beau Monde*. . . . There was none of the Nonsense I ever published, but what they had all by heart.—And in the most elegant & select Library I ever saw, I c.^d not but be flattered to see my GRAND WORKS. . . . In short I had great difficulty to tear myself away from these fair Inchantresses, whose magic spell w.^d have chained me there, to the end of time, if I had not broke thro' it with no little Violence to myself.[140]

As it happened, he might have waited a day to break through the spell. Between Conway and Bangor a wheel flew off the coach, which luckily did not overturn, but the accident delayed his arrival at Holyhead until the evening of the twenty-fifth, after the ferry had left for Dublin.

NOTES

1. *Lit. Illus.*, 7:265 (Letter 18 Oct. 1758). Arthur Young, *A Tour in Ireland* (London, 1780), 115.
2. Henry B. Swanzy, *Succession Lists of the Diocese of Dromore* (Belfast: R. Carswell & Son, 1933), 18. *Journals of the House of Lords in Ireland*, Vol. 5 (Dublin, 1786), 27 May 1782.
3. Collection of Kenneth Balfour. The occasion was commemorated in a painting by Francis Wheatley of the assembled House of Lords.
4. Ibid. The volunteer regiments were first organized in 1778, when a French invasion was feared (Edith Mary Johnston, *Ireland in the Eighteenth Century* [Dublin: Gill & Macmillan, 1974], 150–51).
5. *Lit. Illus.*, 8:203 (Letter Percy to William Scott, 16 Jan. 1783).

6. Ibid., 5–9 (Letters 20 May and 9 June 1782).

7. Collection of Kenneth Balfour. Percy's sermon, based on 1 Cor. 4:1, was a modification of a sermon he had preached at Alnwick in 1776 and Carlisle in 1779.

8. Ibid. ("Observations made by myself on ye Spot in 1782 & 1783"). In 1782 Percy also visited the vicarages of Aghalee, Maghevally, and Segoe.

9. C. E. Brett, "Historic Buildings . . . in the Towns and Villages of Mid Down," Ulster Architectural Heritage Society (July 1974), 26.

10. *Public Advertiser*, 17 Jan. 1782 ("Description of the County of Downe, in Ireland").

11. Bodl. MS. Percy c. 1, ff. 113–14 (Letter Percy to Richard Robinson, Archbishop of Armagh, 10 Aug. 1783).

12. B.L. Add. MS. 32,333, f. 161 (Letter Percy to Cleiveland, 4 Sept. 1782). Nat. Libr. of Wales, MS. 3576E (Puleston MS. 16), f. 20 (Letter Percy to Mrs. Richard Parry Price, 6 Dec. 1782).

13. *Lit. Illus.*, 6:570–71 (Letters Nichols and Percy, 24 April 1782). B.L. Add. MS. 32,329, ff. 122–23 (Letter Andrew Ducarel to Percy, 29 April 1782).

14. Merritt Cox, *An English* Illustrado: *The Reverend John Bowle* (Bern: Peter Lang, 1977), 86.

15. Alnwick Castle MS. 93A/11. John Nichols (*Lit. Illus.*, 8:71) quoted a report in the *Public Advertiser*, 6 Oct. 1781, that Percy had rummaged for material in the Alnwick archives that summer. I have not found the report.

16. *Lit. Illus.*, 6:571–72; 578 (Letters Percy to Nichols, 12 April and 19 June 1783). The article on Cleiveland was published in the second edition of the *Biographia Britannica* (1784).

17. Nat. Libr. of Wales, MS. 3576E (Puleston MS. 16), f. 21 (Letter to Mrs. Price, 6 Dec. 1782). B.L. Add. MS. 32,333, f. 163 (Letter Percy to Cleiveland, 12 Nov. 1782).

18. Percy corresponded with Dr. Heysham for some years after he left Carlisle.

19. The Bible (London: Thomas Baskett, 1754), with a note by Percy on the flyleaf, is in the collection of Kenneth Balfour. Bromwich accompanied Henry as his tutor.

What business Percy was called home about is not clear, but perhaps it concerned Percy's question about the validity of his having taken the bishop's oaths before rather than after he was enthroned at Dromore on 20 June. On 24 October fellow Club member William Scott, whose advice Percy had sought, expressed himself "clearly of Opinion that your Lordship has satisfied all the Requisites of the Acts of Parliament," though he thought it might be prudent of Percy "not to furnish the Objection" against himself "by any unreserved Mention of it." The

Bishop of Waterford, William Newcome, expressed a similar view, noting that he himself was precisely in Percy's circumstances and was "perfectly easy." Depend upon it, he wrote, "these nice points will never be agitated" (collection of Kenneth Balfour).

20. B.L. Add. MS. 32,333, f. 164. Bedfordshire Record Office, OR 2071/315 (Letter Barbara Percy to Mary Orlebar, 13 Jan. 1783).

21. *The Percy Letters*, 8:42–44.

22. Bodl. MS. Percy c. 1, ff. 122–23; Harvard bMS Eng 891 (3) (Letters Percy to William Jessop, 6 April 1784, and James Dodsley, 19 Nov. 1785).

23. *Lit. Illus.*, 7:443, 457. Ritson's work was entitled *Remarks, Critical and Illustrative, on the Text and Notes of the Last Edition of Shakespeare* (London, 1783). In 1782 he had published *Observations on the Three First Volumes of the History of English Poetry*.

24. *Lit. Illus.*, 6:578 (Letter Percy to Edmund Allen, 28 Dec. 1783).

25. Ledger, Goslings Bank.

26. *Lit. Illus.*, 8:207, 209.

27. *Boswell: The Applause of the Jury 1782–1785*, 70–73.

28. *Lit. Illus.*, 6:571.

29. B.L. Add. MS. 32,333, f. 168. Henry was buried in the Protestant cemetery in Marseilles.

30. *Lit. Illus.*, 6:572. *The Letters of Samuel Johnson*, 3:18.

31. Letter Percy to a Mr. Nelson, 20 June, 1783 (both this and the Rogers letter are in the collection of Kenneth Balfour, along with detailed lists of the contents of the parcels). The Percys landed at Donaghadee and spent a short time at Segoe before going on to Dromore (Bedfordshire Record Office, OR 2071/317 [Letter Barbara Percy to Constantia Orlebar, 7 Aug. 1783]; *Lit. Illus.*, 6:577 [Letter Percy to Nichols, 19 June 1783]).

32. B.L. Add. MS. 32,333, f. 170.

According to Joseph Cradock, almost the last time that he saw him, Johnson said that "notwithstanding all the pains that Dr. Farmer and I took to serve Dr. Percy, in regard to his Ancient Ballads, he has left town for Ireland, without taking leave of either of us" (*Literary and Miscellaneous Memoirs*, 1:206–7). It is difficult to give much credence to Cradock's report. Before he left for Ireland in 1782, Percy, far from slighting Johnson, was in touch with him while negotiations for the bishopric were going forward. In 1783 he and his family left for Ireland, not from town but from Carlisle, some 275 miles from London and 260 from Cambridge. It is hard to imagine that Johnson and Farmer would have expected him to undertake such a journey simply for the purpose of taking leave.

Cradock stated also that Percy "blamed Farmer and all at Em[m]anuel for placing his son in a damp apartment, and would attribute his death to that. I was . . . miserable to find such a schism amongst my best friends" (4:293). Quite possibly Percy expressed a wish that Farmer and his colleagues had taken precautions that might have preserved Henry's health; but though he mentioned Henry's lying in a damp bed, nothing in his extant correspondence suggests that he blamed them for placing Henry in a damp apartment and hence for his death. Percy's last *known* letter to Farmer (apparently not the last) shows no sign of resentment (Folger Shakespeare Library, Letter, 24 July 1784). See also Percy's reaction later in this chapter to the news of Farmer's death and *The Percy Letters*, 2:xv–xvii.

33. Collection of Kenneth Balfour ("Observations made by myself"). Bodl. MS. Percy d. 3, f. 240.

34. Bodl. MS. Percy d. 3, ff. 263–78. One of Percy's contributions at Wilby had been to put a carelessly kept register in order.

35. *The Percy Letters*, 8:47 (Letter Percy to Pinkerton, 29 Oct. 1783). *Lit. Illus.*, 6:578–79.

36. *Lit. Illus.*, 6:579. Public Record Office, B. 4/22 (4 Dec. 1783).

37. *Archaeologia* (London, 1785), 7:158–59. *The Banks Letters*, ed. Warren R. Dawson (London: British Museum, 1958), 666 (Letters Percy to Banks, 28 Nov. 1783, and 28 Jan. 1784). Percy had purchased the horns.

38. Collection of Kenneth Balfour ("Improvements made at Dromore").

39. Donald Harman Akenson, *The Church of Ireland Ecclesiastical Reform and Revolution, 1800–1885* (New Haven: Yale Univ. Press, 1971), 28.

40. Swanzy, 134–35.

41. "Improvements made at Dromore." *Lit. Illus.*, 8:14 (Letter, 31 March 1786). Percy's relationship with Lady Moira was much strained in 1790 when he was alleged to have accepted "an evil report" that she had no right to the additional title of Countess of Hastings (Hist. Mss. Comm., Twelfth Report, Appendix: *The Manuscripts . . . of James, First Earl of Charlemont*, 2:119, 131).

42. "Observations made by myself." Akenson, 45, 48, 80, 87–88.

43. Collection of Kenneth Balfour (Letter Percy to William Stafford, 3 Feb. 1789). James Hawkins was Bishop of Dromore from 1775–80.

44. Ibid. ("King's Bench"). Folger Shakespeare Library, Letter Percy to William Jessop, 14 March 1789; B.L. Add. MS. 32,333, f. 177 (Letter to Cleiveland, 10 Feb. 1791).

45. *Lit. Illus.*, 8:241 (Letter to James Macpherson, 21 Aug. 1787). Sturrock, who had been a private tutor at Eton, informed Macpherson that Percy appointed him as a tribute to the memory of Sir John Eliot, who died in 1786. He had been introduced to Percy by the Duke of Northumberland (Alnwick Castle MS., Northumberland Misc. Papers, G/2/55).

46. Gaussen, 252.

47. Woodward's work, published in Dublin, went through four editions in 1787.

48. "Improvements made at Dromore." Neither the purpose of the congress nor Percy's reason for writing anonymously is apparent. Congresses of the volunteer regiments had assembled in Dublin periodically to promote parliamentary reform until the defeat of William Pitt's trade "propositions" in August 1785; perhaps the 1786 venture was intended as a sequel to them (*Annual Register*, 1786, 6–24; R. B. McDowell, *Ireland in the Age of Imperialism and Revolution 1760–1801* [Oxford: Clarendon Press, 1979], 321–24, 330–38).

49. *Lit. Illus.*, 7:461–62 (Letter Lort to Percy, 24 Feb. 1784); *Letters of James Boswell*, 2:324 (Letter Boswell to Percy, 8 July 1784).

50. *The Percy Letters*, 1:42–43 (Letter Percy to Malone, 17 Oct. 1786); Waingrow, *The Correspondence . . . Relating to the Making of the* Life of Johnson, 204–8 (Letter Percy to Boswell, 6 March, 1787). Fellowship date supplied by the Society of Antiquaries.

51. *The Banks Letters*, 666 (Letter Percy to Banks, 28 Jan. 1784); *The Percy Letters*, 1:38 (Letter Percy to Malone, 17 Oct. 1786).

52. *The Percy Letters*, 1:17, 49, 52–53 (Letters Malone to Percy, 2 March 1785 and 22 Dec. 1786; Percy to Malone, 12 Feb. and 14 April 1787). The suggestion to include the prose works came from Malone in a letter of 28 September 1786 (1:32).

53. *Lit. Illus.*, 8:12. Percy was one of the thirty-eight original members.

54. Ibid., 7:304–5, 466–67; 8:231 (Letters Boswell to Percy, 12 July 1786; Lort to Percy, 5 May 1785; Henry to Percy, 13 Sept. 1785).

55. Ibid., 7:771 (Letter 25 Oct. 1787). Campbell, rector of Clones, had made Johnson's acquaintance during a visit to London in 1775 (*D' Campbell's Diary of a Visit to England in 1775*, ed. James L. Clifford [Cambridge: Cambridge Univ. Press], 1947).

56. *The Percy Letters*, 8:67 (Letter 11 Feb. 1786). Vallancey published *A Grammar of the Iberno-Celtic or Irish Language* in 1773.

57. *The Percy Letters*, 1:52 (Letter Percy to Malone, 12 Feb. 1787).

58. Bodl. MS. Percy c. 1, ff. 122–23. Ritson's *Select Collection of English Songs*, though dated 1783, did not appear until September 1784 (Bertrand H. Bronson, *Joseph Ritson Scholar-at-Arms* [Berkeley: Univ. of California Press, 1938], 1:82). Harvard bMS Eng 891 (3 [Letter 19 Nov. 1785]).

59. *The Percy Letters*, 1:41–42. The omissions, Percy informed Malone, were not intentional.

60. *Lit. Illus.*, 8:245.

61. Ibid., 7:4, 500.

62. Joseph Ritson, *A Select Collection of English Songs* (London: 1783), 1:li–lii.

63. Margaret Forbes, *Beattie and His Friends* (Westminster: Constable, 1904), 56. Beattie said that the "hint" of *The Minstrel* came from Percy's essay.

64. Boswell's *Life*, 4:75.

65. *The Correspondence and Other Papers . . . relating to the* Life of Johnson, 310, 313–14, 319–20. Boswell's letter is dated 9 April 1790. Through letters of 12 March, 24 March, and 6 April 1791, Percy persuaded Boswell to modify Johnson's comments on Richard Rolt, Grainger, and his own role in the review of *The Sugar Cane* (393–95, 397–98, 399).

66. *Lit. Illus.*, 7:777, 780.

67. "Improvements made at Dromore."

68. Johnson Birthplace Museum MSS. 16/35–37 (Letters Barber to Percy, 16 Dec. 1788 and 5 Jan. 1789; Percy to Barber, 26 Dec. 1788).

69. *Lit. Illus.*, 8:77 (Letter Percy to Nichols, 2 March 1789); Ledger, Goslings Bank.

70. "Improvements made at Dromore"; Ledger, Goslings Bank.

71. Hist. MSS. Comm., Thirteenth Report, Appendix, pt. 3: *The Manuscripts of J. B. Fortescue, Esq., Preserved at Dropmore*, 1:487 (Letter Marquis of Buckingham to W. W. Grenville, 2 Aug. 1789). Huntington Library, STG Box 29 (28); Nat. Libr. of Ireland, MS. 2022 (Letters Percy to Marquis of Buckingham, 2 Aug. 1789; 11 Feb. 1793).

72. B.L. Add. MS. 32,333, f. 176 (Letter to Cleiveland, 12 May 1788).

73. *Lit. Illus.*, 8:267 (Letter 23 Aug. 1788). Percy seldom attended Parliament from 1783–85 and did not attend at all in 1786 and 1788. Otherwise, except when he was in England, he attended fairly regularly.

74. *Gentleman's Magazine* (March 1790), 191; *Lit. Illus.*, 8:78–87. Percy prepared his remarks for the Reverend P. Parker, prebendary of Kilroot, over whose name they were published.

75. Trinity College, Dublin, MS. 960.

76. *A Sermon Preached at Christ-Church, Dublin, on the 18th of April, 1790, before His Excellency John, Earl of Westmoreland, President; and the Rest of the Incorporated Society, in Dublin, for Promoting English Protestant Schools in Ireland.*

77. Alnwick Castle MS., Northumberland Misc. Papers G/2/50 (Letter Percy to Henry C. Selby, 26 Nov. 1789).

78. *Lit. Illus.*, 7:490, 511 (Letters Percy to Lort, 2 March 1788; Lort to Percy, 13 July 1790).

79. Collection of Kenneth Balfour ("Ecclesiastical Papers").

80. B.L. Add. MS. 32,333, ff. 179–81 (Letters Percy to Cleiveland, 28 Sept. and 10 Oct. 1791). *Lit. Illus.*, 7:718 (Letter Percy to J. C. Walker, 24 Sept. 1791).

81. *Lit. Illus.*, 7:514–15, 516, 518 (Letters Lort to Percy, 24 Aug. and 4 Sept. 1790; Mrs. Lort to Percy, 27 Feb. 1791). B.L. Add. MS. 32,333, ff. 177–78 (Letter Percy to Cleiveland, 10 Feb. 1791).

82. *Isaac Reed Diaries 1762–1804*, ed. Claude E. Jones, University of California Publications in English, (Berkeley: Univ. of California Press, 1946), 10:191.

83. *The Percy Letters*, 1:56–57. The index reference may have been left in through an oversight, but Boswell had intended to reveal Johnson's authorship of the dedications for both the *Reliques* and Reynolds's *Discourses on Painting*, the latter with Reynolds's consent. When Reynolds withdrew his consent, Boswell canceled the page in which both dedications were mentioned (*Life of Johnson*, 4:555–56). It is not apparent that he ever sought Percy's consent.

84. *The Yale Edition of Horace Walpole's Correspondence*, vol. 12, ed. W. S. Lewis and A. Dayle Wallace (New Haven: Yale Univ. Press, 1944), 241.

85. *Lit. Illus.*, 8:82 (Letter Nichols to Percy, 2 July 1789).

86. *Ancient Songs, from the Time of King Henry the Third, to the Revolution* (London, 1790), xix–xxi. Ritson had also questioned the folio manuscript's existence in his 1783 *Remarks* (167).

87. *The Percy Letters*, 8:87–89 (Letter Percy to Pinkerton, 28 July 1792); 95–98 (Letter Pinkerton to Percy, 4 Sept. 1794).

88. *Reliques* (1794), 1:x.

89. Bodl. MS. Percy c. 3, f. 200 (Letter Percy to his nephew, 4 Jan. 1806). It is not clear why Nichols, who was to be paid by Rivington for the printing, should have received half the profits. His turning his share over to Tom suggests that it may also not have been clear to him.

90. Possibly Tom did some work for him in the Oxford libraries, but he was not among those admitted to the British Museum during this period (B.L. Add. MS. 45,870).

91. *Reliques* (1794), 1:x.

92. *The Yale Edition of Horace Walpole's Correspondence*, vol. 42, *Horace Walpole's Miscellaneous Correspondence*, ed. W. S. Lewis and John Riely (New Haven: Yale Univ. Press, 1980), 3:367 (Letter Percy to Walpole, 11 Aug. 1792).

93. *Lit. Illus.*, 7:790 (Letter Thomas Campbell to Percy, 12 June 1793).

94. *Gentleman's Magazine* (July 1793), 662. Percy's family and William Cleiveland appear to have been in Oxford for the installation (B.L. Add. MS. 32,333, f. 185 [Letter Percy to Cleiveland, 21 Aug. 1793]).

95. *Gentleman's Magazine*, loc. cit. A draft of the sermon is in the collection of Kenneth Balfour ("Ecclesiastical Papers").

96. Ibid. (Aug. 1793), 684. "Oxoniensis," the author of the August report, was probably Percy's nephew. Although he claimed to be quoting some ten paragraphs of Percy's sermon from the "joint recollection" of several friends, it is much more likely that he quoted them from Percy's manuscript, to which he could have had access.

97. Ibid. (July 1793), 664.

98. B.L. Add. MS. 32,333, f. 185 (Letter Percy to Cleiveland, 21 Aug. 1793).

99. Ibid.

100. B.L. Add. MS. 34,756, f. 29 (Letter Edward Berwick to Percy, 17 Oct. 1794). *The Percy Letters*, 1:64 n. 4 (Murray died on 6 Nov. 1793). *Lit. Illus.*, 8:309 (Letter Rivington to Percy, 12 April 1794); 6:581 (Letter Percy to Nichols, 12 June 1795).

101. B.L. Add. MS. 32,333, f. 187.

102. Hist. MSS. Comm., Twelfth Report, Appendix: *The Manuscripts . . . of James, First Earl of Charlemont*, 2:256 (Letter Percy to Reverend E. Hudson, 22 Dec. 1794).

103. *Lit. Illus.*, 7:791 (Letter 16 April 1795).

104. The correspondence relating to the Drumsallagh Treasure Trove, until recently in the collection of Kenneth Balfour, is now in the National Museum of Ireland.

105. Letter Percy to Osborne Shiel, 27 Dec. 1794.

106. *Ulster Journal of Archaeology* 48(1985):116–21. Percy's watercolor is also in the National Museum of Ireland.

107. B.L. Add. MS. 32,333, f. 187.

108. *Lit. Illus.*, 6:581 (Letter Percy to Nichols, 12 June 1795).

109. *The Percy Letters*, 2d ed., 1:307–8 (Letter Percy to Malone, 5 April 1794). Between 11 and 26 July Percy received letters of thanks from Isaac Reed, Thomas J. Mathias, the Duke of Leeds, and Horace Walpole (*Lit. Illus.*, 8:293, 297–98, 312–14).

110. *Reliques* (1794). 1:ci–ciii.

111. Ritson made the best statement of his position in *Ancient Engleish Metrical Romanceës*, 1:cix.

112. *The Percy Letters*, 7:72–73 (Letter 1 Oct. 1760).

113. *Critical Review* (Feb. 1765), 123.

114. *Reliques* (1794), 1:41.

115. Ibid., 2:50.

116. Ibid., 1:xvii.

117. Ibid., xii. For a recent defense of Percy's practice, see Zinnia Knapman, "A Reappraisal of Percy's Editing," *Folk Music Journal* 5(1986):202–14.

118. G. E. Bentley, Jr., "Blake and Percy's *Reliques*," *Notes & Queries* 201(Aug. 1956):352–53. Chatterton's biographer E.H.W. Meyerstein suggested that the *Reliques* might almost be considered "the efficient poetical cause" of Chatterton's Rowley (*A Life of Thomas Chatterton* [New York: Scribner's, 1930], 56).

119. Elsie I. M. Boyd, "The Influence of Percy's 'Reliques of Ancient English Poetry' on German Literature," *Modern Language Quarterly* 7(Oct. 1904):80–99.

120. Percy sold £1000 each in India Stock and the Three Percents in order to bring Barbara's dowry up to £3000 (diary, 13 Oct. 1795).

121. *London Gazette*, 17–21 Nov. 1795. Percy's activities during this period are recorded in some detail in his diary.

122. B.L. Add. MS. 32,327, f. 177.

123. Bodl. MS. Percy c. 1, f. 176 (Letter Percy to William Newcome, Archbishop of Armagh, 16 March 1798).

124. Letter Percy to his wife, 1 Jan. 1796 (Beinecke Library, Ms. Vault File). Thomas Shearer and Arthur Tillotson, "Percy's Relations with Cadell and Davies," *The Library*, 4th ser., 15(Sept. 1934):229.

125. *Lit. Illus.*, 7:15 (Letter to Percy, 10 March 1797). The portrait is owned by Kenneth Balfour.

126. Ibid., 5.

127. *Journals of the House of Lords in Ireland*, vol. 8 (Dublin, 1800), 16 Jan. 1797. England and France had been at war since 1792.

128. Charles Dickson, *Revolt in the North: Antrim and Down in 1798* (Dublin: Clonmore & Reynolds, 1960), 103. Gaussen, 252.

129. Bodl. MS. Percy c. 1, ff. 174–77 (Letter Percy to the Archbishop of Armagh, 16 March 1798). B.L. Add. MS. 32,327, f. 178.

130. B.L. Add. MS. 32,327, f. 175. Ambrose's parents had not yet detected signs of the deafness that was seriously to impair his speech.

131. Bodl. MS. Percy c. 1, f. 175. In Dublin on 15 March Percy sent Nichols an essay with conjectures on the migration of swallows and cuckoos and on lightning hurling stones for miles through the air. At Ecton he reviewed William Melmoth's *Memoirs of a Late Eminent Advocate* (*Gentleman's Magazine* [March 1797], 179–80; [July 1797], 586–87).

132. *Lit. Illus.*, 7:35 (Letter Percy to Steevens, 12 Nov. 1797).

133. Ibid., 34.

134. Ibid., 35. Unable to find a record of payment, Percy sent Farmer's nephew, Capt. Joseph Farmer, £96/9/9 representing a balance on his son's account at Emmanuel. The cost of his degree, he wrote, did not much exceed £80, which he believed he had paid (Bodl. MSS. Percy c. 1, ff. 247–51; c. 2, ff. 14–15 [Letters Percy to Capt. Farmer, 15 Nov. 1798 and 20 Feb. 1799]).

135. Bodl. MS. Percy c. 3, f. 58.

136. Ibid., ff. 56–57.

137. Ibid., ff. 58–65 (Letters Percy to his nephew, 20 Feb., 7 and 9 March, and 26 May 1798).

138. *Lit. Illus.*, 7:745–48 (Letters Walker to Percy, 14 and 20 March 1798).

139. Shearer and Tillotson, 227–29; Osborn Collection, Yale University (Letter Percy to Cadell and Davies, 26 April 1797); Ledger, Goslings Bank.

140. B.L. Add. MS. 32,335, f. 5.

CHAPTER XII

Rebellion and Union:
1798–1800

PERCY LANDED AT Dublin on April 27, 1798, and resumed his seat in the House of Lords on May 2, in the midst of one of the more momentous periods in Irish history. Martial law and a 9:00 P.M. curfew were in effect. In scattered pockets about Ireland the long-smoldering Irish discontent, fanned by the success of the French Revolution, was bursting into open rebellion, and the government feared that a landing of French forces would ignite the rest of the country. But the French did not come when they could have been most effective, and the government's arrest in late March of much of the United Irishmen's leadership had left many of the insurgent bands groping with inadequate direction and coordination. The arrest in late May of the young rebel leader Lord Edward Fitzgerald touched off what Percy called "great commotions & disturbances" in Dublin and adjacent counties, but did not provide the unifying force that his followers required. By May 26, with Dromore and much of the rest of the country apparently quiet, Percy had set his sights on returning to his diocese on June 6.[1]

Concerned with the cost of maintaining households in both Ireland and England, and optimistically underrating the rebel threat, he had at first urged Anne and Elizabeth to join him promptly, and Anne's servants did, in fact, arrive in Ireland about the first of June. But with General Sir William Fawcett's troops suffering a disastrous defeat at Wexford on May 30, he advised Anne to wait until she heard from him that all was quiet, and, postponing his own departure, he bought "an easy safe mare" for riding about Dublin and sent to Dromore for a servant to attend him. The other bishops, he noted on June 11, were sending their families to England, and even Lady Camden, wife of the Lord Lieutenant, had set off with her children the night before.

"So you may judge what they think of this Country," he commented to Anne—"However I am in high Spirits & have no fear of the Event."[2]

Walking around Merrion Square on the evening of the tenth, he had overheard Lady Beresford talking from her balcony to Lady Castlereagh and Lady Frances Stewart some distance below her. He did not catch the question, but the answer by Lady Castlereagh was loud enough to be heard across the square: "Yes, Lady Camden goes off to Night, but Lady Lond^{derry} does not go with her." In this way she continued to pour out all the information supposed to have been kept secret.[3]

In the north, though Dromore remained quiet, the rebellion was approaching a climax. On June 7 Crane Brush, captain of the Dromore yeomanry, marched the main body of his men to Hillsborough after leaving James Hall in charge at Dromore and stationing a small group to the south at Banbridge. On June 9, after the rebels took Saintfield only about fourteen miles east, the fear of an attack caused a near panic at Dromore, with the virtually defenseless inhabitants seeking cover behind ditches in the open fields. The few able-bodied men, "undisciplined and unarmed," put on the best fronts they could, stayed on guard, and even sent out patrols on foot and horseback.[4] On June 12 Percy's butler, John Logie, wrote from Dromore that three thousand rebels were within ten miles of Dromore House and were expected any moment. He hoped that Percy would send for the servants, "as the poor wimen is in a very bad way."[5]

The rebels never reached Dromore. On the thirteenth they suffered an overwhelming defeat at Ballynahinch by troops under the command of General George Nugent. Thomas Stott—poet, leader in the bleaching industry, and captain of one of the yeoman companies—notified Percy promptly of the government's victory, and on the same day Meredith Darby, Percy's steward, sent him a description of Ballynahinch after the battle. He had counted seventeen dead in town and in the rebels' campground and had brought back two of the rebels' pokers "all Bloody for to be put along with your Lordship's other Curiositys."[6]

Percy was pleased to learn that his nephew had "behaved like a Heroe" during the alarms around Magheralin by securing weapons from the generals in the nearby encampment, patrolling with his parishioners all night, and staying "forever on the wing." It was a gratification also to know that not a single person from the parish of Dromore—not even any members of the United Irishmen—had joined the rebels at Ballynahinch. The greatest loser by the rebellion, he informed Anne, was Euseby Cleaver, Bishop of Fernes in the province of Dublin, where the rebels took possession of his house and see lands, so that he could expect neither rents nor fines for many years.[7] Concerned to see Dromore better protected for the future, Percy later wrote Lord Castlereagh, the first secretary for Ireland, to ask that the dozen riders who had patrolled at Dromore be enlisted as a cavalry troop under the captain of the yeomanry, and that the government provide them with swords, pistols, holsters, and ammunition. About six weeks later the request was approved.[8]

In Dublin the Earl of Camden was replaced by Lord Cornwallis, who had surrendered to George Washington at Yorktown in 1781. Clearly the rebellion had sent tremors through the English government, and the appointment of a Lord Lieutenant with military experience was considered imperative. On June 22, with the rest of the House of Lords, Percy attended the new Lord Lieutenant's levee, Cornwallis appearing in boots and the military dress of a general of the army. He was unmarried, Percy observed to his wife, "so the Ladies here will have no Drawing Rooms. Perhaps . . . he may fill up the vacancy from among our Irish belles. Tell Eliz. to post over. I hope indeed ye will both of you come soon, now the Rebellion is crushed & extirpated. At least, if, after a few Weeks, ye see all safely returned to peace & quiet." He noted also that no chaplain had accompanied Lord Cornwallis to Ireland: "I suppose no English Clergyman will now venture over for an Irish B[isho]prick. So much the better for the Nation."[9]

Though the rebellion was suppressed, isolated banditti continued to infest the highways and rob the mailcoaches. Percy heard from Barbara that three of his remittances totaling more than £43 had never reached her, all of them apparently taken in holdups. Thus he stayed on at Dublin, attending Parliament regularly, enjoying the company of his fellow bishops, and riding about town on his mare—so steady, he wrote Anne, that one rainy day he rode through the bustle of Dublin with his umbrella up and the mare never started at the flapping of the silk.[10] On July 13 Thomas Apperley's younger son, recently appointed paymaster to Sir Watkin Williams Wynn's Corps of Ancient Britons, stopped by for breakfast, and on July 28, with selected members of Parliament, he dined at Dublin Castle, where Lord Cornwallis placed him by his side and asked him, as senior bishop, to officiate as chaplain. "He was very conversible," Percy noted, but "he will not be a favourite here for he is sober himself & does not push the bottle. They also think him too merciful to the Rebels."[11]

By August 9 Percy had arranged to travel north in the mailcoach on August 14, its postal mission assuring him the protection of a corporal's guard. He notified the Dromore clergy of a visitation on the sixteenth and reached Dromore himself on the fifteenth, after a journey without incident during which he observed the "greatest appearance of peace & plenty all the way." At the visitation the clergy brought good news: their part of Ireland was in "as agreeable a state as possible." A thanksgiving service, however, was not held until November 29, when Percy officiated before the largest congregation, including many Dissenters, ever to have assembled in the cathedral.[12]

By the time of his return to Dromore, any discussion of his family's rejoining him had ended, and by December Anne was urging him to hurry back to Ecton. For Anne the improved health that she enjoyed in England was probably reason enough for her wishing to stay where she was, but perhaps she was also reluctant to give up the company of Barbara's family in a part of England where she had spent most of her life. She must also have been concerned for thirty-three-year-old Elizabeth, whose prospects for marriage seemed more likely to be furthered in England than in Ireland. She was being courted by the much younger Pierce Meade, son of the Earl and Countess of Clanwilliam of Gill Hall near Dromore; but Meade had matriculated at St. John's College—young Tom Percy's college—in January 1797, and was to be graduated in 1799, after a move to Wadham College. As one who aspired to clerical orders, he was likely to remain at Oxford for another year or two while he pursued the degree of Master of Arts. The thought of returning to Ireland could thus hardly have been agreeable to either Elizabeth or her mother.[13]

Percy himself had good reason for not continuing to press for Anne's and Elizabeth's return to Dromore. In the wake of the rebellion, the English government had resolved to move quickly toward a union of England and Ireland similar to that of England and Scotland. Percy, in fact, seems to have believed that the idea of union would be readily accepted, and he set himself the objective of returning to England for his fourth visit when it was accomplished. At the same time setting his finances in order became almost an obsession lest at his death he should leave Anne and their daughters with debts to discharge or with an estate as encumbered as those of William Cleiveland and his own father.

In 1783 he had submitted a memorial to Archbishop Robinson which, in accordance with Church of Ireland practice, charged his successor in the bishopric with about £2375 of the nearly £3170 that he himself was compelled to pay for the see house. At that time he had enumerated his intended improvements of the house and grounds: roughcasting the house and fitting it with gutters and spouts; erecting a barn with a cow house, poultry house, walled coal yard, and a room for fruit; setting out a walled garden of two acres or less to be planted with fruit trees and shrubs; and building a gardener's house and a porter's lodge. He had proposed to spend not more than £1704/8/4. By 1798, however, his projected costs had risen to almost £3000. And he was required to complete the improvements and submit a new memorial to Archbishop Newcome if Anne, Barbara, and Elizabeth were to realize three-fourths of their value from his successor.[14]

Percy's household staff in late 1798 consisted of six men and four women, a congenial group on the whole, even though he found it necessary to dismiss John Logie for his extreme mistreatment of the footman, Hugh Magennis. When the servants held a ball at Dromore House on October 20, Percy interrupted a letter to Anne to slip below stairs and watch them: "Miss Darby & Miss Tibbs far exceed all the rest, among the Ladies," he wrote: "And Hugh Magennis & Dick McGarry carry the Prize of dancing among the Beaux." On September 20, 1799, he and the servants celebrated the birth of Barbara's daughter Anne with a "grand ball and supper" below stairs that did not break up until two in the morning, about three hours after Percy had gone to bed.[15]

The outdoor staff included a night watchman, a gardener, and eight to ten laborers, an augmented force brought in to expedite the work for the memorial. Percy himself was out with his workmen for hours each day and, as he reported to Anne on January 2, 1799, had made numerous new walks on the hill beyond the garden—the "Hill Grove." The nearer grove had been "divided into such a variety of winding walks, that Darby measured them all yesterday & found that we might walk above an English Mile without going out of . . . [it] or setting the foot twice in the same Path."[16] In 1799 he added to the grove a wooden obelisk and urns painted in *trompe l'oeil* by Thomas Robinson and presented by Mrs. Robinson, plus a wooden bust of Anne also in *trompe l'oeil*. Set in one of the glen's shady reverses, the delighted Percy informed Anne, the bust had all the effect of marble. By August he had also converted a circle of trees near the entrance gate into a scene of "uncommon beauty" by cutting a series of small vistas through the trees, each opening on some little landscape, such as the church, the ruined castle, the winding of the river, a cottage surrounded by trees, or the distant mountains.[17]

Though approaching his seventieth birthday, he boasted to Anne on January 2 that he had not had a cough all winter and had never been more hardy and active. He attributed his good health to his activity, his aversion to wine for the first thirty-seven years of his life, and his abstaining from suppers ever since. "I can scarce discover any difference in my personal exertions," he wrote to Anne on their wedding anniversary, "from what they were the Day you made me the happiest of Men by presenting to my heart the loveliest of Women."[18]

In his solitude he welcomed the company of the translator of Dante, Henry Boyd, whom he appointed rector at Rathfriland, and his own nephew, who arrived from England on the morning of June 27, just in time for the 1799 visitation.[19] Fond though he was of young Tom, he could never appreciate his preference for the impecunious fellowship of an Oxford college over the more lucrative living available to him in Ireland. In July 1798, while waiting to return to Dromore, he had felt compelled to threaten his nephew to keep him from leaving his church to go to England: with the government requiring that strict residence be enforced, Percy was beginning a prosecution against another clergyman for desertion. "If you leave," he informed Tom on July 18, "you leave me forever, and your Living likewise." "Poor Tom never thinks about the Main Chance," he lamented to Anne on March 16, 1799. And when Tom, with the residence requirement long since lifted, announced in mid-September his intention of returning to Oxford with Pierce Meade, Percy confided to Anne that he did not find his continuance at Dromore at all necessary: "his Tastes & Persuits are so different from mine."[20]

Firm when he saw his duty or believed himself in the right, at times impatient and querulous, Percy at one point confronted Elizabeth with an ultimatum. In her eagerness to marry Pierce Meade, Elizabeth, who was then thirty-four, seemed to her father to disregard the unalterable demands of prudence. Meade "seems a very amiable young Man," he wrote to Anne on September 27, 1799, as Meade was leaving for Oxford to begin his graduate studies. Yet when Elizabeth, seconded by Anne and Barbara, pressed for consent to the marriage, he made his opposition clear. He hoped that all of them would "attribute to the purest Motives & the most cordial Regard for our dear Eliz.ᵇ happiness that I cannot agree with you all in thinking it wᵈ be prudent or proper to consent to her Union with Mʳ P. M. till he has some Prefermᵗ I think it not unlikely but something may drop within my own gift ere long: In which Case I shᵈ not delay their Union." Nor could he agree, as Barbara proposed, to contribute annually to the support of a young family when he had a mortgage of £1600 to pay off and £200 remaining on William Cleiveland's indebtedness, and when it was essential that he clear his own estate for the benefit of his family. He expressed the hope that the subject would not be proposed to him again until Meade had some preferment, lest they "render it perfectly disagreeable & it end in a total final *Prevention*."[21]

Occupied as he was with his estate, he still found time for some minor literary activity. For Richard Musgrave, at work on a history of the 1798 rebellion, he secured a variety of information about the battle at Wexford from Holt Waring, prebendary of Dromara, and Waring's son-in-law, William Archer.[22] On July 21, 1798, he had initiated a correspondence with the Scottish physician, author, and editor Robert Anderson, whose edition of the British poets had been published in 1795. Noting in his first letter that Anderson had not had access to all the writings of his "beloved friend Dr. Grainger," he offered to send him several poems bequeathed to him among Grainger's manuscripts and to point out others printed anonymously in the periodicals.[23] With Percy's assistance Anderson undertook a revised edition of Grainger's poems, with a life of Grainger. He became one of Percy's most faithful and informative correspondents, introduced him by letter to such Scottish friends as Walter Scott and Thomas Campbell, and visited him three times at Dromore during the first decade of the nineteenth century.

Percy's most significant literary accomplishment of the eighteenth century's final years was unrelated to his activities during those years. It was a legacy of the 1765 *Reliques of Ancient English Poetry*—of the seriousness and perception with which he had approached his nation's poetic heritage. When *Lyrical Ballads* was published in September 1798, the ground was prepared for an assessment of the impact of the *Reliques* on the course of English poetry. Although most of the poems in the *Lyrical Ballads*, including the expanded two-volume edition of 1801, were by Wordsworth, the poem that provoked the most comment was "The Ancient Mariner" of Coleridge, whose "Kubla Khan" and two parts of "Christabel" were already written but were to remain unpublished until 1814. And such in time became the influence of the two poets that whatever influenced *them* was to pass like an inheritance to succeeding generations of poets.

Both poets, even to the very title *Lyrical Ballads*, owed a debt to the *Reliques* that Wordsworth was to acknowledge handsomely in his 1815 "Essay Supplementary to the Second Edition of the *Lyrical Ballads*." Contrasting the *Reliques* with Macpherson's Ossian translations, Wordsworth found it

> so unassuming, so modest in . . . [its] pretensions! I have already stated how much Germany is indebted to this . . . work; and for our own country, its poetry has been absolutely redeemed by it. I do not think that there is an able writer in verse of the present day who would not be proud to acknowledge his obligations to the "Reliques;" I know that it is so with my friends; and, for myself, I am happy in this occasion to make a public avowal of my own.[24]

Wordsworth's praise was not excessive. For him the ballad had become almost a way of thinking poetically. "We Are Seven," "Anecdotes for Fathers," "Expostulation and Reply," "The Tables Turned," the Lucy poems, "Lines Written in Early Spring"—any number of his poems, essentially lyrical, embodied slight but suggestive narratives commonly in the stanza and manner of the ballads, with the action often forwarded through the ballad device of question and answer. Wordsworth was drawn particularly to the Percy ballads that depicted rustic life in what he termed the language of men, free of the poetic diction that he found distasteful in much of eighteenth-century verse: "The Children of the Wood," for example, one stanza of which he quoted in the preface to the second edition of *Lyrical Ballads* to exemplify a worthy subject expressed in appropriate language. Even a few of his longer poems had roots in the *Reliques*: "The Mad Mother" drew its inspiration from the *Reliques*'s "Lady Anne Bothwell's Lament," and "The White Doe of Rylstone" from "The Rising in the North."[25]

Coleridge, too, was attracted to Percy's ballads, but for different reasons. He was fascinated by their supernatural elements and affected more by their archaic than their everyday language. He introduced

"Dejection: an Ode" with the vivid stanza from "Sir Patrick Spence" in which the sailor reports his ominous sighting of "the new moone / Wi' the auld moone in hir arme." In "The Ancient Mariner" he echoed the theme of "The Wandering Jew" and the language of "The An- cient Ballad of Chevy-Chase," "The Battle of Otterbourne," "Edom o'Gordon," and "Sir Cauline," the last of which supplied the name of his heroine in "Christabel."[26]

It is unlikely that Percy, caught up in the controversy over the Anglo-Irish union and concentrating on completing the work for his memorial to the Irish Primate, was even faintly aware of the impact that the *Reliques* was having in Britain and elsewhere. Joseph Cooper Walker mentioned to him on July 1, 1799, that he had seen "The Child of Elle" and Percy's own poem "The Friar of Orders Gray" among a list of the German poet Gottfried Bürger's translations; but translations were legion, and Percy, unfamiliar with German poetry, could hardly have imagined the stimulus that the *Reliques* had provided for poets like Herder and Goethe as well as Bürger.[27] Even an elegant testimonial by Walter Scott, sent on January 11, 1801, in response to a letter from Percy on Scott's forthcoming *Minstrelsy of the Scottish Border*, might reasonably have been undervalued by the elderly Percy as the acknowledgment of a neophyte editor eager to make his mark on the world: when he received Percy's letter, Scott wrote, he felt as he did "when the Reliques of Ancient Poetry were first put into my hands, an era in my poetical taste which I shall never forget. The very grass sod seat to which (when a boy of twelve years old) I retreated from my playfellows, to devour the works of the ancient minstrels, is still fresh and dear to my memory. That you are pleased to approve of my intended work, will prove to me an additional stimulus in the execution."[28]

Almost totally insulated from a revolution in poetry that he had helped to excite, Percy turned to the pressing problems before him. He informed Lord Cornwallis on January 18, 1799, that he planned to support the government's proposal of a union of England and Ireland, for he perceived in a union the only certain security of the church and kingdom in hostile Ireland, as well as a diminishing of the "Monopolizers" of boroughs. Some of "our great men," he wrote Anne on January 21, controlled ten or twelve members of Parliament and, with some important question coming on, would threaten the Lord Lieutenant with opposing it in order to obtain the most unrea- sonable concessions. The mere prospect of a union, he noted, had already served as a spur to the linen industry, which was critical to the welfare of his home county.[29]

He had planned to travel to Dublin for the opening of Parliament, but on January 18, only a little more than two weeks after boasting to Anne of his good health, he came down with a violent cold that hung on for close to a month. He gave the Bishop of Cloyne his proxy in favor of the union, but when the government could secure a majority of only one vote on an amendment to the proposal, it decided that proceeding was too risky and withdrew the proposal until the next session.[30]

The months that followed were filled with bitter politicking, and in County Down the controversy raged with particular fury. After the Marquis of Downshire—Percy's neighbor in Hillsborough— arrived from England on May 19, he was visited by Percy, and he returned the visit on June 14. But when they found themselves on opposite sides of the controversy, there was little further cordiality between them. Percy gave a dinner for the Marquis on August 8 and dined with him the next day at Hugh Moore's; but "because in the order of Toasts, I drank as usual, the *Lord* Lieut. & Prosperity to Ireland, he behaved at Moore's with the most disobliging Shyness. He affects to be angry wth the Lord Lieu.[t] for promoting the *Union*: but I suppose it is, because Government will not pay him his Price for espousing it. . . . As for me I am perfectly easy about his *Liking* or *Disliking*."[31]

On October 10 Percy and his clergy drew up an address to the Lord Lieutenant in support of the union. But he felt some resentment at his neglect by a government that he had consistently supported, perhaps in part because, unlike many of the Irish bishops, he had never been offered an opportunity to exchange his bishopric for another. Although Parliament was to open on January 15, 1800, he decided to wait a few days before attending. "I have no great reason to go out of my way," he informed Anne on December 18, "to oblige Gov- ernmen.[t] who have not shown me the Attention I merited. But thank God, I want nothing from them & that they know."[32]

As the debate in Parliament intensified, petitions in opposition to the union poured into the House of Commons from every part of Ireland. The petition of most concern to Percy resulted from the efforts of the Marquis of Downshire, who called a county meeting at Down- patrick for January 27. Arriving early, Lord Downshire and his fol- lowers took possession of the Town House, closed the doors to keep out the proponents of union, and proceeded to adopt what Percy called a "violent address" in opposition to it. Undeterred, Percy and his group prepared their own supporting petition. Both were to be presented to the House of Commons on February 3.[33]

If the number of opposing petitions during this period is any indication, Irish sentiment was almost wholly unfavorable to the prospect of a union with England. The petition of Percy and his clergy stands almost alone among the two or three dozen printed in the *Journals of the House of Commons of the Kingdom of Ireland*, a small voice hardly audible amidst the din of the opposition. Opponents of the union, as in the Down petition, typically stressed the uncertain consequences of union and the impossibility of turning back once the step had been taken. At such a critical juncture, nearly all the petitioners professed a reverence for the Constitution of 1782, when Poynings' Law was dealt a stunning if not mortal blow and the Irish Parliament gained a large measure of independence. No doubt many shared the view that Samuel Johnson had conveyed to an Irish friend some years before: "Do not make an Union with us, Sir. We should unite with you only to rob you."[34] Whether or not the petitions accurately reflected public sentiment, the government, bent on having its way, had worked effectively toward that end in the year since it had first submitted the idea of union to a preliminary testing. This time, after extensive debate accompanied by antiunion demonstrations in the streets of Dublin, the bill was passed by both houses. Percy, having arrived in Dublin in time for the meeting of the House of Lords on February 5, saw it through to the final vote on March 25.

He was invited to preach before the Lord Lieutenant on Easter Day, a recognition that perhaps compensated for his not being asked to dine at Dublin Castle during the parliamentary session, and he postponed his departure to England to fulfill the engagement.[35] Although he had not completed his improvements at Dromore, it was an opportune moment to interrupt them. Archbishop Newcome, to whom he was to submit his memorial, had died on January 11, and the government could be expected to take some time to appoint a successor. Eager to be with Anne again after their two-year separation, Percy left Dublin as soon as his schedule—and the winds, which delayed him a day or two—would permit. With Anne and Elizabeth in residence at Brighton, where they had gone in the late winter, and Percy stopping to attend to rental properties in Rothwell and Thurmaston, visit the Isteds at Ecton, and conduct business in London, it was mid-May before he rejoined his family.[36]

He stopped in London to ask Cadell and Davies, who had held the manuscript of the life and works of Goldsmith for more than two years, to grant some immediate relief to Goldsmith's niece and a younger brother whom Percy had not known about when he first proposed the edition. They refused, however; and, as Percy noted in a memorandum that he drew up in 1807, they also refused to give him access to the manuscript of his life of Goldsmith, in which he wished to make some improvements. He discovered later that they had turned the manuscript over to Samuel Rose, who, without consulting him, had added a number of passages to it, including extracts from Boswell's *Life of Johnson* in which Percy did not consider Goldsmith to have been treated with proper respect. The edition, already long overdue, was to suffer a further delay. It was not finally published until 1802, although its title page bears the date 1801.[37]

During this shortest of his four visits to England, he took time to look through the archives at Petworth with his nephew in search of material for a new edition of the *Northumberland Houshold Book*, suggested to him by the second Duke of Northumberland—the former Earl Percy—and the Earl of Egremont.[38] For his old friend John Nichols he reviewed in the *British Critic* the third volume of *The History and Antiquities of the County of Leicester*, which Nichols completed and published in 1800. Less a review than a defense of Percy's brother-in-law William Gutteridge against a charge that he misappropriated a Roman milestone near Thurmaston, Percy's anonymous article praises in passing not only Nichols's book but also William Cleiveland—"who had many . . . rare specimens in natural history, of which he was a curious and diligent collector"—and the *History of Worcestershire* by Percy's friend Treadway Nash. At Ecton Percy delighted in turning the pages of illustrated books to show the prints to his three-and-a-half-year-old grandson, Ambrose, whose deafness, Percy noted, left him capable of learning only through his eyes.[39]

With diocesan duties awaiting him and his memorial still to complete, Percy left Ecton for Ireland on September 29, accompanied by Anne and Elizabeth.[40] Under the rotation system established by the Act of Union, he was scheduled to take his seat in the English House of Lords in 1802. Seniority had placed him in the second group of four bishops and one archbishop to serve for one year.

NOTES

1. B.L. Add. MS. 32,335, ff. 23–26 (Letters Percy to his wife, 24 and 26 May 1798). A full account of this period is contained in Thomas Pakenham's *The Year of Liberty: The Great Irish Rebellion of 1798* (London: Granada, 1972). One of the more helpful shorter accounts is in J. C. Beckett's *The Making of Modern Ireland 1603–1923*, new ed. (London: Faber, 1981).

2. B.L. Add. MS. 32,335, ff. 31, 33, 37 (Letters 1, 5, and 11 June 1798).

3. Ibid., f. 37.

4. Ibid., f. 39 (Letter Crane Brush to Percy, 10 June 1798). Bodl. MS. Percy c. 1, ff. 189–91 (Letters James Hall and James Burrowes to Percy, 8 and 10 June 1798); f. 205 (Letter Percy to Viscount Castlereagh, 24 July 1798).

5. B.L. Add. MS. 32,335, f. 44.

6. Ibid., ff. 47–48.

7. Ibid., ff. 55, 59, 60 (Letters Percy to his wife, 20 June, 22 June, and 4 July 1798).

8. Bodl. MS. Percy c. 1, ff. 205–14 (Letter 24 July 1798); f. 218 (Letter J. Straton to Percy, 6 Sept. 1798).

9. B.L. Add. MS. 32,335, f. 58 (Letter 22 June 1798).

10. Ibid., ff. 62, 60 (Letters 9 and 4 July 1798).

11. Letter Apperley to Percy, 8 July 1798 (collection of Kenneth Balfour); B.L. Add. MS. 32,335, ff. 64, 71 (Letters to his wife, 13 and 30 July 1798).

12. B.L. Add. MS. 32,335, ff. 76, 106 (Letters Percy to his wife, 16 Aug. and 4 Dec. 1798); E. B. Atkinson, *Dromore: An Ulster Diocese* (Dundalk: Dundalgan Press, 1925), 78.

13. Meade seems to have become a good friend of Percy's nephew, whom he helped to canvass for a fellowship at All Souls College in March 1799 (B.L. Add. MS. 32,325, f. 145 (Letter Percy to his wife, 16 March 1799).

14. Bodl. MS. Percy c. 1, ff. 113–14. The memorial is dated 10 August 1783.

15. B.L. Add. MS. 32,335, ff. 91–92, 96, 199 (Letters Percy to his wife, 20 Oct. and 2 Nov. 1798; 20 Sept. 1799). Young Anne Isted, born on 13 September 1799, lived only until 27 July 1801 (B.L. Add. MS. 32,327, f. 175).

16. Ibid., f. 121 (Letter 2 Jan. 1799).

17. Ibid., f. 122, 189–90 (Letters 13 Jan. and 22 Aug. 1799). Robinson's watercolor of the obelisk is one of the illustrations in Edward Malins, *Lost Demesnes: Irish Landscape Gardening 1660–1845* (London: Barne & Jenkins, 1976), 131.

18. Ibid., ff. 121 and 155 (Letters 2 Jan. and 24 April 1799).

19. Ibid., ff. 81 and 175 (Letters 28 Aug. 1798 and 1 July 1799).

20. Bodl. MS. Percy c. 3, ff. 72–77 (Letters Percy to his nephew, 14, 18, and 25 July 1798); B.L. Add. MS. 32,335, ff. 146 and 197 (Letters Percy to his wife, 16 March and 17 Sept. 1799).

21. B.L. Add. MS. 32,335, ff. 203, 226–27 (Letters 27 Sept. and 21 Dec. 1799).

22. Percy's correspondence with Musgrave is in the Nat. Libr. of Ireland, MSS. 4156–57.

23. Lit. Illus., 7:71.

24. The Poetical Works of William Wordsworth, ed. Thomas Hutchinson (London: Oxford Univ. Press, 1895), 949.

25. Stephen Maxwell Parrish, The Art of the Lyrical Ballads (Cambridge: Harvard Univ. Press, 1973), 121–23; 226.

26. John Livingston Lowes, The Road to Xanadu (Boston: Houghton-Mifflin, 1927), 244, 249, 331, 332, 336, 338n.

27. Modern Language Review 25(1930):94–95.

28. The Letters of Sir Walter Scott, ed. Sir Herbert Grierson (London: Constable, 1932), 1:108.

29. Bodl. MS. Percy c. 2, f. 11. B.L. Add. MS. 32,335, ff. 127, 205 (Letters 21 Jan. and 10 Oct. 1799). Henry Grattan, Whig leader in the House of Commons, estimated in 1790 that two-thirds of the seats were private property (Paul Johnson, Ireland: A History from the Twelfth Century to the Present Day [London: Granada, 1980], 75).

30. B.L. Add. MS. 32,335, ff. 125, 127, 129 (Letters Percy to his wife, 18, 21, and 25 Jan. 1799).

31. Ibid., ff. 164, 166, 187 (Letters Percy to his wife, 20 May, 31 May, and 16 Aug. 1799). A full account of this period is contained in G. C. Bolton, The Passing of the Irish Act of Union (London: Oxford Univ. Press, 1966).

32. Ibid., ff. 205, 225 (Letters 10 Oct. and 18 Dec. 1799).

33. Ibid., f. 232 (Letter 30 Jan. 1800). The opposing petition was printed in the Journals on 7 February and the supporting petition on 14 February.

34. Boswell's Life, 3:410.

35. B.L. Add. MS. 32,335, ff. 242, 243 (Letters Percy to his wife, 23 and 31 March 1800).

36. Ibid., ff. 253–54 (Letter Percy to his wife, 30 April 1800). "The sweet Infants," he wrote of Ambrose and Anne, "exceed my fondest Expectations, and are the delight of my heart."

37. Shearer and Tillotson, 227–29. Percy prepared the statement to counter what he considered slanderous accounts by Cadell and Davies of his relations with them. He sent copies to Anderson and Malone. Cadell and Davies had agreed to publish the edition promptly when they signed their contract with Percy on 25 October 1797.

38. B.L. Add. MS. 32,335, f. 257 (Letter Percy to his wife, 11 May 1800); Bodl. MS. Percy c. 3, f. 90 (Letter Percy to his nephew, 14 July 1800).

39. *British Critic* (Oct. 1800), 346–61. The editor of the *British Critic* was Robert Nares, Percy's successor as vicar of Easton Maudit. Letter Percy to Barbara Isted, 5 Oct. 1800 (Beinecke Library, Ms. Vault File).

40. *Lit. Illus.*, 8:28 (Letter Percy to Andrew Caldwell, 25 Sept. 1800).

CHAPTER XIII

Last Years:
1800–1811

ALTHOUGH HE LOOKED forward to taking his seat in the English House of Lords in 1802, Percy never ceased to enjoy his house and estate and his position as head of his diocese. The very calm of Dromore, relative to much of the rest of Ireland after the rebellion of 1798, was a gratification: "I am now more & more happy that I have not changed my See," he had written to Anne on March 3, 1799, as he contemplated the nightly disturbances in Antrim and Connaught.[1] And his delight intensified as he was able to share his walks with family and friends: past St. Colman's Well to the south, or north through the walled orchard to the lake, where the swans glided to the shore as he appeared. In his solitude before his return to England he had even grown fond of a litter of suckling pigs romping in a little enclosed park with a chicken that roosted each night on a pig's back. He had not been able to put them to their intended use.[2]

Like others with favors to bestow, Percy did not suffer for want of flatterers. But he had warm friends as well: Thomas Stott and Thomas Robinson in his own vicinity, and Andrew Caldwell, Edward Ledwich, and Richard Musgrave in Dublin, all of whom he could see with some regularity; and Robert Anderson and Edmond Malone, of necessity joined to him mainly through the postal service. Anderson, a genuine Percy enthusiast, arranged for a reissue of both *Northern Antiquities* and the *Key to the New Testament*, only to have his Edinburgh publishers dissolve a partnership before either project had been completed.[3] With Percy's assistance he moved ahead with his work on Grainger, and he tapped Percy for information on Johnson that lent a distinction to the third edition of his *Life of Johnson*, the first two having been heavily dependent on the biographies of Boswell and Hawkins.[4] He paid Percy the first of three visits at Dromore in August

1802, and a year later recalled the visit with an eloquence that suggests, like Scott's tribute, the stature achieved by the editor of the *Reliques* among a generation nurtured on his three volumes: "a visit to such a man, like that of a pilgrim to a distant shrine, forms an era in the life of a private individual." Anderson expressed satisfaction in helping to draw Percy out of his long retirement to assume his place "in the ranks of learning, and to receive renewed testimonies of public gratitude for . . . [his] eminent services to English poetry."[5]

Anderson's view of Percy's renewed activity may have been overstated. Percy's literary work of the period was largely incidental: assistance to Anderson and others, encouragement of young poets, and occasional pieces for the periodicals. He also participated in a book club that met at Dromore House with a rotating chairmanship, and his interest in Swift prompted him to purchase a portrait said to have been painted of Swift while he was a student at Trinity College.[6] Family matters continued to preempt much of his attention. He took time to find a buyer for William Cleiveland's collection of shells.[7] More important, Lady Clanwilliam was pressing for his approval of Elizabeth's marriage with her son. When Percy acknowledged that he could provide Elizabeth with a dowry equal to Barbara's, Lady Clanwilliam, asserting that she would be a second mother to Elizabeth, urged that they move ahead.[8] On April 6, 1801, Percy officiated in his own cathedral at the marriage of Elizabeth and Pierce Meade, whom he was to appoint vicar of Seapatrick in 1803 and rector of Anaghelone in 1805, livings that Meade held concurrently until he became Archdeacon of Dromore in 1810 and gave up the Seapatrick vicarage.

Percy continued his work on his estate, and he submitted a memorial to the new Primate, Dr. William Stuart, either late in 1801 or early in 1802. To his annoyance it did not meet with the prompt approval he had expected. The commissioners, Dr. Stuart informed him—friends of Percy appointed by Percy—had certified that the memorial failed to comply with the law in not setting forth the nature and extent of all improvements to the property.[9]

Percy reacted with some asperity. The Primate, he charged, had delayed unnecessarily and thus made it impossible for him to take up his seat in the English House of Lords according to schedule. He seems even to have hinted that he might try to secure his rights through the courts.

Placed on the defensive, Dr. Stuart replied in kind. He stated on

May 23 that he was in bed with a fever when the commissioners brought him their report, but he attended to it as soon as he was able. "It is singular," he argued, "that your Lordship should now complain of delay, since you might have obtained a Commission last August, and indeed might, & ought to have obtained it many many years ago." Percy, moreover, was free to leave for England at any time after the commission was established. As for himself, Dr. Stuart continued, he would neither willingly do Percy an injustice nor tamely submit to being accused of treating him cruelly, but would act "to set at defiance the most vigorous investigation of a Court of Justice, in which, I conjecture from your Lordships language, this business must be ultimately discussed."

His anger much abated, Percy replied on May 25 that he could not leave Ireland until he knew whether the commission would need "those explanations which, as your Grace has seen, only I could give." Nor had he been in a position to submit his memorial until the improvements to his property were completed. There was no limitation of time, he wrote: if the memorial had been delayed until "the last hour of my Life, no Injury would have been done to my successor." But he would now proceed to execute those parts of it that appeared deficient to the commissioners.

Characteristically, he set to work with a will, and to the commissioners' evident satisfaction. In spite of their harsh exchange, his differences with the Primate were smoothed over also, though perhaps he had already made his best impression on Dr. Stuart when he wrote to him on May 16, 1802, to explain what he thought he had accomplished at Dromore. Once the least of Irish sees, he pointed out, Dromore had become one of the more desirable. Through a careful management of rents and fines the yearly income had been raised from £2000 to £3000. The see house, a mere shell when he and his family moved into it, had been transformed into an attractive home, set in the midst of the improved one hundred twenty acres that it could be said to occupy of the demesne's four hundred. He was not himself asking the full cost of the additions permitted by law, but only three-fourths; and surely it would discourage "all future Improvers if I could not be allowed the very moderate Proportion . . . to which I have confined my Demands for rendering this one of the very best Episcopal Residences in Ireland, and at the same time improved the Revenue of the See to enable my Successor to pay it."

The last words in the correspondence were Dr. Stuart's, and they were kind ones: "every improvement at Dromore is so well and so handsomely executed," he wrote on March 25, 1803, "and will be of such benefit to the Bishop of Dromore. I am much concerned so large a proportion of the expense should fall upon your Lordship."

One of Percy's contributions at Dromore, though hardly admissible in his memorial, was the encouragement of the young for which William Sturrock had praised him in 1787.[10] His hopes for his nephew, particularly after Henry's death, were frustrated by interests that drew Tom from projects to which he seemed to commit himself, perhaps for no other reason than to please his uncle. The most persistent of these was the publication of a fourth volume of the *Reliques*, a project that Percy did not abandon until 1807.[11]

But between 1801 and 1809 three young poets caught Percy's attention and achieved successes that would have been impossible without his support. The first was William Cunningham, a poor weaver's son who, at the age of nineteen, sent Percy a copy of verses asking for the loan of some books. Percy did better than he was asked. He placed Cunningham in the diocesan school of Dromore, where in two and a half years he read the principal Latin and Greek classics. His poem "On the Peace" was printed first in the *Belfast News-Letter* and then in the November 1801 issue of the *Gentleman's Magazine*, which also carried a Cunningham poem in each of its next three issues.[12] In 1804 Cunningham was appointed an assistant teacher in Dr. William Bruce's Belfast Academy, but he had already developed consumption, and he died at Magherabeg, near Dromore, on December 27, 1804. He was buried in the churchyard at Dromore.[13]

In January 1805 the *Gentleman's Magazine* printed verses on Cunningham's death by another Percy protégé, Thomas Romney Robinson, son of the painter Thomas Robinson. T. Romney Robinson, as he signed his poems, had begun contributing to the *Gentleman's Magazine* when he was eight, his own "Verses on the Peace," sent in by Thomas Stott, appearing side by side in the December 1801 issue with Cunningham's ode "On the Approach of Winter." In 1803 Percy sent Nichols two more Robinson poems with a request that he "take off" two dozen copies and send them to him at Dromore.[14]

Robinson's grand poetic year was 1804, which saw the publication of his *Juvenile Poems*. A subscription volume dedicated to Percy, its subscription list probably achieved a record for a work of its kind. Over fourteen hundred people subscribed for more than two thousand copies, the Lord Lieutenant the Earl of Hardwicke leading the list with sixty-three and Percy a commendable second with forty. Anne Percy also subscribed for ten. The volume, of course, bears witness less to Robinson's genius than to his precocity, as well as to the promotional efforts of Percy and the elder Robinson's other friends; but with the Lord Lieutenant and an eminent scholar-bishop carrying its banner to a community eager for recognition, it is not surprising that its infant rhapsodies attracted a following that poets of genuine stature would have envied. As Robinson matured, he abandoned poetry for astronomy and physics and achieved a more durable fame through his invention of the cup anemometer.

Five years later the experience of *Juvenile Poems* was almost duplicated in Connop Thirlwall's *Primitiae; or Essays and Poems on Various Subjects, Religious, Moral, and Entertaining.* An ambitious title for the work of a twelve-year-old—the son of Percy's chaplain Thomas Thirlwall—*Primitiae* was also dedicated to Percy, "the encourager of early genius, and the common patron of literature in general." Connop, as his father wrote in the volume's preface, was taught Latin at three and, at four, read Greek "with an ease and fluency which astonished all who heard him." His subscription list was outstripped by Robinson's, but the total of 384 subscribers for 507 copies was itself a remarkable showing. Percy again took forty copies and this time led all the rest. Other subscribers included Samuel and Barbara Isted and their son Ambrose, and Pierce and Elizabeth Meade and their children John, Thomas Percy, Edward, Theodosia, and Henry. Thirlwall, who became Bishop of St. David's, was a leading religious writer of the nineteenth century. Although he, too, abandoned a poetic career, his contemporaries thought him worthy of a bust by the northwest entrance of Westminster Abbey's Poets' Corner.

Percy continued his own writing intermittently. He reviewed his friend Jane West's *Letters Addressed to a Young Man* in a nineteen-page article, most of it quotations from the book, which the *British Critic* spread out through its issues of September, October, and November 1801. For the May 1802 *Gentleman's Magazine* he contributed a brief memoir of the physician James Johnstone and an introductory note for an essay on the Giant's Causeway by a writer, probably William Richardson, who signed himself "W. R." In the January 1805 *Gentleman's Magazine* he shared with the world his faith in the efficacy of brown paper in the curing of rheumatism, though he concealed his identity behind the initials "B. D." A Mrs. K——— of Oxford Street, he reported, had cured her pains in a few days by wearing a waistcoat of brown paper, and Sir. Wm. P. was said to have covered his ears with it and cured a deafness. He himself had "used the common brown paper, which is made of junk (old rope); it smells of tar, and it is best to rub it smooth with a black glass bottle."[15]

A persistent pain beyond the reach of brown paper and a glass bottle was that inflicted by Joseph Ritson, who in 1802 renewed his attack on Percy in a book entitled, in Ritson's system of revised English spelling, *Ancient Engleish Metrical Romanceës*. In his prefatory "Dissertation on Romance and Minstrelsy," Ritson accused Percy of printing scarcely "one single poem . . . fairly or honestly" and of practicing "every kind of forgery and imposture."[16] Prompted by the ferocity of Ritson's charge, Robert Nares invited Percy to provide him with a rebuttal for the *British Critic*. Percy hung back, however—because of business and his failing eyesight, he informed Nares—but with Nares renewing his invitation every few months, Percy sent him three paragraphs on December 28, 1804, which Nares printed in the January issue as a supplemental article to his own earlier review. They were submitted by a "friend" of Percy, he announced in the magazine.[17] As much a counterattack against Ritson as a defense of Percy's own practice, the three paragraphs addressed only two minor points of Ritson's argument: whether Percy's nephew had seen the advertisement to the fourth edition of the *Reliques* before it was published and whether Steevens, after examining the folio manuscript when it was on display at John Nichols's, was satisfied with the exactness of Percy's transcriptions. As for Ritson, it was argued, he had learned all that he knew about romance from Percy; and because he had never been given the least provocation, his "false insinuations and defamatory assertions" could be accounted for only "from his avowed hatred of *all Priests and Priest craft* (for so he stiled Religion and its Ministers) which he carried to such an horrible excess, that he was engaged in an attempt to prove our blessed Saviour an impostor, when a dreadful paroxysm of frenzy put an end to his existence."[18]

Ritson had died under extraordinary circumstances in September 1803, shortly after setting fire to the manuscripts in his Grays Inn chambers. Convinced, like most of his friends, that Ritson was insane—Nares called him "most unequivocally mad"—Percy did not hesitate to circulate an account of his death which Henry Selby sent to him in April 1804, and which Anderson persuaded R. H. Cromek to publish in the 1810 edition of his *Select Scotish Songs*.[19] Nor was he ever able to countenance any praise of Ritson, direct or indirect. When

Henry Boyd published a memorial poem after Joseph Cooper Walker's death in 1810, Percy rebuked him for his unqualified praise of one who, in an essay read before the Royal Irish Academy in 1805, had held up Ritson's "Dissertation" on romances for approbation without defending Percy against Ritson's abuse.[20]

The problem with his eyesight that Percy had reported to Nares was much more serious than the occasional eyestrain which had disrupted his work as early as 1757. By 1803 he was clearly going blind. Early in the year he had mentioned a "complaint" in his eyes to Andrew Caldwell, who expressed the hope on March 25 that the mild spring weather would alleviate it. By August Anderson had been given a more precise account of Percy's complaint and the measures he was taking to arrest its progress. "The thought of your being confined to a darkened room" Anderson wrote on August 16, "deprived of the sight of one eye, and threatened with the loss . . . of the other, gives me very sincere concern; for I know no man to whom such a privation would be a greater calamity. It would not merely be a heavy private affliction, but a serious public misfortune."[21]

Unfortunately, with cataracts apparently developing in both eyes, withdrawal into a darkened room provided no lasting relief. By October 5, as he informed Malone, Percy saw with the remaining good eye only as through a mist. He continued nonetheless to write most of his own letters, and in January 1804 was even considering a return to England to consult with Nichols about his longstanding literary projects. With his eyesight steadily worsening, however, a trip across the Irish Sea proved impracticable, and he turned the edition of Surrey's poems over to his secretary, young H. E. Boyd, who completed its glossary by December 1805. Any profits from the edition, Percy informed Nichols, were to be divided between Boyd and Nichols's son John Bowyer, the brother of Percy's deceased godson, Thomas Cleiveland Nichols.[22]

Anderson was pleased to learn from Thomas Stott, who visited Edinburgh in the summer of 1805, that Percy had suffered few privations as a consequence of his blindness.[23] He continued to discharge his episcopal duties and to enjoy his family, friends, and garden. He wrote his own letters until 1805, and what he could not read he had a secretary read for him. Except for his eyesight and a fainting spell that he suffered in January 1805, he appeared in excellent health; "how delightful to me," Anderson wrote to him on July 13, 1806, "is the reflection, that, since it is no longer permitted to your Lordship to contemplate the scenery which your taste embellished, you bear the privation with pious resignation, and cheerfully pursue your accustomed walks with health as vigorous and step as firm and light as when I had the happiness to attend you!"[24]

For Anne, her health almost always precarious, there was more reason to be concerned. In February 1803 Edward Ledwich had lamented her indisposition, which he attributed to the relentless wet weather. On January 12, 1805, Percy informed his nephew that she was afflicted with a violent pain in her breast; and by the end of the year she was seriously ill with the gout. She died on December 30, 1806, less than a month before her seventy-sixth birthday and just a day before the Isteds arrived from England to be with her.[25]

A brief entry in Percy's diary by his secretary reveals that he nearly suffocated on January 3, the day before Anne was buried in the cathedral. Whether his attack resulted from the shock of Anne's death or was part of a recurrent pattern cannot be determined, since no other allusions to it have survived and only a few unrelated entries are extant between January 5, 1796, and December 31, 1806. But the loss of Anne after nearly forty-eight years must have been a grievous affliction. Mourned apparently by all who, like Joseph Cradock, had warmed to her "gentleness and joy," she was commemorated in poems by Thomas Stott and Henry Boyd that were published, with a third, anonymous, poem, in the *Gentleman's Magazine*. Stott described her as

> Alike from ostentation free, and pride,
> Humanity her motive—sense her guide.

And Boyd, recalling her voice "nearly tun'd to heavenly praise," expressed a wish that the hope of meeting her in heaven would

> *his* mind sustain,
> Who felt with deepest pang the sudden wound.[26]

Within fifteen months the Percy family was to suffer another loss. Not yet forty, Percy's nephew, having been troubled with head pains throughout the winter, was taken ill with a fever while visiting the Isteds at Ecton, and he died at Northampton on May 14, 1808. Often impatient with his nephew during his lifetime, Percy was generous in death, without totally concealing his disappointment: "He was highly regarded by all that knew him for his very amiable qualities," he wrote in the *Gentleman's Magazine.* "He was a man of learning; and when a boy displayed such proofs of early genius, as, if it had been cultivated, must have given him a distinguished rank among the Poets of his time."[27]

The year 1808 also brought a loss of a different kind. On February 8, a fire consumed John Nichols's warehouse in Red Lion Passage and its entire contents, including the printed sheets of the Surrey and Buckingham editions on which Percy had begun work more than forty years before. Whatever Percy's feelings, just as he was on the point of completing the Surrey edition, they were tempered by the thought of Nichols's calamitous loss, and he extended both sympathy and, somewhat later, money to help Nichols compensate for his misfortune.[28] Luckily, copies of each edition escaped the blaze because they were not in the warehouse at the time, but Nichols, having suffered a loss of nearly £10,000 beyond what was reimbursed by insurance, was in no condition to attempt another printing, as had been done with the *Spectator* edition when the original printing was destroyed by a warehouse fire in 1783.[29]

Percy finished out his life at Dromore, a revered figure who, despite his failing health, enjoyed his family, friends, and position to the end. In 1807 he spent substantial sums of his own to repair the cathedral and to add a section of pews that became known as the Percy Aisle.[30] He contributed his name and money as one of the sponsors of the newly established Belfast Academical Institution.[31] A lithograph of the time depicts him at his pond, tall, gaunt, and unbent by his years, feeding the swans whose presence he must have sensed as much by sound as by sight. An oil painting by Thomas Robinson, with an accompanying poem by Thomas Stott, commemorated a gathering at Dromore House on October 1, 1807, with Percy the seated central figure, and Stott, Robinson, Robinson's son, Lord Castlereagh, Lord Bangor, Edward Ward, and one or two others gathered around him.[32] Edmond Malone kept him abreast of the Club, of which he was the senior member, while Jane West sent him literary news from the Midlands and Anderson from the North.

Anderson and Mrs. West both visited him in 1810, by which time he was undergoing a series of attacks that Meredith Darby, Jr., recorded in Percy's diary. The Bishop, he wrote on November 17, 1810, in the first such entry to survive, had "the usual attack" about five in the morning and many more till eleven. He "did not go to breakfast[;] afterwards had no more till 5 oc. then had another and 2 or 3 till 11 oc. but dined with the family passed the night in perfect ease but never slept. The attacks in general were much milder than heretofore."[33] Darby recorded similar attacks on January 18 and 19 and February 25, a period during which Percy was still able to continue much of his usual activity. He entertained friends who frequently stayed for dinner, kept up his correspondence, and, weather permitting, went for airings in his chaise. In the spring, however, the attacks intensified. On May 15 a very severe attack was accompanied by fainting fits and a violent stomach and intestinal disorder, and on June 14, just before an attack, he nearly suffocated at breakfast.

The Isteds arrived from Ecton on July 11, 1811, and stayed until August 22, with Percy's condition remaining much the same during that period. Then on September 14 he suffered a series of attacks between 11:00 A.M. and 9:00 P.M., and on the twenty-second he was seized with a "stoppage of urine." On the twenty-sixth his condition began noticeably to deteriorate, and with Elizabeth at his bedside, he died peacefully on September 30. He was eighty-two years old.[34]

He was buried beside Anne in the cathedral, where his bishop's robes have been carefully preserved and a plaque on the wall commemorates his nearly three decades of service to the diocese. In the *Gentleman's Magazine* John Nichols devoted a full page to his obituary, and Jane West, Henry Boyd, and "Arsenius" mourned his loss in verse.[35] Thomas Stott, whose poem on Percy's death was published in the *Belfast News-Letter*, erected a monument to him between the River Lagan and the Dublin road; and the townspeople inscribed the new Regent Bridge, close by the cathedral, with a "Memorial of their Respect."[36]

Having fulfilled his wish to leave his estate unencumbered, Percy bequeathed to Barbara and Elizabeth both money and property, the latter acquired through inheritance and purchase and improved by careful management. Under the terms of his will, his books and other possessions were to be divided equally between them, and the sum of £2000 was to go to each of the five Meade grandchildren.[37] The see of Dromore—its income, palace, and demesne improved in his twenty-nine years almost beyond recognition—went to his successor, George Hall, the provost of Trinity College, who died only six days after being consecrated. It passed then to John Leslie, dean of Cork, and in 1819 to James Saurin, dean of Derry, on whose death in 1842 the Dromore bishopric was united with Down and Connor's.

His most enduring legacy, of course, was to the world of letters. All subsequent ballad collections owed much, if not their whole existence, to the *Reliques*, from Herd's and Ritson's in his own century to Scott's, William Motherwell's, and Francis J. Child's in the next. The spark that helped to ignite Chatterton, Beattie, and Blake, worked its same magic on Wordsworth, Coleridge, Keats, Tennyson, Rossetti, and a host of other poets. A fifth edition of the *Reliques*, already in preparation at the time of his death, was published in 1812, the first in a long line of nineteenth-century editions that were to reveal the wonders of early English poetry to succeeding generations. Just as the parcel of old ballads became a household book, so Percy became a household name. Not until the publication of Francis Palgrave's *Golden Treasury* in 1861 was the *Reliques*'s preeminence among English anthologies even remotely challenged.[38] Although yielding that honor to more comprehensive collections, the book that Wordsworth called the redemption of English poetry remains one of the great accomplishments of English scholarship and one of the most influential and readable works of its time.

Wordsworth's praise of the *Reliques* might readily have been turned into an epitaph for Percy himself. But, however pleasing he might have found such a thought, Percy was a scholar only by avocation. Cleric and prelate that he was, he would surely have been better pleased with a couplet from Jane West's tribute in the *Gentleman's Magazine*:

True to the trust the Master-Shepherd gave,
He only dropt his crosier at the grave.

NOTES

1. B.L. Add. MS. 32,335, f. 141.
2. Ibid., ff. 169–70 (Letter to his wife, 15 June 1799).
3. *Lit. Illus.*, 7:126–27, 164, 218 (Letters Anderson to Percy, 6 May 1804; 13 July 1806; and 17 Aug. 1811).

4. Anderson's *Life of Samuel Johnson* was first published in 1795. The third edition did not appear until 1815. Percy's contributions are discussed in Paul J. Korshin, "Robert Anderson's *Life of Johnson* and Early Interpretive Biography," *Huntington Library Quarterly* 36(1973):239–53.

5. *Lit. Illus.*, 7:116 (Letter 16 Aug. 1803).

6. Letter Percy to [M. Wyatt?], 5 Sept. 1802 (Special Collections, Florida State University). Letters Anthony Trail to Percy, 27 April and 5 May 1801 (collection of Kenneth Balfour); Percy to John Price, 24 Nov. 1801 (Bodl. MS. Add. A 64, ff. 255–56). It has not been verified that the painting, which is owned by Kenneth Balfour, is of Swift.

7. *Lit. Illus.*, 8:31 (Letter Philip Luckombe to Percy, 13 Nov. 1800).

8. Letters Lady Clanwilliam to Percy, 6 March and 2 April 1801; Percy to Lady Clanwilliam, 8 March 1801 (collection of Kenneth Balfour). Elizabeth was almost thirty-six at the time of her marriage; Pierce Meade was twenty-four. Percy's dowry for each of his daughters was £3000, but he noted in one memorandum that his portion to each daughter, including properties as well as the initial dowry, would be £20,000 and, in another, £30,000 (Beinecke Library, Ms. Vault File).

9. Letter Dr. William Stuart, Archbishop of Armagh, to Percy, 8 May 1802. Except for Percy's reply, which appears to be lost but can be inferred from Dr. Stuart's letter of 23 May, the correspondence concerning the memorial is in the collection of Kenneth Balfour.

10. Percy's literary influence on the Down community has been described by Amber M. Adams in "Patronage and Poverty: The Case of Patrick Brontë," *Ulster Folklife*, 33(1987):26–31.

11. *The Percy Letters*, 1:214–15 (Letter Percy to Malone, 10 April 1807).

12. *Gentleman's Magazine* (Nov. 1801), 1030; (Dec. 1801), 1124–25; (Jan. 1802), 60; (Feb. 1802), 157–58. England and France agreed on preliminary articles of peace in October 1801.

13. *Lit. Illus.*, 7:145.

14. Ibid., 6:584–85 (Letter 14 May 1803). The poems were published in the May 1803 issue, 454–55.

15. *British Critic* (1801), 286–95, 359–65, 524–29. *Gentleman's Magazine* (May 1802), 475, 387–91; (Jan. 1805), 30. Percy commended Jane West for rejecting the "sentimental wickedness" of Rousseau and Goethe (Bodl. MS. Percy d.8, ff. 80–87). Percy visited the Giant's Causeway with Edward Blakeway on 15 August 1784 (Letter to his wife, 17 Aug. 1784 [Beinecke Library, Ms. Vault File]).

16. Joseph Ritson, *Ancient Engleish Metrical Romanceës* (London, 1802), 1:cix, cxliiin.

17. *Lit. Illus.*, 7:601–7 (Letters Nares to Percy, n.d. April and 9 Sept. 1803; 6 Feb. and 16 Aug. 1804).

18. *British Critic* (Jan. 1805), 99; *Lit. Illus.*, 7:606–7.

19. *Lit. Illus.*, 7:601 (Letter Nares to Percy, April 1803); 7:215 (Letter Anderson to Percy, 22 June 1811). Osborn Collection, Yale University (Letter Selby to Percy, 6 April 1804).

20. *Lit. Illus.*, 7:756–58.

21. Ibid., 8:46; 7:115.

22. *The Percy Letters*, 1:152; Huntington Library, in Mary Mitford, *Recollections*, foll. p. 4 (Letter to Nichols, 12 Jan. 1804). *Lit. Illus.*, 6:586 (Letter to Nichols, 11 Dec. 1805); 8:70.

23. *Lit. Illus.*, 7:157 (Letter to Percy, 3 Sept. 1805).

24. Bodl. MS. Percy c. 3, f. 176 (Letter Percy to his nephew, 12 Jan. 1805); *Lit. Illus.*, 7:166. In the letter to his nephew Percy likened the fainting spell to one he had suffered in 1799.

25. *Lit. Illus.*, 7:829 (Letter to Percy, 3 Feb. 1803); Bodl. MS. Percy c. 3, f. 176; Letter Barbara Isted to Percy, 27 Dec. 1806 (collection of Kenneth Balfour); B.L. Add. MS. 32,337 (diary, 30 Dec. 1806). The 30 December entry, like the others in these last years, is not in Percy's hand.

26. *Gentleman's Magazine* (Jan. 1807), 60–61; (Feb. 1807), 155. Stott, who signed his poem with the pseudonym "Hafiz," was to be satirized by Byron as "grovelling Stott" in *English Bards and Scotch Reviewers*, published in 1809. Several of his poems for Percy—one a New Year's gift for 1805 and another "On an Aeolian Harp Placed in a Window at Dromore House, Nov. 10, 1810"—were published in his *The Songs of Deirdra* (London, 1825). The extant diary entries for the period 1796–1806 are in the Beinecke Library (Ms. Vault File).

27. Ibid. (May 1808), 470.

28. *Lit. Illus.*, 6:587–89; 8:90 (Letters Percy to Nichols, 20 Feb. 1808 and 11 July 1809; Nichols to Percy, 25 Feb. 1808 and 19 July 1809). Percy gave Nichols £50 in Dec. 1809 (Ledger, Goslings Bank, 19 Dec. 1809), and Nichols acknowledged an earlier remittance in his letter of 19 July 1809. Percy seems also to have helped compensate for Nichols's loss from his *History of Leicestershire* (*Lit. Illus.*, 8:89) (Letter Nichols to Percy, 13 Dec. 1808).

29. *Lit. Illus.*, 6:590 (Letter Nichols to Percy, 12 July 1808). Information on surviving copies is contained in *The Percy Letters*, 2:193–94; 3:148. In addition, a copy of the Buckingham edition is in the Queen's University of Belfast, which purchased Percy's library in 1969.

30. Atkinson, 79. Queen's University of Belfast, MS. 1/70 (Letter Percy to Joseph Stevenson, 16 Nov. 1807).

31. Queen's University of Belfast, MS. 1/70.

32. The painting hangs in the library at Castle Ward.

33. Perhaps it was about this time that Percy, according to an unidentified newspaper, resolved to undergo a cataract operation, only to find the surgeon unwilling to risk impeding his recovery from such a serious illness

(collection of Kenneth Balfour). *The Percy Letters*, 1:213–14 (Letter Percy to Malone, 10 April 1807).

34. Letter Elizabeth Meade to Pierce Meade and Barbara Isted, 3 Oct. 1811 (Beinecke Library, Ms. Vault File). An internist who read this account suggests that Percy's illness may have been prostate or urinary tract trouble complicated by gradual heart failure and, finally, kidney failure.

35. *Gentleman's Magazine* (Nov. 1811), 460–61, 483; (Dec. 1811), 556–57.

36. A number of poems, clipped from newspapers and undated, are in the collection of Kenneth Balfour.

37. Public Record Office, Prob. 11/1528 (529). A copy of the will dated 3 November 1810 is in the collection of Kenneth Balfour.

38. Percy's reputation suffered a serious blow when John W. Hales and Frederick J. Furnivall published *Bishop Percy's Folio Manuscript* in 1867–68 and subjected his editorial practices to the close scrutiny that a comparison of his texts and the folio manuscript made possible. Given a hundred years of changing tastes, Percy was facing a jury hardly more sympathetic than Ritson, the lone critic of his day. The reading public for which Percy had compiled the *Reliques* did not much concern itself with the sanctity of texts; but Hales and Furnivall, along with many of their readers, did. Poem by poem, they noted his deviations from the manuscript and ridiculed his interpolations. Percy looked on the text of the folio manuscript, Furnivall wrote, "as a young woman from the country with unkempt locks, whom he had to fit for fashionable society" (1:xvi). The criticism, at times overwrought, was often on the mark. But while it led to a proper caution in accepting Percy's texts, it neither diminished his achievement nor rendered the *Reliques* any less delightful than earlier generations had found it.

Index

Abbott, Francis Lemuel (1760–1803), 293

Abington, Frances (1737–1815), 212

Acton, Laurence, 219

Adam, Robert (1728–92), 245, 248, 249, 263 n.33

Adams, Mr. *See* Adam, Robert

Adams, Amber M., 332 n.10

Adamson, Rev. Daniel (b. 1683?), 13, 14, 15, 35

Addison, Joseph (1672–1719), 25, 31 n.36, 85, 99, 116 n.66

Adlington, William (fl. 1566), 175

Admonition against Swearing, 5

Aesop, 72–73

Aghadery, County Down, 267, 275

Aghalee, County Down, 298 n.8

Agincourt, 290

Akenside, Mark (1721–90), 58

Albin, Eleazar (fl. 1720–38), 27

Aldrich, Dr. Henry (1648–1710), Dean of Christ Church, 7

Alexander the Great. See Lee, Nathaniel

Alfred, King of England (849–899?), 154

"Algerines, The," 270

Allen, Edmund (1726–84), 120, 129, 178–79, 193 n.22, 195 n.42, 206, 248, 250, 272, 273–74, 389

Aln River, Northumberland, 142

Alnmouth, Northumberland, 143

Alnwick, Northumberland, 136, 143, 149, 151, 163, 184, 202, 203, 222, 235 n.71, 249; Boswell and TP meet in, 185, 194 n.34; Johnson misses TP at, 199, 231 n.10; Brisley Tower erected at, 248–49

Alnwick Castle, 134, 162, 217, 219, 224–25, 298 n.15; TP's summers at, 136, 142–45, 149, 151–52, 158, 164–65, 167, 177, 181, 183–85, 188, 238, 254; Duchess's "Laws" for, 158–59

America, ix, 35, 209, 212, 216, 223

Amphlett, Rev. Joseph (b. 1715?), 239

Anaghelone, County Down, 273, 274, 275

Ancaster, Robert Duke of (1756–79), 251, 252

Anderson, Dr. Robert (1750–1830), 312, 319 n.37, 321–22, 327–28, 329, 332 n.4

Anlaff, King of Denmark, 154

Annan, Dumfriesshire, 146

Antiquarian Repertory, The, 188, 211, 243, 261 n.15

Antonine wall, the, 147

Antrim, County, 321

Antwerp, Belgium, 152

Apperley, Ann (Wynn), 212, 288

Apperley, Charles James ["Nimrod"] (1778–1843), 30 n.35, 308

Apperley, Thomas (1730–1816?), 37, 43, 52, 192 n.2; TP's relationships with, 20, 21, 22, 25–26, 30 n.35, 33, 34, 40, 48, 58, 78, 99, 128, 150, 157, 174, 188; acts as messenger, 75, 81 n.34, 99, 108, 135; marriage and family of, 212, 288, 308

Apuleius, 175

Archer, William, 312

Aristophanes, 110

Armagh, Archbishop of [Primate of All Ireland]. *See* Newcome, William; Robinson, Richard; Stuart, William

Armagh, County, 276